The Van Halen Encyclopedia

The Van Halen Encyclopedia

CJ Chilvers

Writers Club Press
San Jose New York Lincoln Shanghai

The Van Halen Encyclopedia

Writers Club Press
an imprint of iUniverse.com, Inc.

For information address:
iUniverse.com, Inc.
5220 S 16th, Ste. 200
Lincoln, NE 68512
www.iuniverse.com

ISBN: 0-595-16669-5

Printed in the United States of America

Contents

v

Acknowledgements

Special thanks to the following people who shared their knowledge, memories, and experiences. Without them, this book would not have been possible: John Q. Adams, Paula Allen, Rick Ames, Eddie Anderson, Andrea Andrajacks, Michael Anthony, Lucas Aykroyd, Stephen Bagiatis, Sonia Bar, Andy Barrett, Pat Baustert, Thomas Bell, Shawn Berman and Rumbo Recorders, James Berry, Valerie Bertinelli, Steve Betz, Martin Bissett, Tony Bowe, Brian Brantley, Bill Broadway, John Bros, Ali Brown, Michael Brown, Timothy Brown, Nik Brownin, Jimmy Cain, Rodney Carr, Guillermo Carrera, Wayne Charvel and WRC Music, Greg Cherone, Mike Clark, David Clausen, Greg Coach, Scott Cook, Brian Costanza, Chris Cothrun, Liza Cozad, A.J. Crumley, Adam Davis, Steve Davis, Rey De Carlo, Jason Degen, Joe Demartini, Darren DePoy, Kevin Derbyshire, Mike DiGiorgio, Mark Dittmer, Ron Dodson, Kevin Dugan, Leon Duran, Joe Duider, Russ Dunn, Jon Dunphy, Kevin Eaton, Linn Ellsworth and Speedster Amplifiers & Boogie Body Guitars, Matt Emanuel, Everyone on the Van Halen Internet Mailing List, Falcon, Jeffery Falk, Chet Farwell, Grant Fisher, Tim Freeman, Mark Fuller, Rick Garcia, Vince Garcia, Andrew Garrett, Scott Gilbert, David Goodspeed, Danny Grabher, Dave Grant, Robin Gregg, Ryan Greenwood, Dominic Griffith and the Global Satellite Network, Neal Hannan, David Harris, Marie "Scrufflove" Hardy, Jeff Hausman and The Inside magazine, Bruce Henne and the Rock Radio Network, Steve Henning, Rob Heuser, Ron Higgins, Chris Hinger, Mark C. Holt, Alfred Hopton, Jeff Hubbard, the Internet Movie Database, Dave Jablinsky, Robert Jackson, Eric Jaye, Ken

"Mr. Big" Jensen, Michael Johnson, Sonia K., Brian Kennedy, Cindy Kennedy, Roger "WWOTR" Kinney, Jon Kohilakis, Greg LaBuda, Drew Lane, Sindre Lausund, Steven Leavitt, Brian Ledgerwood, Dave Lees, Brad Lefler, Michael Leone, Patrick Leone, Jerry Lica, Jim Liotta, Ellen Lloyd, Rob Lomicka, Preston Luber, Bob Lynds, Derrick MacDougal, Ben Manilla and the House of Blues Transmitter Network, Marco, Paul Marshall, Tom Matthews, Claudio Mantovani Matsui, Tom McGinley, Bryan McGuire, Gerri Miller and Metal Edge magazine, Rob Mills, Paul "Mav" Mitchell, MTV, Jim "MULLY" Mullins, Andrea Murphy, the Muscular Distrophy Association, Greg Musi, Andrew Neal, Joseph J. Northrup, Scott Oakley, Tim O'Keefe, Roberto Nakata Olimpio, Fernando Oliveira, Shail Paliwal, Mark Palowich, Gregory Parker, Kerrijo Patten, Ron Peck, Greg "Top Hat" Phinney, Richard Pike and Greasy Kid's Stuff, Eduardo de Souza Pinheiro, Ron Piotrowski, Len Radeka, Eleanor Ramsay and Boston Rock Opera, Butch Renfroe, Greg Renoff, Chris Reppert, Nicole Reynolds, Scott Cory Roberts, Randy Rogers, Scotty "T-Bone" Ross, Brian Rubino, Henry Ruiz, Dave Russell, Jon Schell, Michel Schinkel and the Dutch 5150 Fan Club, Brian Seppman, Chris Sernal, Rich Sewell, Kim Sharman, Billy Sheehan, Dale Shera, Roger Shirin, Ken Smiley, Ernie Smith, Mike Smith, Dave Snider, Kurt Sokolowski, Peggy Souder,, Dennis Stanley, Ian Stanley, Brad Starks and the Official Van Halen Web Site, Mark Stawasz, Kent St. Clair, T.J. Steele, Arvid Steinbach, Maciej Stoinski, Robert Stolz, Scott Swanson, Deborah Szatkowski, Mike Tagler, Jeff Taylor, Mike Taylor, Andrea Teed, Chuck Thomas, Gina Tobin, Greg Tsigaridas, Benny "The Jet" Urquidez, Steve Vai, Edward Van Halen, Eli Vigil, Dave Vincent, Bill Waagmeester, LeDell Wallace, Willie Walter, Brian J. Welch, Tom Welch, Marty Wharton, Alan Wood, Charles Woodward, WRIF in Detroit.

Preface

The first thing you should notice is that this book includes information on all the side projects and former bands of the six past and present members of Van Halen. Don't be surprised to find just as much information about Extreme as David Lee Roth's band or Sammy Hagar's solo career. This stems from the hope that this will be the first unbiased detailed history of the band. No specific era of the band is preferred over the others.

The top Van Halen memorabilia collectors from around the world were asked to contribute all the information they could to this book. The result is the most detailed record of Van Halen and Van Halen-related releases, from singles to EPs, that has ever been compiled. It isn't perfect, though, so to make increasingly more accurate editions of this book, we encourage you to send any information not included in this book to:

The Van Halen Encyclopedia
P.O. Box 79
Oak Lawn, IL 60454
www.vanhalenencyclopedia.com

HOW THIS BOOK IS ORGANIZED

The Timeline
  The timeline is meant to explain the general history of the band, after which more information can be looked up in the rest of the book. The timeline entries are short and simple to tell a concise story that's easily

understood. The more detailed accounts of events will be found in the alphabetical entries.

The Alphabetical Entries

The entries are arranged in a way that will make it easier to find what you're looking for. Every Van Halen song, whether released or unreleased, has its own entry. In some cases an unreleased Van Halen song may be known by two or three titles. In these cases you will find the song under its most common title.

Songs by Van Halen-related and side-project bands do not have their own entries. You will find information about these individual songs under the entry for the album on which the song appears (every album by a Van Halen-related band does have its own entry).

Entries detailing an individual Van Halen member's involvement on another artist's album have been listed under the artist's or band's name. For example, Eddie worked on a Dweezil Zappa album named *Dweezil*. You will find the information about this under the entry "Zappa, Dweezil."

The entries also include six biographies, one for each past and present member of Van Halen. These biographies are not meant to be equal in length or detail. The longest biography is Eddie Van Halen's. This is because there has been a great deal more written about Ed in the past, giving the public much more knowledge of his role in the band. Alex Van Halen's biography is relatively short for similar reasons; he doesn't do many interviews.

The Tours

Though most of this section is self-explanatory, there is one part that may puzzle some people. For each tour there is a listing of whether an audio or video recording was made of each show. These recordings include any recordings circulating in public. It doesn't matter if the recording is an official release or a bootleg. If it's listed, it means that someone in the general public has a recording.

This is not at all meant to encourage bootlegging. The listings are meant to give the reader an idea of how many Van Halen concerts are archived by their fans. DO NOT contact the author or the publisher about acquiring these recordings.

The band has recorded many of their shows but have not provided any details of these recordings. Therefore, only the recordings that have been proven to exist in public are listed.

Introduction

VAN HALEN IS...
David Lee Roth-Lead singer 1973-1985
Sammy Hagar-Lead singer 1985-1996
Gary Cherone-Lead singer 1996-1999
Edward Van Halen-Guitars, Keyboards
Alex Van Halen-Drums
Michael Anthony-Bass Guitar

ALBUMS

Van Halen (1978)
Runnin' with the Devil • Eruption • You Really Got Me • Ain't Talkin' 'Bout Love • I'm the One • Jamie's Cryin' • Atomic Punk • Feel Your Love Tonight • Little Dreamer • Ice Cream Man • On Fire

Van Halen II (1979)
You're No Good • Dance the Night Away • Somebody Get Me a Doctor • Bottoms Up! • Outta Love Again • Light Up the Sky • Spanish Fly • D.O.A. • Women in Love... • Beautiful Girls

Women and Children First (1980)
And the Cradle Will Rock... • Everybody Wants Some!! • Fools • Romeo Delight • Tora! Tora! • Loss of Control • Take Your Whiskey Home • Could This Be Magic? • In a Simple Rhyme • Growth

Fair Warning (1981)
Mean Street • "Dirty Movies" • Sinner's Swing! • Hear about It Later • Unchained • Push Comes to Shove • So This Is Love? • Sunday Afternoon in the Park • One Foot Out the Door

Diver Down (1982)
Where Have All the Good Times Gone? • Hang 'Em High • Cathedral • Secrets • Intruder • (Oh) Pretty Woman • Dancing in the Streets • Little Guitars (Intro) • Little Guitars • Big Bad Bill (Is Sweet William Now) • The Full Bug • Happy Trails

1984 (1984)
1984 • Jump • Panama • Top Jimmy • Drop Dead Legs • Hot for Teacher • I'll Wait • Girl Gone Bad • House of Pain

5150 (1986)
Good Enough • Why Can't This Be Love? • Get Up • Dreams • Summer Nights • Best of Both Worlds • Love Walks In • "5150" • Inside

OU812 (1988)
Mine All Mine • When It's Love • A.F.U. (Naturally Wired) • Cabo Wabo • Source of Infection • Feels So Good • Finish What Ya Started • Black and Blue • Sucker in a 3 Piece • A Apolitical Blues

For Unlawful Carnal Knowledge (1991)
Poundcake • Judgement Day • Spanked • Runaround • Pleasure Dome • In 'n' Out • Man on a Mission • The Dream Is Over • Right Now • 316 • Top of the World

Live: Right Here, Right Now (1993)
Poundcake • Judgement Day • When It's Love • Spanked • Ain't Talkin' 'Bout Love • In 'n' Out • Dreams • Man on a Mission • Ultra Bass •

Pleasure Dome • Drum Solo • Panama • Love Walks In • Runaround • Right Now • One Way to Rock • Why Can't This Be Love? • Give to Live • Finish What Ya Started • Best of Both Worlds • 316 • You Really Got Me • Cabo Wabo • Won't Get Fooled Again • Jump • Top of the World

Balance (1995)
The Seventh Seal • Can't Stop Lovin' You • Don't Tell Me (What Love Can Do) • Amsterdam • Big Fat Money • Strung Out • Not Enough • Aftershock • Doin' Time • Baluchitherium • Take Me Back (Déjà Vu) • Feelin' • Crossing Over (Japan Only)

Best of Volume 1 (1996)
Eruption • Ain't Talkin' Bout Love • Runnin' with the Devil • Dance the Night Away • And the Cradle Will Rock… • Unchained • Jump • Panama • Hot for Teacher (Japan only) • Why Can't This Be Love? • Dreams • When It's Love • Poundcake • Right Now • Can't Stop Lovin' You • Humans Being • Can't Get This Stuff No More • Me Wise Magic

Van Halen III (1998)
Neworld • Without You • One I Want • From Afar • Dirty Water Dog • Once • Fire in the Hole • Josephina • Year to the Day • Primary • Ballot or the Bullet • How Many Say I

WARNER BROTHERS-RELEASED PROMOTIONAL VIDEOS FOR VAN HALEN SONGS:

Van Halen: Runnin' with the Devil • Eruption • You Really Got Me • Jamie's Cryin'
Van Halen II: Dance the Night Away • You're No Good • Bottoms Up!
Women and Children First: Loss of Control
Fair Warning: Hear about It Later • So This Is Love? • Unchained
Diver Down: Intruder/(Oh) Pretty Woman

xvi The Van Halen Encyclopedia

1984: Jump • Panama • Hot for Teacher
5150: none
OU812: Finish What Ya Started • When It's Love • Feels So Good
For Unlawful Carnal Knowledge: Poundcake • Runaround • Right Now
• Top of the World • Top of the World (live)
Live: Right Here, Right Now: Dreams
Balance: Don't Tell Me (What Love Can Do) • Can't Stop Lovin' You •
Not Enough • Amsterdam
Best of Volume 1: none
Van Halen III: Without You • Fire in the Hole • Once

RELATED BANDS AND THEIR ALBUMS

David Lee Roth
Crazy from the Heat (1985)
Eat 'Em and Smile (1986)
Sonrisa Salvaje (1986)
Skyscraper (1988)
A Little Ain't Enough (1991)
Your Filthy Little Mouth (1994)
The Best (1997)

The DLR Band
The DLR Band (1998)

The Blues Bustin' Mambo Slammers

Sammy Hagar
Nine on a Ten Scale (1976)
Collection (1976)
Sammy Hagar (1977)
Musical Chairs (1977)

All Night Long (1978)
Street Machine (1979)
Loud & Clear (1980)
Danger Zone (1980)
Centre Hole (1980)
Standing Hampton (1981)
Three Lock Box (1982)
Rematch (1982)
Red Alert Dial Nine (1982)
Live 1980 (1983)
VOA (1984)
Cruisin' and Boozin' (1984)
Looking Back (1987)
I Never Said Goodbye (1987)
Rematch & More (1987)
Turn Up the Music (1987)
Red Hot! (1992)
Live-Very Live in Concert (1989)
Best of Sammy Hagar (1992)
Unboxed (1994)
Anthology (1994)
Marching to Mars (1997)
The Best of Sammy Hagar (1999)
Red Voodoo (1999)
Ten 13 (2000)

Montrose
Montrose (1973)
Paper Money (1974)
The Very Best of Montrose (2000)

HSAS
Through the Fire (1984)

Los Tres Gusanos

The Dream
EP (1983)

Extreme
Extreme (1989)
Extreme II: Pornograffitti (1990)
Extreme III: III Sides to Every Story (1992)
Waiting for the Punchline (1995)
The Best of Extreme: An Accidental Collication of Atoms? (1998)

Houndstooth

Tribe of Judah

The Timeline

Pre-1978

1914 Eugenia van Beers is born.

1920 Jan Van Halen is born. Though the family name is officially "van Halen," the more common spelling of "Van Halen" will be used throughout the book.

1940s Jan Van Halen tours Europe playing the clarinet and saxophone and eventually touring with a circus troupe. He later meets and marries Eugenia van Beers in Indonesia.

1946 Robert Hagar becomes the bantamweight boxing champion.

10/13/47 Robert and Gladys Hagar give birth to Sammy Roy Hagar, the youngest of four children, in Monterey, CA.

5/08/53 Alexander Arthur Van Halen is born in Amsterdam.

6/20/53 Michael Anthony Sobolewski is born in Chicago, IL.

10/10/54 Nathan and Sybil Roth give birth to David Lee in Bloomington, IN.

1/26/55 Edward Lodewijk Van Halen is born in Amsterdam.

1961 Edward and Alex begin taking piano lessons. Sammy Hagar fights his first amateur boxing match.

7/26/61 Gary Francis Caine Cherone is born in Malden, MA.

2/22/62 After receiving several letters from relatives describing the promised land of California, the Van Halen family leaves Holland with 75 guilders and a piano and immigrates to the U.S. The family spent nine days on the boat to New York. Jan, Alex, and Eddie provided the ship's musical entertainment. From New York the family took a four-day trip by train to California.

10/10/62 David Lee Roth receives his first radio as a birthday present from his uncle Dave. The young vocalist attaches a stick to the dial, so he can change channels without having to get out of bed.

1963 Sammy Hagar begins playing the guitar after seeing Elvis Presley perform on television.

1964 David Lee Roth checks into a clinic for treatment of his hyperactivity. Michael Anthony moves from Chicago to Los Angeles, where he plays trumpet in his high school marching band.

1965 Ed and Al's first band, The Broken Combs, is formed. The group features Ed on piano and Al playing saxophone along with Don Ferris. Brian Hill plays drums and Kevin Hill plays a plastic Emenee guitar. The group dresses in turtleneck shirts, performing lunchtime concerts at Hamilton Elementary School.

1966 Ed begins playing his four-piece St. George drum set, learning the Dave Clark Five's "Glad All Over" and "Bits and Pieces," while Al takes flamenco guitar lessons.

1967 Edward and Alex switch instruments. Edward takes Alex's guitar and gives his brother his drums. Alex reportedly develops an interest in drums after observing The Beatles' Ringo Starr getting all the girls in *A Hard Day's Night* (United Artists, 1964). At some point during the year, Edward is bitten by a German Shepherd in Covina, CA. Jan Van Halen gives the youth a Pall Mall cigarette and a shot of vodka.

1969 David Lee Roth gets his driver's license and routinely borrows his father's car, driving through his neighborhood and singing along with the radio at the top of his lungs.

1970 Three bands compete in a Battle of the Bands contest in Villa Park in Sierra Madre, CA. Edward, Alex, and a rather long-side-bearded Latin bass player make up one of the bands. The Brick is another band on the bill. A concrete basketball court is used as a stage as Edward rips through a version of Cream's "Spoonful" (from *Wheels of Fire*). Midway through the song, Alex takes a drum solo, and Edward and the bass player light up cigarettes. When the solo ends, the pair place their still-lit cigs under the strings of their respective instruments' headstocks. This is a custom practiced by Edward to this day.

1971 The Trojan Rubber Company is formed (named by Edward). They are also called The Space Brothers so they can perform at schools. David Lee Roth, who is told to learn Cream's "Crossroads" and another song by Grand Funk Railroad prior to the gig, is rejected at an audition for the band. Dennis Travis plays bass and occasionally guitar. At one point the band has a keyboard player, but he is kicked out for unknown reasons.

Edward Van Halen attends a Led Zeppelin concert. While watching Jimmy Page play "Heartbreaker," he gets the idea for an advanced system of hammer-ons that will later evolve into his infamous tapping technique.

1972 Mammoth is formed. The band is made up of Eddie, who sings lead and plays guitar, Alex on drums, and Mark Stone as the bassist.

Sammy Hagar joins Denny Carmassi and Ronnie Montrose, fresh from a stint with the Edgar Winter Group, to form Montrose.

1973 David Lee Roth auditions for Mammoth. Ed sees improvement and gives him the thumbs up. Roth leaves the Red Ball Jets to join the Van Halen brothers.

Edward Van Halen attends Pasadena City College in Pasadena, CA.

1974 Mammoth (now wearing sequined pants) kicks Mark Stone out of the band.

Michael Anthony endures a rigorous audition in a Pasadena, CA, garage and accepts an invitation to join the band, quitting his band, Snake, in the process. The quartet decides to change their name because Mammoth is already in use by another band. They pass on Rat Salad to adopt David Lee Roth's suggestion: Van Halen.

4/04/74 The band becomes a regular act at Gazzaris in West Hollywood, CA (now known as Billboard Live), a breakthrough that gets them out of the backyard party scene.

5/74 Montrose releases *Montrose*.

5/17/74 Robin "Rudy" Leiren becomes Ed's first guitar tech after listening to Ed's various band incarnations at Marshall Junior High School.

11/74 Montrose releases *Paper Money.*

5/76 Van Halen is "discovered" by Gene Simmons at the Starwood in Los Angeles, CA. They record a demo at Village Recorder Studios in Los Angeles. Two guitar solos are later recorded at Electric Ladyland Studios in New York, where Eddie has his first exposure to overdubbing, a technique that he feels is very uncomfortable. While in New York, the band performs using Kiss's equipment for S.I.R.'s Bill Aucoin, who passes to sign the band Piper because he sees no commercial potential in the fledgling Van Halen.

5/77 On a rainy Monday night, Van Halen is "rediscovered" by Ted Templeman and Mo Ostin at the Starwood. Unbeknownst to the band, Templeman has also scouted them out the night before. They later record a twenty-five-song demo from which they will pick nine songs for their first album, Van Halen.

1978

January Sammy Hagar releases *Musical Chairs.*

2/10 *Van Halen* is released.

5/24 *Van Halen* is certified gold.

7/23 Edward Van Halen gives his first interview for a national magazine: Guitar Player.

8/19 Sammy Hagar releases *All Night Long.*

10/10 *Van Halen* is certified platinum.

12/10 Van Halen enters the studio to begin recording *Van Halen II.*

12/31 While at a New Year's Eve party at Ted Templeman's house, Edward Van Halen plays an acoustic guitar. Templeman hears him and suggests he write an instrumental on it for *Van Halen II.*

1979

3/23 *Van Halen II* is released.

4/03 *Van Halen II* is certified gold.

5/08 *Van Halen II* is certified platinum.

September Sammy Hagar releases *Street Machine*.

1980
February David Lee Roth forms the Jungle Studs, a group of 14 adventurers consisting of lawyers, accountants, and doctors (Dave is the only musician). They make annual treks that include kayaking Alaskan rivers and climbing mountains in Nepal.

3/26 *Women and Children First* is released.

May While filming a performance for Italian television at the Piper Club in Rome, Italy, David Lee Roth executes a flying leap from Alex Van Halen's drum riser and hits a low-hanging lighting rig, fracturing his nose and giving himself a minor concussion.

5/29 *Women and Children First* is certified gold.

June Sammy Hagar releases *Danger Zone*.

6/02 *Women and Children First* is certified platinum.

12/31 Edward Van Halen gets down on one knee in a bedroom and proposes to Valerie Bertinelli with an $8,000 emerald-cut diamond ring.

1981
4/11 Edward Van Halen weds Valerie Bertinelli at St. Paul the Apostle Church in Westwood, CA. Nicolette Larson sings a love ballad in French composed especially for the bride and groom. The reception for 400 guests is held at the Grayhall mansion (where the movie *Shampoo* was filmed) owned by millionaire Bernie Cornfield in Beverly Hills, CA. Guests at the reception include Norman Lear and One Day at a Time costars Bonnie Franklin and Pat Harrington. Valerie's mother Nancy helps design the five-flavored wedding cake. The couple spends their wedding night at the Beverly Hills Hotel.

4/29 *Fair Warning* is released.

7/07 *Fair Warning* is certified gold.

October The Jungle Studs explore the island of Tahiti.

11/18 *Fair Warning* is certified platinum.

1982

1982 David Lee Roth purchases a twenty-room mansion in Pasadena, CA, worth a reported $7 million. The swank manor boasts exotic stained glass windows, a thirty-meter swimming pool, a tiled hot tub with see-through front, carefully tended shrubs, and lawns decorated with marble benches. A 12-foot plaster reproduction of Michelangelo's David guards the entryway. It was given to David Lee Roth backstage by a female fan at Cobo Hall in Detroit in 1981. A sign on the estate's wrought-iron gate reads: "There is nothing here worth dying for. No Trespassing." Another sign inside the walls proclaims in bold, red lettering: "If you are found here after dark, you will be found here in the morning."

1/13 Sammy Hagar releases *Standing Hampton*.

4/14 *Diver Down* is released.

6/26-27 Van Halen holds rehearsals in Francis Ford Coppola's Zoetrope Studios in Hollywood, CA, in preparation for the *Hide Your Sheep* tour.

10/15 Edward Van Halen's left wrist is x-rayed at Hand Surgery Associates in New York, NY. A fracture is found that results in the cancellation of three shows on the *Diver Down* tour.

10/22 Van Halen Day is declared by Mayor Sara Robertson in Worcester, MA, after WAAF Radio sponsors a 25,000-signature petition to get the band to add a third show at The Centrum.

December Sammy Hagar releases *Three Lock Box*.

1983

March The 5150 Studio is built. It begins as a forty-foot-long room with an adjustable ceiling height of up to 18 feet.

April "Beat It" goes to #1 on Billboard's charts. Two solos are recorded for the song (only one is used), and Eddie does it free of charge.

4/20 Edward Van Halen and Valerie Bertinelli sign paperwork to lease Marvin Hamlisch's Malibu, CA, beach house for the summer of 1983.

Summer Eddie Van Halen writes and records "Strung Out" and three instrumentals for *The Seduction of Gina*, a movie-of-the-week starring Valerie Bertinelli, at Hamlisch's beach house.

1984
1/04 *1984* is released.

February MTV announces their Lost Weekend with Van Halen contest. Entry requirements: a postcard with your name, address, telephone number, and age. The prize: one winner and a guest will spend the weekend with Van Halen.

David Lee Roth begins daily workouts with International Kick Boxing Champion Benny "The Jet" Urquidez.

2/25 "Jump" begins a five-week peak at #1 on the U.S. Billboard's Singles chart.

3/12 *1984* is certified gold and platinum.

3/17 *1984* begins a four-week peak at #2 on Billboard's Top LP chart.

3/20 MTV chooses Kurt Jefferis of Phoenixville, PA, as the winner of their Lost Weekend with Van Halen contest. Jefferis, whose postcard was picked from more than one million entries, passed on offers of clothing, cars, women, and even $5,000 to take his best friend, Tom Winnick. 1,000 runners-up win a copy of *1984*.

3/31 HSAS releases *Through the Fire*.

August Sammy Hagar releases *VOA*.

10/22 *Van Halen* is certified platinum five times over. *Van Halen II* is certified triple platinum. *Women and Children First* is certified double platinum.

10/24 *1984* is certified platinum four times over.

12/31 David Lee Roth releases his first solo album, *Crazy from the Heat*.

1985

1985 Ex-Dream (featuring Gary Cherone on vocals) wins MTV's Basement Tapes contest hosted by Martha Quinn and Tommy Shaw, beating out Henry Lee Summer by one percentage point.

1/23 *1984* is certified platinum five times over.

2/12 Copies of professional audio and video recordings of past Van Halen concerts are delivered to the home of Noel Monk.

April Noel Monk is fired from the Van Halen staff after he and the band cannot reach a suitable contract renegotiation. A short time later, Monk sues the band for $10.1 million, alleging that he has not been given his fair share of merchandising profits (outcome unknown). Kiss's Gene Simmons reportedly tries to become Van Halen's manager.

4/01 David Lee Roth leaves Van Halen (unofficially on April Fool's Day).

Spring Warner Brothers President Larry Waronker suggests to Edward Van Halen that the band drop the name Van Halen now that David Lee Roth is no longer in the band.

6/04 David Lee Roth and Billy Sheehan sit down in Dave's kitchen and begin planning the strategy and formation of Roth's new solo band.

August Edward Van Halen calls Sammy Hagar from Claudio Zampolli's auto shop and invites him to jam with the band at the 5150 Studio. Hagar claims he knew they'd call and ask him to jam and shares the sentiment with both his wife and Ed Leffler. A few days later, he appears and the band plays an unfinished "Summer Nights" and "Good Enough," with Hagar improvising lyrics. 20 minutes later Hagar joins Van Halen. Apparently no love is lost between the band and David Lee Roth. In the bathroom in the 5150 Studio there hangs a photograph of Van Halen while Roth was still in the band and his face is covered with tape. Hagar's joining Van Halen presents a problem for his solo label, Geffen. He has just come off his most successful album to date, *VOA*, and they aren't about to let him go without a fight. After several weeks of negotiations, the label lets him go. Hagar owes Geffen one more solo album, and they get a percentage of *5150*.

September Ted Templeman bets David Lee Roth that the vocalist can't drive his 1951 Mercury lowrider to New York, NY, from Los Angeles, CA, in three days, driving no faster than 55 mph, and arrive in time for the 1985 MTV Video Music Awards. Roth has crew member Larry Hostler ship the car to New York, while he flies out on a plane. Hostler picks up the vehicle after the pair arrive, and Roth drives it to Radio City Music Hall. Upon his arrival the vocalist sticks out his hand to a surprised Templeman and remarks, "Pay up!"

At the awards show, MTV announces Sammy Hagar as Van Halen's new lead vocalist.

11/13 Edward Van Halen places his hands in cement as he is inducted into the Hollywood, CA, Rock Walk. The Rock Walk is located in front of the Guitar Center music store on Sunset Boulevard. Other inductees at the inaugural ceremony include Stevie Wonder, Robert Moog (creator of the Moog Synthesizer), drum king Remo Belli, Les Paul, luthier Frank Martin III, and amplifier creator Jim Marshall. Among the dozens of celebrities on hand to witness the event are Quiet Riot's Frankie Banalli and Carlos Cavazo, Alex and Kelly Van Halen, Michael Anthony, Valerie Bertinelli, the late Ennis Cosby, and Lita Ford.

November Mick Jones begins overseeing production on *5150*.

1986

February Edward Van Halen attends the National Association of Music Merchants show in Anaheim, CA. He presents one of his Kramer striped guitars to Michael Guiterrez, the winner of a contest that 80,000 people entered.

3/24 Van Halen releases *5150*.

4/25 Van Halen tops Billboard's LP chart with *5150*.

5/28 *5150* is certified gold, platinum, and double platinum.

7/04 David Lee Roth releases *Eat 'Em and Smile*.

9/01 David Lee Roth's *Eat 'Em and Smile* is certified gold and platinum.

10/10 *5150* is certified triple platinum.

11/24 Van Halen releases *Live without a Net*.

December Alex and Edward's father, Jan, passes away at the age of 66. Ed and Al go into the studio on the day of his death and play for around 10 hours.

12/20 Linda Duke claims she suffered "acoustic trama" after David Lee Roth's performance at the Great Western Forum in Inglewood, CA, on 12/19/86.

1987

6/23 Sammy Hagar releases an untitled album, later titled *I Never Said Goodbye*.

7/01 *1984* is certified platinum six times over.

1988

1988 Due to conflicting schedules, Edward declines an offer to produce Billy Joel's *Storm Front* album.

February David Lee Roth releases *Skyscraper*.

March Kim Musgrove spends the day at the 5150 Studio after winning MTV's Sammy Hagar's Name My Album contest. Her entry, I Never Said Goodbye, was picked by Sammy and entitled her and a friend to hang out with the band for a day at 5150.

3/29 David Lee Roth's *Skyscraper* is certified gold and platinum.

April While vacationing with Valerie Bertinelli on Turtle Island, located off the Australian coast, Edward Van Halen is infected with the dengue fever virus. Two days later his temperature reaches 105 degrees. He spends five days in the hospital recuperating.

5/16 Sammy Hagar calls in from his car phone when Alex Van Halen and Michael Anthony appear on Rockline. All callers receive an autographed copy of the "Black and Blue" CD. A random drawing of postcards for an additional 150 CDs is also held.

5/24 Van Halen releases *OU812*.

6/25 *OU812* reaches #1 on the Billboard charts.

7/26 *OU812* is certified gold, platinum, and double platinum.

1989

1/18 *5150* is certified quadruple platinum, and *OU812* is certified triple platinum.

2/01 *Van Halen* is certified platinum six times over.

3/14 Extreme releases *Extreme*.

10/15-16 Edward Van Halen and Michael Anthony take part in the First Annual World Music Invitational Pro/Am Celebrity Golf Tournament held at Stonebridge Ranch in Dallas, TX.

1990

4/22 Van Halen opens the Cabo Wabo Cantina in Cabo San Lucas, Mexico.

7/05 *Van Halen II* is certified platinum four times over.

8/07 Extreme releases *Extreme II: Pornogaffitti*.

12/17 Van Halen files a federal law suit against 2 Live Crew contending that the rap act sampled a riff from "Ain't Talkin' 'Bout Love" for their song "The Fuck Shop" without the band's permission. The suit seeks $300,000 in damages for copyright infringement and unfair competition.

1991

January The 5150 Studio is remodeled: A new console is installed, and the size of the studio is doubled, due in part to the addition of a drum room.

David Lee Roth releases *A Little Ain't Enough*.

3/16 Edward Van Halen and Valerie Bertinelli welcome their first son, Wolfgang William Van Halen (named after Wolfgang Amadeus Mozart), at St. John's Hospital in Santa Monica, CA. Wolfgang's birth weight is seven pounds, thirteen ounces.

5/14 Extreme releases *Photograffitti*.

6/13 Van Halen appears on national radio from the 5150 Studio to premiere *For Unlawful Carnal Knowledge*.

6/17 Van Halen releases *For Unlawful Carnal Knowledge*.

6/18 Alex Van Halen places his handprints in cement as he is inducted to the Hollywood, CA Rock Walk.

8/22 *For Unlawful Carnal Knowledge* is certified gold and platinum.

10/23 David Lee Roth attends the opening of Planet Hollywood.

11/08 *For Unlawful Carnal Knowledge* is certified double platinum.

11/28 David Lee Roth attends a memorial for Bill Graham, the legendary concert promoter who was killed in a helicopter crash near the Sears Point Motor Speedway in northern California in the beginning of November.

1992

4/09 Police confiscate the shirt of 19-year-old Shawnn Pierce outside a restaurant in Little Rock, AR. The shirt had been purchased at a Van Halen concert the previous night. Pierce is cited and fined based on an Arkansas state law forbidding public display of obscene material on a motor vehicle or clothing, which is punishable by 30 days in jail and up to a $100 fine.

6/18 Shawnn Pierce appears in municipal court in Little Rock, AR, to receive sentencing for having violated state obscenity laws. Van Halen pays the youth's fine.

8/05 Toto drummer Jeff Porcaro passes away at the age of 38.

8/10 Edward Van Halen attends the funeral for Jeff Porcaro at Forest Lawn Memorial Park in Hollywood Hills, Los Angeles, CA.

8/20 Michael Anthony and Sammy Hagar co-host the Cabo Wabo Rock Radio Festival at the Cabo Wabo Cantina in Cabo San Lucas, Mexico. The Westwood One live special includes performances, interviews, and a Van Halen concert taped in Fresno, CA. After the special leaves the air, live jamming continues.

9/08 Extreme releases *Extreme III: III Sides to Every Story*.

9/09 Van Halen attends the MTV Video Music Awards at the Pauley Pavilion at UCLA in Los Angeles, CA. They are interviewed before and after the show and take home awards for their "Right Now" video, including Best Editing (Michael Sinaway), Best Direction (Mark Finske), and Video of the Year.

11/16 *The Best of Sammy Hagar* is released.

1993

1/23 Van Halen releases *Live: Right Here, Right Now.*

3/03 Van Halen plays the Whisky A GoGo in Hollywood, CA, to celebrate their fifteenth anniversary. See "Whisky A GoGo Anniversary Gig."

3/21 Michael Anthony takes part in the opening of the Bass Centre in Birmingham, England.

4/16 David Lee Roth is arrested and arraigned in New York, NY, for possession of a $10 bag of marijuana in an NYPD drug sweep known as Operation Doubleheader. He was fined $35 and placed on one year's probation.

5/04 *Live: Right Here, Right Now* is certified gold and platinum.

9/20 *Live: Right Here, Right Now* is certified double platinum.

9/29 *Van Halen* is certified platinum seven times over.

10/16 At the age of 57, manager Ed Leffler succumbs to thyroid cancer at Cedars Sinai Hospital in Los Angeles, CA.

10/19 Funeral services for Ed Leffler are held at Hillside Park & Mortuary in Los Angeles, CA.

10/22 Petersen Publishing Company gives away a Chevy C1500 red, white, and black striped project truck in a Hot Rod Hot Trucks Magazine giveaway. The truck is one of only two such beauties in existence. The second belongs to Edward Van Halen.

12/07 Edward Van Halen visits the Rock Walk outside the Guitar Center in Hollywood, CA, to celebrate the induction of Led Zeppelin's Jimmy Page.

1994

1994 Sammy and Betsy Hagar divorce after more than twenty years of marriage.

January Music Man's Sterling Ball donates one of his kidneys to his ailing son, Casey. Eddie Van Halen steers Casey's wheelchair around the hospital for x-rays. Later, Ed would hold a charity golf tournament for kidney ailments.

2/23 Edward assists in groundbreaking ceremonies at the Hard Rock Hotel in Las Vegas, NV, with B.B. King, Chris Isaak, and Hard Rock Cafe founder Peter Morton.

3/08 David Lee Roth releases *Your Filthy Little Mouth*.

3/15 Sammy Hagar releases *Unboxed*.

5/25 Van Halen begins recording *Balance*.

June Ed takes part in Jim Kelley's charity softball event, along with Dan Marino and Warren Moon.

7/11 *Van Halen* is certified platinum eight times over. *1984* is certified platinum seven times over.

August Van Halen considers headlining Woodstock 2, but declines because they feel it would be a logistical nightmare, and they would rather focus on finishing *Balance*.

8/04 *Women and Children First* is certified triple platinum. *Fair Warning* is certified double platinum.

8/17 *5150* is certified platinum five times over. *For Unlawful Carnal Knowledge* is certified platinum three times over.

9/02 Van Halen finishes recording *Balance*.

9/07 Mike Fraser begins mixing *Balance*.

9/23 David Lee Roth appears at an opening of an HMV Music Store.

10/02 Edward Van Halen quits drinking.

10/13 America Online posts a 60-second clip of "Don't Tell Me (What Love Can Do)" available for downloading prior to the release of *Balance*.

1995
1/12 Van Halen appears on Warner/Reprise's Cyber-Talk on America Online.

1/17 Van Halen premiers *Balance* on Westwood One radio. Two hundred forty stations carry the live special from Air Studios in London, England. One hundred twenty contest winners from across the U.S. attend the event.

1/24 Van Halen releases *Balance* and makes a promotional appearance in Paris, France.

1/26 Van Halen rehearses for their "Secret Gig" at the Luxor Theater in Arnhem, Holland.

1/28 Van Halen films the video for "Amsterdam" while walking the streets in Amsterdam, Netherlands. Eddie also receives his first tattoo featuring the name "Wolfgang" over the Van Halen logo. MTV refuses to air the video due to strong drug use references in the lyrics.

February Extreme releases *Waiting for the Punchline.*

3/29 *Balance* is certified gold, platinum, and double platinum.

4/03 Van Halen celebrates the double platinum award given to *Balance* and the sale of more than 60 million Van Halen albums overall at the Museum of Flying in Santa Monica, CA. Joining the band in attendance are Atomic Punks guitarist Bart Walsh and Edward's tech, Matt Bruck.

4/04 Sammy Hagar records new lyrics for the video release of "Amsterdam." Strangely, MTV still refuses to air the video, which is seen only overseas.

4/07 Edward Van Halen is cited and detained for 30 minutes after a .25-caliber semiautomatic handgun (a Baretta) was discovered when his carry-on bag passed through a scanner at the Burbank-Glendale-Pasadena Airport in Burbank, CA.

4/11 Edward Van Halen is charged with unlawful possession of a firearm for allegedly trying to board a United Airlines flight with a loaded gun in his carry-on bag. He pleads no-contest to the charges, is fined $910, and is placed on one year's probation.

8/02 Van Halen is inducted into the Metro Music Cafe in Royal Oak, MI.

10/06 Van Halen places their handprints in cement as the band is inducted into Guitar Center's Rock Walk in Hollywood, CA.

11/17 Sammy and fiancée Kari Karti buy a marriage license at the county clerk's office in San Rafael, CA.

11/29 Sammy and Kari Karti exchange wedding vows on Mount Tamalpais in Marin County, CA. The reception is held at the Mill Valley Outdoor Art Club. Guests include Whoopi Goldberg, Whitesnake's Denni Carmassi, Gary Pihl (formerly with Sammy's solo band and now with Boston), and Starship's Craig Chaquico. At the reception a jam session ensues with some of the guests and all of the members of Van Halen.

12/17 Decked out in a hard hat and an orange safety vest, Sammy Hagar poses for a publicity photo with workers in Santa Rosa, CA. The Department of Transportation employees were hard at work changing the 55 mph speed limit signs to 65 mph as part of Congress's repeal on the 55 mph speed limit law.

1996

1/04 "The Seventh Seal" is nominated for a Grammy in the 38th annual Grammy Awards for Best Hard Rock Performance.

March Sammy writes "The Silent Extreme" (also called "The Hot Zone") for the *Twister* soundtrack. The song is not used.

3/10-13 Van Halen mixes "Humans Being" for the *Twister* soundtrack.

4/01 Sammy and Kari welcome their first daughter. She is named Kama, which in Sanskrit means "love."

6/25 Radio stations across the country announce the breakup of Van Halen.

6/26 SRO Management releases an official statement that Sammy is out of the band and that the original lineup is currently in the studio recording new material. Hagar releases his own press release citing creative differences as the cause for the split.

7/22 Van Halen enters the studio with David Lee Roth to begin recording material for *Best of Volume 1*.

8/02 Van Halen completes the recording of "Me Wise Magic," the first of two tracks with Dave for *Best of Volume 1*.

8/03 Van Halen completes the recording of "Can't Get This Stuff No More," the second track with Dave for *Best of Volume 1*.

8/05 Mixing begins on both new tracks for *Best of Volume 1*.

8/07 *Van Halen* is certified platinum ten times over.

8/08 *1984* is certified platinum nine times over.

9/04 Van Halen with David Lee Roth appears on the MTV Video Music Awards and presents the award for Best Male Video to Beck. The reunited quartet receives a standing ovation from the shocked and delighted crowd. At the backstage press conference, emotions flare as Ed and Dave argue about answers to give the reporters. Frustrated with the reporters' questions, Ed attempts to set the record straight saying that the only thing happening between the band and Dave at the time is the *Best of Volume 1* project.

10/02 David Lee Roth releases an open letter to the public expressing his views on the situation with the band:

An Open Letter from David Lee Roth October 2, 1996

To Whom This May Interest:

You've probably heard rumors that Van Halen and I will not be consummating our highly publicized reunion. And since neither Edward, Alex, nor Michael have corroborated or denied the gossip, I would like to go on record with the following: Eddie did it.

It's no secret, nor am I ashamed of my unabashed rapture at the prospect of resurrecting the original Van Halen. A "couple of songs" was all I knew for sure when Edward and I got together three months ago to write them. At that time, the band tip-toed around me sprinkling sentiments like, "this isn't a sure thing, Dave; this doesn't mean anything long term, Dave; we're still auditioning other singers, Dave." I was cool. I was happy. I was in the moment.

The next thing I knew, the four of us are doing a surprise walk-on at the MTV Awards. I told Edward at that time that I didn't think it was a good idea for the band to go to New York half-cocked; and that I didn't want to imply by our presence that we were "back" if in fact it was just a quickie for old time's sake. Well ain't hindsight always 20/20...Had I asked for something in writing, this wouldn't have happened. Had I acknowledged the occasional icy grip in my stomach, maybe this wouldn't have happened. But I didn't. Like I said—rapture. And, I love these guys.

Do I trust them? That question never entered my mind.

Then, a series of events last week led me to discover at about the same time the press did, that the band, along with their manager, had already hired another lead singer, possibly as long as three months ago. I wonder how he felt the night of the MTV Awards. It certainly explains why on that night Edward looked as uncomfortable as a man who just signed a deal with the Devil. I can't think of a reason Edward would lie to me about being considered for the lead singer when he had already hired someone, and then let me appear on MTV under the impression that there was great likelihood that Van Halen and I were reuniting. As I said, I told him in no uncertain terms that I didn't want to do the MTV gig as a band unless we were, in fact, a band.

And so I apologize to my fans and my supporters, and to MTV. I was an unwitting participant in this deception. It sickens me that the "reunion" as seen on MTV was nothing more than a publicity stunt. If I am guilty of anything, I'm guilty of denial. I wanted to believe it just as much as anyone else. Those who know me know that trickery was never my style.

10/03 Van Halen releases an official press release in response to Dave's open letter.

The Van Halen Response:

We parted company with David Lee Roth 11 years ago for many reasons. In his open letter of October 2nd, we were reminded of some of them. The intention all along was to do two new songs with Dave for the *Best of Volume 1* package. He was never led to believe anything but that. When the four of us were asked by MTV and Warner Bros. to present an award at the 1996 MTV Video Music Awards, the four of us agreed. Dave was never an "unwitting participant." We appeared in public just as we do before releasing any other Van Halen record. For the last two weeks we have been working with someone who we hope will be part of the future of Van Halen, although no final decision can be announced until contractual considerations have been resolved. Van Halen will go forward and create the best possible music we can.

Edward, Alex, Michael

"Me Wise Magic," the first song with Dave since 1984, is released to radio stations across the country. The song had previously been played openly on many U.S. radio stations, all of which received Cease and Desist orders from Warner Bros. immediately afterward.

Extreme officially disbands.

10/04 Ed and Al are interviewed on the KLOS Mark and Brian radio show in Los Angeles, CA, to discuss the situation with David Lee Roth and announce that Gary Cherone is 99.999% locked in as the new lead singer.

10/05 Ed, Al, and Mike are presented with an Outstanding Contribution to Music award at the 1996 Foundations Forum at the Palladium in Hollywood, CA. They are also presented platinum awards for surpassing the 10-million-sales mark for *Van Halen*. Later that day the band is honored with a plaque commemorating the event. The plaque is to be placed in the sidewalk in front of the historic Whisky A GoGo in West Hollywood, CA.

Extreme's Pat Badger releases an open letter to Extreme fans on the Internet explaining Extreme's breakup.

10/08 Tommy Nast, senior vice president and general manager of the Album Network, releases an open letter in response to David Lee Roth's open letter:

Dave,

After reading your letter, I had to tell you it did interest me. It interested me so much I had to write this. To our readers who don't know, since your departure from Van Halen a decade ago, I consider myself a friend to you, to the Van Halen camp, and yes, to Sammy Hagar as well. And because of my friendship with all of you, I had to state the facts I'm aware of that I don't think you know.

I know for a fact that Edward, Michael, Alex, and Ray Danniels did not have a lead singer hired three months ago, since they were running names by me, including yours, to get a temperature on what the spin may be. I know for a fact that one month ago, a singer had not been hired, because Ray, myself, and a potential singer for the band were discussing the possibilities. That person was not Gary Cherone, and because I gave that person my word that I would not give his identity, I will not use it here. But believe me, nothing at this point was set in stone.

Dave, before you insinuate that you were lied to, I have to share my knowledge on the subject. I don't want you to burn a bridge with Van Halen again, without hearing from a neutral party that can go on record and hopefully set it straight.

There are many people who are disappointed (me included) that we will not, at this time, see you reunite full-time with Van Halen or a tour or new album. But, there are also a lot of fans who will be ecstatic to hear the two new tracks you all put together. It is very true that we don't know what the future will hold, and if Van Halen confirms Gary as the new singer, that is their prerogative. But I did have to make it known that Gary was not hired as early as one month ago, no less three.

I wish you well and will always support your musical endeavors.

Your friend,
Tommy Nast

10/17 *Best of Volume 1* is released throughout Japan.
10/18 *Best of Volume 1* is released in the Netherlands.
10/22 *Best of Volume 1* is released in the U.S.
10/28 *Best of Volume 1* and *Video Hits Volume 1* are released in the U.K.

10/29 *Video Hits Volume 1* is released in the U.S.

11/04 *Best of Volume 1* is released in Australia.

11/07 *Best of Volume 1* drops from #1 to #3 on the Billboard charts.

11/08 Sammy Hagar debuts "Salvation on Sand Hill" on the Internet using a new technology called Liquid Audio.

11/15 *Best of Volume 1* drops to #6 on the Billboard charts. Ed, Pat Torpey, and Steve Lukather rehearse at 5150 in preparation for their appearance at the ALS Benefit in Chicago, IL. The band's bass player, Billy Sheehan, is in Australia.

12/13 John Cottrell, the winner of the signed Peavey Wolfgang in Van Halen's Best of Volume 1 giveaway, flies to California to receive the guitar from Edward at 5150.

12/16 Edward and Alex Van Halen shoot a milk advertisement at 5150. The ad surfaces a few years later in a book, *The Milk Mustache Book: A Behind-The-Scenes Look at America's Favorite Advertising Campaign* by Jay Schulberg.

1997
1997 Edward receives the award for Best Rock Guitarist at the 1997 Orville H. Gibson Awards held at the Hard Rock Café in New York, NY. Dave Davies of the Kinks accepts the award on Edward's behalf. Each year's winners are decided by a nationwide panel of magazine editors and music writers. Proceeds from the ceremony go to the Nordoff-Roberts Music Therapy Foundation.

1/04 Fresh from a holiday break, Van Halen returns to 5150 to continue writing and recording new material with Gary Cherone.

1/18 Sammy Hagar and Michael Anthony appear at the 1997 NAMM Convention in Anaheim, CA. Hagar signs autographs in the Washburn booth, while Anthony signs his John Hancock in the Ampeg Booth. Anthony later takes part in the St. Louis Music 75th Anniversary Birthday Bash.

1/28 Pat Boone releases *In a Metal Mood-No More Mr. Nice Guy,* a collection of hard rock cover songs by the 1950s Christian pop idol including Van Halen's "Panama."

4/01 Sammy Hagar signs a record deal with Track Factory.

4/11 Sammy Hagar finishes a month's rehearsing at Hun Sound in San Rafael, CA, in preparation for his upcoming solo tour.

5/01 *Best of Volume 1* is certified gold and platinum.

5/20 Sammy Hagar releases *Marching to Mars.*

7/19 Sammy Hagar throws out the first pitch at a Cleveland Indians baseball game.

10/15 An announcement is made that *Van Halen III* has been completed and turned over to Warner Brothers.

10/23 David Lee Roth's autobiography *Crazy from the Heat* is released.

10/24 Gary Cherone appears on the Internet to answers fans' questions.

10/28 David Lee Roth's *The Best* compilation is released.

12/05 Extreme releases *The Best of Extreme: An Accidental Collication of Atoms?*

1998

February David Lee Roth breaks his wrist while ice-skating at the Wollman Rink in New York's Central Park.

2/19 "Without You," the first release from *Van Halen III,* makes its official radio debut. It was actually released two days earlier to some radio stations, and bootleg copies debuted weeks before this date.

2/23 The first single from *Van Halen III* is released only in Australia.

3/10 *Van Halen III* is released in Japan.

3/12 The Album Network airs the *Van Halen III* premiere party from Billboard Live (formerly Gazzari's) in West Hollywood, CA. The broadcast is heard on hundreds of radio stations throughout the world.

The band performs a show after the broadcast.

3/17 *Van Halen III* is released in the U.S.

5/21 *Best of Volume 1* is certified double platinum and *Diver Down* is certified quadruple platinum.

6/09 The DLR Band releases *The DLR Band*.

August David Lee Roth surprises the patrons of the Lansky Lounge in New York City by taking the stage unannounced to perform a karaoke version of "California Girls" after watching a woman sing "Just a Gigolo."

8/19 *Van Halen III* is certified gold.

9/09 *Van Halen* is re-released on 24k gold CDs and LPs.

11/27 David Lee Roth launches Dave TV, an episodic web site at www.dave-tv.com devoted to Dave's stories and music. Some early Van Halen songs are heard publicly for the first time.

12/27 Gary Cherone joins Nuno Bettencourt, Paul Geary, Mike Mangini, and Pat Badger in an Extreme reunion at Paul Geary's "The Backstage" club in Haverhill, MA. This the first time the band had performed together in four years. The performance includes two Van Halen songs.

1999

1/15 Two videos for "Once" are released on the Internet.

2/08 *1984* is certified platinum ten times over.

3/16 *Van Halen* and *1984* are honored at a RIAA ceremony with a new award, called the "Diamond" award. This new award is bestowed upon albums that have sold at least 10 million copies in the U.S. The band attends the ceremony, which is held at the Roseland in New York City.

3/23 Sammy Hagar releases *Red Voodoo*.

5/17 *Balance* producer Bruce Fairbairn is found dead in his Vancouver home.

June Gary Cherone issues an open letter to Eddie Vedder arguing against Vedder's pro-choice stance on abortion.

6/01 David Lee Roth introduces his new DLR Band to the world with a private performance for 30 friends at Nightingales rehearsal studio in Burbank, CA.

8/02 Danny "Kootch" Kortchmar begins working with the band on their next album as a producer.

10/31 David Lee Roth announces that a law suit has been filed against a former employee for piracy of his image online.

11/05 Gary Cherone leaves the band. Van Halen issues the following press release:

The members of Van Halen have announced that singer Gary Cherone is leaving the band. The band stressed that the departure was both mutual and amicable and they remain good friends. The band is currently working on its next LP and Cherone is pursuing new musical ventures.

The members of the band, Eddie Van Halen, Alex Van Halen and Michael Anthony, expressed their appreciation for Gary's work with the band and wished him well in his future endeavors.

"I had a great time singing with the band and I wish Eddie, Alex and Michael all the best. I'll see 'em in Boston," said Cherone.

Eddie Van Halen said, "Gary is a brother and he and I will continue to have a personal and musical relationship."

11/15 The Houston Chronicle reports that David Lee Roth has received 11 death threats by email while in Lubbock, TX.

11/16 Eddie has his hip replaced in a one-hour surgery while totally conscious. He makes an audio recording of the procedure. In two days he is walking again.

12/27 David Lee Roth records a song for Ashley Abernathy, a girl suffering from leukemia, through the Songs of Love Foundation. Only two copies of the song, titled "Ashley Abernathy" are made, one for Ashley and one for the highest bidder at auction with the proceeds going to Songs of Love. The high bidder, from Japan, paid $3,350 for the track on 8/21/00.

2000

2/06 Ed's new line of amps, Peavey's 5150II, wins Best New Instrument Amplifier of 2000 and Product of the Year for 2000 at NAMM.

Sammy Hagar is named Master Taster of Tequila at the American Tasting Institute's Awards at Carnegie Hall. His various Cabo Wabo Tequilas win 3 awards including Best of Show.

6/20 Trump Marina Casino in Atlantic City issues Van Halen chips. The chips feature the Cherone-era lineup and are valued at $10.

7/07 Mike Hartman, DLR Band guitarist and songwriter, dies at the age of 24, losing his life-long battle with Cystic Fibrosis.

9/19 Remastered versions of the first six albums are released.

10/24 Sammy Hagar releases *Ten 13*.

11/27 Eddie, Valerie, and Wolfgang attend a 'N Sync concert at the MGM Grand in Las Vegas.

Alphabetical Entries

A

A Apolitical Blues-(*OU812* [3:50]) Engineer Donn Landee hung two microphones in the middle of a room, and this song was recorded in approximately 30 minutes for inclusion on the *OU812* album.

This is one of only two Van Halen tracks featuring guitar work from Sammy Hagar. Ed played slide guitar on this song using a 1959 black Airline guitar (purchased at the 1985 NAMM show in Anaheim, CA) through a small Music Man amplifier.

Ted Templeman and Donn Landee recorded the original version of this song with Little Feat 16 years earlier.

This track is included on the CD release, but not the vinyl or cassette releases of *OU812*. It is also on the B-side of the "Black and Blue" single.

ABC in Concert-Gary Cherone hosted this show on 7/17/93. Van Halen was also featured live on a 1988 segment.

Access-Van Halen appeared on the cover of this publication dated March 1995. The issue featured "Just For Laughs," a one-page Gary Cherone interview by Keith Sharp and "Rock's Ultimate Balancing Act," a three-page Van Halen interview by Roy Trakin.

Access Hollywood-Edward Van Halen and Valerie Bertinelli appeared on this television show on 4/20/97 to promote Valerie's Lifetime channel special, "Intimate Portrait." The program also showed clips of Van Halen's 1991 MTV Video Music Awards performance of "Poundcake" from 9/04/91.

On 6/05/98 this show premiered the "Fire in the Hole" video.

Action Now (formerly Skateboarder magazine)-A two-page Van Halen feature by Steven Rosen appeared in the August 1981 issue of this publication. Address: Surfer Publishing Group, 33046 Calle Aviador, San Juan Capistrano, CA 92675-4704.

Addicted to Love-During the *5150* tour, the band played this Robert Palmer cover almost every night backstage before concerts. On 8/08/86 the band played the song on stage in the middle of "Best of Both Worlds." The band also performed this song on 8/11/86, where they proceeded to mimic the dance from the Rober Palmer video for the song.

Aftershock-(*Balance* [5:29]) The lyrics to this song are about Sammy's divorce from his wife Betsy. This track appears in a different place in the song order for the cassette version of the album.
Ed used his MXR Flanger for some parts in the song.

A.F.U. (Naturally Wired)-(*OU812* [4:28]) Alternate titles for this song included "All Fired Up," "Naturally Wired," and "A.F.U."
The song was written around a drumbeat Ed had come up with eight years before recording it for the *OU812* album.

Ain't Talkin' 'Bout Love-(*Van Halen, Best of Volume 1* [3:37]; *Live: Right Here, Right Now* [4:37]) Ed felt this song was the "lamest" song he had ever written. It took him six months to work up the nerve to show it to the rest of the band.
This song was originally written, as was "Loss of Control," to poke fun at the emerging punk scene.
The song was written in one day in the basement of David Lee Roth's parents' home in 1977 (along with the unreleased tune "Bullethead"). Dave's house was often used as a rehearsal space.
A Coral electric sitar was used to double Ed's solo.

In 1985 Minutemen released a cover of this song on *Tour-Spiel* (Reflex) and *Just a Minute Men* (Virgin). In 1989 the song was again released on the album *Post-Mersh, Vol. 3* (SST 165), and again on a 1990 compilation album *Duck & Cover* (SST 263).

2 Live Crew sampled a riff from this song without permission for their 1990 track "The Fuck Shop" and was subsequently sued by Van Halen, who sought $300,000 for copyright infringement. The suite was filed on 12/17/90.

Scatterbrain covered the main riff in this song for "Down with the Ship (Slight Return)" on their 1990 album *Here Comes Trouble*. The song had moderate success on MTV's Headbanger's Ball. They rerecorded the song on their 1994 EP *Mundus Intellectualos* without the Van Halen riff.

The Mighty Mighty Bosstones released their version of this song on their 1992 album *Where'd You Go?* (Taang! 48).

In 1997 the U.K. band Apollo 440 released a song using a sampled riff from this track entitled "Ain't Talkin' 'Bout Dub." The song was used to advertise the women's basketball league, the WNBA. The "Ain't Talkin' 'Bout Dub" CD single (UK Sony SSXCOX6, 1997) features several different remixes of the song. Tracks: • @440 Instrumental Version • Armand Van Helden Moonraker Edit • Escape from New York Edit • Technology Park Remix • Joey the Butcher Remix • Booby Trap Remix

The band Skin released a live version of this song on their CD single *Take Me Down to the River.*

The Moog Cookbook's second album, *Ye Olde Space Bande* (Restless 1997), features a remake of this song with Devo's Mark Mothersbaugh on synthesizer and a computerized voice programmed by Michael Penn.

A recording of Third Eye Blind performing this song is in circulation.

Air Studios-In 1993 at Air Studios in Cleveland, OH, Extreme's Gary Cherone and Nuno Bettencourt performed "Rest in Peace" and "Hole Hearted" during an early morning live broadcast as WMMS spent an entire year celebrating its 25th anniversary.

Air Studios in London, England, hosted the *Balance* premiere party on 1/17/95.

The Album Network-Van Halen appeared on the covers of the 11/01/96 and 2/20/98 issues of this publication. Gary and Ed were interviewed in the 3/08/98 issue.

All Night Long-(Capitol Records 11812, 1978) Sammy Hagar solo album released on 8/19/78. The album spent 9 weeks on the charts topping out at #89. Tracks: • Red • Rock 'n' Roll Weekend • Make It Last/Reckless • Turn Up the Music • I've Done Everything for You • Young Girl Blues • Bad Motor Scooter

All Night Long was reissued in February 1997 (One Way Records, 72438 19094 23). The album features a cover of the Donovan song "Young Girl Blues." Rick Springfield later covered "I've Done Everything for You" on his 1980 release *Working Class Dog* (AYLI-4766), which reached the Top 10. The track was also included on Springfield's 1989 release *Rick Springfield's Greatest Hits* (BMG Music, 9817-2-R).

"Sittin' on the Dock of the Bay" was released on the singles for this album, though it didn't appear on the album. This version of the classic song featured Steve Cropper on guitar and the Boss-Tones (Boston's Brad Delp, Sib Hashiam, and Barry Goudreau) on backing vocals.

All Night Long singles/promos
"I've Done Everything for You," "Sitting on the Dock of the Bay," Capitol SPRO-9077, 12" Vinyl, USA, 1978.

"Sittin' on the Dock of the Bay," "I've Done Everything for You," Capitol 8511, 12" Vinyl, USA, 1979.

All Right Now-This Free cover song was performed in medley format with "You Really Got Me" on 4/29/93 at Wembley Arena in

London, England. Opening act Little Angels joined the band on stage for this performance.

ALS Benefit-This nearly eight-hour benefit on 11/17/96 at the Riviera Theater in Chicago, IL, was held in honor of former David Lee Roth guitarist Jason Becker, who is suffering from Lou Gehrig's disease. The benefit featured Edward Van Halen on guitar, Steve Lukather on guitar and lead vocals, Billy Sheehan on bass, and Pat Torpey on drums. The group was decked out in matching black berets and white tank top undershirts and was billed as The Lou Brutus Experience. The name was chosen during a radio interview the day before at Chicago's WRCX 103.5 (hosted by Lou Brutus). Callers were encouraged to phone in their band name suggestions, with Edward wanting "something sick, but fun." Suggested names included Four Play, Bad Ass Barnyard Animals, and Delicious Vomit.

Edward's appearance began with a televised plea for donations to charity on Jason's behalf that had originally been broadcast at the Muscular Dystrophy Association Telethon on 9/01/96-9/02/96. Becker, who contracted the disease in 1989 and started feeling symptoms shortly before his work on David Lee Roth's *A Little Ain't Enough* album, was confined to a wheelchair and was not present for the event.

As the band took the stage at this former movie theater, Edward kicked things off with a brief rendition of the Munsters theme before launching into "Wipeout." Interestingly, when Sheehan came into the song, the whole band sounded off-key, all playing different lines.

The night before the ALS Benefit, the Lou Brutus Experience made an appearance at the Chicago Hard Rock Café, where Edward donated one of Jason's guitars to be hung on display.

Other performers on the bill included Marty Friedman, Tony McAlpine, Zakk Wylde, Richie Kotzen, and Vinnie Moore. Songs performed by The Lou Brutus Experience: • Wipeout • Good Times, Bad Times • Little Wing • Ain't Talkin' 'Bout Love • She's So Heavy • Fire

Amadeus-David Lee Roth made a cameo appearance as an orchestra conductor in the video for "Eine Kleine Nachtmusik" from this 1984 film (Orion Pictures).

Ambulance Tour-The nickname given by Edward Van Halen for the 1995 *Balance* tour. The name came about because of injuries Alex and Eddie Van Halen dealt with while on the tour. Alex wore a neck brace for much of the tour due to a herniated disk sustained on day after lifting his son to his shoulders. Ed also dealt with a great deal of pain on this tour due to his degenerative hip disease, avascular necrosis. Ed was informed his hip would eventually need to be replaced, but after two series of x-rays in October 1997, doctors determined that the condition had improved and that he could wait. The operation finally took place on 11/16/99.

American Journal-This tabloid television show aired a segment about Eddie and Valerie in 1995.

American Music Awards-In 1991 Van Halen's *For Unlawful Carnal Knowledge* album won the award for Favorite Heavy Metal/Hard Rock Album. Other nominees included Guns 'n Roses *Use Your Illusion 1* and Metallica's *Metallica*. The award was presented by the members of Spinal Tap, while "Runaround" played in the background.
Eddie and Alex Van Halen returned to the American Music Awards on 1/29/96 to present the award for Favorite Female Artist Pop/Rock to Mariah Carey.

American Musical Supply-Edward Van Halen appeared on the spring 1997 cover of this music catalog. Address: 600 Industrial Avenue, Paramus NJ, 07652-3607; Telephone: 1-800-458-4076

Amnesty Is Granted-This unreleased original tune was performed on 7/14/93 at the Jones Beach Theater in Wantagh, NY. The song was later either sold or given to Meatloaf, and a different version of the tune appears on his 1996 release *Welcome to the Neighborhood* (MCA, MCAD-11341).

Amsterdam-1. This song (*Balance* [4:45]) caused quite a bit of trouble within the band. The lyrics, which Sammy Hagar wrote, used the word Amsterdam as a synonym for marijuana and reportedly glorified drug use. It's rumored that this was an insult to the Van Halens, and Ed publicly denounced the chorus in the March 1998 issue of Guitar World magazine. MTV refused to play the video for this song because of the lyrics. Sammy rerecorded the lyrics on 4/04/95, but MTV still refused to play the video. It was also left off *Video Hits Volume 1*.

Filming of the video took place on 1/28/95, while the band walked through the red-light district of Amsterdam during the European promotional tour in support of *Balance*. The band stopped at Hanky Panky's Tattoo Studio, where Sammy had his Bogus Otis tattoo reinked and Edward received his very first tattoo: the Van Halen logo with "Wolfgang" over the top.

2. In Holland, the birthplace of Eddie and Alex Van Halen.

Anabas-In 1988 this magazine devoted an entire issue to the careers of Van Halen and David Lee Roth. Address: P.O. Box 716, Fair Lawn, NJ 07410-9929.

In 1984 they published a book, part of their Look Book series, entitled *Van Halen*.

Ancient Rhythms-A 30-inch-by-60-inch Triptych painting by Maui-based artist Christian Riese Lassen commissioned by Michael Anthony in 1992. Between 750 and 1000 copies of the piece were made.

And the Cradle Will Rock...-(*Women and Children First, Best of Volume 1* [3:31]) "And the Cradle Will Rock..." was our introduction to Eddie Van Halen as a keyboardist. The keyboard parts were played on a

Wurlitzer electric piano. The sound was fed into his MXR Flanger, then his Marshall. Oddly enough, the song's intro was written using a guitar in the band's tour bus. Two keys on the piano were broken while recording because Ed was pounding on them so hard. The Wurlitzer that was used to record this song was used to write another Van Halen song before the release of *Women and Children First*. On the day Eddie bought the piano he wrote "Jump."

On stage the keyboard lines were played by Michael Anthony.

Angel Eyes-(3:04) This unreleased original song was written by David Lee Roth and was believed to be recorded in both 1973 at Cherokee Studios in Chatsworth, CA, and again in 1975 at an unknown location. There is no known public performance of this song, but it was played once backstage for some friends in the band's club days of the mid-1970s. Although they had originally planned to include it on *Van Halen II*, the band decided against doing so because it was too different from the other songs being recorded for that album.

Angelus, Pete-Road manager for Van Halen from 1978 through 1984. Van Halen first met Angelus at Gazzari's during their club days. Angelus, who held a myriad of jobs while with Van Halen (including directing more than one video), was one-half of the solo David Lee Roth video team, The Fabulous Picasso Brothers, and can be seen in some of Roth's solo videos.

Anthology-(Connoisseur Collection VSOP CD 207, 1994 [65:13]) Sammy Hagar solo album featuring songs from 1973 through 1984. Tracks: • Bad Motor Scooter • Rock the Nation • Connection • Paper Money • Eagle's Fly • Keep on Rockin' • Cruisin & Boozin' • Fillmore Shuffle • Red • You Make Me Crazy • I've Done Everything for You • This Planet's on Fire • Heartbeat • Piece of My Heart • Your Love Is Driving Me Crazy • Two Sides of Love • I Can't Drive 55

Anthony, Michael-Much like the Van Halen brothers, Michael Anthony got his start in music at the age of seven by following in the footsteps of his father, Walter. Both were trumpet players, but not for very long. When Mike entered his teens, he stopped playing the trumpet to learn the guitar. Since all his friends played either guitar or drums, Mike logically turned to bass.

Michael's first bass really wasn't a bass at all, but rather a Tiesco Del Ray electric guitar that he relieved of its extra two strings. Though he is left-handed, Mike played the guitar as a right-handed player would. After playing that guitar for a while, Mike's dad sprung for a P-Bass copy by Victoria and a Gibson amp.

By this time Mike's family had moved from Chicago to California twice before finally settling in California. Mike had to give up his wish of becoming a major-league catcher to pursue his musical hopes.

Mike's first band was called Poverty's Children and featured his brother Steve on drums and a lead singer by the name of Mike Hershey. Other bands that Mike belonged to included Black Opal and Balls.

In 1971 Mike met his future wife, Sue, his high school sweetheart. She proposed to him on the way to a McDonald's.

The band that Mike is really known for from his early years is a group named Snake. Since the band was only a three-piece, Mike was the lead singer as well as the bass player. Snake played the same backyard party scene that Mammoth played, but Mammoth got much more popular, much faster. Mike knew Alex Van Halen from a music theory class at Pasadena City College. Snake was opening for Mammoth one night in a high school auditorium when Mammoth's PA system failed. Mike let the band borrow Snake's PA and in turn was befriended by the members of Mammoth.

By this time David Lee Roth had been performing with the Van Halen brothers for a little while, but their bass player, Mark Stone, just wasn't working out. It wasn't long before word hit the street that Dave and the brothers were in search of a new bass player.

"The very first time I jammed with Eddie and Alex, it was in a little garage in Pasadena," Mike recalled in a Rockline interview on 1/20/92. "The garage was so small I could barely even get what little amp I had in there. And these guys just blew me away, the way they were playing. I was like 'I'm just gonna keep up with these guys.' I knew 'em. I had seen their band play many times, I was like, 'Whoa!', blown away that Ed even asked me to jam with them. Al went, 'Would you like to join the band?' and I went, 'Uh…yeah!' I was about 23."

This rounded out Mammoth, which would soon become known as Van Halen.

The band discovered Mike's unique vocals when they asked him to sing background on the unreleased track "She's the Woman." This background sound of bass guitar and vocals would become the foundation of the Van Halen sound that allowed Eddie and Alex to perform their crowd-pleasing riffs.

There have often been complaints that Mike was buried in the mix for most of Van Halen's albums. However, early on Mike did record a bass solo for inclusion on *Van Halen II*. Only part of the solo was used, though, as an introduction to "You're No Good." Though Mike's placement in the mix has always been debated among fans, his concert bass solo has become legendary.

Often seen as more of a physical than musical display, Mike's solos were a mix of whiskey-guzzling, amp-pounding, tumbling ferocity that showcased the most outlandish bass effects.

Several of these performances were filmed, and a progression of these strange solos is clearly evident from tour to tour. One of the earliest known circulating films of Mike's solo from the 1981 *Fair Warning* tour shows that his solos at this time involved freakish lighting and frequent stomps upon the guitar's pickups after the instrument had been thrown to the ground.

During 1983's U.S. festival, the bass solo became a theatrical event. During the solo the chord came out of the bass (Mike was not using a wireless), cutting off the signal and causing dead silence. While Alex filled in with some background drums, Mike's bass tech, Kevin Dugan, ran out with a new guitar and asked Mike to look angry and push him around as if it were the tech's fault. Mike did it and Kevin threw the new guitar to the ground in a faked disgust that could have won an Oscar. The incident even fooled Mike's wife, Sue, who said her goodbyes to Kevin as he went backstage. Just for the record, Kevin is still Mike's tech.

During the *1984* tour, Mike launched his bass from the highest part of the stage, then jumped on it several times. This made it necessary to have two basses to complete each night's solo. It was also during this tour that Mike got the finished version of his infamous Jack Daniels bass.

As a connoisseur of Jack Daniels whiskey, Mike was prompted to build a bass in the shape of a Jack Daniels bottle. Mike built the first version, but Jack Daniels offered to do the graphics for the final version in exchange for Mike's entry into their hall of fame. The guitar made its debut appearance in the video for "Panama."

In the tours that followed, Mike eventually put more music and less theatrics in his solo. On the *F.U.C.K.* tour, Mike played a small rendition of the "Star Spangled Banner." On the *Balance* tour, he played part of Bach's Toccata and Fugue in D minor.

Mike was also involved in a side project band with Sammy Hagar and David Lauser named Los Tres Gusanos. They often played at the Cabo Wabo Cantina and even released a full-length concert video. Mike was replaced with Robert Berry when Sammy left Van Halen.

Michael's family consists of his wife, Sue, and his two daughters. One of his daughters was featured in an Entertainment Tonight episode in 1993 that chronicled a day on tour with Van Halen. Mike has three brothers and a sister: Steve, Robert, Dennis, and Nancy. Dennis appeared in the 1991 MTV special "We're with the Band: Backstage with Van Halen."

When Sammy Hagar joined the band, his love of cars rubbed off on Mike. Mike now owns a Porsche turbo and a 1984 Ferrari Boxer. He also owns "Raging Red," a 1940 custom Ford convertible built by Boyd. This

$200,000 hot rod took 17 people nine months to assemble and features a Corvette engine and a leather interior.

Besides being a connoisseur of fine autos and whiskey, Mike also collects watches. He has more than 80 watches in his collection including Donald Duck, Winnie the Pooh, Mary Poppins, and more than 60 Mickey Mouse watches. He also loves listening to a wide variety of music and cites some modern rock and alternative bands as current influences.

Mike continues to be the backbone of the Van Halen sound; something needed to hold together Ed's solos and Alex's jungle rhythms. In a band that could easily have four successful solo artists, Mike keeps them one unit.

Any Time, Any Place-This unreleased original is a leftover song from the *1984* sessions. It has never been performed publicly.

Aquarian-Van Halen appeared on the cover of the April 1995 issue of this publication.

Arcadia High School-Michael Anthony's high school in Arcadia, CA. It was here that he saw Mammoth perform for the first time during a school carnival.

Arcadia Methodist Hospital-Jan Van Halen was employed at this hospital in Arcadia, CA, cleaning dishes shortly after the Van Halens first arrived in the U.S.

Arnott, Drew-Member of the Canadian duo Strange Advance. Arnott is thanked in the liner notes of *Balance*.

The Arsenio Hall Show-On 7/22/93 Gary Cherone sat in with the World's Most Dangerous Band and performed "More Than Words." Extreme later performed "Get the Funk Out" and "Tragic Comic."

Edward and Wolfgang accompanied Valerie when she appeared on a 1994 episode of the show. Arsenio Hall also introduced Van Halen for their live performance at the 1991 MTV Video Music Awards.

Atomic Punk-(*Van Halen* [3:00]) Ed rubbed his hand back and forth across the strings, while kicking in his MXR Phase 90 to produce the scratchy-sounding riff so prominent in this track. The same effect was also used on *Women and Children First*'s "Everybody Wants Some!!"

Atomic Punks-A Los Angeles based, Dave-era-only, Van Halen tribute band that performed at the second annual Van Halen Mailing List Convention in Las Vegas, NV, on 6/28/97. On 3/14/98 the band was joined by Michael Anthony on stage at the Twenty/20 Club in Pasadena, CA, much to the surprise of the audience. As people crowded the stage, Mike pounded out these tracks with the Dave-era look-a-likes: • Romeo Delight • Feel Your Love Tonight • I'm the One • Ain't Talkin' 'Bout Love • Dance the Night Away • Light Up the Sky • Unchained
In 1999 when David Lee Roth needed a new guitar player to tour with, Atomic Punks' Bart Walsh was his choice.

Australian Guitar-Ed appeared on the cover of this magazine's March/April 1998 issue featuring an interview about *Van Halen III*.

Autograph-Michael Anthony contributed background vocals on the song "Blondes in Black Cars" for this band's 1985 album *That's the Stuff* (RCA, AFK1-7009). Autograph also opened for a large portion of the *1984* tour.

B

Babe Don't Leave Me Alone-(3:00) This unreleased original song was played live on 6/03/76 at The Starwood in Hollywood, CA. It was often used in the band's club set. They recorded the song in 1976 for the Gene Simmons financed demo and in 1977 as part of the 25 song demo for *Van Halen*. The song was never released, and it is not known to have been performed after 1978. Dave used to claim the song was about a girl whose boyfriend dumps her because she was developing a big behind.

Backdoor Shuffle-This is a leftover song from the *Balance* sessions. The music was later used for "Can't Get This Stuff No More" on *Best of Volume 1* with new lyrics written by David Lee Roth.

Back to the Future-(Universal Pictures, 1985) An untitled song Eddie Van Halen originally wrote for the film *The Wild Life* is heard in this film. Marty McFly (Michael J. Fox) travels back in time and pays a visit to his sleeping father (Crispin Glover). Marty McFly, wearing a radiation suit, pulls out a cassette tape labeled "Edward Van Halen." He places it into a Sony Walkman, straps the headphones onto the unknowing ears of his science fiction loving Dad, and cranks it up effectively scaring the living daylights out of his father, who upon seeing the young McFly is convinced he is a space traveler from a far off galaxy.

Back to the Future Part II-(MCA/Universal Pictures/Amblin Entertainment, 1989) Sammy Hagar's "I Can't Drive 55" is briefly heard in this sequel to Back to the Future that starred Michael J. Fox, Christopher Lloyd, and Thomas F. Wilson, with a cameo appearance by the Red Hot Chili Peppers' bassist, Flea. It can be heard when Fox's character, Marty McFly, has returned to 1985 from 2005 to discover that the town of Hill Valley has been turned into a run-down shell of its former self.

Baked Potato Bar and Grill-On 2/25/92 at the Baked Potato Bar and Grill in North Hollywood, CA, Eddie Van Halen joined Steve Lukather on stage to perform several tunes with Lukather's band Los Lobotomies (Steve's side project apart from Toto). Steve humorously coaxed Edward into joining him on stage, introducing him as an "intermediate guitarist." The set list: • Sunshine of Your Love (6:29) • Red House (8:01) • Funk #49 (3:45) • Crossroads (5:10) • Smell Yourself (7:20)

Balance-(Warner Bros. 45760 [52:27]) This album was recorded from 5/25/94 to 9/02/94 and was released on 1/24/95. It debuted at #1 on the U.S. charts. 3.9 million copies have been sold. It was certified gold, platinum, and double platinum on 3/29/95.

The CD and cassette versions of this album have some tracks in a different order. The U.S. vinyl release does not include "Baluchitherium," while the European vinyl release does.

The twins on the cover are actually only one child digitally cloned to create conjoined twins.

Alex Van Halen commented on the cover during a 2/20/95 interview on Rockline. "It's kind of a duality. It has to do with one person. What you do to another, it comes back to you pretty quickly. It has to do with a balance within everybody; the age old struggle between good and evil. And before I get too deep, 'Balance' is really the title of the picture."

At one point the album was going to be named *The Club*, a title dedicated to deceased manager Ed Leffler.

The Japanese version of *Balance* has only one child on the cover because the Japanese took offense at the conjoined twins. The band tossed around the idea of using the second child in the background as a ghost. The Japanese did not like this idea either. *Balance* was the first Van Halen album to hit #1 on the Japanese charts. This version of the album also includes the extra track "Crossing Over."

The landscape on the front cover of the album is actually a moonscape. On the back cover of the album, in the lower right corner, is a can of Coke. It has been rumored that this is a message by the band in reference to their previous troubles with Crystal Pepsi using the song "Right Now" in their commercials, though the rumor has never been confirmed.

The artwork on the CD itself is Leonardo Da Vinci's Vitruvian Man.

Five of the lead vocals on *Balance* were recorded in Vancouver, Canada, so that producer Bruce Fairbairn could spend more time with his family.

Ed did not use his Soldano amp for this album. Instead, he went back to his Marshall, which had restoration work done to it, and also used his new Peavey 5150.

2. A Canadian Van Halen tribute band.

Balance singles/promos

"Don't Tell Me (What Love Can Do)" (edit), "Don't Tell Me (What Love Can Do)" (video version), "Don't Tell Me (What Love Can Do)" (LP version), WB Pro-CD-734, CD, USA, 1995.

"Don't Tell Me (What Love Can Do)" (EP), WEA 41919-2, CD, UK, 1995.

"Don't Tell Me (What Love Can Do)," "Baluchitherium," WEA W0280X, 12" Vinyl, UK, 1995.

"Don't Tell Me (What Love Can Do)," "Baluchitherium," WEA 5439-17956-7, 7" Purple Vinyl, UK, 1995.

"Can't Stop Lovin' You," "Crossing Over," WB 2-17909, CD, USA, 1995. Highest Chart Position: USA #30.

"Not Enough" (CHR Remix No. 1), "Not Enough" (CHR Remix No. 2), WB Pro-CD-7664-R, CD, USA, 1995.

"Not Enough" (promo), CD, Spain, 1995.

"Not Enough," "Amsterdam," WB 2-17810, CD, USA, 1995.

"Can't Stop Lovin' You," "Crossing Over," "Right Now" (live), "Man on a Mission" (live), WB 9362-43510-2, CD, France, 1995.

"Don't Tell Me (What Love Can Do)" (video version), "Dreams" (live), "Top of the World" (live), "Judgement Day" (live), WEA 9362-41924-2, Gold Tin CD #1, France, 1995.

"Don't Tell Me" (edit), "Why Can't This Be Love?" (live), "Panama" (live), "Poundcake" (live), WEA WO280CD 9362-41919-2, Gold Tin CD #2, Germany, 1995.

"Amsterdam" (edit), "Runaround" (live), "Finish What Ya Started" (live), "Love Walks In" (live), WEA WO302CDX 9362-43555-2, Blue Tin CD, UK, 1995. Tracks 2, 3, and 4 taken from *Live: Right Here, Right Now.*

CD1: "Can't Stop Lovin' You," "Best of Both Worlds" (live), "When It's Love" (live), "One Way to Rock" (live), CD2: "Can't Stop Lovin' You," "Crossing Over," "Right Now" (live), "Man on a Mission" (live), WEA WO288CDX 9362-43511-2, Black Tin 2-CD Set, UK, 1995. Tracks 2, 3, and 4 on both CDs are taken from *Live: Right Here, Right Now.*

Bald-A short-lived band of Edward and Al's that was formed in between the Trojan Rubber Company and Genesis.

Ballot or the Bullet-(*Van Halen III* [5:37]) This song's lyrics are based on a Malcolm X speech.

The song features licks played on an electric sitar with a Dobro interspersed throughout. The song was initially written entirely on the Dobro, and it marks the first time Edward has used it on a recording. The solo was performed on Wolfie's miniature Peavey Wolfgang.

The tune ends with Edward again playing slide on the Dobro, and a string can be heard breaking.

Balta, Carol-Nurse at New Start Homes in Chatsworth, CA, who was conned out of her car when a man claiming to know Edward Van Halen promised to bring him by the home to meet the patients. It didn't happen, but when Edward got wind of the story, he went to the home and spent 1½ hours meeting the patients and signing autographs. The event was televised on the show Current Affair in 1994.

Baluchitherium-(*Balance* [4:05]) It has been speculated that Edward borrowed the intro to Trevor Rabin's "Eyes of Love" for this song.

Valerie Bertinelli picked the name for this instrumental. She named it after the largest prehistoric mammal. The baluchitherium was roughly four times the size of an elephant and looked like a cross between a brontosaurus and an elephant (without a trunk).

Originally, this song was supposed to have vocals. Sammy ended up humming the vocals for the chorus, which Ed then adapted for the guitar.

Ed's pet Dalmatian, Sherman, was used at the end of this song. A hot dog was taped to the microphone to attract the dog, and an audio tape of a fire engine was played to induce barking.

Ed used an Albert Lee Music Man guitar with heavy strings tuned down to low A for the song.

Bam-This California music magazine's index of Van Halen-related articles:

10/09/81: "Ted Templeman": four-page Ted Templeman interview by David Gans.

7/16/82: Eddie Van Halen cover. "Edward Van Halen: Heavy Metal Hero": four page interview by Marc Shapiro.

5/85: David Lee Roth cover. "David Lee Roth Gets Crazy on the Beach.": four-page David Lee Roth interview by Kristine McKenna. *Crazy from the Heat* reviewed.

1/01/86: David Lee Roth cover plus article (no author given).

1/31/86: Van Halen cover. "Van Hagar": five-page interview by Jerry McCulley.

3/11/88: David Lee Roth cover. "Diamond Dave and the Skyscraper of Doom.": four-page interview by Jerry McCulley.

7/01/88: Van Halen cover plus article by Dave Zimmer.

9/06/91: Van Halen cover. "Al & Ed's Excellent Adventure.": four-page Edward and Alex interview by Jerry McCulley. "Producer Andy Johns behind the Board at 5150": one-page Andy Johns interview by Pat Lewis.

1/13/95: "A Question of Balance-Van Halen's Family Business Still Thrives": two-page Van Halen feature by Roy Trakin.

7/25/97: "BAM 50." *Van Halen* is ranked #15 in 50 Greatest Albums Ever to Emanate from California poll.

4/10/98: Van Halen feature.

Address: 5951 Canning Street, Oakland, CA 94609; Telephone: 415-652-3810.

Bass Frontiers-Michael Anthony appeared on the cover of the vol. 2, no. 4, 1995 issue of this magazine. The issue features a six-page interview entitled "Van Halen's Secret Weapon, Michael Anthony" by Christopher Buttner.

Address: 6739 Sun Acer Way, Rio Linda, CA 95673; Telephone: 916-992-0233.

Bass Player-In the November 1995 issue of this magazine, Michael Anthony appeared on the cover and was interviewed in a ten-page article by Scott Malandrone entitled "Bottoms Up." The Japanese version of this magazine featured a Michael Anthony interview in its May 1998 issue. Address: P.O. Box 57324, Boulder, CO 80322-7324.

Bay Area Music Awards-Also known as the "Bammies," these music awards are given to individuals from the Bay Area of Northern California. In 1977 Sammy Hagar won the Bay Area Musician of the Year award.

On 3/12/87 at the San Francisco Civic Auditorium, Sammy was nominated for Bay Area Outstanding Vocalist of the Year and Bay Area Outstanding Album of the Year for *I Never Said Goodbye*.

On 3/07/92 at a televised Bammies at the San Francisco Civic Auditorium, Sammy performed "Rock and Roll" and "Eagles Fly" with Neil Schon, Denny Carmassi, Ricki Phillips, and David Lauser. Sammy won Bay Area Male Vocalist of the Year for his work on *For Unlawful Carnal Knowledge*. Other nominees included Gary Floyd (Sister Double Happiness), Chris Isaak, Huey Lewis and Mike Patton (Faith No More/Mr. Bungle). Sammy accepted the award as "Top of the World" (live version) played in the background.

On 3/05/94 also at the San Francisco Civic Auditorium, Sammy performed "High Hopes," "I'll Fall in Love Again," "Three Lock Box," "Goin' Down," "Red," "There's Only One Way to Rock," and "Rock and Roll" with Michael Anthony, ex-Styx guitarist Tommy Shaw, and David Lauser. Again, Sammy won Bay Area Male Vocalist of the Year.

At the same awards ceremony, Hagar received the Arthur M. Sohcot Award (known from 1978 to 1987 as the Board of Directors Award), given in honor of an individual who, through excellence in performance and/or professional activity or through dedicated public service has contributed to the betterment of the local community.

On 3/11/95 the Bammies were held at The Warfield Theater in San Francisco, CA. "High Hopes" was nominated as Outstanding Song of the

Year at the 18th Annual Bay Area Music Awards, along with Counting Crows' "Mr. Jones," Green Day's "Basket Case" and "Longview," and Neil Young and Crazy Horse's "Change Your Mind."

Bayern 3-This German television network aired Van Halen's 5/29/98 performance at Rock Im Park in Nurnberg, Germany, on 6/26/98 and again on 7/21/98.

Beautiful Girls-(*Van Halen II* [3:55]) Originally this song's chorus was "bring on the girls" instead of "beautiful girls." It was in this form that the band recorded it in 1977 for the Warner Brothers demo under the title "Bring on the Girls." The lyrics were slightly different than those on the *Van Halen II* version, but not by much.

This song was used on Saturday Night Live's "Schmitt's Gay Beer" commercial parody.

Beer Drinkers and Hell Raisers-(3:02) This ZZ Top cover tune was performed by Van Halen on 9/18/76 at The Bogart in San Bernardino, CA. It was also performed in Caracas, Venezuela, in 1983. The original song by ZZ Top had tapping in it, long before "Eruption" was recorded. However, Ed had been using the technique before the ZZ Top song was recorded. This is just one of the many debated points in the history of tapping, though neither guitarist is actually considered the originator of the technique.

When Van Halen played the song in their club days, Michael Anthony joined David Lee Roth in singing the lead vocals.

Believe Me-(2:56)*, (4:06) This song was performed on 9/18/76 at The Bogart in San Bernardino, CA. It's also known as "Take It Back." It is not known whether it is a Van Halen original or a cover tune. The band recorded it in *1973 at Cherokee Studios in Chatsworth, CA.

Berle, Marshall-Van Halen's first manager, the nephew of the one and only Milton Berle. Marshall later went on to manage Ratt.

Bertinelli, Valerie-World-renowned actress and Eddie Van Halen's wife. Valerie participates in Van Halen-related activities on the Internet, making her an extremely valuable information resource. When someone asked if she thought Van Halen would ever perform "unplugged" on MTV, she replied, "When pigs fly." She later recited the same phrase in her network movie *Night Sins* as a nod to the Van Halen fans on the Internet.

The Best-(WEA/Atlantic/Rhino) This "best of" compilation from David Lee Roth was released on 10/28/97. The album included one new track, "Don't Piss Me Off." Tracks: • Don't Piss Me Off • Yankee Rose • A Lil' Ain't Enough • Just Like Paradise • Big Train • Big Trouble • It's Showtime! • Hot Dog and a Shake • Skyscraper • Shyboy • She's My Machine • Stand Up • Tobacco Road • Easy Street • California Girls • Just a Gigolo/I Ain't Got Nobody • Sensible Shoes • Goin' Crazy! • Ladies' Nite in Buffalo? • Land's Edge

Best of Both Worlds-(*5150* [4:49]) This song was recorded on an L-Series 1958 rosewood-neck Fender Stratocaster with "5150" carved in the body.

It has been a long-running joke among fans that the song's rhythm sounds a little too much like Kool & the Gang's 1980 hit "Celebrate!"

The Best of Extreme: An Accidental Collication of Atoms?-(A&M POCM-1233) Extreme's "best of" collection released on 12/05/97 in Japan. Tracks: • Decadence Dance • Rest in Peace • Kid Ego • Get the Funk Out • Tragic Comic • Hip Today • Stop the World • More Than Words • Cupid's Dead (Horn Mix) • Leave Me Alone • Play with Me • Hole Hearted • Am I Ever Gonna Change

Best of Sammy Hagar-1. (Capitol C2-80262 [51:38]) Released on 11/16/92, this compilation includes the following tracks: • Red • (Sittin' on the) Dock of the Bay • I've Done Everything for You • Rock and Roll Weekend • Cruisin' and Boozin' • Turn Up the Music • Reckless • Trans Am (Highway Wonderland) • Love or Money • This Planet's on Fire (Burn in Hell) • Plain Jane • Bad Reputation • Bad Motor Scooter • You Make Me Crazy

2. (EMI/Capitol 21097, 1999) Sammy Hagar compilation released on 8/17/99. Tracks: • Red (live) • Plain Jane • I've Done Everthing for You • Rock 'N' Roll Weekend • This Planet's on Fire • You Make Me Crazy • Trans Am • (Sittin' on the) Dock of the Bay • Cruisin' & Boozin' • Bad Motor Scooter (live)

Best of Volume 1-(Warner Bros. 46332 [72:23]) This album was released on 10/22/96 in the U.S., 10/17/96 in Japan, 10/18/96 in the Netherlands, 10/28/96 in the U.K., and 11/4/96 in Australia. It debuted at #1 on the U.S. charts, dropping to #3 on 11/07/96 and then to #6 on 11/15/96. The album features the return of David Lee Roth for two new songs. Sammy stated that this album is what drove him to leave the band. It was certified gold and platinum on 5/01/97 and double platinum in May of 1998. 2.4 million copies have been sold in the U.S.

Originally, this was meant to be a double album, one featuring Sammy-era songs and one featuring Dave-era songs. For unknown reasons, it never materialized in that form.

Alex Van Halen was mostly responsible for picking the songs that would end up on this album.

The band presented approximately 20 songs to Dave to write lyrics to, of which two were chosen. Recording began on 7/22/96.

In a contest to promote this album, 10,000 CDs included a Van Halen guitar pick, 500 of the CDs were autographed, and one lucky contest winner received a black Peavey Wolfgang guitar. The winner, John Cottrell, was given the autographed guitar, an autograph on his winning ticket, a Warner Brothers hat, and a lesson from Ed all at the 5150 Studio on 12/13/96.

The one promotion that went awry was the 500 autographed CDs. Roth mistakenly signed the outside of some of the CD jackets, rendering the giveaway useless. Tour manager Scotty Ross then suggested the rest of the band sign the outside of those same discs and give them to various charities to use as fund-raising items.

The shadowy figure who appears in the photo of Al's drum room in the album's artwork is the album's art director, Stine Schyberg.

The mysterious Sat-Kaur Khalsa thanked in the liner notes is Edward's therapist.

Also in the liner notes describing each of the albums' contents, "Take Your Whiskey Home" is incorrectly listed as "Take the Whiskey Home." Due to another printing error Mike isn't given credit for writing "Jump" and "Panama."

"Runnin' with the Devil" featured a different arrangement, due to a mixing error and the selection of the wrong master tape during the final mastering of the album. It was corrected in a later release of the album.

The Japanese release (WPCR 900) includes "Hot for Teacher."

A Japanese Warner Brothers import cropped up in late 1997 named *Mini Best Of.* The cover was identical to the *Best of Volume 1* cover, but with the colors reversed. It included five tracks, two being karaoke versions (vocals removed). Tracks: • Top of the World • Top of the World (karaoke) • Jump • Jump (karaoke) • Panama

The album was dedicated to the memory of the band's former manager Ed Leffler.

Best of Volume 1 singles/promos
"Me Wise Magic" (promo edit), "Me Wise Magic" (LP version), WB PRO-CD-8474, CD, USA, 1996.

"Me Wise Magic" (edit), "Me Wise Magic" (LP version), "Why Can't This Be Love?" WEA 9362-43795-2, Germany and Australia, CD 1996.

"Can't Get This Stuff No More" (edit), "Can't Get This Stuff No More" (promo), WB PRO-CD-8571-R, CD, USA, 1996.

"Jump," WEA PRCD 483, CD, Germany, 1996.

"Humans Being" (edit), "Humans Being" (album version), WB PRO-CD-8200, CD, USA, 1996.

"Humans Being," "Respect the Wind" (score), WEA, CD, 7/26/96.

"Humans Being" (album version), "Humans Being" (score), "Respect the Wind," WEA WPCR-788, CD, Japan, 7/10/96.

The Best Rock Album in the World...Ever II-(Virgin 40430) "Why Can't This Be Love?" appears on this rock compilation album.

Bettencourt, Nuno-Gary Cherone co-wrote two songs with this former Extreme guitarist, "Pursuit of Happiness" (3:33) and "You" (4:25), for Nuno's solo album *Schizophonic* (A&M 31454 0593, 1996).

Better Off Dead-(CBS Entertainment Productions, 1985) This comedy starring John Cusack and David Ogden Stiers features the song "Everybody Wants Some!!" from *Women and Children First* during a scene when Lane Myer (Cusack's character) is daydreaming while working at a hamburger joint. He pretends he is a mad scientist in the vein of Baron Frankenstein, turning a raw hamburger patty into a "living" rock and roll beefcake. The stop-animation scene features the burger jamming on a striped guitar, similar to Edward's "Shark" guitar seen on the *Women and Children First* cover, and singing "Everybody Wants Some!!" Originally, the tune was uncredited, but when the video (Twentieth Century Fox, 7083) was re-released to the general public on 8/26/97, credit for the song's usage had been added.

Between Us Two-This unreleased original song is a leftover from the *Twister* soundtrack sessions in 1996.

Biff Malibu-The name of Michael Anthony's alter ego, coined by David Lee Roth. Michael was given the moniker because he reminded Roth of "those perfect jocks you see out on the beach."

Big Bad Bill (Is Sweet William Now)-(*Diver Down* [2:44]) Dave got the idea to cover this Jack Yellen/Milton Ager song after hearing it broadcast from a Kentucky radio station one day while listening to his Walkman.

Edward used a Gibson hollow-body on this track, and Michael used a large acoustic bass, similar to those used by Mariachi bands. Al played drums with brushes, a jazz standard.

Jan Van Halen played clarinet on this track.

Big Breakfast-This British Channel 4 television program aired a 20-minute Paula Yates interview with Sammy Hagar and Eddie Van Halen on 4/10/95.

Big Fat Money-(*Balance* [3:54]) The solo on this track was recorded in one take on a Gibson ES-335 through Ed's Marshall. Ed was fooling around with some suggestions from Bruce Fairbairn, while unbeknownst to him, Bruce was taping his first attempt. Fairbairn decided he liked what he heard.

A lot of thought went into the coin sound at the end of the song. Everyone crowded around the recording console where they dropped quarters, dimes, nickels, and pennies until they got the perfect sound.

Big Trouble-(3:36) There were two studio versions of this unreleased original song recorded. It was first recorded for the 1977 Warner Brothers demo and then rerecorded during the *Diver Down* sessions in 1982. This song was intended for *Diver Down* and later for *1984*, but appeared on neither. It's often considered by fans to be the best song the band never released. Other than its title, the tune is not related in any way to "Big Trouble" from David Lee Roth's *Eat 'Em and Smile* album.

The Big V-The first incarnation of the Van Halen Fan Club (1978-1979). Five dollars got you a one-year membership, which entitled you to a quarterly newsletter, 8-inch-by-10-inch photographs of each band member, a world tour book, a band biography, and a Van Halen button.

Bill & Ted's Excellent Adventure-(Interscope Communications/Nelson, 1989) The Extreme song "Play With Me," in a form a bit different from the version on their first album, *Extreme*, is heard near the end of the movie during a chaotic scene at a San Dimas, CA, mall, where several famous figures from history are exploring in 1989. The film stars Keanu Reeves and Alex Winter as Bill and Ted, two adolescents who travel through time collecting historical specimens for a high school report.

Amusingly, Van Halen earns several mentions throughout the movie.

The song appears on the soundtrack (A&M Records 3915, 1989 [3:31]).

Other artists contributing to the soundtrack included Tora Tora, Shark Island, and Power Tool. All the artists (including Extreme) were relatively unknown at the time.

Billboard-Van Halen articles have appeared in this publication on 4/27/85, 12/23/89, and 1/06/90.

Billboard Live-This club that now stands where Gazzari's used to stand hosted Van Halen's *Van Halen III* premiere party on 3/12/98. The premiere, which included interviews and previews of the album, was broadcast over hundreds of radio stations. After the broadcast segment was finished the band launched into a surprise performance; their first public performance with Gary Cherone. The set list: • Romeo Delight • Without You • One I Want • Mean Street • Unchained • Fire in the Hole • I'm the One • Dance the Night Away • Feel Your Love Tonight • Ain't Talkin' 'Bout Love

Billboard Music Awards-Paul Schaffer, who incidentally has been a very good friend of Valerie Bertinelli, presented Van Halen with the award for Top Album/Rock Artist in 1991. The award presentation was taped while the band was on tour in Memphis, TN.

Black and Blue-(*OU812* [5:24]) This was the first single released from *OU812*. Along with "Sucker in a 3 Piece," this song was highlighted by the media as being too lyrically suggestive for children attending the Monsters of Rock tour.

Blood from a Stone-This unreleased original song is a leftover from the *Van Halen III* sessions.

The Blues Bustin' Mambo Slammers-David Lee Roth's experimental band assembled after the shortened *Your Filthy Little Mouth* tour. It cost Dave $500,000 to put this together. Originally, he planned to take the show to such places as Rio and Monaco and to tour through April 1996, but the tour was cancelled after the relatively poor turnout at the December 1995 shows. Tour Dates (1995):
Ceasar's Palace, Lake Tahoe, CA: 10/13, 10/14
Bally's, Las Vegas, NV: 10/19, 10/20, 10/21, 10/22, 10/23, 10/24, 10/25
Foxwood's Resort and Casino, CT: 11/03, 11/04
MGM Grand, Las Vegas, NV: 12/23, 12/24, 12/25, 12/26, 12/27, 12/28, 12/29, 12/30, 12/31

Bob Hope Chrysler Classic-Edward took part in this celebrity golf tournament in 1994, portions of which were broadcast on NBC.

Bocephus Mode-Named after Hank "Bocephus" Williams Jr., this is a state of mind that's just a little bit less crazy than 5150 mode. As a child Hank Jr.'s dad nicknamed him "Bocephus," an Indian name. It became the country music equivalent of "5150 time." Van Halen made several references on television and in concert to the expression and even appeared in the video for the Hank Williams Jr. song "My Name Is Bocephus."

Bogus Otis-The name of Sammy Hagar's tattoo. It is a bird that resembles a cross between a chicken and the Road Runner. It is located on his right bicep.

Boogie Booger-One of two instrumental tunes Ed remembers his first band, The Broken Combs, writing and performing.

Books-
Jumping for the Dollar by John Shearlaw (biography. Zomba, 1984)
The Mighty Van Halen by Buzz Morrison (48-page biography with photos. ISBN 0-89524-229-X. Cherry Lane, 1984)
Van Halen by Iain Blair (64-page binder-style, oversized biography and photo scrapbook. ISBN 0-517-45864-0. Beekman House, 1984)
Van Halen by J.D. Considine (160-page biography. ISBN 0-688-04299-6. Quill, 1984)
Van Halen by Philip Kamin and Peter Goddard (126-page biography and photo album. ISBN 0-7737-1082-5. Stoddart, 1984)
Van Halen by Philip Kamin (ISBN 0825302420. Olympic Marketing Corporation, 1984)
The Van Halen Scrapbook (64-page fact, photo, and interview book. ISBN 0-451-82102-5. Starbooks, 1984)

Van Halen by Gordon Matthews (145-page biography with 16 pages of photos. ISBN 0-345-32176-6. Ballantine, 1984)

Van Halen by Jim Palmer (27-page photo and fact book. ISBN 1-85099-004-2. Anabas, 1984)

Van Halen by Phil S. Tene (64-page photo, quotation, and statistic book. ISBN 0-88188-296-8. Robus, 1984)

Van Halen Live (64-page photo scrapbook (no text). ISBN 9-99596-581-X. Freezz Frame, 1984)

Masters of Heavy Metal (191 pages of interviews reprinted from Guitar Player magazine. 19 pages of Edward Van Halen interviews and 4 pages of Michael Anthony interviews. ISBN 0-688-02937. Quill, 1984)

Van Halen by Michelle Craven (32-page biography. ISBN 0-86276-274-X. Proteus Books, 1984)

Metal Shots (32-page photo scrapbook with 6 pages dedicated to Van Halen. ISBN 0-88188-372-7-Robus, 1985)

Van Halen by Annene Kaye (ISBN 0671550314. Pocket Books, 1985)

Van Halen by Annene Kaye (Rock Bio Series) (ISBN 0-67155-032-2. Julian Messner, 1985)

Van Halen (Rock 'N' Roll Favorites) by Consumer magazine editors (ISBN 0517458640. Outlet, 1985)

Van Halen-David Lee Roth by Philip Kamin (32-page biography and photo collection. ISBN 0-88188-391-3. Robus, 1985)

Van Halen by Michelle Craven (ISBN 0-94639-151-3. Cherry Lane Books, 1985)

David Lee Roth: What A Guy! by Mimi Kasbah (75-page photo and quotation book. ISBN 0-345-33255-5. Ballantine, 1986)

Eddie Van Halen by Dan Hedges (Biography. ISBN 0-39474-130-7. Vintage Books, 1986)

Van Halen by Michelle Craven (ISBN 0-84643-007-X. Beekman, 1991)

Guitar Wizards by Larry DiMarzio (1993, Player magazine special [Japanese])

1,000 Great Guitarists by Hugh Gregory (Edward Van Halen entry. Published in the U.K. by Balafon Books, Miller-Freeman, 1994)

The Best of Metal: The Essential CD Guide (144-page guide that lists Van Halen among the who's who of metal)

Van Halen: Excess All Areas by Malcolm Dome (144-page biography and photo book. ISBN 1-898141-85-1. Castle Communications, 1994)

1984: The Ultimate Van Halen Trivia Book by Lucas Aykroyd (ISBN 1-55212-089-9. Trafford, 1996)

Crazy from the Heat by David Lee Roth (359-page autobiography. Released on 10/23/97. ISBN 0-7868-6339-0. Hyperion, 1997)

Guitar World Presents: Van Halen (208-page biography. ISBN 0-7935-8081-1. Hal Leonard, 1997)

Also see "Comic Books" entry.

Bootlegs-The band's official stance on bootlegs is negative. Eddie has often stated clearly that he believes fans should not bootleg and that the quality of the recordings is so poor that it's not an accurate representation of the live performances.

Unlike many rock bands, Van Halen has not allowed fans to record live performances. Still, the bootleg trade in Van Halen material is just as lively as for any other band. Recordings from as far back as 1973 are traded. The buying and selling of bootlegs is generally looked down upon by fans.

To get information about Van Halen bootlegs, please visit www.vhboots.com.

Born into Exile-(NBC, 1997) "And the Cradle Will Rock" was featured at the beginning of this television drama starring Talia Shire and Gina Philips in a scene in which a cheerleader is dared to jump off a cliff with her shirt off in front of her friends. It aired on 3/17/97.

Born on the Bayou-(2:13) This Creedence Clearwater Revival cover was played several times throughout the *F.U.C.K.* tour in 1991 and 1992.

Boston Gets a Grip-(1996) Gary Cherone's side project band Houndstooth recorded "Dream On" for this Aerosmith tribute album, which has never been released.

Boston Music Awards-Extreme won the award for Outstanding Hard Rock/Heavy Metal Act in both 1986 and 1987. Gary Cherone was nominated for an award in 1999 for his work on *Van Halen III*.

Boston Rock Opera-Gary joined the Boston Rock Opera's production of *Jesus Christ Superstar* in 1994 in the lead role of Jesus. It began a long association with the group that continues to this day.

The company returned in 1996 with a completely new staging presented at the Lansdowne Street Playhouse at Mama Kin (a club co-owned by Aerosmith) and with Cherone again playing the role of Jesus. It was his first public singing engagement since Extreme's 1995 tour and was a coming-out party of sorts for Cherone who was still in rehabilitation from surgery for a node on his vocal cords.

The Boston Rock Opera had been presenting the two-hour tragic-comic take on the last days of Jesus Christ since 1991. The company continues to showcase Boston-area talent with original interpretations of rock opera. On 12/11/94 at the Middle East Downstairs in Cambridge, MA, Cherone appeared in Boston Rock Opera's presentation of *A Quick One While He's Away*, an operetta by The Who in which Cherone played the forgiving husband of a philandering wife. The 12-minute piece was presented twice during Boston Rock Opera's Rock 'n' Roll Circus fundraiser.

Cherone returned to the stage in the Boston Rock Opera's *Another Night at the Opera* on 8/01/99 where he performed Alice Cooper's "Second Coming" and "Ballad of Dwight Fry" as Francis Caine.

He also made an appearance at the Boston Rock Opera's benefit for stroke victim Mikey Dee and performed "Ziggy Stardust," "Love Reign O'er Me," "All You Need Is Love," and two songs from *Jesus Christ Superstar*.

When the group revisited *Jesus Christ Superstar* in 2000, Gary performed as Judas Iscariot.

Bottoms Up-1. (*Van Halen II* [3:04]) The band frequently used this tune recorded for *Van Halen II* as their encore on the 1978 tour. A live video was made for the song.
2. The name of a Van Halen tribute band.

Boxtalk-Eddie and Alex Van Halen were interviewed for this television show in 1995.

The Brain Box-A small black box outfitted with a pair of headphones and a pair of glasses that sends the listener into an electronic drug-like state of nirvana. Both Sammy and Edward own such a device, which was developed by D.E. Gorges. The device is used by Sammy at the beginning of his "Hands and Knees" video.

Break Out-This German rock magazine's index of Van Halen-related articles:
4/93-5/93: Van Halen cover, three-page feature "Van Halen Einzigartig," by Markus Baro. European tour dates. *Live: Right Here, Right Now* reviewed by Markus Baro.
2/95-3/95: Van Halen cover. "Van Halen Der Kampf Zwischen Gut und Bose": three-page feature by Marco Magin. "Extreme Die Vierte Seite Der Geschichte": two-page Extreme feature by Marco Magin.
Address: Postfach 1250, D-69236 Neckarsteinach, Germany.

Bright Lights, Big City-(7:37) This cover song was frequently heard on the 1980 *World Invasion* tour, though the most well-known recording of it is from the 3/24/80 performance in Spokane, WA. It's also known as "Big City Blues."

Bring on the Girls-(3:48) This song would later become "Beautiful Girls" on *Van Halen II*. It was recorded as "Bring on the Girls" for the 1977 Warner Brothers demo.

Broderick, Tom-An early tech for Eddie Van Halen. He gave a very revealing interview about the band's early days in issue #8 of The Inside magazine.

Broken Combs-Eddie and Alex Van Halen's first band, formed in 1965. Ed played piano and Alex played saxophone with Don Ferris. Brian Hill played drums, and Kevin Hill played a plastic Emenee guitar. They performed lunchtime concerts at Hamilton Elementary School dressed in turtleneck shirts.

Brown Sugar-This Rolling Stones cover, from the album *Sticky Fingers* (FC-40488, 1971), was performed by the band in their club days. An April 1975 recording exists in a private collection.

Bruck, Matt-Ed's guitar and amplifier tech. The pair met while team-mates on the same softball team (he followed Edward in the batting order).

Bruderhof-A New York based commune that believes listening to "popular music" will earn you a place in hell. Van Halen leased a GIII Lear Jet from the sect during the *Balance* tour.

Bullethead-(3:40) This unreleased original was performed on 12/31/77 at The Whisky A GoGo in West Hollywood, CA, as well as on at least one occasion during the *Van Halen* world tour. It's sometimes known as "Bang Bang."

Burrn Magazine-Edward and Gary appeared on the cover of the February 1998 issue of this Japanese magazine. Gary was interviewed by Kaz Hirose.

C

Cabo Wabo-(*OU812* [7:03]; *Live: Right Here, Right Now* [7:58]) Alternate titles for this track included "Face Down in Cabo."

This song was written two days prior to being recorded. It was recorded on a "Villagecaster," a homemade hybrid in Ed's guitar collection featuring a Fender Villager 12-string neck married to a Fender Telecaster body with Schecter pickups. Ed had his amplifier in a separate room from him and Mike during recording. This track marks the first appearance of a Wah pedal in a guitar solo on a Van Halen album.

Cabo Wabo Cantina-This is the cantina built in Cabo San Lucas, Mexico, once owned by Van Halen and now co-owned by Sammy Hagar and Marco Monroy. The grand opening on 4/22/90 was hyped by MTV in their Cabo Wabo contest and Viva Van Halen Saturday. Van Halen filmed two commercials to advertise the contest, and opening night was broadcast on MTV. Before the opening the band did a rehearsal concert for some lucky customers.

MTV flew 10 winners and their guests down for the occasion, and the band was joined on stage by several big name musicians including Steve Lukather, Boston's Brad Delp, Lita Ford, and Dweezil Zappa. Many other famous folks were on hand including Kip Winger, Cheap Trick's Robin Zander, and Ratt's Robin Crosby. Among the songs performed were: • Best of Both Worlds • Summer Nights • Finish What Ya Started • Panama • Rock and Roll • Wild Thing • Born to Be Wild

On the second anniversary of the club, 5/21/92, the band appeared for the second and final time at the Cabo Wabo Cantina. They performed: • Poundcake • Judgement Day • Waiting for the Bus • Man on a Mission • There's Only One Way to Rock • Cabo Wabo • Runaround • Finish What Ya Started • Best of Both Worlds • Top of the World • You Really Got Me

• Satisfaction • Mississippi Queen • Communication Breakdown • Dazed and Confused

Michael, Alex, and Edward sold their shares of the club to Sammy and Monroy shortly thereafter. The band remained affiliated with the club until Sammy's departure on 6/26/96.

Sammy appeared from time to time to perform including on 5/12/90 and 10/13/94. Occasionally, he'd also perform with his side band Los Tres Gusanos including at shows on 2/25/92, 5/20/92, 8/18/92, 8/19/92, 8/20/92, 10/18/95, 10/19/95, 10/11/96, 10/12/96, and 12/13/96-the last three featuring Robert Berry on bass. On 12/31/95 Sammy kicked off the 1996 New Year at Cabo Wabo by jamming with Guns 'n' Roses' Duff McKagan and Matt Sorum as well as Stevie Salas.

McKagan, Sorum, the Sex Pistols' Steve Jones, and John Taylor provided most of the entertainment with their punk band Neurotic Boy Outsiders. Their set consisted of Sex Pistols' and other cover tunes.

After their hour and a half set, McKagan swapped his rhythm guitar for a bass as Hagar joined them to tear through four songs: • Summertime Blues • Wild Thing • Rock and Roll • Roadhouse Blues

After Sammy's split with Van Halen, he began playing the club much more frequently. He now uses the venue to showcase new songs and albums, as well as his annual birthday bash.

Café Americain-Eddie Van Halen appeared on an episode of this show in which his wife starred. In a short scene, Eddie is seen playing guitar at a customer's table and is asked to leave by Valerie's character. As he is being kicked out, Ed mutters some phrases in Dutch. An English translation of his lines is available on the Internet.

The show was broadcast in Holland on 4/25/94 and during sweeps week on 11/06/93 in the U.S. Edward's appearance wasn't originally planned and is only half a minute long.

Café Wha?-A small nightclub in New York's Greenwhich Village owned by David Lee Roth's uncle Manny. Roth spent several summers there as a child. Many now-legendary performers got their start and/or were discovered at the café including Bob Dylan, Jimi Hendrix, and Steve Van Zandt.

California Bicyclist-Sammy Hagar appeared on the cover of the September 1989 issue of this magazine, though there was no related article. Address: 490 Second Street, Suite 304, San Francisco, CA 94107; Telephone: 415-546-7291.

CAMM Magazine-David Lee Roth was interviewed and appeared on the cover of the April 1991 issue of this now-out-of-print Chicago-area magazine that was celebrating its first anniversary.

Can't Get This Stuff No More-(*Best of Volume 1* [5:14]) Glen Ballard came up with the concept for this song. It was the second song David Lee Roth recorded with Van Halen for the *Best of* album.

Dave brought several palm trees into the studio for inspiration while writing the lyrics.

This song features the first-ever appearance of a Talk Box on a Van Halen record. It was run by guitar tech Matt Bruck because Edward's mouth wasn't big enough for the tube. The music for this track was originally recorded as "Backdoor Shuffle" for the *Balance* album. The *Best of's* version features brand new lyrics by Roth.

Can't Stop Lovin' You-(*Balance*; *Best of Volume 1* [4:07]) The song came about when producer Bruce Fairbairn asked Edward for a pop tune for *Balance*. Rather than dig through his mountains of tape, Edward wrote the music from scratch. It was one of the last tracks recorded for the *Balance* album.

The "Ray" Sammy refers to at the end of the song is Ray Charles, who had a hit with the Don Gibson original, "I Can't Stop Loving You." Ray's version sold 2 million copies and topped the U.S. charts for five weeks in 1962. It was certified as the year's best-selling single.

Edward used an EBMM equipped with a piezo pickup to get the acoustic/electric rhythm sound in this song.

When Edward's guitar was delivered to the set of the video for this song, he opened the case and discovered it had arrived without a strap. Kevin Dugan was called upon to rig something together to enable Edward to properly hold the guitar.

This video also marked the first time a little person had been used in a Van Halen video since the Dave era. It was produced by Fiz Oliver and directed by Peter Christopherson.

Captain Beyond-An influential band that the members of Van Halen listened to and covered in concert during the club days of the mid 1970s. Captain Beyond was an all-star band of sorts that included Rod Evans (Deep Purple) on vocals (later vocalists included Marty Rodriguez and Willy Daffern), Lee Dorman and Larry Rheinhart (Iron Butterfly) on guitars, and Bobby Caldwell (Johnny Winter) on drums.

Captain Beyond released three albums: *Captain Beyond* (Capricorn CP-0105, 1972), *Sufficiently Breathless* (Capricorn CP-0115, 1973), and *Dawn Explosion* (Warner Bros. 3047, 1977 reprinted as One Way 33639, 1997).

Cathedral-(*Diver Down* [1:20]) This instrumental was recorded on a 1961 Fender Stratocaster (using echo and chorus effects) and was performed by Eddie hammering notes on the fretboard with his left hand while simultaneously rolling the volume knob off and on with his right hand. Ed did two takes, and the volume knob froze completely at the end of the second take due to the heat generated from rolling it on and off.

CBS This Morning-In 1990 Ed was shown in a preview for Valerie Bertinelli's upcoming sitcom Sydney.

In 1991 the promotional "Top of the World" video from the Dallas Free Show was aired on this program.

Centre Hole-(Capitol 11599) This Sammy Hagar album was released in 1980 and included the following tracks: • Red • Catch the Wind • Cruisin' and Boozin' • Free Money • Rock and Roll Weekend • Fillmore Shuffle • Hungry • Pits • Love Has Found Me • Little Star/Eclipse

Channel V-This Australian television network's index of Van Halen-related broadcasts:

1/98: Alex and Gary are interviewed during the "Without You" video shoot by Ian Meldrum on The Drum.

4/20/98: Van Halen interviewed.

6/15/98: "Fire in the Hole" video premiere on Launchpad.

6/20/98: Van Halen live and documentary footage.

6/21/98: Van Halen report.

Cherone, Gary-After Sammy Hagar left the band, Van Halen's manager, Ray Danniels, had an idea for a replacement. It seems that Ray also managed a Boston band named Extreme. The lead singer was described as having the stage presence and energy of a young David Lee Roth and the vocal range of Sammy Hagar. A singer with a voice Eddie Van Halen sometimes refers to as "angelic."

Gary Francis Caine Cherone was born and raised in Malden, Massachusetts, a city seven miles north of Boston, to a blue-collar, Italian, Catholic family on 7/26/61. His Mother worked as a phys-ed teacher and his father served as a master sergeant in the U.S. Army. The third of five brothers, Gary arrived just eleven minutes after his fraternal twin. Gary was a quiet and creative child who developed a talent for drawing in elementary school.

As a teenager, Gary found his calling singing in bands as early as age 15. His influences included Roger Daltrey, Freddie Mercury, and Steven Tyler. He paid a lot of dues on the club-circuit fronting a pop rock outfit known as The Dream. They released a six-song vinyl E.P. A collector's item, the recording has recently quadrupled in value.

In the summer of 1985, Gary and his drummer, Paul Geary, joined forces with guitarist Nuno Bettencourt and bassist Pat Badger to form Extreme. They quickly gained notoriety for their energetic shows, which earned them opening spots for Aerosmith, Poison, and White Lion. It also earned them the award for Outstanding Hard Rock/Heavy Metal Act at the Boston Music Awards for both 1986 and 1987.

The band was further awarded for their talent in November 1987 with a recording contract from A&M Records. They spent January and February of 1988 in the studio recording with producer Mack, of Queen and Billy Squier fame, and engineer Bob St. John, who was involved with the band's early demos. The result was their debut release, *Extreme*, which sold 300,000 copies.

While their first album was impressive as debuts go, it was merely a warm-up for their 1990 bombshell release, *Extreme II: Pornographitti*. The album showcased the band's diversity, featuring the funk-metal of "Get the Funk Out"; the acoustic ballad heard 'round the world, "More Than Words" and; hard rock stomps like "It('s a Monster)" and "Decadence Dance." The album sold a monumental 4 million copies and gave the band a great excuse to take their show to a worldwide audience. What followed the album was a 25-country tour, which included an opening spot on David Lee Roth's *A Little Ain't Enough* tour.

On April 20, 1992 Extreme appeared at the Freddie Mercury Tribute Concert held at London's Wembley stadium. It was one of the biggest rock events that year raising AIDS awareness and funds for the Terrence Higgins Trust, a leading AIDS charity. The estimated television audience worldwide was over one billion. Extreme stole the show performing a twenty-minute medley of Queen songs. The majority of the massive crowd sang along knowing every note. It was indeed a celebration of Queen's music and Freddie Mercury's extraordinary talent.

Later, Gary also got to perform "Hammer to Fall" on stage with the remaining members of Queen. This was truly a highlight of his career and just a taste of what it might be like to sing with a legendary band.

Their next album, 1992's *Extreme III: III Sides to Every Story*, would finally put Gary in the spotlight. The album was divided into three sides displaying three different sides to the band. The third side, entitled "The Truth," was Gary's chance to stretch the boundaries of his vocal capacity. The album and subsequent tour were lavish events.

In 1994 he began his acting career by starring as Jesus in the Boston Rock Opera's production of *Jesus Christ Superstar*. However, he had incorporated his beliefs into his music long before the play. From "Watching, Waiting" on Extreme's first album to "There Is No God" on Extreme's last album, religion is a big part of Gary's music, but it's not the only part. Gary's lyrics have dabbled in politics, sex, and religion sometimes within the same song.

Gary and Extreme stripped down their sound to its bare minimum for 1995's *Waiting for the Punchline*. Gary came out swinging with his gloves-off approach on this album. His lyrics were honed and his sound was raw. Extreme set the tone for other bands going into the studio in 1995 who threw away their effects to be heard in their most basic forms.

The *Waiting for the Punchline* tour took a toll on Gary's voice and a polyp developed on his vocal cords, a common problem that arises for rock and roll singers after years of wear and tear on the road. In November of 1995, he had surgery and recovered swiftly. Not long after, he appeared in another production of *Jesus Christ Superstar*. Again Gary played the title role.

In the year that followed, the band went on to do separate projects. Nuno Bettencourt left Extreme to pursue his solo career. Extreme broke up, leaving Gary available to join Van Halen.

It wasn't quite love at first listen, though. The demo Ed sent Gary to audition on was sent back to some lackluster reviews at 5150. However,

Gary had been promised an in-person audition. The day he arrived, he sang a handful of songs from the two previous eras. The band suddenly found themselves jamming on what would later become "Without You."

From the outset, the chemistry was obvious. Another plus was Gary's down to earth, unassuming personality and willingness to be a team player, an aura the rest of the band immediately responded to.

During the recording of *Van Halen III*, Gary stayed at Ed's guesthouse. Whenever Ed was inspired to write, Gary was there to help. When the press began knocking on the studio doors throughout 1997, Gary did very few interviews. Thankfully, he proved himself to the band and then to the fans. The talent that Extreme fans had known for a decade, Van Halen fans could finally experience for themselves.

However, *Van Halen III* was not typical Gary fare. Many fans and critics argued that Gary vocals weren't a good fit for Van Halen. Most fans held out hope for another album, but the band and Gary decided to part ways in 1999. For the first time the band had lost a singer amicably.

Chevrolet-The band performed this ZZ Top song, from the album *Rio Grande Mud* (Warner Bros. 3269, 1972), in their club days.

Cinco de Mayo 2000 Video-Performance video of Sammy Hagar and the Waboritas released in August of 1999. Filmed by Jeth Weinrich, the director of Van Halen's video for "Not Enough," the video is a 1 hour, 20 minute performance at Cabo Wabo.

Circus-This magazine's index of Van Halen-related issues:
8/31/78: Van Halen cover. "Rock Roundup in Texas": six-page feature on First Annual Texxas Jam.
10/10/78: David Lee Roth cover. "Heavy Metal Meltdown-Van Halen Takes On Black Sabbath" by Scott Cohen. This article was run again in another issue under the title "Van Halen's Challenge of 1978."
10/31/78: Sammy Hagar feature.

11/14/78: "Van Halen's Fantasies Have All Come True" by Stan Soocher.

1/02/79: "A Gallery of Guitar Heroes": Edward Van Halen profiled by Stan Soocher. Ed poster.

1/09/79: Eddie Van Halen cover. "Eddie Van Halen's Really Got Guitars": two-page feature on Edward's equipment by Stan Soocher.

2/20/79: Interview about *Van Halen II* by Stan Soocher.

1/22/80: David Lee Roth/Eddie Van Halen cover. Van Halen poster.

5/13/80: David Lee Roth cover. "Head for the Bomb Shelters! It's Van Halen!": three-page David Lee Roth interview by David Fricke.

7/22/80: *Invasion* tour dates

8/26/80: David Lee Roth cover. "Life on Planet Van Halen": three-page Van Halen feature. This issue was called "Van Halen Exclusive Color Scrapbook."

10/28/80: David Lee Roth interview.

12/31/80: *Invasion* tour feature plus dates.

5/31/81: Tour dates. *Fair Warning* tour announcement.

6/30/81: *Fair Warning* tour dates.

7/31/81: Eddie Van Halen/David Lee Roth cover. "Van Halen's Teen Hearts" by Philip Bashe.

9/30/81 "Know Nothing Roth": David Lee Roth feature. "Face to Face with Van Halen's David Lee Roth": two-page David Lee Roth interview by Gerald Rothberg. "Music Gear": Edward's gear briefly explained.

2/28/82: 1981 poll results.

4/30/82: "Music Gear: Eddie Van Halen."

5/31/82: "Sammy Hagar Beats a Path to Stardom": three-page Sammy interview by George Arthur. Sammy Hagar tour dates.

6/30/82: "Van Halen Hits a Crossroads": three-page feature by Andy Secher.

7/31/82: David Lee Roth cover. "Van Halenizing the Rock World": one-page Van Halen feature.

8/31/82: Van Halen cover. "Jekyll and Hyde: Rock Stars On and Off Stage": one-page feature on Edward Van Halen by Philip Bashe. Edward Van Halen poster. *Diver Down* tour dates. "Stage Pass": three-page review of Texxas World Music Festival featuring Sammy Hagar by Pete Oppel.

9/30/82: David Lee Roth cover. *Diver Down* tour article plus dates. "Special Report: 3-Ring Rock and Roll Circus-Van Halen Hit Middle Age": two-page feature by Philip Bashe. Short feature on Van Halen and Scorpions meeting backstage by Richard Hogan.

10/31/82: "Head for the Bomb Shelters! It's Van Halen!": reprint of two-page feature by David Fricke (originally appeared in 5/13/80 issue). *Hide Your Sheep* tour dates.

11/30/82: David Lee Roth cover. Short Van Halen feature.

12/31/82: "Van Halen: Torn between Two Worlds": two-page feature by Steve Gett and Richard Hogan.

1/31/83: David Lee Roth cover. Article about Ed's wrist injury and Dave road stories.

2/28/83: David Lee Roth cover. Two-page Van Halen feature by Andy Secher. 1982 poll results.

3/31/83: "Van Halen: Biggest US Band?": one-page Van Halen feature. "Photo Journal" by Richard Hogan. Short feature on Dave's chaps and stage banter. "Hagar Unlocks Stardom": one-page Sammy Hagar feature by Dan Hedges. *Three Lock Box* reviewed. "Back Pages": short feature on Van Halen canceling European leg of 1983 tour.

4/30/83 David Lee Roth on the cover. "A Van Halen History": three-page Van Halen timeline by Philip Bashe.

5/31/83 David Lee Roth cover. "Van Halen: Crowd-pleasers or Egomaniacs?": one-page Van Halen feature. "Guitar Clinic": one-page look at Ed's guitar technique by Arlen Roth.

6/30/83: David Lee Roth cover. "Van Halen Enter the Studio, Secretly": two-page feature by Dan Hedges. "Drum Beat": one-page look at Al's drumming style by Carmine Appice.

7/31/83: "Van Halen: Rising Stock, Level Heads": two-page feature by Dan Hedges. "Back Pages": short feature on rumor of Neal Schon and Eddie Van Halen working together on a project by Lou O'Neill Jr.

8/31/83: "Van Halen: 'I Shocked the Sheriff'": two-page feature at Us Festival. "Back Pages": short feature on EVH and recording of *1984* by Lou O'Neill Jr.

9/30/83: Article about *1984* and an Alex Van Halen wedding photo.

10/31/83: David Lee Roth on the cover. Reprint of 7/31/81 article.

11/30/83: "How Van Halen's Album Hit a Studio Deadlock": three-page Van Halen feature by Dan Hedges. "Guitar Clinic": one-page feature on Edward's harmonic technique.

12/31/83: Eddie Van Halen/David Lee Roth on the cover. Dave interview.

1/31/84: Article about Starfleet project.

2/29/84: *1984* feature. Tour dates and poll results.

3/31/84: Eddie Van Halen/David Lee Roth on the cover. *1984* tour feature and dates.

4/30/84: David Lee Roth on the cover. Dave interview. Eddie's Kramer ad. Tour dates.

5/31/84: David Lee Roth cover. *1984* tour feature and dates.

6/30/84: Eddie Van Halen/David Lee Roth on the cover. Feature article. Tour dates. Article about HSAS.

7/31/84: Eddie Van Halen on the cover. Tour dates. "Eddie Van Halen Probes His Past and Present": seven-page feature by Richard Hogan. Words to HSAS' "Top of the Rock." HSAS' *Through the Fire* reviewed.

8/31/84: *1984* tour feature.

9/30/84: "Stage Pass": Van Halen at Madison Square Garden.

10/31/84: David Lee Roth on the cover. "Van Halen": eight-page Van Halen feature and photo spread.

11/30/84: Sammy Hagar's *VOA* reviewed.

12/31/84: David Lee Roth on the cover. (No Van Halen content.)

1/31/85: Article about David Lee Roth on Van Halen videos and *Crazy from the Heat* EP. Sammy Hagar article.

2/28/85: Eddie Van Halen on the cover. Poll results.

4/30/85: Article about David Lee Roth on *Crazy from the Heat* and next Van Halen album.

5/31/85: Article about *1984*.

6/30/85: Debut of Alex's Ludwig ad.

10/31/85: (16th Anniversary Special) Five-page Van Halen live report by Richard Hogan. "Photo Journal": short feature on David Lee Roth by Jeff Tamarkin.

5/31/86: "David Lee Roth to Van Halen: Why Can't This Be Rock?": three-page David Lee Roth interview by Richard Hogan.

6/30/86: Eddie Van Halen cover. "Rock on the Road: The Summer of '86": short features on Van Halen and David Lee Roth tours by Dan Daley. "Stage Pass": Three-page live review by Dan Hedges.

7/31/86: Eddie Van Halen cover. "The 'New' Van Halen Goes Cross-country": five-page interview by Michael Smolen. Edward and Sammy centerfold. Report on Van Halen's decision to skip videos for *5150*. *5150* reviewed by Richard Hogan.

9/30/86: David Lee Roth/Sammy Hagar cover. "Inside David Lee Roth's New Band": four-page feature on Dave by Richard Hogan. "Van Halen: Happy Again with Hagar": six-page feature on Van Halen by Ben Liemer.

11/17/86: Eddie Van Halen/David Lee Roth cover. "Eddie Van Halen Probes His Past and Present" (17-year retrospective): seven-page Edward feature by Richard Hogan, originally printed in 7/31/84 issue. David Lee Roth tour dates. "Front Pages": short features on Autograph opening for Van Halen on *1984* tour and the projects of Sammy Hagar's former solo band members. *1984* reviewed. "Guide to Stars' Pickups": short feature on Edward's gear.

1/31/87: Eddie Van Halen on the cover. Articles about Van Halen and David Lee Roth. *Live without a Net* ad.

2/28/87: Eddie Van Halen cover. "Roth Beats Van Halen for Comeback of the Year": two-page interview with David Lee Roth by Dave Ford. "Van Halen Triumps and Disappoints": two-page Van Halen feature by Daina Darzin. Edward Van Halen wins top honors in 1986 Readers' Poll: Best Guitarist and Best Keyboardist. Van Halen the band also takes top honors as Biggest Disappointment of the Year while David Lee Roth wins Comeback of the Year. David Lee Roth tour dates.

3/31/87: "The Top Rockers of All Time-The 80's": one page Van Halen entry and one-page David Lee Roth entry. Short entry on Van Halen/David Lee Roth feud in "Back Pages."

1992: "Van Halen: Standing on Top of the Polls": Eddie Van Halen is voted Best Guitarist, Best Keyboardist and Most Valuable Player.

11/30/92: Sammy Hagar/Eddie Van Halen cover. "Stage Pass": two-page feature on Extreme live by Dan Hedges. Lyrics to "Poundcake." "Jitters Before Ninth Van Halen Tour": two-page feature on Van Halen by Corey Levitan. "King Edward, the First": two-page Edward feature by Corey Levitan. "Sammy Come Lately": one-page Sammy feature by Corey Levitan. "Mike Gets Noticed": one-page Michael feature by Corey Levitan. "Alex, the Other Van Halen": one-page Alex feature by Corey Levitan. "Hailin' Edward": one-page feature praising Edward's guitar strengths by various guitarists. "Sailin' with Van Halen": one-page photo history on Van Halen. Tablature to Extreme's "Hole Hearted."

Address: 115 East 57 Street, New York, NY 10022.

City of Hope Benefit-This benefit on 10/16/96 in Universal City, CA, was broadcast on VH1 on 3/08/97. Edward made an appearance and performed on the following songs: • I Fought the Law • Stay with Me • Bitch • Come On Everybody • Gimme Some Lovin' • Gloria • Get Back

The benefit concert honored VH1 president John Sykes. The music industry as a whole selects one person to honor each year, and it is the responsibility of that individual to organize a benefit of their choice to raise money for the City of Hope Hospital, the leading medical and research center in the U.S.

Other performers included Late Night with David Letterman band leader Paul Schaffer, who also acted as musical director, Steve Winwood, John Mellencamp, Bryan Adams, Bon Jovi's Richie Sambora, Sheryl Crow, drummer Max Weinberg, ex-Eagles vocalist Don Henley, and Melisssa Etheridge among others. Gary Cherone watched from the audience.

While most of the performers took part in every song, Edward did not. He instead chose to sprinkle licks and provide solos to only the songs listed above. He played through a small amplifier and switched back and forth between a cream-colored Peavey Wolfgang and a white Peavey Wolfgang Special prototype.

On "I Fought the Law" (sung by Mellencamp), Edward played the cream Wolfgang and shared guitar duties with Adams and Sambora.

For the Rolling Stones classic "Bitch," Edward played a little more in the background on lead guitar, while Crow belted out a raspy vocal. Edward wrapped up the song with an extended solo.

"Come On Everybody" (written by Eddie Cochran and Jerry Capehart) featured Adams on lead vocals. Edward switched to the Wolfgang Special and provided some serious whammy bar induced soloing.

"Gimme Some Lovin'" again featured Edward on the Wolfgang Special prototype while Steve Winwood handled lead vocals.

The Van Morrison classic "Gloria" featured Mellencamp on lead vocals, Henley on drums, and Sambora and Edward sharing lead guitar.

The Beatles' "Get Back" was the show's encore and was completely unrehearsed. Sambora stepped to the front to sing lead (along with Etheridge), and he and Edward again shared lead guitar duties.

CNN-This television network's index of Van Halen-related broadcasts:
3/30/94: Sammy Hagar featured on a Showbiz Today segment.
1995: Short feature about Edward's short haircut.
11/04/96: Ed and Alex interview.

3/98: Segment of Showbiz Today devoted to *Van Halen III*.
4/04/98: Van Halen interviewed on Latin American CNN.
9/28/98: Interview with Gary Cherone posted to www.cnn.com

Collection-(Capitol 1C 038-82 216, 1976; EMI 82216, 1983) Sammy Hagar solo compilation album. Tracks: • Keep On Rockin' • Urban Guerilla • Flamingos Fly • China • Silver Lights • All American • Confession (Please Come Back) • Young Girl Blues • Rock 'n' Roll Romeo

Comic Books-
Van Halen: June 1990, Rock Fantasy Comics. 31-page black and white comic book.
Van Halen II: October 1990, Rock 'N' Roll Comics/Revolutionary Comics. 32-page black and white comic book.
Van Halen: May 1993, Hard Rock Comics/Revolutionary Comics. 36-page color comic book.
Sammy Hagar: 1993, Hard Rock Comics All Star Special #1 (part 1 of 2).

Communication Breakdown-This Led Zeppelin cover was performed by the band at the Cabo Wabo Cantina in Cabo San Lucas, Mexico, on 5/21/92.

Concert Shots-A three-page feature on David Lee Roth and Van Halen by Mary Toledo entitled "The Halens and the McRoths" was published in this magazine in 1986.

Cosmopolitan-David Lee Roth was interviewed in the August 1986 issue of this magazine.

Could This Be Magic?-(*Women and Children First* [3:08]) This song represents the first time Ed recorded with slide guitar (Ted Templeman's idea). He practiced it for a few days, but really didn't know how he'd play the song until the time came. This song prepared him for the next song on which he used a slide: *Fair Warning*'s "Dirty Movies." Dave accompanied Ed by playing acoustic rhythm guitar. The band tossed around the idea of having a horse sounding off or a cow mooing at the end of the track.

It was raining on the day of recording, so the band opened the bay windows of the studio to add some "outside sound" to the song.

Nicolette Larson helped with background vocals-the first time an outside artist had appeared on a Van Halen recording. In 1978 Ed made a guest appearance on Nicolette's album *Nicolette* (coincidentally produced by Ted Templeman and engineered by Donn Landee) and is listed as "?" in the album's credits.

Countdown Café-Ed and Alex were interviewed on this Dutch radio program from the 5150 Studio in 1992. Van Halen was later interviewed in another appearance in January 1995, just before the Secret Gig in Arnhem, Holland.

Crazy from the Heat-1. (Warner Bros. 25222, 1985) Produced by Ted Templeman and recorded at Power Station, New York, NY, this was David Lee Roth's first solo album. The album entered the charts on 2/23/85 and stayed on the charts for 33 weeks, reaching #15 on the U.S. charts and #91 on the U.K. charts. Tracks: • Easy Street • California Girls • Just a Gigolo/I Ain't Got Nobody • Coconut Grove

The idea for this album was reputedly thought up while Dave was vacationing on the beaches of Mexico. While listening to the Beach Boys, a bodyguard suggested to Dave that he should cover "California Girls." Roth, in turn, presented the idea to Warner Brothers President Larry Waronker and *Crazy from the Heat* was born, debuting shortly thereafter at #43 on the Billboard charts. Roth's philosophy was that most albums contain no more than four good tracks on them. He cut off the flab, so to speak, resulting in this EP containing the aforementioned quartet of good material. Reportedly, Dave titled his EP *Crazy from the Heat* after seeing an early 1930s Warner Bros. cartoon about two mice on a beach who were going crazy from the heat.

While the media and fans speculated that this release might have been a signal that Van Halen was breaking up, Dave spent just as much time refuting such claims as he did hyping the album. He referred to the EP as something to occupy his time while the band recuperated from the recent *1984* tour. Whether he changed his mind or was merely putting up a smoke screen to hide his intentions, he did indeed leave the band a scant four months after the EP's release.

"California Girls," a #3 hit in the U.S. for the Beach Boys from their 1965 Capitol release, features background vocals by Christopher Cross and the Beach Boys' own Carl Wilson. The video for the song premiered on MTV on 12/31/84. It was directed by The Fabulous Picasso Brothers, Pete Angelus and David Lee Roth.

The video was filmed entirely on location at Venice Beach in Southern California. Angelus and Roth approached this video from a theatrical standpoint, wanting to present characters you could see for only 5 seconds and feel as though you knew them. One of these characters, the Latin youth dressed in breakdancing clothing, got his film start in *Breakin'* (Cannon Group, 1984).

"Just a Gigolo/I Ain't Got Nobody" features horns arranged by Edgar Winter, who played keyboards on three of the EP's four cuts. Edgar also teamed up with Roth as bandleader for the Blues Bustin' Mambo Slammers for Dave's Vegas-style lounge act in 1995. The video for this song was directed by The Fabulous Picasso Brothers. It earned Dave six MTV Video Award nominations at the September 1985 awards show, though he didn't win in any category.

The "California Girls" (remix) on the B-side of the "California Girls" single differs in that the order of the verses and chorus has been changed. The instruments have also been mixed differently, with the guitar lines standing out more than the A-side version.

The "Just a Gigolo/I Ain't Got Nobody" (remix) B-side from the single of the same name is similar to the "California Girls" (remix) in that the order of the verse and chorus sections has changed and the instruments have been remixed.

A spoof of "Just a Gigolo/I Ain't Got Nobody" entitled "Just A Big Ego" was recorded by Bob Rivers and Peter Zipfield, a pair of radio disc jockeys working for WAAF in Boston, MA. Released in 1985, the single was backed with "Can We Talk?"

2. A movie Dave wrote. Dave's original idea was for him to star in the movie and to have Van Halen do the soundtrack. This concept changed after he left the band. CBS Theatrical Films was to co-produce with The Fabulous Picasso Brothers. It was to be filmed in Acapulco, Mexico, and the Virgin Islands among other places. Its motto was: The movie, like our name, will be a combination of fine art and pizza delivery. It was to be a comedy featuring music by Nile Rodgers and Dave's as-of-then-yet-unnamed band with Billy Sheehan and Steve Vai. "Goin' Crazy" was supposed to be the title track to the movie. An open audition for the lead female role was held at the Palladium in Hollywood, CA. Roughly one thousand five hundred women showed up. Dave and Pete Angelus were present to help decide. Reportedly, the film crew was to include *Rocky*'s editor and *Arthur*'s art director.

3. The title of David Lee Roth's autobiography (Hyperion, 1997).

Crazy from the Heat singles/promos
"California Girls," "California Girls" (Remix), WB 7-29102, 7" Vinyl, USA, 1985. Highest chart position: #3 in USA, #68 in UK.

"California Girls," "California Girls" (promo), WEA 1011, 7" Vinyl, Spain, 1985.

"Just a Gigolo/I Ain't Got Nobody" (promo edit), WB 7-29040, 7" Vinyl, USA, 1985. Highest chart position: #12 in USA.

"Just a Gigolo/I Ain't Got Nobody," "Just a Gigolo/I Ain't Got Nobody" (promo edit), WB P 1967, 7" Vinyl, Japan, 1985.

"Just a Gigolo/I Ain't Got Nobody" (promo remix), "Just a Gigolo/I Ain't Got Nobody," WB 7-29040, 7" Vinyl, USA, 1985.

Creem-This magazine's Van Halen-related article index:
7/78: Van Halen feature.
8/78: Full page ad for *Van Halen*.
3/80: Van Halen feature.
7/80: David Lee Roth cover. "Remnants of the Flesh Hangover If You hate Van Halen, You're Wrong": six-page Van Halen feature by Dave DiMartino. *Women and Children First* reviewed.
10/80: Van Halen feature.
2/81: Van Halen poster.
3/81: Eddie Van Halen/David Lee Roth cover. Poll results.
5/81: Eddie Van Halen cover. "Guitar Heroes": Edward featured in four-page article by Rick Johnson.
Summer 1981: Van Halen on the cover.
9/81: Van Halen cover. *Fair Warning* reviewed by Jeff Nesin.
10/81: Van Halen cover. "Van Halen Gets Even with Everyone": six-page feature by J. Kordosh.
11/81: David Lee Roth cover. "Rock Shots": Van Halen feature.
1/82-2/82: "Guitar Heroes of Rock 'N' Roll."
3/82-4/82: Van Halen cover. "Special Edition: Rock Shots Van Halen Goes Friendly": five-page photo spread.
5/82-6/82: Van Halen cover. "Special Edition: Van Halen": entire issue devoted to Van Halen.
8/82: Van Halen feature.
9/82: Van Halen cover. "David Lee Roth and the Philosophy of Diving Down: Hang 'Em High, Hump 'Em Low": eight-page David Lee Roth interview and *Diver Down* review by Sylvie Simmons.

11/82: Van Halen cover.

3/ 83: Van Halen cover.

4/83-5/83: Van Halen cover. "Closeup: Metal Music Only You Can Save Van Halen, Maybe": four-page feature by J. Kordosh.

8/83-9/83: Van Halen on the cover. "Closeup: Metal-The New Wave."

9/83: David Lee Roth cover. Us Festival report.

11/83: Van Halen cover. "Creem Rock-Shots.": twelve-page Us Festival feature. David Lee Roth pinups.

12/83-1/84: Van Halen on the cover. "Van Halen: So Live You Can Lick It!": six-page Van Halen live feature. Sammy Hagar pinup. David Lee Roth pinup. "Closeup: Rock Shots"

1984: "Closeup: Heavy 100": Van Halen feature.

1984: "Closeup: Rock Chronicles '84": Van Halen feature.

5/84: Van Halen cover. "It's 1984-Do You Know Where Your Van Halen Is?": feature by Rick Johnson. Video feature. "Closeup: Metal Rock 'N' Roll"

7/84: David Lee Roth cover. "Rock Shots": Van Halen feature.

8/84: Van Halen cover. "Closeup: Van Halen.": special all Van Halen issue.

10/84: David Lee Roth cover.

12/84: "Rock Shots": Van Halen feature.

1985: Van Halen cover. "The Best of Creem Metal": Van Halen feature.

1/85: Van Halen cover. "Closeup: Metal Rock 'N' Roll. Strong & Silent": two-page article by Steve Gett.

2/85: David Lee Roth cover. "Rock Shots": Van Halen feature.

3/85: Van Halen cover.

4/85: David Lee Roth cover. "David Lee Roth: & The Gleeby Shall Rock": five-page Dave interview by Billy Altman. *The Wild Life* soundtrack reviewed. Two Van Halen singles reviewed. "Kiss & Tell": short feature on Edward and Valerie on the town.

6/85: "Closeup: Metal Rock 'N' Roll": David Lee Roth feature.

7/85: Van Halen cover. "Closeup: Metal Rock 'N' Roll": Van Halen feature. David Lee Roth article.

1986: Eddie Van Halen cover. "Guitar Heroes."

1986: "Rock Shots: Van Halen & David Lee Roth: The Noise and the Fury!": special edition on Van Halen and David Lee Roth bands.

3/86: Van Halen cover. "Give Us Van Halen!": six-page Van Halen interview by Dave DiMartino.

7/86: "Van Halen on Their Utter Van Halen-ness: Metal Q & A": five-page Van Halen interview by Dave DiMartino. "Closeup: Metal"

8/86: David Lee Roth cover.

10/86: David Lee Roth cover. "David Lee Roth's Revenge": four-page Dave interview by Roy Trakin.

11/86: David Lee Roth cover.

1988: Van Halen cover. "Closeup: Metal Special Edition 1988, Monsters of Rock: Those Amazing Collosal Men": two-page Monsters of Rock feature by Donna Sclair. "Van Halen Eat You Alive": four-page band interview by David Sprague. Scorpions and Van Halen poster.

5/94: Gary Cherone appears with Nuno Bettencourt in a photo spread titled "The Naked Truth."

Address: P.O. Box 1064, Birmingham, AL 48012.

Crossing Over-(*Balance* [5:03]) This song was included on only the Japanese version of *Balance* and as a B-side to the "Can't Stop Lovin' You" single.

Ed wrote and recorded some of the song in 1983 after a friend committed suicide. It was revived after the death of long time band manager Ed Leffler. Ed's recorded parts include his playing the drums and singing. The rest of the song was recorded in 1994. Ed's music is in the left channel, and Al's drums and Sammy's singing are in the right channel. Sammy really loved the song and wanted to remove "Take Me Back (Déjà Vu)" from *Balance* and put "Crossing Over" in its place.

Crossroads-(3:20) A partial version of this Cream cover song was performed on 5/31/86 at the Kemper Auditorium in Kansas City, MO, toward the end of "Ain't Talkin' 'Bout Love." The song was also played several times during the *F.U.C.K.* tour.

Cruisin' and Boozin'-This Sammy Hagar album was released in 1984 and re-released in 1992 (CEMA 9092) and includes the following tracks:
• Keep On Rockin' • Cruisin' and Boozin' • You Make Me Crazy • Reckless • Bad Reputation • Red • Rock and Roll Romeo • Twentieth Century Man • Never Say Die

Crystal Pepsi-The song "Right Now" was used to promote this product in commercials. The band didn't want the song to be used but were informed that another group would rerecord the song and collect the money from the ads. Reluctantly, the band allowed Pepsi to use the song.

Current Affair-This show televised the incident involving a con man who claimed to know Eddie Van Halen swindling the New Start Homes (see "Balta, Carol" entry). The show was aired in April 1994.

D

Daddy Long Legs-One of the names Kiss bassist Gene Simmons wanted to give Van Halen upon "discovering" them in 1976.

The Daily Show (Comedy Central)-In 1996 this show aired clips from Ed and Al's MTV interview about the breakup with Dave to make jokes about the band and Gary Cherone. On 5/21/97 Sammy Hagar was interviewed about the breakup with Van Halen and his solo album *Marching to Mars.*

Dance the Night Away-(*Van Halen II; Best of Volume 1* [3:04]) This is the only track from the *Van Halen II* album written completely in the studio. The song was inspired by Fleetwood Mac's "Go Your Own Way." David Lee Roth originally wanted to name this song "Dance, Lolita, Dance." It was Edward's idea to call it "Dance the Night Away."

In the live video for this song, the editor makes an obvious mistake by confusing Ed's new "false harmonic" technique with regular harmonics. This is not the only editing mistake, but is by far the most noticeable.

The Wedgies released a 6 song CD in 1997 to celebrate the Green Bay Packers' placement in the Super Bowl-all rock songs with tongue-in-cheek lyrics. Track #5 was entitled "Take Us All the Way" and was sung to the tune of "Dance the Night Away."

Dancing in the Streets-(*Diver Down* [3:43]) Ed used a Mini Moog synthesizer in conjunction with his echoed guitar for the music in the song. He initially wanted the music to be for an original song. However, Dave and Donn Landee talked him into using it for this cover tune.

Danger Danger-Gary Cherone provided background vocals on this group's 1992 album *Screw It* (Epic ZK-46977).

Danger Zone-(Capitol Records 12069, 1980) This Sammy Hagar solo album spent 12 weeks on the charts beginning on 6/21/80 and peaking at #85.

The initial run of this album included a poster that featured the names of lucky Hagar-ites.

"Bad Reputation" was featured in the 1980 satire *Up the Academy* (Warner Bros.) and "Love or Money" features Neal Schon on lead guitar. Tracks: • Love or Money • Twentieth Century Man • Miles from Boredom • Mommy Says, Daddy Says • In the Night (Entering the Danger Zone) • Iceman • Bad Reputation • Heartbeat • Run for Your Life • Danger Zone

Datehead-The nickname of Michael Anthony's *F.U.C.K.* tour bass tech, Craig DeFalco. According to DeFalco, he used to wear a spikey "palm tree" hairdo when his band played the club scene, which prompted his friends to dub him Datehead. The moniker has been with him ever since.

The Dave Clark Five-The band that inspired Edward and Alex to get into rock and roll.

Davesickle-The guitar David Lee Roth used from time to time for live performances of "Ice Cream Man." This steel-stringed electric/acoustic was shaped and painted like a popsickle.

Dave TV-A combination of images and Real Audio technology, this Internet broadcast has introduced fans to several unreleased Van Halen and David Lee Roth tunes. Located at www.dave-tv.com, the broadcasts include a series of pictures accompanied by approximately 30 minutes of music, stories, and classic Dave-style clowning.

David Lee Roth (the video)-A 30 minute compilation of four videos from *Crazy from the Heat* and *Eat 'Em and Smile* as well as an interview.

The videos included: • Just a Gigolo/I Ain't Got Nobody • California Girls • Yankee Rose • Goin' Crazy

David Lee Roth Fan Club-In 1985 the premiere release of the membership kit included a package of colored feathers, a numbered club card, and a flyer for merchandise.

Dazed and Confused-This Led Zeppelin cover was performed by Van Halen at the second anniversary celebration of the Cabo Wabo Cantina on 5/21/92.

Delta Sonic-This band released a song about Van Halen titled "VH" on their 2000 EP *Onward Into Obscurity*.

Demos-Van Halen recorded at least four demos before the release of *Van Halen* in 1978.
   Cherokee Demo (1973) Tracks: • Take Your Whiskey Home • Simple Rhyme • Angel Eyes • Believe Me
   This is the band's earliest-known studio work is believed to have been recorded at Cherokee studios, located on a farm in Chatsworth, CA. The tape was given to Michael Anthony just before he tried out for Mammoth, and he was told to learn all the songs on it. More than likely Anthony's predecessor, Mark Stone, recorded the bass lines on these tracks.

   Hound Dog Demo (1974/75)
   It is not known for sure what songs were recorded during this particular studio session, which took place at the now defunct Hound Dog Studio located on Colorado Boulevard in Pasadena, CA, (although it is rumored that the session yielded two or three different versions of "Ice Cream Man" along with two other unknown tracks). "Ice Cream Man" was a staple of David Lee Roth's prior to his teaming forces with the Van

Halen brothers. He used to perform it at the Pasadena, CA, Ice House solo on an acoustic guitar.

The Hound Dog Studio, a rather modest affair with a small mixing console and a couple of soundproofed rooms, was run by a gentleman known only as Bill, who was heir to a construction fortune, and an engineer known only as Russell, who was known to have a severe sinus problem. It is quite probable that the studio based its name on a velvet painting that hung within its walls. The mock tapestry featured a group of dogs sitting around a smoky table playing poker.

Gene Simmons Financed Demo (1976) Tracks: • House of Pain • Runnin' with the Devil • Babe Don't Leave Me Alone

Gene Simmons wanted to try producing a band and thought Van Halen was the next big thing (though he wanted them to change their name). They recorded this demo sometime around May 1976 at Village Recorder Studios in Los Angeles after an evening gig at The Starwood. Two guitar solos were later recorded at Electric Ladyland Studios in New York. While in New York, the band performed (using Kiss's equipment) for S.I.R's Bill Aucoin, who passed to sign the band Piper. However, the band didn't know what was going on and kept performing in Los Angeles without a copy of the demo to show other labels. To this day Simmons jokingly states that Van Halen still owes him the money he fronted to produce the tape.

Warner Brothers Demo (1977) Tracks: • Feel Your Love Tonight (3:48) • Show Your Love (4:00) • Runnin' with the Devil (3:18) • Voodoo Queen (3:33) • Little Dreamer (3:13) • Last Night (3:25) • Somebody Get Me a Doctor (3:59) • Light in the Sky (4:35) • Get the Show on the Road (2:55) • Babe Don't Leave Me Alone (3:00) • Big Trouble (3:38) • On Fire (3:56) • She's the Woman (2:59) • I Want to Be Your Lover (3:00) • D.O.A. (4:07) • Bring on the Girls (3:48) • We Die Bold (3:01) • Young and Wild (2:35) • Let's Get Rockin' (3:07) • Put Out the Lights (3:36) •

House of Pain (3:27) • Piece of Mind (3:57) • In a Simple Rhyme (4:39)
• You Really Got Me (2:42) • Happy Trails (1:12)

This is the 25-song demo from which the tracks for *Van Halen* were
picked. The instrumental tracks were recorded in one day, and the vocals
were recorded the next day. "Ain't Talkin' 'Bout Love" was written after the
demo was recorded.

On some bootlegs of this demo, the date 10/26/77 is given as the date
the demo was recorded. This date is almost certainly not the date it was
recorded. No one officially connected with the demo has spoken publicly
about the details behind the recording of it.

Detroit Rock City-"Runnin' with the Devil" appears on the soundtrack (Polygram 546389, 8/03/99) to this film (New Line, 8/13/99).

Diamond Dave-David Lee Roth's nickname. According to the vocalist,
he's had it since childhood.

Dick in the Dirt-Van Halen performed a jam of this song from Sammy
Hagar's *VOA* album on 12/13/91 at the Miami Arena in Miami, FL.

"Dirty Movies"-(*Fair Warning* [4:06]) This, Edward's second instance
of recording with a slide, was recorded on a Gibson SG with a Les Paul
Junior neck. Eddie couldn't reach high enough up on the fretboard, so he
had Ted Templeman hold the guitar's lower horn while he sawed it off
with a hacksaw.

This is one of only two Van Halen songs with quotation marks around
the title. The other is "5150" from 5150.

Decadent Dub Team sampled parts of this song for their 1990 tune
"Money."

Mr. Bungle covered this song on 5/27/90 at the Moon Saloon in San
Fransisco, CA. A bootleg recording of this show is in circulation among
Mr. Bungle fans.

Dirty Water Dog-(*Van Halen III* [5:24]) The working title for this song was "Swamp Groove." Ed and Gary began writing the song when in New York City. The title "Dirty Water Dog" was used because Ed and Wolfie, while in New York, ate the street vender hot dogs, known as dirty water dogs, every day.

Edward added a counter rhythm in the intro created by scratching a pool brush on the sidewalk outside the home of engineer Robbes Steiglitz. Robbes followed Ed with a microphone as the guitarist scratched his way down the walkway.

Sharp-eared listeners will hear the handle fall off the broom. Ed was unscrewing it while scratching and accidentally dropped it twice. Listen even closer and you'll hear him say "Shit!" though the "t" sound was cut out.

Ed used a cream Wolfgang prototype with single-coil pickups through a Whammy pedal and an MXR compressor before plugging right into the board on most of this track except the solo, which was performed on a standard Wolfgang through a 5150 amp.

Ed reused a riff from his appearance on Saturday Night Live, on the song "Stompin' 8H," on this track.

Diver Down-1. (Warner Bros. 3677, US/K 57003, UK [31:14]) Released on 4/14/82, *Diver Down* spent 65 weeks on the charts, peaking at #3 on U.S. charts (entering on 5/08/82) and at # 36 on U.K. charts (entering on 5/01/82). 4 million copies have been sold in the U.S. The album was re-mastered and re-released on 9/19/00.

It's safe to say this is easily the band's least favorite album. Of the 12 songs, five are cover tunes. Though the album sold well and led to a large tour, the band seemingly felt that none of the songs on it were worthy of an appearance on *Best of Volume 1*.

The entire LP was recorded in 12 days at Amigo Studios (now known as Warner Brothers Recording Studios) at a cost of approximately $46,000. It was the first Van Halen album to sell 1 million copies before the tour. The album also helps the band set a record for most consecutive platinum-selling albums at Warner Brothers Records.

The cover art, which is the international symbol to alert boats of a diver below the surface of the water, was chosen because the band had a message: though it may not be noticeable on the surface, there's something going on underneath. The live photo on the back of the album was taken when Van Halen opened for The Rolling Stones on 10/24/81 at the Tangerine Bowl in Orlando, FL.

The number of cover tunes on this album was arguably the proverbial straw that broke the camel's back, cementing Edward's desire to build his own studio.

2. Van Halen tribute band.

Diver Down singles/promos
"(Oh) Pretty Woman" (mono), "(Oh) Pretty Woman," WB, 7" Vinyl, USA, 1982.

"(Oh) Pretty Woman" (mono), "(Oh) Pretty Woman," WEA, 7" Vinyl, Italy, 1982.

"Pretty Woman" (without "Oh"), "Happy Trails," WEA W 17909, 7" Vinyl, Italy, 1982.

"(Oh) Pretty Woman," "Happy Trails," WB WBS50003 (ZCA 1509S), 7" Vinyl, USA, 2/06/82. Highest chart position: #12 in USA on 4/17/82.

"(Oh) Pretty Woman," "Happy Trails," WEA P-1618, 7" Vinyl, Japan, 1982.

"(Oh) Pretty Woman," "Dancing in the Street," WB GWB 0433, 7" Vinyl, USA, 1982.

"Dancing in the Street," "The Full Bug," WB, 7" Vinyl, USA, 5/22/82. Highest chart position: #38 in USA.

"Dancing in the Street" (mono), "Dancing in the Street," WB 7-29986, 7" Vinyl, USA, 1982.

"Secrets" (mono remix), "Secrets" (remix), WB 7-29929, 7" Vinyl, USA, 1982.

"(Oh) Pretty Woman," "Happy Trails," WB PRO-A-1006, 12" Vinyl, USA, 1982.

"Dancing in the Streets," "Where Have All the Good Times Gone?" WB 17954, 7" Vinyl, USA, France, Holland, Germany, 1982.

"Secrets," "Big Bad Bill (Is Sweet William Now)," WB 92 99297, 7" Vinyl, USA 1982.

"Dancing in the Streets," "Big Bad Bill (Is Sweet William Now)," WEA K 17957, 7" Vinyl, UK, 1982.

"Dancing in the Street" plus five non-Van Halen tracks, WEA Muziek Expres Super-6 Single, 7" Vinyl, Holland, 6/82.

The DLR Band-1. David Lee Roth's solo band circa 1998, which included guitarists John Lowery, Terry Kilgore, and Mike Hartman, bassist Tom Lilly, and drummer Ray Luzier.
2. (Wawazat!! WACD 1217) The DLR Band's self-titled debut album released on 6/09/98. The album debuted at #172 on the charts with 8,000 copies sold in the first week. Within a year the album had sold 65,000 copies. It marked a return to the hard rock guitar-virtuoso sound that made *Eat 'Em and Smile* such a classic rock album. The album was

engineered, mixed, and mastered by Erwin Musper, who had just come off a short stint mixing some of *Van Halen III*. Tracks: • Slam Dunk! • Blacklight • Counter-Blast • Lose the Dress (Keep the Shoes) • Little Texas • King of the Hill • Going Places... • Wa Wa Zat!! • Relentless • Indeedido • Right Tool for the Job • Tight • Weekend with the Babysitter • Black Sand

The first single, "Slam Dunk," reached #1 on the FMQB and Album Network airplay charts for three weeks. The second single "Relentless" also debuted in the top ten on these charts.

Some of the lyrics to "Lose the Dress (Keep the Shoes)" were first printed in Dave's autobiography *Crazy from the Heat*. "Tight" was originally "Private Parts," an unused song written for *Howard Stern Private Parts: The Movie*.

Bettie Page, the popular pin-up girl of the 1950s, graces the cover of the album.

The DLR Band singles/promos

"Slam Dunk!" "King of the Hill," WaWaZat!! WACD 101-2, CD and Cassette, USA, 3/20/98

"Relentless," WaWaZat!!, CD, USA, 6/30/98.

D.O.A.-(*Van Halen II* [4:07]) This song was on the band's 25 song Warner Brothers demo tape. On the demo, though, the lyrics are in some cases completely different from the final version and in other cases mumbled, suggesting the song still needed to be refined a bit from Dave's aspect. Maybe this is the reason this song was left off *Van Halen*.

Doin' Time-(*Balance* [1:41]) This Alex Van Halen instrumental wouldn't have made it onto the album if Ed and Bruce Fairbairn hadn't pushed for it. Alex did not originally intend for it to be on *Balance*.

Dolby, Thomas-Ed performed on Dolby's album *Astronauts & Heretics* (Warner Bros. 24478, 1992) Tracks: • Eastern Block (Sequel to Europa and the Pirate Twins, 1981) (5:18) • Close but No Cigar (4:25)

Ed played lead guitar on "Eastern Block" and shared guitar duties with Larry Treadwell on "Close but No Cigar." All his parts were recorded in a single evening at 5150. On 5/25/92 Virgin records released a two part CD single (VSCDG 1410/665 246/ PM 515) that included two different edits of "Close but No Cigar."

"Europa and the Pirate Twins" (the song to which "Eastern Block" is the sequel to) appeared on Dolby's 1983 release *The Golden Age of Wireless* (Capitol Records, 12271) and peaked at #67 on the U.S. charts.

Dolby was born Thomas Morgan Dolby Robertson and of British parentage on 10/14/58 in Cairo, Egypt. His biggest hit to date was 1982's "She Blinded Me with Science" (from 1983's EP *Blinded By Science* [Harvest 15007] and later appearing on The Golden Age of Wireless), which peaked at #5 on the U.S. charts. Dolby asked Eddie for his help after assisting the guitarist with two keyboard tunes during the *For Unlawful Carnal Knowledge* sessions.

Dolby spent time as the keyboardist for Bruce Woolley & The Camera Club and the Lene Lovich band (1979-80). The 1986 film *Howard the Duck* (MCA/Universal Pictures/Lucasfilm) featured music by Dolby (billed as Dolby's Cube). He is married to Kathleen Beller (Kirby Colby on Dynasty).

Don Kirshner's Rock Concert Series-In 1982 Jim Ladd interviewed David Lee Roth for this show.

Don't Call Us, We'll Call You-(3:52) This Sugarloaf cover was performed by Van Halen on 9/18/76 at The Bogart in San Bernardino, CA.

Don't Tell Me (What Love Can Do)-(*Balance* [5:56]) The song was inspired by the suicide death of Nirvana's Kurt Cobain, and it is about how his death affected Sammy Hagar.

The video for this song premiered on MTV New Year's Eve at midnight in Times Square. This was the first video from *Balance*. With the exception of one person (the main character), all of the troubled youths appearing in this film were portrayed by real gang members. The segments with the band were filmed at Hollywood National Studios in Hollywood, CA. The video was directed by Peter Christopherson and produced by Catherine Finkenstaedt and Fiz Oliver.

On the day of filming, MTV interviewed the band for an upcoming MTV News segment, and Ed gave an interview for Guitar for the Practicing Musician magazine.

Down and Out in Beverly Hills-The David Lee Roth song "California Girls" from the album *Crazy from the Heat* appeared in this film.

Down in Flames-(4:25) This unreleased Van Halen original was played several times throughout the 1978 tour. The chords immediately following the solo were used on "You're No Good." The song was also played on 12/31/77 at the Whisky A GoGo in West Hollywood, CA. An alternate title that has been used for the song is "Stop Tryin'."

The Dream-The first incarnation of Extreme, featuring Gary Cherone on lead vocals, Peter Hunt on guitar, Paul Mangone on bass, Mika Watson on keyboard, and Paul Geary on drums.

According to legend, sometime around 1984 or 1985 the CBS network aired a program about the music business and one of the featured bands was named The Dream, which was not this incarnation of the same name. Geary sold the rights to the name to CBS for $50,000 which he, Cherone, and company, used to make a video for "Mutha."

In the band's very next gig, the banner (or possibly bass drum) that featured "The Dream" emblazoned on it was altered: the "The" had a large X through it (X-Dream), which was later modified to Extreme.

In 1983 the band released an EP that included the tracks: • See the Light • Mutha • Show Me Your Love • Say Goodbye • The Mask • Why

In 1985 "Mutha" was submitted to MTV's Basement Tapes, a contest in which unsigned bands submitted videos to the young network, which in turned aired the best ones in a head-to-head contest. Viewers then called in during each round to vote for their favorite video. "Mutha" won the grand prize, beating out then-unknown Henry Lee Summer by 1% of the total votes.

Nuno Bettencourt and Pat Badger joined after a Halloween show in which members of different Boston bands got together and did a tribute show. The guys performed as Aerosmith. "Mutha" later found its way to Extreme's first major-label release, *Extreme*, as "Mutha (Don't Wanna Go to School Today)."

The Dream Is Over-(*For Unlawful Carnal Knowledge* [4:00]) Ed used a prototype Bob Bradshaw preamp on the rhythm track of this song.

Though this song does not appear on the *Live: Right Here, Right Now* album, it does appear on the *Live: Right Here, Right Now* video.

Dreams-(*5150*; *Best of Volume 1* [4:54]; *Live: Right Here, Right Now* [4:49]) This song was written by Ed, Sam, and Mick Jones (who also helped produce the *5150* album). Ed met Jones (who was nicknamed "The Duke" by the band) through Sammy at an MTV Awards show. Originally, the verse section was part of the solo section. It was Jones's idea to change them. Eddie had just begun to write "Dreams" when Dave left the band.

It was recorded on a 1912 Steinway 7-foot B Grand, MIDI-ed to an Oberheim OB-8. The song also features a Kramer Ferrington acoustic/electric guitar.

During the Gulf War, several pilots played the song in the cockpit of their aircraft, using it for inspiration prior to engaging in combat.

Though the band didn't film a video for the *5150* version of the tune, the Navy's aerial stunt team, the Blue Angels, created a video of their own for "Dreams," which they used to promote their 40th anniversary. The video was quickly picked up by MTV and placed into relatively heavy rotation.

The band filmed a video for "Dreams" as it appeared on the *Live: Right Here, Right Now* album. Filmed at a "secret" gig at the Whisky A GoGo in West Hollywood, CA, this video featured the band returning to its roots. The video was directed and produced by Stan Kellum and Carloyn Mayer Beug. The band incurred more costs than initially expected due to the extra police officers who had to be called in to help control the mini riot on the Sunset Strip that evening.

Dreamworlds-This 2-part documentary made by England's Soot Golley took a look at the portrayal of women in music videos. Several Van Halen videos were attacked in the presentation, and the film as a whole claimed that only women who dressed like prostitutes or sluts were hired to appear in rock videos, citing the "Poundcake" video as an example.

"Hot for Teacher" was used to demonstrate the opinion that male bands sometimes revert to their childhood and portray their teachers or female classmates as strippers.

David Lee Roth's "California Girls" video was presented as proof that it is common practice to portray women as objects rather than people. Another of Roth's videos ("A Lil' Ain't Enough") was used to demonstrate the idea that women used in videos are interchangeable and not considered as individuals.

Motley Crue videos were also used in the film, as were several other rock videos set to rap and pop music.

Drive!-Sammy Hagar appeared on the cover of this magazine on 2/23/93. Bill Auda wrote a one-page feature on Hagar's 1967 Shelby GT-500 entitled

"Sammy Hagar's '67 'Red Rocker'." Address: 3470 Buskirk Avenue, Pleasant Hill, CA 94523; Telephone: 510-934-3700.

Drive My Car-This Beatles cover was reportedly played in Van Halen's club days.

Drop Dead Legs-(*1984* [4:13]) This song was first recorded by Edward, Alex, and Donn and then played for Ted, Dave, and Mike the next day.

Drum!-Alex Van Halen was featured on the July/August 1991 cover of this magazine. Alex was interviewed by Greg Rule in a seven-page article entitled "Bashing, Crashing and Smashing with Finesse: Alex Van Halen." Alex was also interviewed in the February 1998 issue of the magazine. Address: 12 South First Street #417, San Jose, CA 95113; Telephone: 408-971-9794.

Drums & Drumming-Alex Van Halen appeared on the July/August 1988 cover of this magazine. Alex was interviewed by Andy Doerschuk in a nine-page article entitled "Keeping It in the Family." "Get Up" was transcribed.

Dugan, Kevin-Michael Anthony's tech since 1980. Kevin was interviewed in issue #3 of The Inside. Before joining forces with Mike, Kevin worked for many acts including Fleetwood Mac and the Raspberrys.

Dumpster-Eddie Van Halen and Valerie Bertinelli's dog in the late eighties. The dog got his name because Valerie found him in the trash while filming the made-for-television movie *Shattered Vows* (1984).

E

Eagles Fly-Sammy used this song for years as his solo during Van Halen shows. While on the *F.U.C.K.* tour, he sang it solo. During the 1993 tour, the band played the full song, and during the 1995 tour, the band joined in toward the end of the song.

Earache My Eye-This Cheech and Chong cover song was played by Van Halen on the 1981 *Fair Warning* tour.

Earsay-This British Channel 4 television program aired a 20-minute interview with David Lee Roth on 7/25/84.

Eat 'Em and Smile-(Warner Bros. 25470-2,1986) This was David Lee Roth's first full-length solo album. Produced by longtime Van Halen producer Ted Templeman and released on 7/04/86, the album spent thirty-six weeks on the charts beginning on 7/26/86. It topped out at U.S. #4 and U.K. #28.

This album featured Steve Vai on guitar, Billy Sheehan on bass, and Greg Bissonette on drums. Originally, this was going to be the soundtrack for Roth's movie *Crazy from the Heat*. Billy Sheehan was the first person Dave contacted to form a band and put together the soundtrack; he and Roth were to be the core of the band, responsible for the songwriting, getting other band members, etc.-an idea that slowly became less and less a reality as time went on. Interestingly, Sheehan didn't know Roth had left Van Halen and phoned Edward Van Halen the day prior to his meeting with Roth to discuss the project with him. It was then that he learned the vocalist had struck out on his own.

Sheehan, who was in his band Talas at the time, remembers it as being a really active week in his own life. Besides Sheehan's getting the call from Roth, Talas had just done a personal showcase for Clive Davis of Arista

Records, and Danny Goldberg of Goldmount Records (who later went on to manage Nirvana) offered them a major-label record deal. Two days after that, Talas was offered the opening slot on Yngwie Malmsteen's tour by the William Morris Agency.

Steve Stevens was the first guitarist considered for the band, but the idea fell through for unknown reasons. Ex-Whitesnake guitarist John Sykes (who had already jammed with Dave a couple of times) was also considered. Sheehan suggested former Frank Zappa and Alcatrazz guitarist Steve Vai, with whom, coincidentally, he had wanted to do a solo project while in Talas.

Once Vai was in the band, the Roth/Sheehan core expanded to include Vai, and eventually dwindled down to just Roth calling all the shots. No one is really sure why this occurred, but Sheehan feels that had the nucleus remained as planned with him, Roth, and Vai at the helm, the band could very well have continued successfully, quite possibly to this day.

Sheehan and Vai were then instructed by Roth to go forth and find a drummer. Ads were placed in various newspapers and trade magazines and were answered by Dave's secretary. Approximately 200 drummers including Roxy Petrucci, who later went on to join Vixen, auditioned at S.I.R. for the spot all trying out on the same drum kit. Greg Bissonette, a positive, upbeat individual and one of Sheehan's favorite human beings, was chosen. He was a player both Vai and Sheehan knew right away was the best man for the job. Amazingly, at band rehearsals the very next day, Bissonette already knew all of the songs.

The cannibal-like tribesman cover art was inspired by one of Dave's Jungle Studs trips to Borneo.

Sheehan was very pleased with the working environment for this album. He, Vai, and Bissonette would work on the music, and Roth would interject here and there with comments like "That sounds cool; do more of that," or "That's a good chorus; that isn't. Let's keep the good part of that."

"Shy Boy," originally a Talas composition that appeared on their 1983 release *Sink Your Teeth into That* (Important Records 149-03), wasn't changed too drastically from its original form. The rhythm track under the solo was changed from D major to B minor (Dave's idea). Sheehan wrote the song right after Talas' stint opening for Van Halen on the1980 *Invasion* tour, and the track was obviously very Van Halen influenced (in the same vein as "I'm the One").

"Ladies Night in Buffalo?" came about when Sheehan, Vai, Bissonette, Roth, Larry Hostler, and several others were hanging out at Roth's Pasadena, CA, house one evening drinking some "skunk beer" left over from the 1983 Us Festival. Sheehan had just returned from spending Thanksgiving in his hometown of Buffalo, NY. The group was talking back and forth, and Sheehan remarked that while in Buffalo, he had gone out for Ladies Night. The concept of such an event taking place in Buffalo, NY, was very humorous to the group, and a song was eventually built around the phrase.

The lyrics for "Yankee Rose" were written in a New York City hotel room. Roth called Sheehan and asked the bassist to come to his room and work on some lyrics with him. "Firecrackin' on the Fourth of July" was one line contributed by Billy.

Two tracks that were considered for inclusion on the album but didn't make the cut were a cover of "Kids in Action," written by Kim Mitchell (from Toronto, Canada's Max Webster), and another cover originally written by the late Irish guitarist Rory Gallagher. Tracks: • Yankee Rose • Shyboy • I'm Easy • Ladies' Night in Buffalo? • Goin' Crazy! • Tobacco Road • Elephant Gun • Big Trouble • Bump and Grind • That's Life

The video for "Yankee Rose" was directed by The Fabulous Picasso Brothers. The convenience store sequence at the beginning of the video took approximately 20 hours to shoot and was filmed at a small "Mom and Pop" establishment in West Hollywood, CA. David Lee Roth's "I'll take a glazed doughnut and a bottle of anything" line was originally scripted as, "I'll take a glazed doughnut and a bottle of Jack," but was changed because of concern about how it would be handled by MTV and that it might get censored (thanks in part to Tipper Gore and the PMRC's music lyric censorship campaign). In addition, the grocer's "Son of a biscuit" line (said just after swallowing a breath mint) was overdubbed. If you watch closely, you'll see that he mouths something slightly different. The grocer is played by the brother of Harry Perzigian, a former writer for The Jeffersons television sitcom who was convicted of supplying cocaine to actor Carol O'Connor's late son, Hugh, in the late 1990s.

The stage sequences were filmed in San Bernardino, CA, to a packed house of screaming fans. This was Billy Sheehan's first on-camera performance, and he and the band naturally gave it their all from the very first take (not realizing there were going to be many more takes afterward). He was so sore the day following filming that he couldn't even walk downstairs. He had to sit and scoot his way down any stairways he encountered. Sheehan used a custom-built Yamaha BB3OOOS bass for this video as well as all the other videos from *Eat 'Em and Smile*. It was outfitted with a Gibson EBO-style pickup in the neck position and a DiMarzio Model P-style pickup in the middle. Each pickup was wired separately, requiring two separate jacks on the body. The bass was also used as his backup while on the album's supporting tour.

The video for "Goin' Crazy!," directed by The Fabulous Picasso Brothers, was the first video from the album.

The sequence at the end of the video, in which the band is overtaken by all sorts of people, was planned but was kept secret from Diamond Dave and the band. The surprised looks on their faces were real, and amazingly they were able to keep their composure enough to pull it off on the first take.

The custom-made flame guitar used by Vai in this video was sculpted from a Stratocaster body by Performance Guitars. It was fitted with a maple fingerboard and one humbucking pickup. Also seen in this video was Vai's custom-made "Steve Eye" guitar, which was stolen just prior to the start of the *Eat 'Em and Smile* tour.

The video for "That's Life" was also directed by The Fabulous Picasso Brothers. This video includes clips from past videos and performances, including some with Van Halen.

Eat 'Em and Smile singles/promos
"California Girls," "Just a Gigolo/I Ain't Got Nobody," "Yankee Rose," WEA W7650, 12" Vinyl, France, 1986.

"Yankee Rose," "Shyboy," WB 7-28656, 7" Vinyl, USA, 7/04/86. Highest chart position: #16 in USA.

"Yankee Rose," "Yankee Rose," WB Pro-A-2523, 12" Vinyl, USA, 1986.

"Yankee Rose," "Shyboy," WEA P-2139, 7" Vinyl, Japan, 1986.

"Yankee Rose," "Shyboy," WEA W8656, 7" Vinyl, UK, 1986.

"Goin' Crazy," "Goin' Crazy" (promo), WB Pro-A-2564, 12" Vinyl, USA, 1986.

"Goin' Crazy," "Goin' Crazy" (promo), WB 7-28584, 7" Vinyl, USA, 1986.

"Goin' Crazy," "Loco Del Calor!" WB 7-28584, 7" Vinyl, USA, 1986. Highest chart position: #66 in USA on 10/18/86.

"That's Life," "Bump and Grind," WB 7-28511, 7" Vinyl, USA, 1986. Highest chart position: #85 in USA on 12/06/86.

"That's Life," "Asi' Es La Vida," WEA P-2201, 7" Vinyl, Japan, 1986.

"Tobacco Road," "Tobacco Road" (promo), WB Pro-A-2547, 12" Vinyl, USA, 1986.

"Yankee Rose" (reissue), WB, USA, 11/88.

Eat Thy Neighbor-This unfinished, unreleased original was one of three tracks written for the then-untitled *5150* that David Lee Roth began vocal work on prior to his departure from the band.

Egos and Icons-Van Halen was featured in this Canadian special on an unknown date.

Eighteen-This Alice Cooper cover was reportedly played by Van Halen throughout 1974 and 1975 during their dance party days, prior to being signed.

89 A Revista Rock-Van Halen appeared on the cover of this Brazilian magazine that also included a Van Halen article in its 7/98 issue.

Emeril Live-Sammy Hagar made an appearance on this Food Network television program on 3/30/99. Sammy is good friends with the show's host, chef Emeril Lagasse, who had cooked at Hagar's wedding reception.

E! News-This television show's index of Van Halen-related broadcasts:
1992: Segment about Ed's golfing.
1993: Ed and Valerie at Emmy Awards.
1994: David Lee Roth interviewed and feature on *Your Filthy Little Mouth*.
9/11/96: Report of Sammy leaving the band and Dave reunion using footage of the band's Rock Walk induction.
3/26/98: Report of *Van Halen III* debuting at #4 on the charts.
1/02/99: A Sammy Hagar interview is featured.

Entertainment Tonight-Index of this television show's Van Halen-related broadcasts:

1982: Feature on Ed and Val's one year anniversary.

1982: Edward feature.

3/09/82: Dave interviewed from his bedroom.

1983: Feature on *The Seduction of Gina*.

1983: Ed and Valerie interview

5/29/83: Us Festival Dave interview before show.

1986: *5150* tour in San Francisco.

1986: Ed shown in 1983 footage during his wife's *I'll Take Manhattan* promo.

1990: Ed shown in his wife's Sydney promo.

1992: Grammy nomination interview in airport.

1993: Van Halen in Dallas. Backstage interviews and some concert footage shown.

11/05/93: Feature on Ed's appearance in Café Amercain.

4/94: Feature on Ed and Sterling Ball from the Pediatric Kidney Charity event.

4/95: Sammy interviewed after Great Woods Center show in Mansfield, MA, on 4/04/95.

5/09/96: Ed and Valerie at *Twister* premiere in Los Angeles, CA.

Entertainment Weekly-This magazine's index of Van Halen-related articles:

10/93: Feature about Ed making a guest appearance on the television show Frasier.

10/18/96: Van Halen cover. "Van Wailin'": seven-page Van Halen feature by Chris Willman and Dan Snierson.

1/10/97: "Musical Mikes": one-page feature on breakup and reconciliation with David Lee Roth.

4/11/97: "A Guitar Hero Picks His Bride": one-page feature on Edward and Valerie's 16 years of marriage.

1997: Sammy Hagar's *Marching to Mars* reviewed.
1997: "What Makes Sammy Run?": one-page Sammy Hagar interview.
Address: Time, Inc., 1675 Broadway; New York, NY 10019.

EQ-Eddie Van Halen appeared on the cover of this publication's February 1996 issue. The issue included "A Question of Balance," an eight-page Ed interview by Steve La Cerra. Address: 2 Park Avenue, Suite 1820, New York, NY 19916.

Eruption-1. (*Van Halen*; *Best of Volume 1* [1:42]) This instrumental introduced the guitar genius of Eddie Van Halen to the world. Half of the song was used in Warner Brothers promotional video for the band's first album. It was used as an introduction to the band and the set of succeeding videos. Eddie is introduced first, followed by Alex, Mike, and then Dave.

The song wasn't originally planned for inclusion on the album. Ed used to play it live during the band's club days, and one day while he was warming up with the piece for a gig at the Whisky A GoGo, producer Ted Templeman overheard it and suggested it be put on the record. It was recorded twice.

The long descending growl at the end was created using a Univox EC-80 echo unit that Ed housed in an old WWII practice bomb that he picked up from a junkyard. The Univox works off of a cartridge like tape, similar to an 8-track tape.

2. A North Carolina-based Van Halen tribute band.

3. The magazine published by the first Dutch Van Halen fan club, active between 1983 and 1984. Four issues were published by Jan Stoffer, founder of the club and consultant to the current Dutch fan club, 5150.

4. A Van Halen tribute album showcasing Bart Walsh and Ralph Saenz of the tribute band The Atomic Punks. The album features classic tracks set to a continuous dance beat. Tracks: • Jamie's Cryin' • Dance the Night Away • Somebody Get Me a Doctor • (Oh) Pretty Woman • Eruption • Ain't Talkin' 'Bout Love • You Really Got Me • Unchained • Feel Your

Love Tonight • Everybody Wants Some!! • Panama • Atomic Punk • Romeo Delight • Light Up the Sky • On Fire • Atomic Punk (reprise) • Bottoms Up • Ice Cream Man • I'm the One • Hot for Teacher • Runnin' With the Devil • Beat It

ESPN2-This network aired an interview with Michael Anthony on 7/18/98. He was interviewed during a funny car race in Denver on 7/17/98.

Everybody Wants Some!!-1. (*Women and Children First* [5:05]) If you've ever wondered what a video for this song might look like, check out the movie "Better Off Dead," a CBS release from 1985 starring John Cusack. There's a claymation sequence in which a guitar-playing hamburger sings this song.

The opening guitar effect was the same as in "Atomic Punk," but instead of Eddie rubbing against all the strings, he rubbed just the low E.

The drum/vocal interlude was completely ad-libbed. Dave came into the studio on the day of recording with the vocals unprepared, so he just winged it. Dave has stated the actual lyrics were not sung perfectly in favor of the more mumbled words to add more feel to the song.

The track was used in a commercial (available for viewing online) for Boylan's Birch Diet Beer.

2. (Cherrydisc Records CH 5794-2, 1997) Though not the first Van Halen tribute album, this was the first mass-produced tribute album. It was released on 10/07/97. Tracks include: "Eruption" on keyboard by the Reverend Ed Broms, "Could This Be Magic?" by Trona, "Jamie's Cryin'" by Jajuya, "Everybody Wants Some" by Talking to Animals, "Atomic Punk" by Cherry 2000, "Why Can't This Be Love?" by Gigolo Aunts, "Beautiful Girls" by Red Time, "Take Your Whiskey Home" by Honkeyball, "Jump" by Mary Lou Lord, "Somebody Get Me a Doctor" by The Ghost of Tony Gold, "Mean Street" by Elbow, "Feel Your Love Tonight" by Fuzzy, "Panama" by Captain Rock, "Little Guitars" by The

Vic Firecracker Orchestra, "Dance the Night Away" by Tom Leach, "Romeo Delight" by Sam Black Church, and "Eruption" by Crick Diefendorf.

Evil Eye-Ed co-wrote this Black Sabbath song, from the album *Cross Purposes* (Capitol 77806, 1994), with Tony Iommi.

Extra-This television show's index of Van Halen-related broadcasts:
1995: News about Ed's hip.
6/95: Van Halen in Paris
7/95: Ed and Valerie in a promo for Val's movie *The Haunting of Helen Walker.*
10/95: Van Halen's Rock Walk induction.

Extreme-1. Gary Cherone's band prior to joining Van Halen.
2. (A&M 5238, 1989) Extreme's self-titled debut album, which was released on 3/14/89. While this album had striking similarities to the Van Halen sound, it really didn't showcase this band's talent. "Play with Me" went on to be a signature song for the band, landing, on the *Bill & Ted's Excellent Adventure* soundtrack (with an alternate version of the song). The videos for "Kid Ego (East Coast Remix)," "Little Girls," and "Mutha (Don't Wanna Go to School Today)" can be found on the home video compilation *Photograffitti*. Two videos were made for "Kid Ego," which were directed by Nigel Dick and produced by Lisa Hollingshead for Propaganda Films. One of the videos featured a remixed version, called the East Coast version, of the song for censorship purposes.
The video for "Little Girls" was also by directed by Nigel Dick and produced by Lisa Hollingshead for Propaganda Films.
"Mutha (Don't Wanna Go to School Today)" was directed by Jim Shea and produced by John Hopgood for Planet Pictures. It was filmed at Hammerjack's in Baltimore, MD, after a show at the now-defunct club.

The Japanese release of this album included different cover art, and the vinyl Japanese release didn't include "Play with Me."

Tracks: Little Girls • Wind Me Up • Kid Ego • Watching, Waiting • Mutha (Don't Wanna Go to School Today) • Teacher's Pet • Big Boys Don't Cry • Smoke Signals • Flesh 'n' Blood • Rock a Bye Bye • Play with Me

Much like Van Halen, Extreme went into the studio with about 27 songs for the first album. Some of the songs that didn't make it appeared on later albums including "Lil' Jack Horny" and "Suzi," which later surfaced on *Pornograffitti*, plus "Our Father," which was used on *III Sides to Every Story*. Other songs that didn't make the cut included: "Adam and Adam," "Baby Love," "Music Isn't Mine," "Body Chemistry," "Funky Metal Holiday," "Mr. Bates," "Never Be Wrong," "Nice Place to Visit," "Sex and Love," "Simon Sez," "Strong as You," "Time Will Tell," "What Can I Say."

Extreme singles/promos
"Kid Ego" (censored), "Kid Ego" (LP version promo), A&M 17717, CD, USA, 1989.

"Little Girls" (edit) (promo), A&M 17830, CD, USA, 1989.

"Mutha (Don't Wanna Go to School Today)" (promo), A&M 17874, CD, USA, 1989.

Extreme II: Pornograffitti-(A&M 75021 5313, 1990) This Extreme album was released on 8/07/90, certified gold on 5/17/91, platinum on 6/18/91, and double platinum on 10/26/92.

After more than six months in the racks, this album was going largely unnoticed. The album's third single, "More than Words," was released to a small Boston radio station on 3/12/91 (eventually certified gold on 5/17/91). Interest in the band escalated ten fold, catapulting them into the limelight and establishing Nuno Bettencourt as what some critics and guitar magazines called "the new Eddie Van Halen." "More than Words" went to #1 the week of 5/29/91. It was the #7 single on Billboard's year-end pop singles charts. It spent 24 weeks on the U.K. charts and reached #2.

This album was the band's first concept album. Social issues were the premise to the album, illustrated thusly: A lad named Francis gets his girl-friend pregnant. The different emotions and experiences he goes through are what make up the songs on the album. For instance, "When I'm President" is Francis's way of questioning what constitutes power. The song "Hole Hearted" is meant to be separate from the rest of the album, kind of an outside observance of Francis.

"Money (In God We Trust)" features a cameo by Janet Jackson, who says the opening lines on the track. Guitarist Nuno Bettencourt repaid the favor by lending his guitar talents to Jackson's "Black Cat."

Gary sang the song "When I First Kissed You" with a cold.

Pornograffitti was recorded at Cortland Recording in Massachusetts and the Scream in Los Angeles, CA.

The two videos for "Decadence Dance" were directed by Alex Winter (of *Bill & Ted's Excellent Adventure*) and Tom Stern and were produced by Steve Carter for Propaganda Films. The difference in the two videos involves a scene in which Gary Cherone flings animated snot, which seems to hit the camera and slide down the screen. The uncensored ver-sion can be found on *Photograffitti*.

The video for "Get the Funk Out" was re-released after the popular "More than Words" called for the band to show a little more of their funk metal side.

The last video made was for the song "Hole Hearted."

The vinyl U.S. release of this album did not include "Hole Hearted." Tracks: • Decadence Dance • Li'l Jack Horny • When I'm President • Get the Funk Out • More than Words • Money (In God We Trust) • It('s a Monster) • Pornograffitti • When I First Kissed You • Suzi (Wants Her All Day What?) • He-Man Woman Hater • Song for Love • Hole Hearted

Extreme II: Pornograffitti singles/promos
"Decadence Dance," "Get the Funk Out," "When I'm President,"
A&M CS 18050, Cassette, USA, 1990.

"Get the Funk Out" (promo), A&M 75021 7295 2, CD, USA.

"Get the Funk Out" (LP promo), A&M 75021 7431 2, CD, USA.

"Get the Funk Out" (What the Funk? mix), "Get the Funk Out"
(album version), A&M 75021 7320 2, USA.

"Get the Funk Out" (What the Funk? mix), "Get the Funk Out"
(album version), A&M, 7" Vinyl, Spain.

"More than Words," "More than Words" (remix), A&M 75021 1552
4, Cassette, USA, 3/12/91.

"Hole Hearted," "Get the Funk Out," A&M 8716, 7" Vinyl, USA.

"Get the Funk Out," "Li'l Jack Horny," "Mutha" (remix), A&M 390
613-2, CD, UK.

"Get the Funk Out," "Li'l Jack Horny," A&M 737, 7" Vinyl, UK.

"Get the Funk Out," "Li'l Jack Horny," A&M AMMC 737, Cassette,
USA and UK.

"Get the Funk Out," "More than Words" (remix), A&M 75021
15527, 7" Vinyl, USA.

"Get the Funk Out," "Li'l Jack Horny," "Little Girls" (edit), A&M AMX 737, 12" Vinyl, UK.

"Get the Funk Out," "Li'l Jack Horny," "Nice Place to Visit," A&M AMP 737, 12" Vinyl, UK.

"Song for Love," A&M 390 684-2, CD, Germany.

"Song for Love," A&M, 7" Vinyl, UK.

"Hole Hearted," "Get the Funk Out" (remix), A&M AM 839, 7" Vinyl, UK.

"Decadence Dance" (edit) (promo), "Decadence Dance" (album version), A&M 75021 8102 2, CD, USA.

"Decadence Dance," "Money (In God We Trust)," "More than Words" (a capella with Congas), "Decadence Dance" (album version), A&M CD 773, CD, UK

"Decadence Dance," "Money (In God We Trust)," A&M AM 773, 7" Vinyl, UK.

"Decadence Dance" (promo), A&M AM-DJ-773, 7" Vinyl, UK.

"Decadence Dance," "Money (In God We Trust)," "Decadence Dance" (album version), "More than Words" (a capella with congas), A&M AMY 773, 7" Vinyl, UK. Tour information included.

"Decadence Dance," "Money (In God We Trust)," A&M AMMC 773, Cassette, UK.

"More than Words," "Nice Place to Visit," A&M AM 7922, A&M AMMC 792, A&M AMCD 792, 7" Vinyl and Cassette, UK, 7/91.

"More than Words," "More than Words" (remix), A&M AM 8693, 7" Vinyl, USA.

"More than Words," "Nice Place to Visit," "Little Girls," A&M AMYDJ 792, 12" Vinyl, A&M 792, CD.

"More than Words," "Hole Hearted," A&M 31458 0678-2, CD, USA.

"More than Words," "Nice Place to Visit," "Little Girls," "Mutha (Don't Wanna Go to School Today)" (remix), A&M AMX 792, 12" Vinyl, UK.

"More than Words," "Hole Hearted," A&M PCDY-1027, 3" CD, Japan.

"More than Words" (remix), "Kid Ego," "Nice Place to Visit," A&M AMCD 764, CD, UK.

"Hole Hearted," A&M, 7" Vinyl and CD, France.

"Hole Hearted" (promo), A&M 75021 5313 4/2, CD, USA.

"Hole Hearted," "Suzi (Wants Her All Day What?)," A&M 390 7337, 7" Vinyl, Germany.

"Hole Hearted," "Suzi (Wants Her All Day What?)," A&M 750211564 4, Cassette, USA.

"Hole Hearted," "Suzi (Wants Her All Day What?)," A&M, CD, Australia.

"Hole Hearted," "Get the Funk Out" (12" remix), "Suzi (Wants Her All Day What?)," "Sex 'n' Love," A&M AMCD 839, CD, UK.

"Hole Hearted," "Get the Funk Out" (12" remix), "Suzi (Wants Her All Day What?)," "Sex 'n' Love," A&M AMY 839, 12" Vinyl, UK. Poster included.

"Hole Hearted," "Get the Funk Out" (remix), A&M AMMC 839, Cassette, UK.

"Hole Hearted," "More than Words" (a capella with congas), "Suzi (Wants Her All Day What?)," A&M 390 733 2, CD, Germany.

"Song for Love," "Love of My Life" (featuring Brian May), A&M AM 6982, 7" Vinyl, A&M AMY 6983, 12" Vinyl, A&M AMCD 698, CD, A&M AMMC 698, Cassette, UK.

"Song for Love," "Sex 'n' Love," A&M 390-684-7, 7" Vinyl, Germany.

"Song for Love" (edit), "Get the Funk Out" (12" remix), "Sex 'n' Love," A&M 390 684-2, CD, USA.

"Song for Love," "Get the Funk Out" (12" remix), A&M, CD, Germany.

ExtraGraffitti (EP) "Get the Funk Out," "Decadance Dance" (edit), "Mutha" (remix), "Little Girls" (edit), "Kid Ego," "Nice Place to Visit," "Message from Extreme," A&M PCCY-10155, CD, Japan, 1990.

Extreme III: III Sides to Every Story-(A&M 31454 0006, 1992) Extreme's third album was released on 9/08/92 and certified gold on 12/04/92.

Recorded in part in Miami, FL, and produced by Nuno Bettencourt, the concept for this album attempted to address things like militarism and racism on three sides called "Yours," "Mine," and "The Truth." The first side is made up of mostly hard rockers and addresses topics like racism, assassination, and government corruption. The second side is made up of ballads and touches on themes like parental abandonment, lost love, and the death of God. The third side is a combination of both, made up of three thematically related songs featuring a 70-piece orchestra and recorded in one day at Abbey Road Studios in London, England. The orchestra was assembled and directed (with assistance from Bettencourt) by Mike Moran, best known for his orchestral arrangement for Queen.

The three-sided concept was born approximately one month after the band finished their second album, *Pornograffitti*. The initial plan was that the first side would be guitar-oriented, the second side would explore a more atmospheric side of the band, and the third side would use an orchestra.

"Peacemaker Die," which deals with the thought that peace has become more of a fashion then a reality, includes a speech by Martin Luther King, Jr. The band was concerned that the King estate wouldn't allow it to be used in the song, but after Gary Cherone spoke with King's son Dexter, who was worried about how people would interpret the song, Dexter was more than willing to allow its use.

The album ran too long to fit on a CD, so there's an extra track, "Don't Leave Me Alone," on the cassette version. Another version of "Cupid's Dead" was recorded with a six-piece horn section playing counterpoint to many of the guitar lines. This version was later released in Japan.

Videos were made for "Rest in Peace," "Stop the World," and "Tragic Comic" (released only in Japan).

Tracks: "Yours": • Warheads • Rest in Peace • Politicalamity • Color Me Blind • Cupid's Dead • Peacemaker Die, "Mine": • Seven Sundays • Tragic Comic • Our Father • Stop the World • God Isn't Dead? • Don't Leave Me Alone, "The Truth": Everything Under the Sun: • Rise 'n' Shine • Am I Ever Gonna Change • Who Cares?

The live show on the supporting tour was split into three parts: traditional Extreme rockers; an acoustic set; and a set featuring the Heavy Metal Horns (saxophonists John Vanderpool and Henley Douglas, trombonist Hikaru Tsukamoto, and trumpeter Garrett Savuluk). At one point during part three of the show, Gary Cherone and Savuluk regularly treated the crowd to a musical call-and-response duel.

Extreme III: III Sides to Every Story singles/promos
"Rest in Peace" (edit), "Rest in Peace" (album version)(promo), A&M 31458 8015 2, CD, USA, 1992.

"Stop the World" (radio edit) (promo), "Stop the World" (edit), "Stop the World" (album version), A&M 31458 8097 2, CD, USA, 1992.

"Am I Ever Gonna Change" (promo), A&M   31458   8123   2, CD, USA, 1992.

"Rest in Peace" (new radio edit), A&M 31458 8070 2, CD.

"Rest in Peace," "Peacemaker Die," A&M, 7" Vinyl, Germany, 1992.

"Rest in Peace" (radio edit), "Rest in Peace" (album version), "Peacemaker Die," "Monica," A&M AMCD 0055, CD, UK, 1992.

"Stop the World" (radio edit), "Christmas Time Again," "Warheads," "Don't Leave Me Alone," A&M AMCD 0096, CD, UK, 1992.

"Stop the World," "Christmas Time Again," A&M AM 0096, 7" Vinyl, UK, 1992.

"Tragic Comic" (radio edit), "Help!" "When I'm President" (live), "Tragic Comic," A&M CDR 0156, CD, UK, 1992.

"Tragic Comic" (radio edit), "Hole Hearted" (horn mix), "Rise 'n' Shine" (acoustic), "Tragic Comic" (album version), A&M CD 0156, CD, UK, 1992.

"Tragic Comic," "Help!" "Hole Hearted" (horn mix), "Don't Leave Me Alone," A&M, USA, 1992.

"Tragic Comic" (radio edit), "Hole Hearted" (horn mix), "Rise 'n' Shine" (acoustic), "Cupid's Dead" (horn mix), "When I'm President" (live), "Help!" A&M POCM-1024, CD, Japan, 1992.

"Am I Ever Gonna Change" (edit), "Am I Ever Gonna Change" (album version), A&M, UK, 1992.

Eyes of the Night-(4:34) This unreleased original was performed on 5/30/76 at Pasadena Community College and 6/03/76 at The Starwood in Hollywood, CA. At the 6/03/76 performance, Dave explained, "This song here is part one of our two-part rock opera. It's about a guy who is in love with the lady across the street, but he doesn't have the nerve to tell her. All he does is watch her with a pair of binoculars."

F

Fabulous Picasso Brothers-The two-man videomaking team created by David Lee Roth and former Van Halen associate Pete Angelus. The pair were responsible for all of Dave's videos from the *Crazy from the Heat* and *Eat 'Em and Smile* albums. According to Dave, "Picasso" stood for "high art," and "Brothers" was used because it made the title sound like pizza delivery. The concept was that their art wound up somewhere in between the two.

Faces Rocks-This magazine's index of Van Halen-related articles:

4/84: David Lee Roth cover. "Van Halen: High Kickin' with David Lee Roth and the Boys": five-page David Lee Roth interview by Mikael Kirke. Two Van Halen posters.

6/84: David Lee Roth cover. "David Lee Roth: Faces Interview of the Month": seven-page interview by Martha Quinn. (Reprinted from MTV broadcast).

8/84: Sammy Hagar/David Lee Roth cover. "HSAS: Superstars Just Want to Have Fun To": four-page HSAS feature by Mikael Kirke. "My Lost Weekend with Van Halen": four-page feature on Kurt Jefferis (the winner of the MTV Lost Weekend with Van Halen contest) by Ann Kolson.

9/84: David Lee Roth cover. Edward and Alex feature.

3/85: Sammy Hagar feature.

4/85: David Lee Roth cover. "In the Court of the Palace Roth": four-page David Lee Roth interview by Laura "Legs" Gross. Two Dave posters.

6/85: David Lee Roth cover.

8/85: David Lee Roth cover. Five-page feature on "Just a Gigolo/I Ain't Got Nobody" video by Frank Lovece.

10/85: Eddie Van Halen/David Lee Roth cover. "The Party's Over": four-page Van Halen feature by Lee Sherman & Lorena Alexander.

8/86: Eddie Van Halen / David Lee Roth cover.

9/86: David Lee Roth cover. "Rock's Hottest Property Just Got Hotter": two-page David Lee Roth interview by Lorena Alexander.

10/86: Eddie Van Halen/Sammy Hagar cover. "Van Halen on with the Show": two-page feature by Gary Graff.

12/86: David Lee Roth cover. "David Lee Roth Going For the Gusto": three-page David Lee Roth interview by Lorena Alexander. Two Dave posters. Two-page feature on "Yankee Rose" video and lyrics by Lee Sherman.

10/88: "The Anatomy of a Supergroup": three-page Van Halen feature by Laura "Legs" Gross.

Address: 211 East 43rd Street, New York, NY 10017; Telephone: 212-986-6830.

Faces Rocks Presents Metal Muscle-Van Halen appeared on the cover of this publication's fall 1985 issue. A centerfold and various other photographs were also included. Address: 211 East 43rd Street, New York, NY 10017; Telephone: 212-986-6830.

Fachblatt Musik Magazine-This German magazine's index of Van Halen-related articles:

4/93: Van Halen cover. "Live on Stage": six-page Van Halen live feature.

12/96: Van Halen cover. "Der NeuAnfang": seven-page Van Halen feature. Edward pinup.

Fair Warning-1. (Warner Bros. 3540 [30:48]) This album took a mere 12 days to record at a cost of approximately $40,000. It was released on 4/29/81 and reached #6 on the U.S. charts (entering the charts on 5/30/81) and #49 on the U.K. charts (entering on 5/31/81). 3.4 million copies of this album have been sold in the U.S. It was certified gold on 7/07/81, platinum on 11/18/81, and double platinum on 8/04/94. The album was re-mastered and re-released on 9/19/00.

The cover art was Alex's idea after he saw a painting in a book called The Brain from the Time-Life series (published in 1964). The cover was taken from a piece by self-taught artist William Kurelek (1927-1972), a mentally unstable painter whose family immigrated to Canada from the Ukraine. Initially, Alex planned to use only the scene featuring a man ramming his head into a brick wall, but later expanded the idea to include several different images from the scene. The original painting hangs in the hospital where *The Elephant Man* (Brooksfilms, 1980) was filmed.

Most of Kurelek's work (a lifelong Christian) revolved around a single theme-Jewish immigrants carving a life for themselves on the prairie. This painting was no exception; bathed in symbolism, it is made up of more than a dozen scenes depicting violence, death, war, and religion. In addition to scores of paintings, Kurelek also created lithographs and tapestries and illustrated children's books. In 1991 four of his pieces were depicted on Canadian postage stamps.

Much of this album was written in the early morning hours when Ed and Donn Landee would retreat to the studio after the rest of the band had gone home. This practice signaled a turning point in Van Halen's career, Edward was becoming increasingly frustrated about not being able to express himself the way he wanted to; he felt he was growing musically but was being suppressed by Ted Templeman and Roth. Tensions between the guitarist and the vocalist increased, and Edward briefly considered quitting the band. Alex convinced him to stick it out, and *Fair Warning* was the result. However, the anger and unhappiness comes through in the music, giving the album its dark undertones. The *Fair Warning* sessions were also the seed for Edward's desire to have his own studio, and in fewer than three years, 5150 Studio became a reality in his own backyard.

Live videos for "Unchained," "So This Is Love?," and "Hear about It Later" were filmed at the Oakland Coliseum during a three-night stint in Oakland, CA (6/11/81-6/13/81). The videos later debuted on an episode of the Don Kirshner Rock Concert Series television program. A fourth video is rumored to exist, but no known broadcasts of it are in existence.

Photos from the shooting of this unknown video appeared in the first issue of The Inside magazine.

2. A Chicago-based Van Halen tribute band that performed at the 1996 First Annual VHML Convention held in Chicago, IL.

Fair Warning singles/promos
"Hear about It Later," "So This Is Love?" WB WBS49751, 7" Vinyl, USA, 1981.

"So This Is Love," "Hear about It Later," WB HS 3540, 7" Vinyl, USA, 1981.

Farm Aid-Sammy Hagar and Eddie Van Halen appeared at the first production of this now-annual event on 9/22/85 at the University of Illinois in Champaign, IL. The concert raised approximately $9 million for America's farmers.

They performed a cover of Led Zeppelin's "Rock and Roll" (backed by Hagar's solo band). In addition, Edward performed an unaccompanied solo that was cut from the live broadcast only moments after he began, due in part to Hagar's constant verbal obscenities. Upon completion of the solo piece, Hagar announced to the audience that he was joining Van Halen.

Fast Times at Ridgemont High-(Universal Pictures, 1982) (Full Moon/Electra 60158-2, 1982) Sammy Hagar performed "Fast Times at Ridgemont High" (3:36), the title song on this movie's soundtrack. Other artists contributing to the soundtrack included Billy Squier, Quarterflash, the Go-Go's, and Oingo Boingo among others.

Eddie Van Halen was asked to contribute music to the soundtrack, but he didn't know anything about the request until it was too late.

The soundtrack began a 20-week run on the charts on 8/28/82, topping out at #54.

Feelin'-(*Balance* [6:36]) Sammy thought this was the most important song on *Balance*.

Feels So Good-(*OU812* [4:27]) This was the third song written for *OU812*. The video for the song was filmed on a sound stage in Hollywood, CA. This video featured the only known video appearance of Ed's Charvel Frankenstrat outfitted with a striped headstock.

Feel Your Love Tonight-(*Van Halen* [3:40]) This song was on the 25 song Warner Brothers demo. The only major difference in the demo and final versions occurs during the break (on the demo version). When Dave is singing without instruments, there's hand clapping to keep the beat.

Fifteen Minute Van Halen University-A joke of David Lee Roth's around 1981 in which the lead singer declared that the band was going to open a college that taught you only what you would remember seven years after graduation. The make-believe institution also offered a special graduate course extension called "Buyer Beware" and a two-minute extension course in law.

5150-1. Van Halen's seventh album (Warner Bros. 35394 [43:02]). It took three and a half months to record and was released on 3/24/86. *5150* spent 64 weeks on the charts and reached #1 on the U.S. charts three weeks after its release. This was Van Halen's first #1 album. On the U.K. charts, the album's highest position was #16. 6.9 million copies have been sold in the U.S. It was certified gold, platinum, and double platinum on 5/28/86; triple platinum on 10/10/86; quadruple platinum on 1/18/89; and platinum five times over on 8/17/94.

The album introduced the band's new lead singer, Sammy Hagar. Ed originally toyed with the idea of having Patty Smythe take over as lead vocalist, but apparently she wasn't comfortable being in a band with three men. Australia's Jimmy Barnes was another proposed choice; however, Ed felt Barnes wasn't right for the type of music he writes. Edward also tossed around the idea of doing an album with a different vocalist for each track. Singers considered included Phil Collins, Joe Cocker, Mike Rutherford, and Pete Townsend, but it would have been a scheduling nightmare, and Al convinced Ed that it would work for only one album, which wouldn't be feasible.

The band decided against making videos for *5150* because they wanted the fans' first visual experience with Sammy Hagar to come from a live performance. Several videos were shown on MTV, most taken from Van Halen's first live video, *Live without a Net*, and a video made by the Blue Angels using "Dreams" as the accompanying music.

Longtime Van Halen producer Ted Templeman came to one band rehearsal and heard four or five songs, but was unable to produce *5150* because he already had a contract with David Lee Roth. Other producers considered included Quincy Jones, Nile Rodgers, and Rupert Hine before the band selected Mick Jones, who was Sammy Hagar's idea.

Originally, the band wanted to name the album Best of Both Worlds but decided against it because it might have been seen as misleading or as having some kind of religious connotation. *5150* was Sammy Hagar's idea.

Alex's drum kit was made primarily of Simmons electronic drums. The kit consisted of a double Simmons kick drum setup rounded out by five Simmons toms. This was all hooked to a Simmons SDS-5 through a Yamaha power amp. The setup also included a 6½-inch-by-14-inch rosewood Tama snare. The head, like all of Al's acoustic drum heads, was a taped Ludwig black dot. His Paiste cymbal setup included a 40-inch gong, a 24-inch ride, two 20-inch crashes, a 20-inch rude crash, a 20-inch China, and 15-inch Sound Edge High Hats. Most of the hardware was Ludwig with Ghost Pedals. His sticks of choice were Promark 5A oak sticks. The choice to go with electronic drums was due partly to the size of the 5150 Studio, which was too small to house a full-size acoustic kit. It has since been remodeled to accommodate a drum room.

Mike used a Spector J-Bass, an Apostrophe 5-string bass, and an 8-stringed aluminum-neck Kramer bass for most of this album. All of his bass lines on this album were recorded without a pick. His main amp was a Mesa Boogie D-180, run through a Flagg Systems bass reflex cabinet. He also used a Pearl Octaver.

Effects-wise, Edward had his Echoplex, a Lexicon PCM 42, a TS Engineering Trigger, and a Roland DC 30 analog chorus/echo all at his disposal during recording. Add to that a Music Man Music Machine practice amp, a pair of Marshall heads on a single stack, and a Laney KLIPP guitar head with a Guild/Hartke cabinet housing pushing four 10-inch speakers.

Keyboard-wise, Edward's studio setup included one Steinway piano, which acted as a master keyboard to a MIDI setup that included a Prophet VS, a Roland D-50, a Yamaha DX711, a Yamaha TX816, and a MIDI-fied Oberheim OB-8. A Yamaha MJC8 (MIDI junction controller) directed the MIDI flow to and from the synthesizers and two Roland MC-500 sequencers. The TX816 consisted of eight tone modules that were routed through a Yamaha 8-channel mixer before being sent, along with the audio outputs of all the other synths, to a BOSS BX-800, which acted as Edward's main keyboard mixer. Session ace Steve Porcaro served as Edward's informal keyboard and sequencer advisor.

2. The California statute for holding those with grave mental disabilities involuntarily for 72 hours and sometimes longer pending further psychiatric evaluation. Many police departments across the U.S. use the term to indicate insanity in suspects. The album *5150*, the song, and the studio are all named after this code.

3. A Canadian Van Halen tribute band.

5150 singles/promos
"Why Can't This Be Love?" (extended version), "Get Up," WEA 920 463-0, 12" Vinyl, Germany, France, 1986.

"Why Can't This Be Love?" (extended version), "Get Up," WEA W8740P, 12" Vinyl, UK, 1986.

"Why Can't This Be Love?" "Get Up," WB 28740-7, 7" Vinyl, USA, 1986. Highest chart position: #3 in USA and #8 in UK.

"Why Can't This Be Love?" (promo), "Why Can't This Be Love?" WB PRO-A-2453, 12" Vinyl, USA, 1986.

"Love Walks In" (edit), "Love Walks In" (edit) (promo), WB 7-28626, 7" Vinyl, USA, 1986.

"Love Walks In" (edit), "Love Walks In" (album version), WB PRO-A-2542, 12" Vinyl, USA, 1986.

"Summer Nights," "Summer Nights" (promo), WB PRO-A-2523, 12" Vinyl, USA, 1986.

"Dreams," "Inside," WB 7-28702, 7" Vinyl, USA, 1986. Highest chart position: #22 in USA and #62 in UK.

"Dreams" (edit), "Inside," WEA P-2120, 7" Vinyl, Japan, 1986.

"Love Walks In," "Summer Nights," WB 28626-7, 7" Vinyl, USA, 1986. Highest chart position: #22 in USA on 10/04/86.

"Dreams" (album version), "Dreams" (edit), WB PRO-A-2483, 12" Vinyl, USA, 1986.

"Dreams" (extended), "Inside," WEA W8642T, 12" Vinyl, UK, 1986. VH patch included.

"Dreams," "Inside," WEA W8624P, 12" Vinyl "Spacecar" picture disc, UK, 1986.

"Best of Both Worlds," "Best of Both Worlds," WB PRO-A-2477, 12" Vinyl, USA, 1986.

"Best of Both Worlds" (live), "Rock and Roll" (live), WB PRO-A-2622, 12" Vinyl, USA, 1986.

"5150,""5150," WB PRO-A-2586, 12" Vinyl, USA, 1986.

"Intro/Best of Both Worlds" (from *Live Without a Net*), "Best of Both Worlds" (edit), WB 7-28505-B, 7" Vinyl, USA, 1986.

"Dreams" (album version), "Dreams" (edit), WB 7-28702, 7" Vinyl, USA, 1986.

"5150"-(*5150* [5:44]) This song was recorded on an L-Series 1958 Fender Stratocaster with "5150" carved in the body that Ed also used for "Best of Both Worlds." The song was written in drop-D tuning, but for this track the guitar was tuned down to D, with the low E string being tuned to C.

Eddie was in a hotel in New York, possibly for his appearance on the Late Night with David Letterman show, when he initially came up with the main riff to this song. He called Sammy from his room at 3:00 a.m. and played it to the vocalist over the telephone.

The performance of this song on the *Live without a Net* video is often considered by fans to include one of the best solos Ed has ever played.

The 5150 Fan Club-The Dutch Van Halen fan club. Originally, they went by the name Dutch Fan Club Federation or DFF, which has since been abandoned. The club was started in November 1989 and approved by Warner Music in Holland. The club publishes a magazine called 5150 every three months. The subscription rate is $25 a year. By the end of 1997, 44 issues had been published. 5150 includes the latest news, interviews, bootleg reviews, and more.

The magazine is written in Dutch, but there are occasionally some parts in English. Every subscriber is given a chance to win a signed copy.

Van Halen performed a special show, inviting all of the fan club's subscribers, on 1/27/95 at the Luxor Theatre, in Arnhem, Holland. Known as the Secret Gig, this show was organized by Warner Brothers Benelux and Holland's Veronica Radio.

Each of 5150's subscribers was sent a special invitation that allowed him or her and one guest entrance to the show. The set list: • Seventh Seal • Judgement Day • Don't Tell Me (What Love Can Do) • Amsterdam • Panama • Top of the World • Feelin' • Best of Both Worlds • Ain't Talkin' 'Bout Love

The 5150 Studio-The studio designed by Donn Landee and built in 1983 up the road from Ed's home. The 5150 Studio boasted, at the time, a 1969 UREI United Recording console with a couple of extra cue busses feeding into an Ampex 1200 24-track, a 3M Model 56 16-track, and a couple of Ampex 2-tracks. The outboard effects included a couple of Eventide Harmonizers, UREI 1176 limiters, and an EMT 140 echo chamber. The microphones included Neumann U-48s, a U-87, Sennheiser 421, a couple of Shure 545s, and a London C-12. The monitors consisted of JBL components inside of Auchsberger cabinets with H&H power amps. The studio was remodeled in 1991 when a drum room was added (formerly a raquetball court).

As of 1995 the studio was outfitted with two Studer A820-2 24-track, 2-inch analog mixers equipped with Dolby SR. The console was a 48-input, 24-monitor custom design by Brent Averill. It was based on API op amps and equipped with GML automation. Control room monitors were designed by George Augspurger and powered by H&H 800 amps. The outboard gear included UREI 1176 limiters, GML stereo EQs and AMS delay lines. Microphones included Shure SM57s, Neumann U87s, and some vintage AKG C-12s.

Finish What Ya Started-(*OU812* [4:20]; *Live: Right Here, Right Now* [5:50]) Alternate titles for this track included "Baby, Come On" and "Come On, Baby."

This is one of only two Van Halen tracks featuring Sammy Hagar on guitar (he used a Gibson acoustic).

This is the only Van Halen song on record that Ed recorded without using a pick; the entire track, including the guitar solo, was fingerpicked. The solo also features a technique never heard previously from Edward: chickin' pickin' (a bluegrass and country music staple).

Valerie Bertinelli used this as the theme song to her 1990 sitcom Sydney.

Two versions of this video were released, both in black and white. The less common version of the two is slightly letterboxed and features more shots of the women seen in the other version. The other version appears on *Video Hits Volume 1*.

This is the only known Van Halen video featuring Sammy Hagar playing a guitar. Edward is featured in a cowboy hat and boots as he fingerpicks through the guitar solo on a red and white Teisco Del Ray.

The video was directed by Andy Morahan, who at the time was well known for his work with a George Michael video. It was produced by Luc Roeg and Steve Brandman.

Firehouse-Van Halen performed this Kiss cover song on 9/18/76 at The Bogart in San Bernardino, CA.

Fire in the Hole-(*Van Halen III* [5:27]) Ed used a Wolfgang Special on this track, which was either very similar to or the same as the one used at the City of Hope Benefit. The guitar features a Steinberger TransTrem.

The song was mixed at 5150 on 6/04/97, though mixing was attempted at another studio prior to this date.

When asked about the ending of the song, Michael Anthony added, "It's kind of a Pink Floyd parody. Ed called the studio from another studio line and we recorded him over the telephone." The lyrics at the very end of the song were inspired by the Bible passages in James 3:3-6.

The song was used in the movie *Lethal Weapon 4*. The song's video centered around a *Lethal Weapon 4* theme. The video was only played a few times on MTV and was more likely to be seen in small clips during television shows that promoted *Lethal Weapon 4* in July 1998.

The song was also used in a Japanese car commercial for the Skyline Sports 4 Door.

First Reflection-This magazine's 12/97 issue featured an article about Eddie Van Halen's bathroom studio entitled "M-20: The 20-bit ADAT Is Here."

Fischer, Dr. Truman-Edward Van Halen and David Lee Roth's scoring and arranging professor at Pasadena Community College. His motto was: If it sounds good, it is good.

FMQB-This magazine's index of Van Halen-related issues:
4/19/96: "Humans Being" reviewed.
5/09/97: Sammy Hagar cover.
5/23/97: Sammy Hagar cover. *Marching to Mars* review. "Marching to Cabo": one-page photo spread on *Marching to Mars* record release party at the Cabo Wabo Cantina.
Address: Executive New, F-36, 1930 East Marlton Pike, Cherry Hill, NJ 08003; Telephone: 609-424-9114.

The Fool in Me-Van Halen reportedly played this Robin Trower cover in their club days. No known recordings exist.

Fools-(*Women and Children First* [5:55]) This song was originally called "I Live with Fools" and was frequently performed during the band's club days.

Footage-(PolyGram POVM-1020, 1996) Japan-only Extreme video release in VHS and laserdisc. Tracks: • Hip Today • Cynical • Rest in Peace (performance version) • Stop the World • Tragic Comic • Hole Hearted

Footloose-(Paramount Pictures, 1984) (Columbia 39242, 1984) Sammy Hagar's "The Girl Gets Around" appears on the soundtrack for this movie. The song is credited as being written by Sammy and D. Pitchford. The soundtrack entered the charts on 2/18/84 spending 61 weeks there and reaching #1 on 4/21/84.

The Footloose soundtrack boasted six Top 40 hits, including two #1 hits: "Footloose" by Kenny Loggins and "Let's Hear It for the Boy" by Deniece Williams. The album spent 27 weeks in the Top 40, 20 weeks in the Top 10, and 10 weeks at #1. Sammy's track was never released as a single. The soundtrack was also released on vinyl in Japan (30AP-2888).

48 Hours-This television news program featured a story on 3/27/97 that involved a Learjet leased by Van Halen on the *Balance* tour.

For Unlawful Carnal Knowledge-(Warner Bros. 26594 [52:08]) This album was released on 6/17/91 and debuted live on national radio from 5150 on 6/13/91. It was produced by Andy Johns, Ted Templeman, and Van Halen. This album was the third Sammy-era Van Halen album in a row to reach #1 on the U.S. charts. It has sold 3.8 million copies in the U.S. It was certified gold and platinum on 8/22/91, double platinum on 11/8/91, and triple platinum on 8/17/94.

This album came after a yearlong break for the band. Eddie claims that he barely picked up the guitar in that time. When the band decided to start the new album, they decided to first pick a producer. They knew of

Andy Johns from his work with Led Zeppelin, and he came to work so quickly that the band was taken by surprise and had nothing written for the album. The entire process from recording to mastering took 361 days.

The band eventually wrote enough songs to make this a double album, which is why they brought in producer Ted Templeman. He convinced the band to finish enough songs for one album and release it.

At one point the band wanted to try recording at a different studio, but Ted talked them into staying at 5150.

The album was done one song at a time in that each song was completed before moving on to the next.

Originally, the slang term "fuck" was suggested as the title, much to Alex's dismay. Boxer Ray "Boom Boom" Mancini informed Sammy that the word was actually an acronym for "for unlawful carnal knowledge," which the band then chose as the album's title. However, fans usually refer to the album simply as "Fuck."

The first pressing of the CD had gold or white lettering on the outer cover and a chalkboard full of phone numbers pictured within the liner notes. One of the numbers on the chalkboard received so many calls that new pressings of the CD had to be made excluding the chalkboard. The newer pressing featured white lettering on the outer cover. The same changes had to be made for the cassette version of the album, which originally had silver lettering.

The album won the Best Rock Album award at the Billboard Music Awards on 12/17/91 from Memphis, TN, and Best Hard Rock Performance with Vocal at the 1992 Grammy Awards.

Except for "Spanked," Mike used his 1964 Fender Precision bass and his 1964 Fender Jazz bass to record this album.

Sammy used a handheld Peavey microphone in the control room for most of the vocals on this album.

Al's drum tracks were recorded with 23 different microphones placed at various locations around his kit.

Except for four songs, Ed used a 1989 Soldano SLO-100 amplifier to record the entire album. Other amps included the Peavey 5150 prototype and his 1969 Marshall Super Lead. He recorded dry, adding touches from an AMS Echo and his Evantide H3000 Harmonizer afterward. His main cabinet was a 75-watt Marshall JCM 800 slant cabinet. Other effects used included a T.C. Electronics 2290 delay.

For Unlawful Carnal Knowledge singles/promos
"Poundcake" (promo), WB PRO-CD-4884, CD, USA, 1991.

"Poundcake," "Pleasure Dome," "Interview," WEA 9362-40126-2, CD, Germany, WEA 9362-40126-0, 12" 45 rpm Vinyl, UK, 1991.

"Runaround" (promo), WB PRO-CD-4922, CD, USA, 1991.

"Top of the World" (promo), WB PRO-CD-5027, CD, USA, 1991.

"Top of the World," "Poundcake," WB 9 19151-4, Cassette, USA, 1991.

"Man On a Mission" (promo), WB PRO-CD-5407, CD, USA, 1991.

"Right Now" (single mix), "Right Now" (edit) (promo), WB PRO-CD-5150, CD, USA, 1991.

"Right Now," "Right Now" (edit), "Man on a Mission," WB, Cassette, USA, 1991.

"Top of the World," "Why Can't This Be Love?" "When It's Love," "Dreams," WEA W0066TB, 12" Vinyl, UK, 1991. Badge and sticker included.

Foxey Lady-Van Halen performed this Jimi Hendrix cover on 7/31/86 in East Rutherford, NJ.

Fox (Network) Specials-On 2/20/94 Fox aired Adventures in Paradise in which David Lee Roth made an appearance.

On 12/31/95 as a part of the Fox New Year's Eve in Vegas special, "Dreams" from the band's 1995 pay-per-view concert was played 10 minutes before midnight.

Francine-Van Halen performed this ZZ Top cover on 9/18/76 at The Bogart in San Bernardino, CA.

Frasier-Eddie Van Halen did a voice-over as "Hank" in this TV show's 7th episode entitled "Call Me Irresponsible," written by Anne Flett and Chuck Ranberg and directed by James Burrows. Hank had a problem with his neighbor, but never got around to talking about it because he couldn't hear himself over the radio. The episode was broadcast on 10/28/93.

Freddie Mercury Tribute-Extreme performed a medley of Queen songs at this tribute concert on 4/20/92 at Wembley Stadium in London, England. Other acts that performed included Def Leppard, Metallica, Guns 'n' Roses, Elton John, George Michael, and Roger Daltrey. The show was seen on Fox and MTV. A 175-minute video of the show is available.

From Afar-(*Van Halen III* [5:19]) For the solo of this song, Ed used the same Ripley guitar he had been using since the mid-1980s, possibly the same guitar used to record "Top Jimmy."

Two other versions of this song were recorded: one on an acoustic guitar and one on a piano.

Mixing on this track was completed on 6/05/97.

The Full Bug-(*Diver Down* [3:18]) According to Roth the title is a slang term. It refers to success. To succeed at something, you've got to give it everything you have, make the maximum effort, do everything possible, get the full bug.

The guitar intro was performed by David Lee Roth, marking the last time he would record a guitar track on a Van Halen album. The harmonica solo was also performed by Roth.

Funk #49-David Lee Roth claimed this James Gang cover song was part of Van Halen's repertoire while responding to a patron's request for the song during a Whisky A GoGo appearance on 12/31/77. The claim has since been supported by others. No recorded version is known to exist.

Für Elise-Ed incorporated this Ludwig van Beethoven piece into his solo on numerous occasions during the *5150* tour as a private joke between himself and Al. Early in the tour, the two had a disagreement about what key the piece was in. Al claimed the piece had been written in B flat, while Ed insisted it had been written in A minor.

G

Gateway Commercial-David Lee Roth's image makes an appearance in this television ad that debuted in August of 2000. The commercial hypes the image editing capabilities of Gateway's Photoware package. The commercial shows a man trying to impress a woman by showing her photos of him with various celebrities. In the obviously doctored photos, he's seen with Lassie, Marilyn Monroe, Evander Holyfield, and finally David Lee Roth, with an autograph that reads, "Keep It Real! Dave."

Genesis-The name of Ed and Al's high school band. Al used to play Cream's "Toad" (a drum instrumental from the album *Fresh Cream* [Polygram, 827 576-2]) before Edward launched into Cream's "Spoonful," also from *Fresh Cream.*

Gentlemen of Leisure-Episode 3 of Dave TV revealed this unreleased Van Halen tune, reportedly from a 1974 demo.

Gentlemen's Quarterly (GQ)-A six-page David Lee Roth interview by Steven Daly entitled "Mr. Saturday Night" appeared in the May 1996 issue of this magazine. Address: 350 Madison Avenue, New York, NY 10017.

George-One of two Burmese cats owned by Edward and Valerie Van Halen in the late 1980s.

The Geraldo Rivera Show-On 4/27/97 Valeri Kendall (Alex Van Halen's ex-wife) was interviewed along with several other women in a segment about drug addiction entitled "Crank Crazed Women."

Get Down Tonight-This KC and the Sunshine Band cover song was a staple of the band's club sets prior to being signed.

Get the Show on the Road-(2:53) This unreleased original was occasionally used to open the band's performances. It was recorded as part of the band's 1977 demo for Van Halen. A bootleg of a 6/10/77 live performance at the Whisky A GoGo in West Hollywood, CA, also exists. The song contains vocal elements from "Romeo Delight."

Get Up-(*5150* [4:35]) Recorded on a Steinberger GL-2T.

Girl Gone Bad-(*1984* [4:43]) Eddie got the inspiration for the song's main riff while on tour in South America in 1983. Not wanting to wake his sleeping wife while in their hotel room, he slipped into the closet and hummed the riff into a pocket cassette recorder. The band premiered an instrumental version of the song at the1983 Us Festival.

Ed used the same 1958 Gibson "Flying V" guitar on this track that he used on "Hot for Teacher."

Give to Live-(*Live: Right Here, Right Now* [5:39]) This Sammy Hagar song from his *I Never Said Goodbye* album was used as his solo throughout the *F.U.C.K.* tour and was included on the *Live: Right Here, Right Now* album.

Glitter-Dave TV introduced this unreleased Van Halen tune on 12/10/98. Reportedly only Dave owns the original recording made in 1974, though another version may have been recorded later.

Goin' Home-This Ten Years After cover song was Eddie's showpiece during the band's backyard party days prior to being signed.

Good Enough-(*5150* [4:00]) The low E string on the "1984" Kramer guitar Ed used to record this song was actually a .060-gauge bass string.

Good Morning America-In 1988 this program aired at least two segments on Van Halen's Monsters of Rock tour. Van Halen was also featured in a 1992 segment.

Good Morning Australia-Sammy Hagar made an appearance on this show on 5/18/98.

Gossip Show-This E! Network program falsely reported on 2/11/98 that Gary Cherone was no longer in Van Halen. The photo of Gary used in the episode was actually a photo of Nuno Bettencourt.

Graffiti-David Lee Roth appeared on the cover of the September 1986 issue of this magazine for a five-page interview by Craig Lee. Earlier, in its May 1986 issue, this magazine reviewed *5150*.

Grammy Awards-In 1985 Sammy Hagar helped present the award for Producer of the Year to Lionel Richie at the 27th Annual Grammy Awards. In 1992 *For Unlawful Carnal Knowledge* won in the Best Hard Rock Performance with Vocal category. On 1/04/96 "The Seventh Seal" was nominated for a Grammy in the 38th annual Grammy Awards for Best Hard Rock Performance.

The Grind-This Tommy Bowen cover song was reportedly played by the band in the early years.

Grossi, Nancy-The band's seamstress on the *1984* tour.

Growth-(*Women and Children First* [:15]) Although not officially credited on the album as a song, this little piece was meant to be followed up on the next album, but never was. It fades out on the vinyl and tape versions, but the full 15 seconds can be heard on the CD version. Alternate title: "Tank."

On 8/15/86 at the Centrum in Worcester, MA, Van Halen performed a full-length version of this song in concert with Sammy Hagar on rhythm guitar.

Gudbuy T' Jane-This Slade cover tune from the album *Slayed?* (Polydor CF5524 1972) was performed and recorded on 9/18/76 at The Bogart in San Bernardino, CA, and on 6/10/77 at the Whisky A GoGo in West Hollywood, CA.

Guitar-(Formerly known as Guitar for the Practicing Musician) Index of this magazine's Van Halen-related articles:
4/84: Sammy Hagar cover and feature. "Your Love Is Driving Me Crazy" transcribed.
5/84: Eddie Van Halen cover. "Breaking All the Rules": eight-page Edward interview by John Stix. "Little Guitars" transcribed.
6/84: "Van Halen: *1984*": record review.
8/84: HSAS' *Through the Fire* reviewed.
9/84: "Eddie Van Halen" poster and feature.
11/84: "Panama" transcribed.
4/85: Eddie Van Halen cover. "Eddie Van Halen MVP": four-page interview by John Stix. "Jump" transcribed. Edward wins The Phil Collins Tuxedo for Versatility award in the Ignoble Prize Awards, along with being voted into the Hall of Fame. Van Halen wins The Tarnished Metal Medallion for Top 40 Metal Act of the Year.
10/85: "And the Cradle Will Rock" transcribed.
8/86: "Van Halen: *5150*": record review.
9/86: Van Halen cover. "Van Halen": ten-page interview with Edward, Sammy, and Michael by John Stix. "You Really Got Me" transcribed. Autographed 5150 guitar giveaway.
11/86: "Research & Development": Commentary on split with David Lee Roth and *5150*. "Ice Cream Man" transcribed.
12/86: David Lee Roth's "Tobacco Road" transcribed.

3/87: David Lee Roth's "Ladies Night in Buffalo?" transcribed.

4/87: Eddie Van Halen poster. Feature by John Stix. "5150" and David Lee Roth's "Shy Boy" transcribed. *5150* voted Guitar Album of the Year; Edward voted Most Valuable Player; "Dreams" places third, Roth's "Yankee Rose" places fifth, "5150" places seventh, and "Shy Boy" places tenth for Guitar Solo of the Year in The Ignoble Prize Awards IV.

12/87: "The Last of the Pre-Van Halen Bands": two-page Michael Anthony interview by John Stix. "Eruption" transcribed.

6/88: David Lee Roth's "Skyscraper" transcribed.

7/88: Top 50 Albums of All Time. *Van Halen* is voted #1, *5150* is voted #6, and *Fair Warning* takes #29 in this readers' album poll.

9/88: *5150* reviewed. "Get Up" transcribed.

10/88: "Van Halen: *OU812*": record review

11/88: Eddie Van Halen/Sammy Hagar cover. "Acting Naturally": ten-page Edward interview by John Stix. "Black and Blue" transcribed. "Five Years of Rock Guitar": guitarist feature including Edward, with a transcribed excerpt from "Drop Dead Legs."

12/88: David Lee Roth's "Damn Good" transcribed.

4/89: "Spanish Fly" transcribed.

5/89: "The Fountain": nine-page Edward interview by John Stix. "Ain't Talkin' 'Bout Love" and David Lee Roth's "Hot Dog and a Shake" transcribed.

Winter 1989: Guitar Classics II. "Panama" transcribed. "Breaking All the Rules": eight-page Edward interview by John Stix (originally published in May 1984 issue).

1/90: Extreme's "Mutha (Don't Wanna Go to School Today)" transcribed.

9/90: Eddie Van Halen cover. Edward poster feature and "Music Appreciation" by Wolf Marshall. "Hot for Teacher" transcribed.

Winter 1990: Guitar Classics Volume III. "The Last of the Pre-Van Halen Bands": two-page Michael Anthony interview by John Stix (originally published in December 1987). "Eruption" transcribed (also originally appeared in December 1987 issue).

12/90: Extreme's "Decadence Dance" transcribed.

1991: Guitar Classics IV. "Eddie Van Halen MVP": four-page Edward interview by John Stix. "Little Guitars" transcribed.

4/91: David Lee Roth's "A Lil' Ain't Enough" transcribed.

7/91: "In the Eye of the Storm": eight-page Michael Anthony interview by John Stix. "Mean Street" transcribed.

8/91: Eddie Van Halen cover. "Edward Van Halen New Priorities": seven-page Edward interview and poster feature. "Poundcake" transcribed.

11/91: "Van Halen: *For Unlawful Carnal Knowledge*": record review. "Runaround" transcribed. "In the Listening Room": Sammy Hagar reviews selected cuts.

Spring 1992: Guitar Classics VI. "Jump" transcribed.

3/92: Eddie Van Halen cover. "In the Listening Room": various guitarists give their opinions of past Van Halen songs. "Runnin' with the Devil" transcribed.

8/92: "316" transcribed. Eddie Van Halen poster.

2/93: Eddie Van Halen cover. "Eddie Van Halen Jam Master Flash": five-page interview by John Stix.

4/93: "Right Now" and Extreme's "Tragic Comic" transcribed.

6/93: Eddie Van Halen cover. "Coming at You Live": nine-page interview with Alex, Michael and Sammy by John Stix. "Sammy Drills Eddie": Sammy Hagar interviews Eddie Van Halen (6 pages). "Best of Both Worlds (live)" transcribed. "Van Halen *Live: Right Here, Right Now*": record review.

9/93: Eddie Van Halen cover. "Scuddlebuddies: Edward Van Halen Interviews Steve Lukather": eight-page interview. "Sound F/X": one-page feature by Eric Mangum on how to recreate Edward's sound for "316" from *Live: Right Here, Right Now* (song also transcribed).

Spring 1994: Guitar Classics Volume VIII. "The Fountain": six-page Edward interview by John Stix (originally published May 1989). "Push Comes to Shove" transcribed.

3/94: Eddie Van Halen cover. "Artless Art and the Zen of Van Halen": five-page Edward technique exploration by ex-Megadeth guitarist Jeff Young. "Street Noise": feature on Jimmy Page's induction into Guitar Center's Rock Walk that Eddie attended.

8/94: "Van Halen & Young": "Street Noise" feature.

1995: Guitar Classics Volume XI: The Ultimate Van Halen Issue! Eddie Van Halen cover. Five articles reprinted from 1985, 1986, 1988 and 1993. 1984 "Music Appreciation." Seven songs transcribed.

3/95: Eddie Van Halen cover. "Eddie Van Halen Day One: At Work/Day Two: At Play": feature by H.P. Newquist. "Van Halen: Balance" record review." Don't Tell Me (What Love Can Do)" transcribed.

6/95: "Van Halen": "Street Noise" write-up.

8/95: "Six-String Sex Toys": short Edward feature. "Grounded": one-page feature on Edward's hip by H.P. Newquist.

8/96: "Humans Being" transcribed.

9/96: "Groundwire:…and Someone Said Fair Warning": one-page review of Roth's return to Van Halen by H.P. Newquist.

10/96: "Groundwire: Off Balance": a timeline of the breakup with Sammy.

1/97: Eddie Van Halen cover. "Push Comes to Shove": nine-page interview by Steven Rosen. "Van Halen Classic Riffs from the Original Guitar Hero": seven-page technique examination. "Groundwire": feature on David Lee Roth and Van Halen open letters to the press and on *Best of Volume 1* giveaway.

6/97: "One More Way to Rock": Sammy Hagar interview by Greg Pedersen.

1998: Ed and Gary interview in the Japanese version of the magazine.

3/98: "New Man, New Band, New Van": Edward interview by Sandy Masuo. "Cherone Phones Home": short Gary feature.

Address: P.O. Box 53063, Boulder, CO 80322-3063; Web Site: http://www.guitarmag.com

Guitar.com-This web site published a two-part video interview and guitar lesson with Sammy Hagar in November 2000.

Guitarist-This U.K. magazine index of Van Halen-related issues:
5/93: Ed and Mike on cover and in feature article.
3/95: Eddie Van Halen cover. "Edward! 'I Do What I Like...'": Eddie interview.
6/98: Eddie Van Halen interview

The Guitar Magazine-Eddie Van Halen appeared on the cover of this U.K. magazine in December 1996. It also featured "Revolution in the Ed," an eight-page Edward interview by Steven Rosen; "Brown Sugar" a two-page feature on Ed's gear; and "Ed Bangers," a one-page review of *Best of Volume 1*, song by song. Address: Dingwall Avenue, Croydon CR9 2TA.

Guitar One-This magazine's index of Van Halen-related articles:
1996: Volume 3: Edward Van Halen cover. "Ain't Talkin' 'Bout Love" transcribed.
4/98: Edward Van Halen/Gary Cherone cover and interview.
8/98: "Fire in the Hole" transcribed.
Address: 10 Midland Avenue, Port Chester, NY 10573-1490.

Guitar Player-This magazine's index of Van Halen-related articles:
11/78: Eddie Van Halen's first guitar magazine interview by Jas Obrecht.
5/80: Eddie Van Halen cover. Eddie becomes the youngest guitarist ever to be featured on the cover of Guitar Player magazine.
12/82: "Playback: *Diver Down*": four-page Edward interview by Jas Obrecht.

1984: Eddie Van Halen cover. "Legends of Guitar": special Jimi Hendrix and Edward Van Halen issue.

7/84: Eddie Van Halen cover. "Eddie Van Halen Wants You!": six-pages of guitar tips from Edward Van Halen. "Eruption" and "Spanish Fly" transcribed by Steve Vai.

Winter 1986: Eddie Van Halen cover. "Positively Van Halen": special all-Edward issue. Reprinted transcriptions of "Eruption" and "Spanish Fly" by Steve Vai.

12/86: *5150* voted Best Guitar Album in 1986 Readers' Poll.

10/87: Eddie Van Halen/Sammy Hagar cover. "Eddie Van Halen and Sammy Hagar": twelve-page Edward and Sammy interview by Jas Obrecht.

5/91: "Eddie Gets a New Axe to Grind": five-page feature on Edward and Ernie Ball Music Man guitar by Tom Wheeler.

8/91: Eddie Van Halen cover. "Eddie!": eleven-page Edward interview by Jas Obrecht.

1993: Best of Guitar Player. All-Edward issue. "Judgement Day" transcribed.

5/93: Eddie Van Halen cover. "An Audience with Edward": nine-page Edward interview by James Rotondi. "Halen Frequency": one-page feature on Ed's live rig by Matt Bruck (as told to James Rotondi). "Van Halen Lesson": six-page feature on Edward's rhythm and lead techniques by Jesse Gress. "Ed Notes": nine-page look at past interviews with Edward by Jas Obrecht.

3/95: Eddie Van Halen cover. "Sorcerer's Apprentice": ten-page Edward interview by Dweezil Zappa. "Grateful Ed": six-page Edward interview by Chris Gill.

Address: P.O. Box 50376, Boulder, CO 80323-0376; Telephone: 1-800-289-9839.

Guitar School-This magazine's index of Van Halen-related articles:
4/89: Edward Van Halen feature. "I'm the One" transcribed.

11/89: "(Oh) Pretty Woman" transcribed.

1/91: Extreme's "He Man Woman Hater" transcribed.

5/91: Extreme's "More than Words" transcribed.

7/91: David Lee Roth's "It's Showtime" transcribed. Ernie Ball Music Man EVH guitar featured.

11/91: "You're No Good" transcribed.

3/92: Peavey EVH 5150 amplifier highlighted.

Address: Harris Publications, Inc., 1115 Broadway, New York, NY 10010.

Guitar Shop-This magazine's index of Van Halen-related articles:

Spring 1994: Eddie Van Halen cover. "Brown Out: Inside the Van Halen Rig": seven-page feature on the Music Man guitar and 5150 amplifier by Pete Brown.

7/97: Eddie Van Halen cover. "Van Halen Talks!": Edward interview. Review of Peavey Wolfgang.

Spring 1998: Eddie Van Halen on the cover. "Eddie Breaks Down *Van Halen III*." Ed reviews the making of the songs on *Van Halen III*.

Address: 10 Midland Avenue, Port Chester, NY 10573-1490.

Guitar World-This magazine's index of Van Halen-related articles:

1/81: Eddie Van Halen cover. "Eddie Van Halen the New King of Heavy Metal Guitar": five-page Edward interview by John Stix.

11/82: Eddie Van Halen cover. "Eddie Van Halen": five-page interview by Tim Bradley. Photo of Edward with Allan Holdsworth.

1/84: Eddie Van Halen cover. "Edward Van Halen Drops the Bomb on Heavy Metal": five-page Edward interview.

3/84: "Brian May Brings Out the Stars": seven-page Brian May and Starfleet Project feature by Steven Rosen.

11/84: One-page feature on Edward's surprise performance with the Jacksons on their Victory tour.

1985: Eddie Van Halen cover. "Guitar Heroes": special guitar hero collection featuring Edward among the 100 guitarists interviewed.

7/85: Eddie Van Halen cover. "The Life and Times of Edward Van Halen": twenty-page Edward interview by Steven Rosen. "Edward's Producer on the Brown Sound: 'I Just Let the Tapes Roll'": one-page Ted Templeman interview by Gene Santoro. "A Halenesque Axological Ontology: The Technical Anatomy of the Brown Sound": one-page Rudy Leiren interview by Steven Rosen. "Billy Sheehan's Bass-Eye View of Edward Van Halen: From One Hammer-on to Another": three-page Billy Sheehan feature about the secrets of Ed's techniques by Joe Lalaina. Guitar solos to "Jump" and "Hot for Teacher" transcribed. Pull-out poster and detailed description of Edward's Charvel Frankenstrat.

11/85: "Cruising the NAMM Show with Edward Van Halen": two-page feature on Eddie at NAMM by Steven Rosen. "Tune-Ups": short feature on Ed donating guitar to Hard Rock Café. "Edward V. Jams Again": short feature on Ed jamming at an after NAMM club.

9/86: Eddie Van Halen cover. "On the Road with Edward Van Halen": eleven-page Edward interview by Steven Rosen. "Sammy Hagar: The Guitar Player as Mouth": one-page Sammy feature by Steven Rosen. "Michael Anthony: Bass with a Human Face": one-page Michael interview by Steven Rosen. "A Van Halen Axology": four-page Eddie Van Halen gear feature by Steven Rosen. *5150* reviewed.

11/86: "Edward and Les": five-page Les Paul interview conducted by Edward Van Halen (written by Steven Rosen). David Lee Roth's *Eat 'Em and Smile* reviewed.

1/87: "Edward Builds His Ax": three-page feature on Edward assembling a guitar from scratch by Steven Rosen.

6/87: NAMM report.

5/88: Edward's rig featured.

7/88: Eddie Van Halen cover. "Ed. Eddie. Edward.": twenty-six-page Edward interview by Bud Scoppa and Billy Cioffi. "Atomic Junk": four-page feature on Edward's guitars. "Michael Anthony: Playin' in the Dirt":

two-page Michael Anthony interview by Bud Scoppa. "Summer Nights" transcribed.

2/90: Eddie Van Halen cover. "The Monster of Rock": nineteen-page Edward interview by Joseph Bosso and poster. "Eddie on the Record": one-page feature with Edward reviewing each Van Halen album. "The Van Halen Blind-fold Test": one-page feature with Edward listening to four pieces of music and playing "name that guitarist." "Guitar World's Movers & Shakers 1980-1990": guitarist feature with one-page Edward overview from 1982. "The Top 50 of the 80s": Guitar World's Top 50 albums poll. *1984* was voted #1, David Lee Roth's *Eat 'Em and Smile* #8, *Fair Warning* #37, and *Women and Children First* #48. "Beat It" transcribed. Three of Edward's guitars featured in pull-out poster.

7/90: Eddie Van Halen cover. "Guitar World's Greatest Hits": excerpts and quotes from past Edward interviews.

9/90: "Club Van Halen": one-page feature on Cabo Wabo by Katherine Turman.

11/90: Extreme feature.

4/91: Extreme's "Pornograffitti" transcribed.

6/91: "Ball's Deluxe": three-page Edward interview by Brad Tolinski. *Van Halen* is voted #2 in "The 25 Greatest Rock Guitar Records!": by Guitar World editors Brad Tolinski, Harold Steinblatt and Jeff Gilbert. "Ice Cream Man" transcribed.

8/91: "Master Class": a guitar lesson from Eddie Van Halen.

9/91: Eddie Van Halen cover. "Lord of the Strings": ten-page Edward interview by Brad Tolinski. "Dude with No Tude": one-page Matt Bruck interview by Brad Tolinski."Whipper Snapper": one-page Ted Templeman interview by Brad Tolinski. "Iron Mike": seven-page Michael interview by Brad Tolinski. Extreme's "Hole Hearted" transcribed.

1/92: Extreme's "More than Words" transcribed. *For Unlawful Carnal Knowledge* is voted #3 in Best Rock category of the Top 40 Albums of 1991 by the Guitar World staff.

3/92: Eddie Van Halen cover. "Van Halen: On Top of the World": nine-page Edward and Michael interview by Brad Tolinski. "Kings of the Road": three-page feature on Edward and Michael's live rigs. Edward is proclaimed Most Valuable Player and Best Rock Guitarist in the 1991 Readers' Poll. *F.U.C.K.* also wins best Rock Guitar Record, and Michael Anthony ties with the Red Hot Chili Peppers' Flea for 5th place in the Best Bass category. "Whammy Bar": write-up on Dallas free show. "Finish What Ya Started" transcribed.

4/92: Eddie Van Halen cover. "Guitar Legends: The Complete Van Halen: The Making of a Guitar Genius": 15 years worth of articles and photos from Guitar World magazine.

6/92: Short feature on Dr. Jim Schumacher, a brain surgeon who offered a brain surgery lesson in exchange for a guitar lesson from Edward.

8/92: "The Top 50 Heavy Metal Albums.": *Van Halen* is ranked at #5, *Fair Warning* at #28, and *Eat 'Em and Smile* at #37 in this poll by the Guitar World staff.

12/92: Extreme's "Stop the World" transcribed.

5/93: "King of the Road": nine-page Edward interview by Alan Di Perna. "Won't Get Fooled Again" transcribed.

10/93: Eddie Van Halen cover. "Beetle Juice": short feature on Edward's one-time bug-related ear problem. *1984* is voted #18 in the Top 25 Classic Rock Albums poll. "Wild Stringdom": one-page guitar lesson by Edward.

12/93: "Whammy Bar": short feature on Edward trading a guitar lesson for a brain surgery lesson.

1993-1994: Eddie Van Halen cover. "Guitar Buyer's Guide. The Axe Museum": eight-page Edward interview and guitar feature by Alan Di Perna.

3/94: "Celebration Day": short feature on Edward at Jimmy Page's Rock Walk induction. "Like a Hurricane": short feature on Edward at Neil Young's 7th Annual Bridge School Benefit. Edward wins Most Valuable Player, Best Rock Guitar, and Best Solo in the 1993 Reader's

Poll. Van Halen also takes 2nd in the Best Live Band category and *Live: Right Here, Right Now* takes 5th in the Best Rock Album category.

5/94: "Unbox of Rocks": one-page feature on Sammy Hagar's *Unboxed* by Jeff Gilbert. Edward is voted #1 by Guitar World's editors in The Top 100 Most Important People in Guitar.

2/95: Eddie Van Halen cover. "Cut and Dry": eleven-page Eddie interview by Tom Beaujour with Greg Di Benedetto. "Somebody Get Me a Doctor": one-page feature on Ed's Marshall restoration by Ritchie Fliegler.

3/95: Edward voted Best Rock Guitarist in 1995 Readers' Poll. "Hot for Teacher" transcribed.

4/95: "Hammer-Ons of the Gods": one-page Edward feature by Brad Tolinski.

5/95: "Eruption" transcribed. Edward interview (originally printed in 7/95 issue).

7/95: "Whammy Bar": news of Edward's gun arrest in Burbank, CA.

8/95: "Whammy Bar": news of Edward's impending hip replacement surgery.

11/95: "Ed's Wood": six-page Edward interview and a look at the Wolfgang by Tom Beaujour.

2/96: "Whammy Bar": short feature on David Lee Roth and the Blues Bustin' Mambo Slammers. "The 50 Greatest Rock Guitar Records." *Van Halen* is voted one of the 10 greatest rock guitar records of the 70s and *1984* one of the 80s 10 best by a panel of judges made up of Pantera's Diamond Darrell, Gun 'n' Roses' Slash, Metallica's Kirk Hammett, Megadeth's Marty Friedman and Korn.

3/96: Edward is voted Most Valuable Player, Best Rock Guitarist and Best Haircut in the 1996 Readers' Poll. In addition, "Baluchitherium" takes 4th place for Best Solo and *Balance* wins Best Rock Album.

4/96: Eddie Van Halen cover. "Best of Both Worlds": fourteen-page Edward interview by Billy Corgan (Smashing Pumpkins). Corgan reviews *Fair Warning*. Corgan and Edward poster. The Inside magazine is mentioned in "Whammy Bar."

5/96: "The Dirty Dozen": one-page Edward feature. "Can't Stop Lovin' You" transcribed.

6/96: "Whammy Bar": news on Edward winning award at Orville H. Gibson Awards.

10/96: "Runnin' with the Devil" transcribed.

12/96: Eddie Van Halen cover. "Eruptions": nine-page Edward interview by Steven Rosen. "Whammy Bar": news on Edward's hip surgery and *Best of Volume 1* videos. Edward poster.

1/97: "Whammy Bar": humorous write-up on proposed Van Halen name changes. "Unchained Melodies": eight-page Edward interview by Steven Rosen. "You Really Got Me" transcribed.

2/97: "Can't Get This Stuff No More" transcribed.

3/97: "Jason Becker Benefit Concert": write-up on Jason Becker ALS Benefit by Robert Dye. Edward wins Best Rock Guitarist in the 1997 Readers' Poll, as well as placing second as Most Valuable Player and Best Hard Rock/Metal Guitarist. Van Halen places second in best Guitar Albums of 1996 with *Best of Volume 1* and the album takes third in the Hard Rock/Metal category; "Humans Being" is voted Best Solo and David Lee Roth/Van Halen war takes second place in the Biggest Disappointment, losing to Metallica's "Load." "Humans Being" solo transcribed.

4/97: "Van Whosis?": one-page feature on humorous Van Halen name combinations contest. "Ain't Talkin' 'Bout Love": ten-page Sammy Hagar interview by David Huff.

5/97: "Master Pieces": twenty famous guitars overviewed by Brad Tolinski, Harold Steinblatt, and Tom Beaujour, one of which is Edward's Franky.

1/98: Eddie Van Halen cover. "Tune Ups": short feature on Ed's hip. "For Those About To Rock": a short Eddie Van Halen interview about *Van Halen III*.

2/98: "The Lord's Player": a short Eddie Van Halen interview about *Van Halen III*.

3/98: Edward cover. "Three of a Perfect Pair": Edward interview by Vic Garbarini.

4/98: Edward reviews *Van Halen III* track by track. "Without You" transcribed.

9/98: "Eruption" transcribed.

10/99: Eddie on cover and interview.

3/00: A reader's poll of the "Best of the Millennium" places Eddie at the #4 position for Best Guitarist, *Van Halen* at #5 for Best Album, and "Eruption" places #3 for Best Solo.

Address: P.O. Box 58660, Boulder, CO 80322-8660; Telephone: 303-678-0439; Web Site: http://www.guitarworld.com

Guitar World Acoustic-Transcriptions of two Van Halen acoustic tracks have been featured in this magazine. Issue number 26 featured a transcription to "Neworld" and issue 28 (11/98) featured a transcription of "Spanish Fly." Issue 27 (8/04/98) included an article about the band.

H

Hagar, Sammy-Born in Monterey, CA, on 10/13/47, Sammy Roy Hagar was the youngest of four children born to Gladys and Robert Hagar. His father, Robert, was a professional boxer, a southpaw who fought under the name Bobby Burns. Robert fought Manuel Ortiz seven times for the world bantamweight championship, winning the championship sometime in the 1940s. Sammy grew up in his father's boxing footsteps in Fontana, CA. He has stated a few times in interviews that his father was an alcoholic steel worker who divorced his mother when Sammy was nine.

At the age of sixteen, Sammy decided to see if boxing was his true calling. He got his driver's license, searched for his father, and convinced him to stop drinking long enough to begin training. Sammy lied to the boxing commission, telling them he was 18. He didn't follow through on this career, though, partly because he feared he would end up like the older boxers he knew and partly because his mother threatened to kick him out of the house if he boxed. Though Sammy's love for boxing remains to this day, his true calling was as the "Red Rocker."

Before graduating from Fontana High School, Sammy had already formed his first bands. He cites Elvis Presley and Mick Jagger as being the driving forces behind his wish to be a musician. He cites Eric Clapton as the reason he picked up the guitar at 16. His first guitar was a Gibson SG.

Influenced by The Rolling Stones, The Beatles, and The Who, Sammy formed the Fabulous Castiles with friend Ed Mattson as his first band. This band progressed into another band named Skinny. Other bands that Sammy belonged to in these early years included the Justice Brothers, Manhole, Cotton, Jimmy, Dust Cloud, and the Sammy Hagar Band.

About 1968 he moved to the San Fransisco area and played in clubs. Sammy caught his big break in 1972 when Montrose formed. Ronnie Montrose had just left the Edgar Winter Group to form his own band.

Sammy auditioned with a new song he'd just written, "Bad Motor Scooter." Montrose's self-titled debut album came out in 1973. The album *Paper Money* followed, but Sammy wasn't happy.

Though Montrose opened new doors for him, he preferred to be in charge. In 1975 he left Montrose to form his own band. He made a demo tape, and Phil Charles at KSAN in San Fransico played it. John Carter of Capitol records heard it and made an offer. All the other members of Montrose, with the exception of Ronnie Montrose himself, would eventually join Sammy's solo act. These players included Bill Church on bass, Alan Fitzgerald on keyboards, and Denny Carmassi on drums.

The band opened for Thin Lizzy, Kansas, Kiss, Foghat, Queen, Electric Light Orchestra, Heart, and Boston for two tours. The band also performed at a festival with Van Halen.

The early years of Sammy's solo career were embraced more in the U.K. than in the U.S. When Sammy signed a contract with Geffen records, he lost popularity in the U.K. and gained more success in the U.S. To fulfill contract requirements, Sammy released several compilation albums.

Sammy's obsession with cars eventually landed him the job with Van Halen. His mechanic, Claudio Zampolli, suggested to Eddie Van Halen that Sammy would make a good replacement for David Lee Roth. Ed invited Sammy to a "business meeting," which evolved into a jam session. Having found their new front man, the band began recording what would be their first #1 album. In fact, every Van Halen studio album recorded with Sammy Hagar reached #1.

In 1990 Sammy and the band opened the Cabo Wabo Cantina (Sammy's idea). The club, once owned by the entire band, is now owned by Sammy and Marco Monroy. He still performs there from time to time, on his birthday or whenever he just feels like it.

His marriage of 20 years to Betsy ended in the early 1990s, and Sammy remarried. His family now consists of his wife, Kari, his two sons, Aaron and Andrew, and his daughter, Kama.

Many claims have been made about his departure from Van Halen in 1996. One thing that has been agreed upon by both sides was Sammy's dislike of the idea for the *Twister* soundtrack. He believed it was a rip-off to make fans buy an entire CD of extremely diverse songs when only two songs really mattered to them. Whether Sammy was taking care of personal business (the birth of daughter Kama) or whether he just refused to come to work (as the band has stated) possibly will remain a point of debate forever. What can't be denied is 11 years of great music, five albums, and a giant piece of Van Halen history.

In 1997 Sammy went back to being a solo artist with the release of *Marching to Mars*. The albums and the tours that followed proved Sammy was where he wanted to be in his career and in his life.

Hang 'Em High-(*Diver Down* [3:28]) This song is essentially the same as "Last Night," a song recorded for consideration on Van Halen. However, the lyrics are completely changed. The lyrics are reported to be a tongue-in-cheek stab at Clint Eastwood.

Hans Valen-Australian-based Van Halen tribute band no longer in existence.

Happy Trails-(*Diver Down* [1:03]) This song was originally included on the band's 1977 Warner Brothers demo tape as a joke. They had played all the songs they could for consideration in the album, and this was all that was left.

Hard Copy-In 1995 this television show aired a report on "Andi," Ed's supposed mistress, who offered naked pictures of Ed, claiming they'd been together for two years. Another segment, aired in 1994, featured a report on a con man who was posing as a friend of Edward's to bilk unwitting persons of their property.

Hard 'N' Heavy Videos-This weekly video show featured a segment known as the "Trick or Treat Bag" that involved the guest host for that particular week reaching into a bag of items related to that host. The idea was for the individual to remove one item at a time and talk about each one to the television audience.

David Lee Roth was the host during one particular broadcast in 1990. When he reached into the bag, in typical Diamond Dave fashion he encouraged the home audience to join in at home by reaching into their pants, the pants of the person besides them, etc., ending his remarks by stating that he was going to reach into his own pants after the show.

Hard Rock-David Lee Roth and Van Halen appeared on the cover of this magazine dated 12/86. A satirical breakup review was given in an article entitled "David Lee Roth vs. Edward Van Halen." Address: 475 Park Avenue South, 8th Floor, New York, NY 10016.

Hear about It Later-(*Fair Warning* [4:33]) This song was originally written on a keyboard. It was later recorded on a Fender Stratocaster.

The video for this song was one of three live videos released for this album recorded at the Oakland Coliseum in Oakland, CA, during a three-day stint, 6/11/81 through 6/13/81.

Heart-Sammy Hagar co-wrote two songs on this band's *Brigade* album (Capitol 91820, 1990). Sammy co-wrote "The Night" with Denny Carmassi and Ann and Nancy Wilson. He co-wrote "Fallen from Grace" with Jesse Harms and Denny Carmassi. The album spent 49 weeks on the charts beginning on 4/21/90 and reaching #3. The same tracks appeared on Heart's live release *Rock the House Live!* (Capitol 95797, 1991). This album was recorded in Worcester, MA, on 11/28/90 and began its 7-week run on the charts on 10/12/91 reaching #107.

Heartbreak Hotel-(2:50) This Elvis Presley cover was performed by the band in South America during the 1983 *Diver Down* tour.

Heavy Metal-1. (Columbia Pictures, 1981) (Full Moon/Asylum 90004, 1981) The Sammy Hagar track "Heavy Metal" appeared on this soundtrack to the movie of the same name. This track also appeared on Sammy's solo album *Standing Hampton*, though in a different form.

Other artists contributing to the soundtrack included Journey, Black Sabbath, and Cheap Trick. The soundtrack began a 28-week run on the charts on 8/08/81 reaching its highest chart position at #12.

2. Eddie Van Halen and David Lee Roth appeared on the cover of this magazine's Spring 1985 issue. The three-page feature article was entitled "Van Halen: Are They the Ultimate in Metal?" Two other short features appeared under the names "Metal Madness" (Eddie Van Halen and Sammy Hagar) and "Headbanging Happenings" (Van Halen and David Lee Roth). Address: D.S. Magazines, Inc., D.S. Building, 105 Union Avenue, Cresskill, NJ 07626.

Heavy Metal Heroes-This magazine's index of Van Halen-related articles:

2/85: Eddie Van Halen cover. Ed poster and interview.

6/85: David Lee Roth cover. Dave poster and interview.

7/86: Eddie Van Halen cover. "Van Halen Back in High Gear": six-page band interview and pin-up.

12/86: Eddie Van Halen cover.

Address: Charlton Building, Derby, CT 06418.

Heavy Rock-This Spanish magazine's 4/98 issue featured a Van Halen interview.

Help Wanted: Kids-"Jump" played on a radio during a barbecue scene in this 1986 television movie.

Here's Just What She Wanted-(5:10) This unreleased original was performed and recorded on 12/31/77 at the Whisky A GoGo in Hollywood, CA. Alternate titles include "Just What You Wanted" and "Here's Just What You Wanted."

Hey, Hey It's Saturday-This Australian television show interviewed Van Halen when the band was in Launceston, Tasmania, in April 1998. Sammy Hagar appeared on the same show on 5/16/98.

Hideaway-This Cream song was reportedly the first blues song Edward learned to play on guitar.

Highway Star-This Deep Purple cover was performed by the band during their club days and once on 5/20/92 at the Cabo Wabo Cantina in Cabo San Lucas, Mexico.

History of Rock and Roll-This television special which originally aired on PBS in 1994, featured Eddie Van Halen in "Episode 7: Guitar Heroes." Later in the series, a clip from the *5150* tour was used.

Hit Mag-The band was interviewed for this magazine in 1984.

Hit Parader-This magazine's index of Van Halen-related articles:
10/79: "Spin Addict": by James Spina. *Van Halen II* reviewed.
11/79: Story about *Van Halen II* going platinum.
5/80: "Van Halen They Live by Night": by Regan McMahon. Stories from WMMS radio interview in Cleveland.
10/80: "Instant Discography: Van Halen"
12/80: "Van Halen: Who Are These Guys and Why Are They So Famous?": two-page Van Halen feature.
1/81: "Rock 'n' Roll Hit Parade": Sammy lists his 10 favorite albums.

3/81: David Lee Roth cover. "Van Halen They Live by Night": three-page Van Halen feature by Regan McMahon (originally appeared in 5/80 issue).

9/81: Van Halen cover. "The Wild Bunch": four-page band interview by Andy Secher.

1981: Van Halen cover. Yearbook 1981. "Van Halen They Live by Night": four-page interview by Regan McMahon (originally appeared in 5/80 and 3/81 issues).

9/82: David Lee Roth cover. "Van Halen Wild & Wonderful": four-page Van Halen feature by Eliot Sekular. Lyrics to "Dancing in the Street."

11/82: "Heavy Metal Happenings": Sammy talks about recent concerts in an article by Andy Secher. "Eddie Van Halen": one-page Eddie feature by Andy Secher.

12/82: "Hollywood Knights": Van Halen feature.

Spring 1983: Van Halen cover. Hit Parader Annual. "Van Halen Wild & Wonderful": four-page Van Halen feature by Eliot Sekular (originally appeared in 9/82 issue). Lyrics to "(Oh) Pretty Woman."

5/83: Eddie Van Halen cover. "Eddie Van Halen in Search of the Lost Chord": three-page Eddie Van Halen interview by Marc Shapiro.

8/83: David Lee Roth cover. "Trouble in Paradise": four-page Van Halen feature by Andy Secher.

11/83: "Animal Magnetism": Van Halen feature.

Fall 1983: "Special: Heavy Metal Rules": two-page band feature by Andy Secher.

1/84: Eddie Van Halen cover. Van Halen feature.

3/84: Sammy Hagar/HSAS feature.

4/84: David Lee Roth cover. "The High Life": three-page David Lee Roth interview by Andy Secher.

5/84: Van Halen feature.

8/84: David Lee Roth cover. "Heavy Metal Happenings": short features on Van Halen and Sammy Hagar. "Van Halen too Hot to Handle": four-page Van Halen feature by Ron Hunt.

9/84: "The Rock Brigade": Van Halen feature.

Fall 1984: David Lee Roth cover. Van Halen feature.

12/84: Van Halen cover. "Van Halen Living on the Edge": three-page Edward interview by Don Mueller.

Winter 1984: Eddie Van Halen cover. "Eddie Van Halen One Step Ahead": two-page Eddie Van Halen interview by Marc Shapiro.

Spring 1985: Van Halen cover. Hit Parader Annual.

4/85: David Lee Roth cover. "Heavy Metal Happenings": short feature on Dave. "David Lee Roth Just a Gigolo": five-page Dave feature by Paul Hunter.

9/85: Van Halen cover. "Hit Parader Heavy Metal Hot Shots."

1/86: "Van Halen-A Kingdom Divided": three-page Van Halen breakup feature by Paul Hunter. "Hit Parader Heavy Metal Hot Shots": Van Halen feature.

3/86: "Hit Parader Heavy Metal Hot Shots": Van Halen feature.

4/86: "A New Beginning": two-page Van Halen interview by Andy Secher.

5/86: Van Halen cover. "David Lee Roth-Turning Up the Heat": two-page feature on David Lee Roth by H.R. Fraser. "Van Halen Back to Basics": four-page Van Halen interview by Andy Secher.

6/86: "For Better or Worse": two-page Van Halen interview by Andy Secher.

7/86: "David Lee Roth a Time of Decision": two-page Dave interviewby Andy Secher.

9/86: Eddie Van Halen cover. "David Lee Roth vs. Van Halen: The War Heats Up": four-page review on breakup by Rob Andrews.

11/86: "Van Halen Behind the Scenes": one-page Van Halen feature by Jodi Beth Summers.

Fall 1986: Van Halen cover. Hit Parader Annual. "Back to Basics": three-page Van Halen feature by Andy Secher. "Turning Up the Heat": two-page David Lee Roth feature by H.R. Fraser.

12/86: "David Lee Roth Angry No More": one-page David Lee Roth feature by Rob Andrews.

Winter 1986: Hit Parader Yearbook. Four pages of Van Halen quotes. Lyrisc to "Hot for Teacher."

4/87: "The Next Step": two-page Van Halen interview by Rob Andrews. Lyrics to "Best of Both Worlds" and David Lee Roth's "Goin' Crazy."

Summer 1987: Hit Parader Annual. "Van Halen the Next Step": one-page Van Halen feature by Rob Andrews.

Fall 1987: Eddie Van Halen cover. "Guitar Gods. Edward Van Halen the Living Legend": one-page Edward interview.

9/88: Eddie Van Halen/Sammy Hagar cover. "Van Halen The Monsters of Rock": four-page interview by Andy Secher.

11/88: "Van Halen Behind the Scenes": one-page Van Halen feature by Winston Cummings.

7/90: "Van Halen Feeling the Heat": two-page Van Halen feature by Bryan Harding.

9/94: "Van Halen Joining the Club": two-page Van Halen feature by Dan Wilson.

1997: Two-page feature on Edward and Gary.

7/97: Van Halen feature.

Address: Charlton Building, Derby, CT 06418.

Hits magazine-This magazine's index of Van Halen-related articles:
7/08/96: Sammy talks about his breakup with the band.

7/15/96: Van Halen manager Ray Danniels responds to Sammy's statements in previous issue.

3/27/98: Van Halen on cover. Not much Van Halen content.

Holdsworth, Alan-Edward helped this guitar player get signed to Warner Brothers Eddie was supposed to coproduce Holdsworth's first album along with Ted Templeman and Donn Landee, but while Van Halen was touring South America in 1983, Holdsworth couldn't wait and forged ahead without him.

Honolulu Baby-(2:44) One version of this unreleased original was recorded on 6/03/76 at The Starwood in Hollywood, CA. It has also been called "Kissin' and Squeezin'."

During this particular performance, Dave explained the inspiration behind the song. He had fallen in love with a woman from Waikiki and wanted to write a song about her. He couldn't think of anything that rhymed with Waikiki, so he titled the song "Honolulu Baby." Dave concluded the song's introduction by saying, "With any luck we'll release this next summer and get a hit!"

Hot Bike-Sammy Hagar was featured on the June 2000 cover of this motorcyle magazine.

Hot for Remixes: A Tribute to Van Halen-(Cleopatra, 9/12/99) A companion to the tribute album *Little Guitars*. It features dance and industrial remixes of classic Van Halen songs.

Hot for Teacher-1. (1984 [4:42]) Ed used a 1958 Gibson "Flying V" guitar on this track.

To simulate the quiet interludes live (recorded using the neck pickup on the V turned down low in the studio), Edward used a Roland echo unit with the volume turned down, which he activated from his pedal board.

The single peaked on the U.S. charts at #56.

The band Slow Roosevelt covered this song on a double CD charity release titled *Come on Feel the Metal*. The CDs featured 35 Dallas/Ft. Worth bands playing covers from the 1970s and 1980s. The album's proceeds went to the American Cancer Society.

The video for this song was directed by Pete Angelus and David Lee Roth and produced by Jerry Kramer.

More than 80 people were selected for the various roles in this video (taken from a tryout of several hundred hopefuls), which was filmed over a four-day period at John Marshall High School in Los Angeles, CA.

Interestingly, the school had been closed prior to Van Halen's filming the video there. The city didn't have the funds to reopen the school, so the band contributed an undisclosed amount (on top of the money they paid to rent the school for filming) to the city to help reopen it.

The voice of Waldo was the late Phil Hartman.

The model who played the teacher in this video was Wayne Gretzky's wife, Janet Jones.

Some of the children chosen to portray Van Halen as youths were: Beto Lovato (Alex), Bill Bookmeyer (Dave), and Brian Hitchcock (Eddie). According to legend, by the third day of filming the four actors were walking and talking just like their respective counterparts. The actor playing Mike wore one of Michael's earrings for the video, Bookmeyer lost the pair of sunglasses given to him by Dave for use in the video, and after the shoot was over, Edward gifted Hitchcock with one of his own guitars.

In one classroom scene where the teacher is dancing on the desk, a black board is featured with the numbers 20-9-8-19-25-12-15-8. Each of these numbers corresponds to a letter of the alphabet. If you read the encoded word from right to left, you'll notice it spells "holy shit." This is the only known instance of such "hidden" gimmicks in a Van Halen video.

The choreographed dancing scene featuring the band in maroon wedding style tuxedos was reportedly dubbed "Dave and the Pips" by the members of Van Halen.

The hot rod's burnout at the end of the video was totally unplanned. The car's owner was not too pleased, to say the least. The hot rod, named "as Tom's Tub Two" was put up for auction at DavidLeeRoth.com in the fall of 2000.

Another video was made for this song from a live performance on 8/18/84 at Castle Donington, England, during the Monsters of Rock. More than an hour of footage from this concert was filmed and preserved in the Warner Brothers and Noel Monk vaults, though only the video of this song has ever been released.

2. Dutch-based Van Halen tribute band featuring Peter Van Wheelden on guitar.

Hot Rod Hot Trucks-Eddie Van Halen appeared on the cover of the Summer 1993 issue of this magazine. The issue had a seven-page feature on the Van Halen Van Hauler truck giveaway by Kevin Wilson entitled "Van Halen Van Hauler." There was also a centerfold of the truck. Address: 8490 Sunset Boulevard, Los Angeles, CA 90069.

Hots on for Nowhere-The band performed this Led Zeppelin song, from the album *Presence* (Swan Song SS-8416, 1976), in their club days.

Houndstooth-Gary Cherone's side project band formed after Extreme's *Waiting for the Punchline* tour. The band played Sinatra-like material. They were recruited for an Aerosmith tribute album, for which they performed a cover of "Dream On." Former Extreme drummer Mike Mangini played on the track.

In 1996 the band played an AIDS benefit in Boston. The songs that were performed: • My Funny Valentine • You Can't Take That Away from Me • I Wish I Were in Love Again • I've Got the World on a String • A Foggy Day in London Town

House of Blues-On 6/28/94 in Hollywood, CA, this club played host to the David Lee Roth band featuring Rockette Ritchotte on guitar, Ron Wikso on drums, James Hunting on bass, and Brett Tuggle on keys. The concert was broadcast live on Los Angeles's 97.1 KLSX and hosted by Jim Ladd. Wikso and Ritchotte are members of the Jay Bolan Band, a classic rock cover band that plays the Los Angeles area.

This $9 million club located on the Sunset Strip looks like a decrepit tin shack. The tin was reportedly taken from an old cotton gin in Clarksdale, MI, from the same crossroads where blues legend Robert Johnson was said to have sold his soul to the devil.

Financed in part by Jim Belushi, Joe Walsh, and Dan Akroyd, it is the third such establishment started by Hard Rock Café cofounder Isaac Tigrett (the first is located in a blue and white 19th-century clapboard-style home near Harvard Square in Cambridge, MA). Shows are frequently sold out far in advance. The club also hosts a restaurant and gift shop, and the walls are lined with a myriad of blues and folk memorabilia.

Set list: • Big Train • Panama • Experience • She's My Machine • A Little Luck • Your Filthy Little Mouth • Just a Gigolo/I Ain't Got Nobody • Sunburn • Beautiful Girls • Hey, You Never Know • Night Life • Just Like Paradise • Land's End • Ain't Talkin' 'Bout Love • California Girls • Ice Cream Man • Jump

Edward has also played at the same location. On 1/18/97 he performed "Hard to Handle" as well as another unknown tune with James Belushi and the Sacred Hearts at a private party for Peavey representatives.

House of Blues Radio Hour-Sammy and Edward were interviewed for the House of Blues Radio Hour sometime in mid-February 1994 by the show's producer, Ben Manilla, at Edward's 5150 Studio. The show was broadcast on the syndicated radio show on 4/23/94 and 4/24/94.

The pair discussed their foundations in the blues, and the event featured several Van Halen songs, in addition to cuts by ZZ Top, Cream, Jimi Hendrix, and Stevie Ray Vaughn.

Sammy and Edward also interspersed some blues-singing and guitar-playing throughout the interview, including a riff Edward made up after a discussion about three chord blues. Edward played a quick riff from Cream's "Hideaway," and Sammy and Edward performed a portion of Jimmy Reed's "Baby What You Want Me to Do?" and another song made up on the spot about the House of Blues.

The House of Blues Radio Hour has 170 affiliates nationwide and is a production of the House of Blues Transmitter Network, in partnership with Ben Manilla Productions and CBS Radio Productions.

House of Pain-(*1984* [3:18]) This song was regularly played during the band's club days of 1976 and was included on *1984* at Alex's insistence. The *1984* version features different lyrics and a different musical arrangement. The early version was recorded as part of the Gene Simmons financed 1976 demo at Village Recorder Studios in Los Angeles and Electric Ladyland Studios in New York. Another early version was recorded on the band's 1977 Warner Brothers demo.

Houses of the Holy-This Led Zeppelin cover song was reportedly played by the band in their early years.

Howard Stern-Broadcast on radio and television, the Howard Stern show has hosted members of Van Halen for years. Index of Van Halen-related shows:

(On Radio)

7/12/92: David Lee Roth appears.

1/11/93: David Lee Roth appears on Stern's birthday broadcast.

6/10/94: David Lee Roth performs three songs.

4/94: Sammy Hagar appears.

9/26/95: David Lee Roth appears.

9/09/96: David Lee Roth appears.

5/21/97: Sammy Hagar appears.

10/20/97: David Lee Roth appears.

1/29/98: Eddie and Alex Van Halen appear during Howard's birthday broadcast from the set of the "Without You" video.

3/17/98: Van Halen appears on the same day *Van Halen III* is released.

6/12/98: David Lee Roth appears.

3/09/99: Sammy Hagar appears.

(On Television)

9/26/96: David Lee Roth appears.

10/03/96: David Lee Roth appears (part 1).

10/04/96: David Lee Roth appears (part 2).

7/16/97: Sammy Hagar appears (part 1).

7/17/97: Sammy Hagar appears (part 2).

2/06/98: Eddie and Alex appear on Stern's birthday broadcast.

5/18/98: Van Halen appears.

5/19/98: Van Halen appears.

Howard Stern Private Parts: The Movie-(Northern Lights Entertainment/Paramount Picture /Rysher Entertainment, 1997) Howard Stern made his film debut in this movie, based on his 1996 book of the same name, which opened on 3/07/97.

Private Parts: The Album (WB 9 46477-2), released on 2/25/97, featured old and new cuts by several artists including Deep Purple, Marilyn Manson, Green Day, Ozzy Osbourne, Type O Negative, The Ramones, Cheap Trick, Ted Nugent, AC/DC, and, of course, Van Halen doing "Jamie's Cryin'."

In addition to "Jamie's Cryin'," two other Van Halen tracks were featured in the movie: "Dance the Night Away" and "You Really Got Me."

David Lee Roth also wrote the song "Private Parts," but it wasn't used. It was later debuted on the Howard Stern show in 1997.

How Many Say I-(*Van Halen III* [6:04]) Though the press proclaimed this as the first time Ed had sung lead vocals on a Van Halen recording, the actual first time was for the *Balance* track "Crossing Over." This was the first song on the album for which the music was written after the lyrics. The last verse in the song was originally the first verse.

HSAS-A one-time project album featuring Sammy on vocals, Journey's Neil Schon on guitar, ex Billy Squier bassist Kenny Aaronson, and Santana drummer Michael Shrieve. Schon's choice for drummer was originally Denny Carmassi, but Hagar passed, not wanting to create a Montrose clone. They recorded the album *Through the Fire*. An HSAS concert on 11/14/83 from the San Jose Arena in San Jose, CA, was televised on MTV. Tour dates (1983):

Warfield Theater, San Fransisco, CA: 11/10, 11/11, 11/12

San Jose Civic Auditorium, San Jose, CA: 11/14 (Broadcast on MTV), 11/15, 11/16

Marin Center, San Rafael, CA: 11/20, 11/21

huH-This magazine's index of Van Halen-related articles:

2/95: Van Halen cover. "Interview with the Van Halen": five-page interview by Adrianne Stone. "Might as well Jump Back": one-page Van Halen discography review by Chris Cook.

12/96: Eddie Van Halen cover. "Three Men and a Maybe": six-page Edward and Alex interview by Sandy Masuo.

Address: 2812 Santa Monica Boulevard, Suite 204, Santa Monica, CA 90404.

Humans Being-(*Twister* Soundtrack; *Best of Volume 1* [5:10]) Sammy's first lyrical attempt for "Humans Being" was entitled "The Hot Zone." Director Jan de Bont, however, specifically requested no tornado content in the lyrics, so Hagar went back to work and came up with a new set of lyrics built around the title that Ed came up with, "Humans Being." The song was mixed from 3/10/96 to 3/13/96.

There are two versions of the video for this song filmed on 4/10/96, produced by Rhonda Hopkins, and directed by Rocky Schenck. The first, which debuted on MTV on 4/17/96, contains clips from the movie *Twister* interspersed throughout. The second, included on the band's *Video Hits Volume 1*, does not include the *Twister* footage.

If you look closely, near the end of the second guitar solo just as Edward begins a tapped passage, you'll notice that a string on his Wolfgang is broken.

I

Ice Cream Man-(*Van Halen* [3:18]) The acoustic intro on this John Brim penned, Elmore James recorded, track was played by David Lee Roth. He performed this intro live on a variety of acoustic/electric guitars tuned to open E. On rare occasions he would pull out his infamous Dave-sickle, a steel-string acoustic/electric that looked like a giant ice cream bar.

For over 20 years fans wondered about the lyrics of this song. Speculation about one line in the song led to dozens of theories. The mystery was cleared up by the band in 1999. Dave is actually singing, "I got puddin' pie banana, dixie cups, All flavors and pushups too."

I Can't Drive 55-The band performed this Sammy Hagar cover from his *VOA* album (Geffen 24043, 1984) throughout their tours with Sammy.

If You Can't Rock Me-The band performed this Rolling Stones cover in their club days. Recordings exist of a 1974 performance and a 1976 performance at the Hilton in Pasadena, CA.

I'll Wait-(*1984* [4:41]) This is one of two songs Dave and Ted Templeman wanted left off *1984*. They felt that Ed shouldn't be concentrating on keyboards so much. But Edward and Donn Landee were adamant about its inclusion on the album. The other song was "Jump." In June 1984 "I'll Wait" peaked at #13.

The song is about the girl wearing men's underwear in a Calvin Klein underwear advertisement. Roth tacked the picture next to his Sony Trinitron TV and wrote the lyrics to her.

The song was first recorded by Edward, Alex, and Donn and played for Ted, Dave, and Mike the next day.

I'm So Glad-This Cream cover was often played in medley form with "Somebody Get Me a Doctor" on the *Diver Down* tour. When played at the Us Festival on 5/29/83 in San Bernardino, CA, this medley also contained an early instrumental version of "Girl Gone Bad." Another version of the song was performed during the *Right Here, Right Now* tour.

I'm the One-(*Van Halen* [3:44]) This track used to be called "Show Your Love" when the band performed it during their club days and when it was included on their 25-song Warner Brothers demo.
Four Non-Blondes recorded a cover of this song, which can be found on the soundtrack (Fox Records) to the 1994 movie *Airheads*.

In a Simple Rhyme-(*Women and Children First* [4:33]) Ed played a 12-string Rickenbacker electric for this song.
Originally, Ed had more of an acoustic intro for this song, but changed it because he felt the band might be labeled as trying to sound like Led Zeppelin.
This song was on the band's 1977 25-song Warner Brothers demo. The lyrics are sung a bit differently, and an extra verse is present on the demo.
The song was played often in the backyard party days. The first known recorded version of this song appeared on a 1973 demo that is believed to have been recorded at Cherokee Studios in Chatsworth, CA, and was then titled simply "Simple Rhyme."

In Concerto-On 1/30/95 at The Factory in Milan, Italy, Van Halen performed a small, televised concert. The Factory is one of the few small clubs Van Halen performed in with Sammy Hagar. The set list: • The Seventh Seal • Judgement Day • Don't Tell Me (What Love Can Do) • Amsterdam • Panama • Feelin' • Best of Both Worlds • Ain't Talkin' 'Bout Love

I Never Said Goodbye-(Geffen 24144, 1987) This Sammy Hagar solo album, originally untitled but called Sammy Hagar by many, was released on 6/23/87. It was produced by Sammy Hagar and Eddie Van Halen. The album entered the charts on 7/11/87 for a 23-week stint, topping out at #14. It was certified gold on 9/15/87.

Sammy owed this solo album to Geffen as part of a deal made between Geffen and Warner Brothers when the vocalist joined Van Halen. Besides a studio album, Hagar also kicked around the idea of recording a live album with various musicians and made up of some of his favorite songs.

The album was named *I Never Said Goodbye* by Kim Musgrove. She submitted the winning entry in an album-naming contest sponsored by MTV. The first printing of the album did not include the title, though later runs did. Musgrove's name was supposed to appear in the credits of the named run, but for unknown reasons it didn't.

The album was recorded at A&M Studios in Los Angles, CA, and over-dubs were done at One Studios in Los Angeles and The Record Plant in Sausalito, CA. Now known as Plant Studios, the studio opened on Halloween 1972.

Edward played a Steinberger bass on the entire album, and contributed a short tapped lead solo section to the song "Eagles Fly." The bass lines were reputedly played through two separately located acoustic amplifier stacks owned by Blue Cheer. Los Tres Gusanos skins-pounder David Lauser laid down most of the drum tracks. Omar Hakim provided drum overdubs on "Back into You" and "Hands and Knees." Keyboards were played by Jesse Harms. Michael Anthony added background vocals to this album but was not credited.

Sammy used a Kramer Baretta with a single volume knob (Edward Van Halen style) for most of the guitar parts through Ed's 100-watt Marshall Super Lead amp and his effects rig. He also used a red Sammy Hagar-model Hamer, outfitted with a Kahler bridge on "Hands and Knees" (this guitar was used to record all the guitar parts on *VOA*). A 1953 Gibson Hawaiian guitar tuned to open E was used to play lap slide on "Standin' at the Same Old Crossroads," the solo in "Boys Night Out," and a few background licks on "Privacy." Incidentally, this same guitar was used on "Bad Motor Scooter" from Montrose.

The video for "Hands and Knees" featured an appearance by Edward, Alex, and Michael, as well as the Brain Box (see "Brain Box" entry). Portions of the video for "Give to Live" were filmed at the Rose Bowl in Pasasdena, CA. The only other video made for this album was for "Eagles Fly." Tracks: • When the Hammer Falls • Hands and Knees • Give to Live • Boy's Night Out • Returning Home • Standin' at the Same Old Crossroads • Privacy • Back into You • Eagles Fly • What They Gonna Say Now

Geffen released a promotional CD for this album titled *Sammy Hagar Returns Home* (Geffen Pro-CD-2832, 1987) that included an interview and the following tracks: • Give to Live • Boy's Night Out • Returning Home • Eagles Fly • Back into You • Privacy

I Never Said Goodbye singles/promos
"Give to Live," "When the Hammer Falls," Geffen 7-28314, 7" Vinyl, USA, 1987. Highest chart position: #23 in USA.

"Give to Live" (extended mix), "Standin' at the Same Old Crossroads," Geffen, 12" Vinyl, USA, 1987.

"Eagles Fly," "Hands and Knees" (fade), Geffen P2323, 7" Vinyl, Japan, 1987.

"Eagles Fly" (promo), "Eagles Fly" (edit/fade), Geffen PRO-A-2854, 12" Vinyl, USA, 1987. Highest chart position: #82 in USA.

In for the Kill-(5:55) The band performed this Budgie cover on 12/31/77 at the Whisky A GoGo in Hollywood, CA.

In Melbourne Tonight-Sammy Hagar appeared on this Australian television show on 5/18/98.

In 'N' Out-(*For Unlawful Carnal Knowledge* [6:05]; *Live: Right Here, Right Now* [6:20]) Though many fans and critics alike interpreted these lyrics as sexually suggestive, they actually deal with how ironic it is that it costs money to be born and to die.

Mike considered this to be the hardest song on the album to play because of all the sixteenth notes. He used an Extra Heavy Fender or Dunlop pick on this track.

Inside-(*5150* [5:02]) The horns at the beginning of this song were sampled on a Fairlight keyboard, and the main riff was played on an Emulator.

The words spoken in the background of this track have been transcribed and are available at various sites on the Internet.

The Inside-The official international Van Halen magazine's index of articles:

#1: Interview with Michael Anthony, "Growing Up with the Van Halens," "A Day at 5150," Van Halen timeline, Sammy's *Unboxed*, lost Van Halen video, Trojan Rubber Company. (Spring 1995)

#2: Peavey Wolfgang reviewed, interview with Alex, 1984 Lost Weekend. (Summer 1995)

#3: Interview with Sammy Hagar, interview with Kevin Dugan, the Peavey Wolfgang, guide to Cabo San Lucas. (Fall 1995)

#4: Interview with Eddie Van Halen, interview with Dennis Anthony, David Lee Roth live in Las Vegas, Sammy's birthday bash, timeline #3, tour damage reports, early Van Halen flyers. (Winter 1996)

#5: Interview with Sammy Hagar, NAMM report, the Us Festival, timeline #4, Ed, Al, and Michael's live rigs. (Spring 1996)

#6: The breakup timeline, Dave quotes, Roth's friends talk about Diamond Dave, Interview with Chris Stuba, Star Fleet Project, Rich Wyman (Fall 1996)

#7: Interview with Eddie Van Halen, Interview with Michael Anthony, interview with Alex Van Halen, Gary Cherone background, Sammy Hagar update, fan poll. (Winter 1997)

#8: Special club days issue. Review of 1977 Warner Brothers demo, a look at 5150 Studio, Sammy Hagar's *Marching to Mars* reviewed, *Balance* tour rider featured. (Summer 1997)

#9: Special guitar issue. Eddie's guitars part one, the making of the "Hot for Teacher" video, opening night at Cabo Wabo, Timeline #5, Edward NAMM feature (originally published in November 1985 Guitar World), official Van Halen Web site feature, Dave's 1981 birthday party. (Fall 1997)

#10: *Van Halen III* reviewed, interviews with the whole band at 5150, interview with Scotty Ross. (Spring 1998)

#11: Interviews with Mike and Ed, *Van Halen III* premiere party, tour article about Australian dates, (Summer 1998)

#12: Interview with Gary, Van Halen soundchecks, Club Days Part #2, Timeline #6 (Fall 1998)

#13: Michael Anthony interview, review of early tourbooks, interview with Dweezil Zappa, early photos of Ed and Alex. (Winter 1998)

#14: The *Van Halen* Tour issue. (Spring 1999)

#15: Special photo issue. (Winter 1999)

#16: Review of the short-lived Gary-era, interview with *Balance* engineer Mike Plotnikoff, what other guitarists have to say about Ed. (Summer 2000)

Address: 1739 E. Broadway Rd Suite 105, Tempe, AZ 85282; Telephone: (602) 655-9300; Web site: http://www.vanhalenstore.com

Inside 5150 Studio-This promotional video accompanied the first pressing of the *Live: Right Here, Right Now* concert video. A replica backstage pass was included with the promotional package. The video included an interview from the 5150 Studio, as well as a live performance of the band playing The Who's "Won't Get Fooled Again."

iSong-A line of CD-ROMs that teaches guitar through examples and interaction. The Van Halen CD-ROM includes: "Ain't Talkin' 'Bout Love," "Ice Cream Man," "Beautiful Girls," "Feel Your Love Tonight," "Jamie's Cryin'," and "Dance the Night Away."

In-Sync-This magazine about watches featured Michael Anthony on the cover of its December 1997/January 1998 issue. The magazine interviewed Anthony about his place in the history of Van Halen and his love of Disney watches.

International Musician and Recording World-This magazine's index of Van Halen-related articles:

3/83: "Eddie Van Halen": four-page Edward interview by John Stix.

1/84: Van Halen cover. "1984": four-page Edward interview by Stewart Jaffey. "One Man Moving Van": one-page Patrick Whitley interview by Paul Gallotta.

3/84: Eddie Van Halen cover.

1/86: Van Halen cover. "Van Halen A.D. (After Dave)": six-page Van Halen feature by Michael Smolen.

Address: 242 West 38 Street #1400, New York, NY 10018.

Interview Discs-These are recordings that contain no music, only interviews with the band.

Van Halen: The Interview (Bakta Bak Recordings CBAK 4071, UK, 1995)

Though released on 11/17/95, this interview took place just before the release of *OU812* in 1988. The interview revolved around the Monsters of Rock tour and the new album.

Clock Interview Disc (Bakta Bak Recordings, UK, 1995)

Released on 11/24/95, this disc captures the band discussing the same topics as in *Van Halen: The Interview.*

Music Maker Invites You to Meet Van Halen at Plumb Crazy (no serial #, WEA, 7" Vinyl)

97.7 Htz FM Interview (CG Publishing 8013, 8/17/99)
This is a series of Canadian radio interviews by Kristy Knight. Tracks: • David Lee Roth: Feb 94 • Michael Anthony: May 95 • Sammy Hagar: June 97 • Sammy Hagar: October 97

In the Midnight Hour-This Wilson Pickett cover was originally slated for inclusion on *Diver Down* and later on *1984*. But due to reasons known only by the band, it was dropped both times. It was reportedly played live on the *Diver Down* tour, though no known recordings exist.

Intimate Portrait-Val, Ed, and Wolfgang Van Halen appeared in this hour-long Lifetime network television special devoted to Valerie's life. The program originally aired on 4/20/97 and reportedly received the highest ratings in the series' history.

Intruder-(*Diver Down* [1:39]) This instrumental was recorded when it was determined that the band needed an intro for the "(Oh) Pretty Woman" video because the video ran longer than the length of the song.
Effects included Eddie twirling his tremolo bar and rubbing a can of Schlitz Malt Liquor beer against the strings as well as massive doses of feedback.
The working title for this song was "Jams IV."

I Remember-This unreleased original is a leftover from the *Balance* sessions recorded in 1994.

The Island Ear-Van Halen appeared on the cover of this publication dated May 1995.

It's Not Over 'til It's Over-This unreleased original is a leftover from the *Van Halen III* sessions.

It's Only Rock 'N' Roll-This Rolling Stones cover was performed on 2/01/89 at the Tokyo Super Dome.

It's Your Thing-The band used to play this Isley Brothers tune while trying to earn enough money to perform original material.

I Wanna Be Your Lover-(3:25) (3:00)* This unreleased original was recorded live on 1/18/77 and 2/08/78 at unknown locations in Pasadena, CA. The song also appears on the band's 1977 Warner Brothers demo*.

I Want Some Action-This unreleased tune from the *5150* sessions is essentially another version of "Stompin' 8H," a song Ed performed on Saturday Night Live. The song was released to the public in bootleg form in February 1999.

J

Jack Attack-Term used by Michael Anthony in the early 1980s when he had a craving for Jack Daniels whiskey.

Jackson, Michael-Eddie Van Halen appeared on Michael Jackson's *Thriller* (Epic 38112, 1982) album for the song "Beat It" (4:30). The album spent 122 weeks on the charts, starting on 12/25/82. It went to the #1 position in both the U.S. and U.K. The single "Beat It" hit the charts on 3/12/83, lasting 15 weeks and reaching #1 in the U.S. and #3 in the U.K.

Edward's involvement with this project was done at the request of Grammy Award-winning producer/songwriter Quincy Jones and Michael Jackson. Ed did not ask for, nor did he receive, any money for his contribution.

Van Halen as a band was on a short break from their *Diver Down* tour at the time, and after a short series of phone calls from Jones and Ted Templeman, Edward and Donn Landee went to Westlake Studios in Los Angeles, CA, to lay down a guitar solo for the song sometime between August and November 1982. It was Landee who convinced Edward to take part in the session. Steve Lukather handled bass and rhythm guitar, and Jeff Porcaro played drums on the track.

Upon arriving at the studio, Edward sat down at the mixing console, with Landee to his right and Jones on his left, and listened to a rough mix of the song. Jones explained to Edward where he wanted the solo to occur, over one chord, and Edward responded with a suggestion that they add a verse section with some chord changes underneath. Jones liked the idea, and Edward recorded two solos, letting Jackson and Jones pick the one they liked better, which turned out to be the second. An old Marshall amplifier and cabinet were used, though not his trusty Super Lead, and the solos were played on Edward's Charvel "Franky" along with an Echoplex.

Edward was also asked to appear in the accompanying Bob Giraldi directed video, which had a cast of 150 extras and was filmed at a cost of $160,000, but the remaining members of Van Halen nixed the idea.

It has been heavily debated over the years whether Edward's involvement with Jackson was the driving force that bridged the gap between soul and rock music and whether his work with the vocalist broke down the color barriers on MTV. However, it should be noted that "Billie Jean" (the second single from Thriller, behind the Jackson/Paul McCartney duet "The Girl Is Mine") was the first Michael Jackson video to be shown on MTV, not "Beat It" (the third single). "Beat It" didn't receive attention from the video channel for more than a month after "Billie Jean" initially hit the #1 position on the charts and the accompanying video began being broadcast.

"Beat It" won Record of the Year and Best Pop Rock Vocal Performance, Male, at the 1983 Grammy Awards. *Thriller* won Album of the Year at the 1983 Grammy Awards and spent 37 weeks at #1 selling more than 40 million units.

"Beat It" was rereleased as a single, "Beat It (Moby's Sub Mix)" (6:11), on the Australian *They Don't Care about Us* (Epic Records, 663206 2) in 1996.

Here, "Beat It" kicks off with Edward's solo (32 seconds), treated to heavy doses of echo, all by itself before launching into the dance-mix flavorings of the newly remixed track. Bits of the solo are also interspersed throughout the song. The tune ends with a sampled segment of the solo, played over and over until the fade out.

On 7/13/84 Eddie appeared on stage with Michael Jackson when the *Thriller* tour came to Texas Stadium in Irving, TX. Among the 39,601 people in attendance was The Artist. Eddie performed "Beat It" and jammed with Tito Jackson. The pair traded licks, with Jackson throwing passages at Ed with his guitar behind his head and back, while Eddie would chuckle and respond with a note shower of his own.

Jam Entertainment News-Sammy Hagar appeared on the cover of the 12/31/91 issue of this publication, which featured a two-page article on

Van Halen by Dennis Walking. Address: P.O. Box 151720, Altamonte Springs, FL 32715-1720; Telephone: 407-767-8377.

Jamie's Cryin'-(*Van Halen* [3:30]) This was the only track from the first album written in the studio. It came together in approximately 20 minutes and was based on a riff Edward had been working on. The rhythm track for this song was recorded on Eddie's Ibanez Destroyer "Shark." Mike used a pick on the song's bass track.

A video was made for the song as part of the band's Van Halen promotional video set. This video differs from the others in the set in a few ways. Eddie uses his Charvel "Franky" instead of his usual Explorer. Dave gets much more playful with the camera in this video, forfeiting any control over his own hip movement.

Parts of this song were sampled by Tone Loc for his song "Wild Thing" (4:25) from 1989's *Loc'ed after Dark* on Island Records. Ed found out about it while watching MTV. After rightfully raising a stink, Van Halen was thanked on subsequent copies of the album, but they were not paid. The sample then reappeared on Weird Al Yankovic's "Isle Thing," released on May 25, 1989, and was included on Weird Al's *UHF* album. The "Isle Thing" single featured "Hot Rocks Polka" as the B-side.

The Bingo Boys also sampled parts of this song in their 1991 tune "No Woman, No Cry."

Wesley Willis had his own take on this song, using it on his track "Casper, the Homosexual Friendly Ghost" from his album *Spookydisharmoniousconflicthellride* (ULG 17734, 1996).

Jam Music-This web site featured a Gary Cherone interview on 8/25/98. URL: http://www.canoe.ca/JamMusic

Jam TV-This web site's index of Van Halen-related articles:
1/13/95: "Hagar Says the Right Thing": interview with Sammy about Balance by John Sakamoto.

8/15/95: "Sobering Thoughts": interview with Eddie Van Halen about his hip by John Sakamoto.

6/27/96: "Van Halen Back with David Lee Roth": article about Sammy's departure.

7/02/96: "Parting Ways with Van Halen": article about Sammy's departure.

8/14/96: "Alex Van Halen Files for Divorce."

9/05/96: "Van Halen Wary of Saying Roth Is Back for Good": article about 1996 MTV Video Music Awards appearance by Van Halen.

10/03/96: "Open Letter from David Lee Roth""Van Halen Reunion 'A Stunt'": short summary of David Lee Roth's open letter about the breakup. "Extreme Split Fuels Van Halen Rumors": brief article about Gary Cherone joining Van Halen.

10/07/96: "Van Halen Confirms New Singer": article about Gary Cherone as new singer.

10/12/96: "Backstage Blowup Was Last Straw, Says Van Halen": article about David Lee Roth's departure.

10/31/96: "Battling Van Halen Hit Charts at No. 1": article on *Best of Volume 1*.

3/22/97: "TV Mogul Producing New Van Halen Album": article about Mike Post.

3/12/98: "Sassy!": article about Sass Jordan auditioning for Van Halen.

3/19/98: "The Old New Van Halen": article about Gary Cherone and *Van Halen III* by Jane Stevenson.

8/25/98: "Van Halen's New Kid in Town": article about Gary Cherone by Jane Stevenson.

URL:http://www.canoe.ca/JamMusicArtistsV/vanhalen.html

Jam with Van Halen-(Total Accuracy, 1997) This release allows you to sing or play guitar over basic Van Halen tracks recorded by an unknown band. Tracks: • Ain't Talkin' 'Bout Love • Runnin' with the Devil • You

Really Got Me • Somebody Get Me a Doctor • Jump • Panama • Why Can't This Be Love? • Right Now

Japan Televised Concert-Broadcast only on Japanese television, this 1988 Japanese concert was considered for a live video. Edward felt it was poorly mixed, though. He spent two months mixing and editing, but the video was never released. Tracks: • There's One Way to Rock • Summer Nights • Panama • A.F.U. (Naturally Wired) • Why Can't This Be Love? • Mine All Mine • Drum Solo • "5150" • When It's Love • Eagles Fly • I Can't Drive 55 • Best of Both Worlds • Ed's solo • Black and Blue • You Really Got Me

Jape-A term used by Edward, Sammy, and Donn Landee to describe the addition of effects on finished tracks. Ed describes the term as "fairy dust." Basically, it just refers to effects that smooth things out.

Jean Genie-(4:54) The band performed this David Bowie cover in 1976 at the Hilton in Pasadena, CA.

Jeff Porcaro Benefit-Hosted by Porcaro's former band Toto, the Jeff Porcaro Tribute featured, among others, Edward on guitar; Simon Phillips on drums; Steve Lukather on guitar; and vocal performances by George Harrison (who also played some guitar), Don Henley, and David Crosby. The event was held on 12/04/92 at the Universal Amphitheater in Universal City, CA.

The benefit was held to honor the recently deceased Porcaro and to help raise money for his family to assist in paying his medical and funeral costs. The show featured many lengthy jams as this all-star cast pulled out all the stops and just enjoyed playing music in the drummer's honor. Ed's set list: • Fire (4:15) • Ain't Talkin' 'Bout Love (4:03) • Hold the Line (15:12) • With a Little Help from My Friends (10:00)

John and Leeza-Ed, Valerie, and Wolfie appeared on this television program in September 1993.

Johnson, Edwin-Edward Van Halen has purchased artworks painted by this New York based artist.

Jon Stewart Show-On 2/10/95 Van Halen appeared on this show. Filmed that same day at the Paramount Lot in Los Angeles, CA, the spot featured Eddie Van Halen and Sammy Hagar being interviewed. Segments that appeared before the interview showed the band rehearsing for the *Balance* tour (the segments were staged).

On 4/27/95 in another episode, Van Halen performed "Amsterdam," "Aftershock," and "Can't Stop Lovin' You" (partial).

Jordan, Sass-The first singer Van Halen considered to replace Sammy Hagar when he left the band. Although she claims she wasn't auditioning, she sang a few songs at 5150 to new music Ed and Alex had written. She told the band that she didn't think a female singer would work in Van Halen. She was never asked to join the band.

Josephina-(*Van Halen III* [5:38]) This song was added to the *Van Halen III* album at the last minute to replace "That's Why I Love You." The album's release date was pushed back from 2/24/98 to 3/17/98 to accommodate this change.

The song is about the parents of the band members and their past, little-known lives. Gary's mother's name happens to be Josephina.

The music for the song involved many subtle sounds including the sound of leader tape being yanked through piano strings during the chorus.

Judgement Day-(*For Unlawful Carnal Knowledge* [4:41]; *Live: Right Here, Right Now* [4:51]) This was the first song written in the studio for the *F.U.C.K.* album.

The two-handed lick leading into the solo (appearing at 2:50) and again at the end of the track (4:22) features Ed tapping chords onto the fretboard and was originally part of his tray-table guitar solo on the *1984* tour.

The day after the band recorded this track, the first Eddie Van Halen Music Man guitar prototypes began arriving at the 5150 Studio.

Jump-(*1984*; *Best of Volume 1* [4:04]; *Live: Right Here, Right Now* [4:26]) Parts of "Jump" had originally been written on the back of a tour bus in the late 1970s/early 1980s. However, the band had always felt the song didn't quite fit any of the albums they'd been working on. David Lee Roth and Ted Templeman were the biggest opponents of Ed's keyboard songs and consistently vetoed recording this song for more than two years.

When Ed gained control in the studio by building 5150, he was able to record more with just Alex and Don Landee. One day the three laid down the basic tracks to the song and presented it the following day to Dave, Mike, and Ted. Whether the rest of the band truly loved the song or felt somewhat compelled to record it is not known, but soon Dave was writing lyrics for it.

David wrote the lyrics around a single phrase: "go ahead and jump." He came up with the line after watching the news and seeing a man on top of the Arco Tower threatening to commit suicide. The vocalist thought that there's always at least one person in the crowd telling the guy to "go ahead and jump."

Ed recorded the song using an Oberheim OBX-A keyboard. The solo was spliced together from at least two different takes. The ending of the song has a history all its own. The main riff for "Top of the World" was written around the ending of "Jump." However, the ending of "Jump" had also been heard before during the 1983 Us Festival when Ed played it at the end of "Dance the Night Away."

"Jump" spent 5 weeks at #1 on the charts. The single was certified gold on 4/03/84.

The video for "Jump" (the first from *1984*), produced by Robert Lombard and directed by Pete Angelus, debuted on 12/31/83. It was filmed using 16mm hand-held cameras at The Complex in Santa Monica, CA. The entire cost for the video was a little more than $6,000 (though David Lee Roth liked to claim the total cost was only $600).

The video version of the song differed slightly from the album version.

Sharp-eyed viewers will also notice Edward's keyboard is quite dusty, proof that it's the music that's most important, not the image.

When it came time for Sammy Hagar to sing the song in concert on the *5150* tour, he used to pull a person out of the crowd to sing for him. After this tour he was comfortable enough to sing it on his own.

Aztec Camera recorded an acoustic version of the song as a B-side to their "All I Need Is Everything" single and later included it on their live album, *Backwards and Forwards*, and on the compilation album, *Retrospect*. When Aztec Camera performed the song live, vocalist Roddy Frame would introduce it as "an American folk song about girls who commit suicide."

The group Bus Stop released a techno/dance version of "Jump" (Festival, 1795) in 1999.

"Jump" was on an Australian compilation album named *Throbbin' '84*, released at the beginning of 1984.

The song also appeared on the compilations *Slammin' Sports Jams Vol. 1* (Simitar, 1998) and *Best of Superstars Vol. 1* (1999 from Germany).

Jungle Studs-A group of 14 individuals gathered by David Lee Roth who traveled the world on exotic adventures. In addition to Roth, the Jungle Studs roster included a research chemist from a university in Atlanta, GA, a Vietnam veteran, a doctor, and a lawyer.

Juxtapoz-A review of David Lee Roth's *The Best* was featured in the Spring 1998 issue of this art magazine.

K

Kalvitis, Stass-The Russian music teacher who gave Edward and Alex their first piano lessons. Edward and Alex practiced at home on a German-made Rippen piano.

Keegan, Mike-Eddie Van Halen's tech since 1997. Mike had previously worked for Nuno Bettencourt. He used to play guitar in a Van Halen tribute band.

Keenen Ivory Wayans-Sammy made a taped appearance on this television show on 8/28/97, which was broadcast on 8/30/97, performing "Marching to Mars."

Keep Playing that Rock and Roll-The band performed this Johnny Winter cover on 9/18/76 at The Bogart in San Bernardino, CA.

Kendall, Valeri-Alex Van Halen's first wife. Al reportedly proposed to her only two weeks after they met; it was love at first sight.

Kerrang!-This magazine's index of Van Halen-related articles:
1984: "Kerrang! Extra #1": *1984* tour photos by Ross Halfin.
1/26/84-2/08/84: "Rock in USA": mention about *1984* tour rehearsals.
8/09/84-8/22/84: Article by Malcome Dome and photos about Kerrang! contest winner.
12/26/85-1/08/86: Van Halen cover. "The Story of Sam and Dave": seven-page band interview by Sylvie Simmons.
1/09/86-1/22/86: Van Halen cover. "Heat Strokes": three-page David Lee Roth feature by Arlett Vereecke.

7/24/86-8/06/86: *Eat 'Em and Smile* tour article by Arlett Vereecke. The article's layout and photos were later used on the David Lee Roth bootleg *Do You Like My New Band?*

6/25/87-7/09/87: Sammy Hagar cover. "All American Sam": four-page Sammy interview. Sammy's *I Never Said Goodbye* reviewed.

8/13/88: David Lee Roth cover and feature by Mick Wall.

6/15/91: Van Halen cover and feature, "U.S. Rock Giants in Shock Carnal Comeback!"

1/30/93: Van Halen cover. "Van Halen: A UK Tour at Last!": short feature on Van Halen U.K. tour. "Top 100 Heavy Metal Trax of All Time": Extreme's "Get the Funk Out" ranked at #76. "In the Here and Now": four-page Van Halen feature by Steffan Chirazi.

1/14/95: Van Halen article.

4/01/95: Eddie Van Halen article titled, "I'm Still Alive!"

3/18/98: Eddie Van Halen interview.

Address: Greater London House, Hampstead Road, London NW1 7QZ; Telephone: 01-387-6611

Keyboard-The April 1984 issue of this magazine featured a two-page Eddie Van Halen interview by Bob Doerschuk entitled "1984."

Keyboard World-The July 1988 issue of this magazine featured Eddie Van Halen on the cover, with a six-page interview by Alan di Perna entitled "Crazy Eddie?" The issue also featured "Eddie's Keyboard Korner," a one-page keyboard rig feature by Alan di Perna. "Love Walks In" is transcribed. Address: 1115 Broadway, New York, NY 10010; Telephone: 212-807-7100.

Kiss My Ass-This is a Kiss tribute album (Polygram/Mercury 314 522 393-2, 1994) for which Extreme performed the Kiss song "Strutter" (4:39). The album was released on 6/21/94 and featured performances by Anthrax, Garth Brooks, Dinosaur, Jr., Extreme, Gin Blossoms, Lenny

Kravitz, The Lemonheads, The Mighty Mighty Bosstones, Yoshiki, Toad the Wet Sprocket, and Shandi's Addiction.

"Strutter" featured Extreme's trademark funk rock sound. They also threw in the main riff from "God of Thunder" and the chorus of "Shout It Out Loud" and at the end Gary "sings" the drum intro to "Love Gun."

Kramer Guitar magazine-Eddie Van Halen is featured in this magazine's March 1985 issue with John McEnroe and Vita Geralitas.

L

La Grange-(6:04) The band performed this ZZ Top cover on 5/30/76 at Pasadena City College.

Larry King Live-David Lee Roth was interviewed on this television program in 1988, just after the release of *Skyscraper*.

Larson, Nicolette-Eddie Van Halen performed the solo on "Can't Get Away from You" (3:10) for the album *Nicolette* (WB BSK 3243, 1978) as a favor to Ted Templeman.

Born 7/17/52 in Helena, MT, and raised in Kansas City, MO, Nicolette Larson, who relocated to San Francisco, CA, in 1974, released four albums on the Warner Brothers label and two on MCA. She also spent time as a session vocalist with Neil Young and Linda Ronstadt.

Nicolette, which went gold, was Larson's most successful album. The album was produced by Ted Templeman and engineered by Donn Landee. It entered the charts on 11/18/78, remaining there for 37 weeks and reaching #15.

Larson performed background vocals on the Van Halen track "Could This Be Magic?" She also performed an original composition, written just for the occasion and sung entirely in French, at Ed and Valerie's wedding.

Nicolette died on 12/16/97 due to complications of cerebral edema. She was 45 years old.

Last Child-(2:45) The band performed this Aerosmith cover on 9/18/76 at The Bogart in San Bernardino, CA.

Last Night-(3:24) This unreleased original was an early version of "Hang 'Em High" with completely different lyrics. One version was performed on 6/10/77 at the Whisky A GoGo in West Hollywood, CA. The song was recorded for the band's 1977 Warner Brothers demo.

Late Night with Conan O'Brien-In 1993 Ed and Valerie appeared on this show to promote one of Valerie's movies.

Late Night with David Letterman-Van Halen-related broadcasts:
1/01/85: David Lee Roth interviewed.
5/16/85: Ed sits in with band and performs "(Oh) Pretty Woman," "Jump," "You Really Got Me," and "Sunshine of Your Love."
6/27/85: Valerie interviewed. Ed sits in with band and performs "Panama," "Crossroads," "(Oh) Pretty Woman," and "Sunshine of Your Love."
8/07/87: Sammy Hagar performs "Boys Night Out" and is interviewed.
4/23/91: David Lee Roth performs "Tell the Truth."
3/30/94: Sammy Hagar performs "High Hopes" with a red EVH Music Man guitar.
8/10/95: Van Halen performs "Not Enough" and "Jump."
5/23/97: Sammy Hagar is interviewed and performs "Little White Lie."

Later in LA-On 5/29/92 Sammy Hagar and Eddie Van Halen appeared on this show, hosted by Bob Costas, to give their first network interview. A few years later, while Valerie Bertinelli was being interviewed on the same show, Eddie and Wolfie made an appearance. Since Wolfie answered some questions, this could be considered his first interview.

The Legend of 1900-Ed contributed two guitar solos to the Roger Waters song "Lost Boys Calling" for the soundtrack (Sony 66767, 10/12/99) to this film.

Leiren, Rudy-Ed's tech from junior high school through most of the 1980s. He was known to Ed as Rude (pronounced like "Rudy"). Besides various album thank-you's, the only known appearance of this nickname appears on the body of one of Edward's black and white guitars from the *Fair Warning* tour. It is painted in black letters and is located on the inside of the neck cavity, where the neck bolts on to the body.

Les Paul & Friends-Broadcast on the Cinemax network on 8/18/88 from the Brooklyn Academy of Music in Brooklyn, NY, then released on video (A Vision 50197-3), Eddie Van Halen performed at this tribute to the father of the electric guitar. Other performers on the roster included Pink Floyd's David Gilmour, the Stray Cats' Brian Setzer, B.B. King, and Steve Miller, among others.

Ed had been seen the night before at Fat Tuesday's watching Les perform. Fat Tuesday's is a club at which the Les Paul Trio used to perform every Monday night, but which has since been closed.

During the tribute Ed performed "Cathedral" and an instrumental version of "Hot for Teacher" (swapping licks with Jan Hammer) and took part in the star-studded encore.

Less Than Zero-The David Lee Roth song "Bump and Grind" was featured in this movie (20th Century Fox, 1987) but did not appear on the soundtrack.

Lethal Weapon 4-This film starring Mel Gibson, Danny Glover, Chris Rock, Rene Russo, and Joe Pesci featured the *Van Halen III* track "Fire in the Hole." Scenes and characters from the movie were used throughout the song's video. Though the video wasn't shown in its entirety during MTV's

Lethal Weapon 4 special, another special, shown on a cable movie channel, about the making of the movie did include some parts of the video.

Let Me Swim-The band performed this Cactus cover, from the album *Cactus* (Atlantic 18P2-2758, 1970), in their club days. This song is often mislabeled on bootlegs as "Oceanside."

Let's Get Rockin'-(3:07) This unreleased original was a fast-paced rocker recorded for the band's 1977 Warner Brothers demo. Live performances of the song were recorded at the Golden West Ballroom in Norwalk, CA, in 1976 and at the Whisky A GoGo in West Hollywood on 6/30/76. The song is sometimes called "Ain't No Stoppin'."

Life-The 11/82 issue of this magazine, reprinted in the David Lee Roth autobiography *Crazy from the Heat*, featured "Rock's Rowdiest Rogues," a photo essay of life on the road with Van Halen by Nancy Griffin. The issue causes a great deal of controversy. Several elderly readers cancel their subscriptions. Several hotels cancel the band's reservations after seeing the destruction the band had inflicted on rooms in the photos.

Lifestyles of the Rich and Famous-Michael Anthony was featured on this television show on 6/04/95.

Light in the Sky-(4:35) This unreleased original bears no resemblance to *Van Halen II*'s "Light Up the Sky." "Light in the Sky" was recorded for the band's 1977 Warner Brothers demo and included a guitar introduction for which Ed may have used his MXR Flanger.

Light Up the Sky-(*Van Halen II* [3:09]) Eddie wrote the main riffs for this song immediately after the recording of *Van Halen*. The rest of the song was written completely in the studio.

A Little Ain't Enough-(Warner Bros. 9 26477, 1991) David Lee Roth's third full-length solo album after his departure from Van Halen. It began its 19-week run on the charts on 2/02/91 (U.S.) and 1/26/91 (U.K.). It reached its highest chart position on 2/16/91 at U.S. #18 and 1/26/91 at U.K. #4. Tracks: • A Lil' Ain't Enough • Shoot It • Lady Luck • Hammerhead Shark • Tell the Truth • Baby's on Fire • 40 Below • Sensible Shoes • Last Call • The Dogtown Shuffle • It's Showtime! • Drop in the Bucket

Rumors surrounded the auditions for the album. People wondered who would be the next in a line of guitar heroes to play for Dave. Jason Becker, one of the little-known guitarists in Cacophony (Marty Friedman, later of Megadeth, was the other), sent in a demo tape that included "Hot for Teacher," "Skyscraper," and "Panama." He was asked to audition in person. He performed "Hot for Teacher," "Panama," "Just a Gigolo," "Yankee Rose," as well as some new songs and won the nod to fill the slot.

At first Dave and the band stayed at a luxury hotel while recording in Vancouver, British Columbia. However, when he noticed how other bands staying at the same hotel were being pampered, Dave insisted that his band stay at the worst hotel possible while recording the album (Dave's room cost $15 per night). Dave felt that it would give the album a harder edge.

The original name of the album was Cut 'n Out, but some thought the artwork on the cover, a devil with scissors positioned in a precarious way, was a little too suggestive. Bob Rock produced the album after having just completed Metallica's self-titled album. The album was recorded at Little Mountain Studios where AC/DC was recording next door with producer Bruce Fairbairn. Angus Young inspired at least one solo, on the song "Last Call." Jason was asked to contribute any new material he had written, so he presented "Drop in the Bucket" and "It's Showtime!" which ended the album.

Rob Nevil (Nevil Brothers) and Craig Goldy (Dio) were also used as songwriters on the album. Steve Hunter, referred to Roth by Becker, was brought in to play slide guitar.

Dave built huge climbing walls in the studio so he could enjoy his rock climbing hobby while working on the album.

Shortly after recording the album, Jason Becker's health took a turn for the worse as a result of ALS. Though he had been experiencing symptoms before the recording of the album, the symptoms got worse and he could not to tour with Dave.

The year 1991 was a notorious one for bad concert turnouts. Dave suffered from this. Even though his show offered Extreme and Cinderella as opening acts, it wasn't enough, and ticket prices were slashed. Eventually, the tour was cut short.

Videos from this album included "A Lil' Ain't Enough," "Sensible Shoes," and "Tell the Truth." Dave really went all out for the first video, "A Lil' Ain't Enough." It featured close to 90 women (in various states of undress), eight little people, a huge wall of Marshall amps (later recreated on the tour), and a remix of the song.

Dave once commented that much of the video's script was improvised, including his idea of filming himself being massaged by five Asian women. Soon after the video's debut, Dave hosted a segment on MTV wearing the same high suspenders shown in the video.

Dave also commented about the ending of the video, which shows him on October 10, 2021 during his final tour. He is shown as an old, fat, spandex-clad cowboy. According to Roth this is not what he expects of himself, but what others expect of him-to die like Elvis.

The video for "Sensible Shoes" was much more low-key. It was filmed entirely in black and white and included only a few of Dave's trademark women. The women in this video were later featured in a cable special about how women are portrayed in rock videos.

The video for "Tell the Truth" featured live footage from the 1991 *A Little Ain't Enough* tour. It was also filmed entirely in black and white. This is the only video from this album in which other members of the band are shown.

The tour featured Joe Holmes (who later went on to replace Zakk Wylde in Ozzy Osbourne) and Dezi Rexx of D'Molls fame. Rexx was fired shortly after the tour began. He never stated why he was fired but later teamed with Danny Johnson of Private Life (who replaced Steve Vai in Alcatrazz) to work on a demo produced by Andy Johns (who had just finished producing Van Halen's *F.U.C.K.* album).

A Little Ain't Enough singles/promos
"A Lil' Ain't Enough" (promo), WB PRO-CD-4622, CD, USA, 1991.

"Tell the Truth," "Tell the Truth" (blues remix), WB, CD, USA, 1991.

"Tell the Truth" (edit), "Tell the Truth," WB PRO-CD-4868, CD, USA, 1991.

"A Lil' Ain't Enough," "Baby's on Fire," WB, France, 1991.

"A Lil' Ain't Enough," WEA, 12" Vinyl, UK, 1991.

"A Lil' Ain't Enough," "Tell the Truth" (blues remix), WEA 7599-21842-2, CD, Germany, 1991.

"Tell the Truth (Blues Remix)" features vocals that have been stripped and replaced with quotations from the movie *Crossroads* (Columbia Pictures, 1986), which features guitar work by Steve Vai.

Little Dreamer-(*Van Halen* [3:22]) When this song was dcmoed for Van Halen, David Lee Roth ended the song by asking, "Are you experienced?"

Little Guitars-1. (*Diver Down* [3:47]) Ed recorded this song using his original red, white, and black-striped Charvel "Franky" and a miniature Gibson Les Paul copy hand-built by Dave Petschulat. Effects included a

Roland Chorus/Echo unit. The lyrics were inspired by the acoustic intro. David Lee Roth felt the piece had a Mexican flavor in it, so he wrote "Little Guitars" for a senorita. The line "Can't crow before I'm out of the woods, but there's exceptions to the rule" is an American saying that's been in use for many decades. Its basic meaning is that a crow flying through the forest won't make any noise; otherwise it will draw attention to itself and could get eaten. It will wait until it's out in the open before crowing, but there are exceptions to this rule.

2. (Shrapnel, 9/19/00) Tribute album featuring rock stars that have been influenced by Van Halen. Tracks include: "Unchained" by Jack Russell, Dweezil Zappa, Marco Mendoza, and Eric Singer; "I'm the One" by Mark Slaughter, Doug Aldrich, Tim Bogart, and Frankie Banali; "Dance the Night Away" by Joe Lynn Turner, Reb Beach, Marco Mendoza, and Gregg Bissonette; "Light Up the Sky" by Doug Pinnick, Yngwie Malmsteen, Billy Sheehan, and Vinnie Colaiuta; "Panama" by Jani Lane, George Lynch, Tony Franklin, and Gregg Bissonette; "Hot for Teacher" by John Corabi, Bruce Kulick, Tony Franklin, and Gregg Bissonette; "Runnin' with the Devil" by Stephen Pearcy, Jake E. Lee, Tim Bogart, and Frankie Banali; "Pretty Woman" by Gunner Nelson, Matt Nelson, Albert Lee, Tony Levin, and Aynsley Dunbar; "Atomic Punk" by Fee Waybill, Brad Gillis, Tim Bogart, and Frankie Banali; "So This Is Love?" by Jeff Scott Soto, Blues Saraceno, Tony Franklin, and Eric Singer; "Little Guitars" by David Glen Eisely, Mitch Perry, Marco Mendoza, and Eric Singer.

This album was also released as *Tribute to Van Halen 2000*. Remixes of these songs can be found on *Hot for Remixes: A Tribute to Van Halen*.

Little Guitars (intro)-(*Diver Down* [:42]) This instrumental was played on a nylon string guitar much as was "Spanish Fly." Ed remembers being very frustrated trying to write this piece. It was a prime example of his hearing something in his head that he was unable (at first) to transfer to the guitar. Amazingly, the piece has no overdubs. The tremolo-picked sequence (a classical technique called "frailing") involves Eddie tremolo-picking the high E, B, and D strings (open), while performing hammer-ons and pull-offs on the low E string with his left hand.

Live-Sammy Hagar was interviewed in the August 1997 issue of this magazine. Van Halen was interviewed in the July 1998 issue.

Live for the Music-This Bad Company cover was performed by the band on 9/18/76 at The Bogart in San Bernardino, CA.

Live 1980-(Capitol C2-48432, 1983) Sammy Hagar solo album. Tracks: • Twentieth Century Man • Trans Am (Highway Wonderland) • Plain Jane • Love or Money • This Planet's on Fire (Burn in Hell) • In the Night (Entering the Danger Zone) • Space Station #5 • The Danger Zone

Live: Right Here, Right Now-(Warner Bros. 45198) Released on 1/23/93, this album has sold 2.5 million copies in the U.S. It was certified gold and platinum on 5/04/93 and double platinum on 9/20/93. The home video *Live: Right Here, Right Now* (Warner Reprise Video 38290-3) was released on 1/23/93. The video was released on laserdisc (Reprise 38290-6). The DVD version was released on 6/08/99. "There's Only One Way to Rock" is titled "One Way to Rock" for this album.

Most of this album was recorded on 5/14/92 and 5/15/92 at Selland Arena in Fresno, CA, though some songs may have been recorded during earlier tours. At first only a live video had been planned. Westwood One radio network recorded the audio for both shows to be used in a broadcast from the Cabo Wabo Cantina on 8/20/92. The recordings were mixed by Ed, Alex, and Jon Ostrin at 5150.

The broadcast became known as the Cabo Wabo Radio Festival and included interviews with Sammy Hagar and Michael Anthony. Sammy and Mike also led a jam session during the broadcast with Bret Michaels (Poison), Richie Kotzen (Poison), David Lauser, and Craig Chaquico (Big

Bad Wolf, Starship). When the Fresno recordings were aired, the fan response was very positive. The recordings sounded much warmer and fuller than past live recordings the band had made. Encouraged by the reaction of the fans, the band decided to release the recordings as a live album. The album would also give the band an excuse to tour Europe without releasing a new studio album. The release date of the video was pushed back to coincide with the album.

Andy Johns was brought into the studio to mix the final album tracks, which consisted mostly of the songs from the Fresno show. The final mix differed from what was heard on Westwood One.

Europe was bombarded with Van Halen ads on television, in posters, in magazines, and even on the subway. A special package for those who bought the first pressing of the video included a replica backstage pass and an extra video that included interviews and live footage from the 5150 Studio. (see "Inside 5150 Studio" entry)

Some fans were quick to criticize both the album and the live video due to the video's hectic editing and the album's crowd noise and over-polished sound.

Live: Right Here, Right Now singles/promos
"Dreams" (live), "Dreams" (edit) (promo), WB PRO-CD-6158, CD, USA, 1993.

"Dreams" (promo), "Judgement Day," "Ain't Talkin' 'Bout Love," "There's Only One Way to Rock," "Right Now," WB PRO-CD-6154, CD, USA, 1993.

"Won't Get Fooled Again," WB PRO-CD-5961, CD, USA, 1993.

"Jump" (live), "Love Walks In" (live), "Mine All Mine" (live and previously unreleased), "Eagles Fly" (live), WEA 9362-40771-2, CD, WEA

9362-40772-2, CD with pick and poster, WEA 9362-40796-2, CD in thin, silver case with backstage pass, Germany, 1993.

"Jump" (live), "Love Walks In" (live), "Mine All Mine" (live), "Eagles Fly" (live), WEA WO155CDX, CD in silver tin, UK, 1993. Includes backstage pass.

"Dreams" (live/edit), "Judgement Day" (live), WB 9 18592, 7" Vinyl, Cassette, and CD, USA, 1993.

"Dreams" (live/edit), "Right Now" (live), "One Way to Rock" (live), "Dreams," WEA 9362-40941-2, CD, Germany, 1993.

"Jump" (edit), WEA, 3/13/93.

"Jump" (live), "Love Walks In" (live), WEA W0155/5439-18594-7, 7" Vinyl, Germany.

Live-Very Live in Concert-(Capitol CDL-57245, 1989) (51:37) Sammy Hagar solo album. Tracks: • I've Done Everything for You • Red • Rock and Roll Weekend • Make It Last/Reckless • Turn Up the Music • Bad Motor Scooter • Love or Money • Plain Jane • Twentieth Century Man • The Danger Zone • Space Station #5

Live without a Net-(Warner Home Video 3-38129) This live concert video was filmed on 8/27/86 at Veterans Memorial Coliseum in New Haven, CT. The band wanted their fans' first visual experience with new singer Sammy Hagar to be in concert instead of through MTV. This video was the best of both worlds. MTV used parts of the video for individual videos for songs from the *5150* album.

The video was released on 11/24/86. It was certified gold on 12/22/86, platinum on 2/25/87, and double platinum on 1/23/90. Tracks: • There's

Only One Way to Rock • Summer Nights • Get Up • Drum Solo • "5150" o Best of Both Worlds o Bass Solo o Panama o Love Walks In o Guitar Solo o I Can't Drive 55 o Ain't Talkin' 'Bout Love • Why Can't This Be Love? • Rock and Roll

Looking Back-(Geffen 9241271, 1987) Sammy Hagar solo album. Tracks: • I'll Fall in Love Again • There's Only One Way to Rock • Heavy Metal • Remember the Heroes • Baby's on Fire • Three Lock Box • Two Sides of Love • I Can't Drive 55 • I Don't Need Love • VOA

Looney Tunes Promo-(Warner Bros. Pro-705, 1978) This Van Halen promotional album, pressed on red vinyl, is known as the Looney Tunes Promo because the label on side A features a picture of Elmer Fudd with the words "Looney Tunes" over his head. The words "Merrie Melodies" appear beneath him (a similar logo can be seen in many Warner Brothers cartoons). A similar release with Porky Pig in place of Fudd is also rumored to exist. The black album jacket and side B label both feature the first incarnation of the Van Halen logo: the words "Van Halen" under-lined and sporting short lightning-bolt appendages on the "A" letters (created by Alex).

The album itself was given out at promotional parties sponsored by Warner Brothers and was sent to radio stations, magazines, etc. At the pro-motional parties, guests were handed a bag of promotional goodies as they walked in the door, and this was one such item included in the bags in early 1978. Tracks: Side A: Runnin' with the Devil • Eruption • Ice Cream Man; Side B: You Really Got Me • Jamie's Cryin'

Los Endos-This Genesis cover was performed by Alex Van Halen on 10/20/88 at the Richmond Coliseum in Richmond, VA, as part of his drum solo.

Loss of Control-(*Women and Children First* [2:36]) Originally written around the same time as "Ain't Talkin' 'Bout Love," this song pokes fun at the punk rock scene.

The video for this song (which was never commercially released) features the band in surgical outfits.

Los Tres Gusanos-(English translation: "The Three Worms") This was a side project band made up of Sammy Hagar, Michael Anthony, and David Lauser. Others would occasionally join the band on stage during performances. This band was always meant to be a fun outlet from Van Halen's usual huge productions. The band performed mainly at Cabo Wabo, even releasing a video for their Sammy Hagar birthday performance in 1995. Their set lists consisted primarily of Sammy Hagar solo tunes, with a handful of Montrose and similar classic rock songs. Show dates at the Cabo Wabo Cantina: 2/25/92, 5/20/92 (The Beach Boys and Spryo Gyra's Grover Washington, Jr. were in town during the gig). 8/18/92, 8/19/92, 8/20/92 (Cabo Wabo Rock Radio Festival), 10/18/95, 10/19/95, 10/11/96-This was Sammy's first appearance with Los Tres Gusanos following his departure from Van Halen and was the first performance of his scheduled three-day annual birthday bash engagement at his Cabo Wabo Cantina. Robert Berry took the place of Michael Anthony on bass. Sammy debuted a new oversized Washburn acoustic/electric prototype guitar that was flown into Cabo San Lucas the day of the show, a birthday present from Washburn.

Guns 'n' Roses drummer Matt Sorum sat in on the gig, performing a drum solo and the remaining tunes of the set. An over excited fan also managed to sneak his way on stage to praise the Red Rocker, and Hagar handed him the microphone, letting him sing a couple of lines of "Roadhouse Blues."

10/12/96-The second night of the 1996 birthday bash was supposed to be a free, unplugged gig, and it almost was. Hagar spent most of the evening on an acoustic/electric, while Berry and guest guitarist Damon Johnson (Brother Cane) both played solid-body electrics.

Loren Adams, the man who coined the phrase "What is understood, need not be discussed" (seen on the *Live: Right Here, Right Now* album cover and quoted by Sammy numerous times), opened the evening with three instrumental accordion pieces: "Charge of the Light Brigade," "A Christmas Song," and "Someday." Adams also opened the festivities for Van Halen at the Cantina's grand opening on May 20, 1990.

10/13/96-The final gig of the birthday bash and also the most jam-packed, for this was the evening of Hagar's 49th birthday, and he was determined to do it up right. The set began with the packed house singing "Happy Birthday" as the Red Rocker took the stage.

Damon Johnson took over lead vocal duties at one point, serving up a tasty version of the Lynard Skynard classic "Sweet Home Alabama," and Matt Sorum once again showed off his tremendous drumming skills as he pounded the skins for the set's grand finale.

Other show dates:

3/04/94 Trocadero Club, San Francisco, CA

Opening Act: Craig Chaquico

Starship's Craig Chaquico not only opened, but also sat in on a couple of songs with Los Tres Gusanos at this gig.

1/12/96 Hard Rock Café, Universal City, CA

Billed as the first U.S. performance of Los Tres Gusanos, Sammy, Michael, and David Lauser took part in the grand opening festivities of this Hard Rock Café at the Universal Citywalk. In actuality, however, the first known U.S. performance of the Gusanos took place at the aforementioned Trocadero Club.

The ceremony began with a parade featuring the Los Angeles All-City Marching Band and 1,000 music students, each playing a Washburn guitar. The axes were donated by the Hard Rock Café to the National Academy of Recording Arts & Sciences Foundation's Grammy in the Schools' program.

The Gusanos then took the stage, where Hagar led the students in a giant guitar lesson before ripping into the first song of their short set, "I Can't Drive 55."

Sammy and Michael each donated an autographed guitar to be displayed. Other Van Halen items at the establishment include a bass drum and several platinum record awards.

Loud & Clear-(Capitol 25330, 1980) Sammy Hagar solo album. Tracks: • Rock and Roll Weekend • Make It Last • Reckless • Turn Up the Music • I've Done Everything for You • Young Girl Blues • Bad Motor Scooter • Space Station #5

The Love-This unreleased original was a song Sammy used for his solo on the *Right Here, Right Now* tour. It was debuted at the World Theater in Tinley Park, IL, on 7/30/93 and was later performed at the Cal Expo Amphitheater in Sacramento, CA, on 8/22/93.

The Love Book-The November 1984 issue of this magazine featured Eddie Van Halen on the cover. Articles included "Eddie and Val: Is Rock Ruining Their Romance?" a two-page Edward and Valerie feature with an Edward and Valerie pinup, and "David Lee Roth Exposed!" a one-page feature with David Lee Roth pinup. Address: 105 Union Avenue, Cresskill, NJ 07626.

Love Machine-What a national newspaper once nicknamed Edward in the early 1980s.

Love Walks In-(*5150* [5:09]) Sammy's lyrics for this song were inspired after reading "Aliens among Us" by Ruth Montgomery (reprint edition: Fawcett Books, 1993).

Mike used an Apostrophe 5-string bass on this track.

Lucille-(2:51) This Little Richard cover was performed by the band on 5/05/81 at the Civic Center in Providence, RI.

Lukather, Steve-Ace session guitarist, guitarist for the band Toto, and good friend to Eddie Van Halen. Lukather teamed up with Eddie to produce Steve's first solo album, *Lukather* (Columbia 465657-2, 1989). Eddie performed on the song "Twist the Knife," which was a reworking of the song Eddie performed during his Saturday Night Live performance, "Stompin' 8H."

Other musicians on the album included the members of Steve's side project, Los Lobotomies: David Garfield on keyboards, John Pena on bass, Lenny Castro and Chris Truillo handling percussion, and Simon Phillips on drums.

Steve has stated in an interview that he sang background vocals on the Hagar-era Van Halen albums.

LUVHUBBY-What the personalized license plates of Valerie Bertinelli's black Mercedes Benz once read.

M

Mach 1, 2, and 3-Terms denoting the three main eras of Van Halen: Dave, Sammy, and Gary. The terms may come from the movie *This Is Spinal Tap*, in which the term "Mach 2" was used in a similar way. "Mach 3" (or "III") was coined in 1996 by The Inside magazine and was even suggested as the title for the band's new album, which was later named *Van Halen III*.

Mad Anthony's Café-A small tent, strung with colored Christmas lights, located on Michael Anthony's side of the stage (backstage) complete with wet bar, featuring an unlimited supply of Jack Daniels, that the bassist uses when he's on a "break." It was originally started by bass tech Craig DeFalco and was used by Michael and the road crew during Ed's guitar solo. At one time it was known simply as "The Anthony Bar."

Make It Last-Van Halen performed this Montrose cover on several occasions during the *5150* tour.

Malibu Beach-The name of former guitar tech Zeke Clark's stage pit on the *5150* tour. This is where Zeke monitored each night's performance and provided maintenance on Edward's guitars while on the road. Roughly 14 guitars were kept here each night as backups for Ed's three main stage guitars (the 5150 Kramer, the 1984 Kramer, and a Steinberger GL2-T), as well as an effects rack that was designed by Clark, Bob Bradshaw, and Andy Brauer.

Mammoth-Van Halen's original name. When Mammoth was formed, David Lee Roth and Michael Anthony had yet to join the band. Eddie acted as both lead singer and guitarist, Alex was the drummer, and Mark Stone was the bass player. A year after the band formed, David Lee Roth was hired as the lead singer. Two years after the band's forming, Mark Stone was fired and Michael Anothony was hired as the bass player. Shortly after Mike joined, the band changed their name to Van Halen (Roth's idea, after rejecting Edward's idea, Rat Salad).

Man on a Mission-(*For Unlawful Carnal Knowledge* [5:04]; *Live: Right Here, Right Now* [4:49]) This song was developed from a riff Ed had come up with on a bass. The riff itself begins the song and also appears just before the guitar solo. Ed used a prototype Peavey 5150 amplifier on this track and Mike used his 1964 Fender Jazz bass.

Man on the Silver Mountain-This Rainbow cover was performed by the band in their club days.

Marching to Mars-(Track Factory TRKD-11627, 1997) Sammy Hagar's first album after splitting from Van Halen was recorded at the Record Plant Recording Studios in Sausalito, CA, and Studio X, CA. Hagar financed the album himself at a cost of $480,000 so that record companies wouldn't have an influence on the recording process. Sammy then shopped for a label when he felt the album was ready. In June 1997, only one month after the fledgling label released this album, the Track Factory terminated its joint venture with MCA/Universal, and Hagar was subsequently picked up by MCA. The album was released on 5/20/97 and entered the charts on 5/26/97, peaking at #18.

"Little White Lie" featured the Grateful Dead's Mickey Hart on drums, Roy Rogers on slide guitar and dobro, Huey Lewis on harmonica and Guns 'n' Roses' Slash (who recorded his parts on 2/22/97) on guitar duties with Sammy.

"Salvation on Sand Hill" featured Brother Cane's Damon Johnson on rhythm guitar (he also cowrote the song).

"Who Has the Right?" was written by Hagar, Jesse Harms, and ex-Starship guitarist Craig Chaquico. Mr. Big's Eric Martin, along with Starship vocalist Mickey Thomas, helped lay down background vocals.

"Would You Do It for Free?" featured funk bass master Bootsy Collins.

"Leaving the Warmth of the Womb" was performed entirely by Hagar, Carmassi, bassist Bill Church, and guitarist Ronnie Montrose, marking the first time the original members of Montrose had recorded together since Hagar left that band to pursue a solo career in 1975.

"Kama" features Guns 'n' Roses drummer Matt Sorum, Mike Landau on guitars, and Thomas, Harms, Hagar, and his son, Aaron on background vocals.

"On the Other Hand" featured another appearance by Damon Johnson, this time on acoustic and slide guitars, along with Hart and Giovanni Hidalgo on percussion.

"Both Sides Now" was cowritten by Hagar and Harms and featured Hidalgo, Hart, and Luis Conte on percussion.

"Marching to Mars" was cowritten by Hagar and Hart (who also provided sequencing), percussion was handled by Hildalgo and Hart, and background vocals were done by Arnie's Army, Derrek Hawkins, Harley Dinardo, Dave Cartategui, and Sammy's wife, Kari.

The cover art, which featured a pair of flaming boots on the front, the planet Mars on the back, and an overall red motif, had special significance. It was designed to symbolize the return of the Red Rocker.

The number 13 that appears in the liner notes stands for Sammy's 13th solo album, not including the best-of compilations released by Capitol records (Unboxed was counted because it had two new songs).

The Japanese release of this album featured two additional tracks: an instrumental entitled "Ether" and "Wash Me Down."

The Japanese single for "Little White Lie" featured a live, in-studio version of "Rock Candy" recorded by the briefly reformed Montrose. Tracks: • Little White Lie • Salvation on Sand Hill • Who Has the Right? • Would You Do It for Free? • Leaving the Warmth of the Womb • Kama • On the

Other Hand • Both Sides Now • The Yogi's So High (I'm Stoned) • Amnesty Is Granted • Marching to Mars

Marching to Mars singles/promos
"Little White Lie" (promo), Track Factory TRK5P-3964, CD, USA, 4/23/97.

"Marching to Mars" (radio edit), "Marching to Mars" (album version), Track Factory TRK5P-4011, CD, USA, 1997.

"Little White Lie," "Rock Candy," Track Factory MVCE 9002, CD, Japan, 1997.

"Little White Lie," Track Factory GRK5P-3964, 7" Vinyl, 1997.

"Both Sides Now" (radio edit), "Both Sides Now" (album version), Track Factory TRK5P-90091, CD, USA, 1997.

Martin, Dan-Guitar collector and historian who owns St. Charles Guitar Exchange in St. Charles, MO. Martin regularly supplies Edward with vintage guitars, basses, and amplifiers and has been doing so since July 1982.

Maximum Guitar-In the July 1997 issue of this magazine, Sammy Hagar appeared on the cover for a feature on his *Marching to Mars* album entitled "Red Storm Rising" by David Huff. Parts of "You Really Got Me" and "Unchained" are transcribed. In the September 1997 issue, Sammy Hagar's "Little White Lie" is transcribed. Address: Harris Publications, Inc, 1115 Broadway, New York, NY 10010.

Maybe I'm a Leo-The band performed this Deep Purple song, from the album *Machine Head* (Warner Brothers 2607, 1972), in their club days. A recording of a performance in 1974 has been circulating.

May, Brian-On 4/21/83 and 4/22/83, Eddie Van Halen joined Brian May, Fred Mandel, Alan Gratzer, and Phil Chen in an informal jam session that would later become a three-track mini-LP titled *Brian May and Friends: Star Fleet Project* (EMI MLP-15014, 1983). The album entered the charts on 11/19/83 and lasted for nine weeks, reaching its highest chart position at #125 (U.S.) and #35 (U.K.). Tracks: • Star Fleet (8:02) • Let Me Out (7:15) • Blues Breaker (12:53)

"Star Fleet" was released as a single with "Son of Star Fleet" (4:24), a shortened instrumental version, as a B-side. The single reached its highest chart position at #65 (U.K.).

All three tracks were included on a Brian May two-CD set released in 1992 entitled *Back to the Light* (Parlophone 8 80381 2 6). The first CD contained "Blues Breaker" along with two other May solo cuts, and the second CD (sold separately) included the other two tracks with an additional May solo cut.

All three tracks were also included on Brian May's *Resurrection* album. This album includes five other May tracks and is out of print, though The Inside magazine stocks the CD in its merchandise catalog.

The project was initially inspired by a science fiction show Brian May's son, Jimmy May, was watching on Central TV in England. Brian was inspired by the ending of the show's theme song, written by Paul Bliss. He decided to make a rock version of the song.

"Star Fleet" was recorded on the first day and "Let Me Out" and "Blues Breaker" were recorded on the second day. "Blues Breaker" was inspired by Eddie and Brian's love of Eric Clapton and John Mayall's *Blues Breakers* album (London LC 500009). Ed used his Franky and a Marshall amp to record his parts.

Originally, the recordings were never meant to be released. However, upon securing permission from Ed, Brian released the songs on 10/31/83. Some collectors claim to have copies of the mini-LP that vary in design and color.

MDA Telethon-Edward made an appearance on the 31st Annual Jerry Lewis "Stars Across America" Muscular Distrophy Association (MDA) Labor Day Telethon in support of Jason Becker, who is suffering from amyotrophic lateral sclerosis (Lou Gehrig's disease), also known as "ALS." The telethon was taped at CBS Television City in Hollywood, CA, and aired on 9/01/96 and 9/02/96. Edward's segment was taped in Richmond, CA, on 8/31/96.

Becker, the one-time guitarist for David Lee Roth, played guitar on *A Little Ain't Enough* but was forced to pull out of the supporting tour when he was diagnosed with the disease shortly before the tour began.

It was with Becker, who has lost almost all muscular control and is now confined to his bed, that Edward made a heart-wrenching plea to help find a cure for ALS by donating to MDA.

Jason's fight with ALS began one night in May 1989 when he was awakened from sleep with an intense cramp in his left calf. He'd had cramps in the past, but this one stayed with him the remainder of the night. Upon getting out of the bed the following morning, he noticed that his calf felt tired and lazy.

Shortly thereafter he toured Japan with his band Cacophony, comprised of himself and fellow virtuoso Marty Friedman, who now holds down the lead guitarist slot in Megadeth.

Cacophony released two albums: 1987's *Speed Metal Symphony* (Shrapnel SH-1031) and 1988's *Go Off!* (Shrapnel SH-1040) before parting ways. Following the tour, Jason left Cacophony to concentrate on his own music. All the while the lazy feeling in his left leg remained.

Jason's first solo effort after the disbanding of Cacophony was entitled *Perpetual Burn* (Shrapnel SH-1036).

In November 1989 the guitarist moved from Richmond, CA, to Los Angeles to record with Roth. It was then that he went to see a doctor about his calf.

After a series of tests, it was determined that he had ALS. Jason pressed on, undaunted and enjoying the dream he was living: writing and recording with Diamond Dave. His condition was worsening, but he didn't give up.

By March 1990, while in Vancouver to record for *A Little Ain't Enough*, Jason was taking 100 vitamins each day and was getting a shot of B-12 in his leg, administered by Steve Hunter, who played rhythm and slide guitar on the album. Later that year, by then walking with a cane and growing increasingly tired, Jason, knowing he wouldn't be in any shape to tour, returned to Richmond.

In January 1991 Jason recorded a cover version of the Bob Dylan classic "Meet Me in the Morning" for Guitar Recordings with Steve Hunter, Brett Tuggle, and Matt and Greg Bissonette.

By June 1991 Jason was using two canes and walking very slowly. It was around this time that a friend of his (Mike Bemesderfer) introduced the guitarist to a computer, making it possible for Becker to still create music (he was by then unable to play his guitar without intense physical pain). In late summer Jason reluctantly began using a wheelchair.

Becker composed his second album entirely on computer, completing it in October 1991. He recorded almost all of it with his right hand only (he had lost the use of his left hand and arm). Entitled *Perspective*, the album features three symphonic pieces with a full orchestra of almost 100 violins, cellos, brass, woodwinds, bells, harp, and piano. There are also appearances by the Bissonette brothers and Steve Perry. Shrapnel artist Michael Lee Firkins recreated some of Jason's parts on the album, which also included portions of earlier material recorded by Jason himself.

Perspective (JB Music) was released in 1996, and Jason feels it's the best thing he's ever written or recorded.

MDA is the world's leading voluntary health agency, sponsoring neuromuscular disease research. They support hundreds of research projects at universities and medical centers throughout the U.S. and abroad, seeking the causes of, and treatments for, 40 neuromuscular diseases. The 1996 telethon raised $49,146,555.

Mean Street-(*Fair Warning* [4:55]) This song was originally called "Voodoo Queen" and had completely different lyrics. The song in its original format can be found on the band's 1977 Warner Brothers demo.

Parts of this song were sampled in the song "Stomp" on the 1996 *Foundations Forum Sampler CD*.

Dream Theater covered this song on a limited edition outtakes CD, released by drummer Mike Portnoy as a Christmas 1998 gift to their fan club.

Niacin, a group that includes Billy Sheehan and Steve Lukather, covered this song on their album *Deep* (Magna Carta, 2000).

Meatloaf-"Amnesty Is Granted," a song Sammy Hagar wrote and often played on tour with Van Halen, eventually found its way on to Meatloaf's *Welcome to the Neighborhood* album (MCA MCAD-11341, 1995). The song (6:09) was recorded in New York, with Sammy co-producing, playing guitar, and singing background vocals.

M.E.R. 3rd Anniversary Concert-Eddie Van Halen took part in this concert sponsored by the Malibu Emergency Room, on 5/12/85 in Malibu, CA, that also featured performances by the Beach Boys' Brian Wilson, Private Life and Crosby, Stills & Nash veteran Stephen Stills. Edward performed "Born in East L.A." and "Wild Thing" with comedian Cheech Marin (of Cheech and Chong). The two were introduced by Valerie Bertinelli. Ed also played an early version of "Summer Nights" during soundcheck.

Metal Edge-This magazine's index of Van Halen-related issues:

5/86: Van Halen cover. "The New Van Halen Revamped, Revitalized and Ready to Rock": three-page Van Halen interview by Gerri Miller. "David Lee Roth Makes a Crazy Movie": one-page feature on Dave's casting call for *Crazy from the Heat* by Gerri Miller.

6/93: Extreme cover. "Backstage Interview: Extreme Rocks New York": four-page Extreme interview by Gerri Miller. "Eddie Van Halen on the Record": four-page interview with Edward by Gerri Miller.

9/94: Eddie Van Halen/Alex Van Halen cover. "Van Halen on the Golf Course and on Stage for Charity": three-page feature on the Edward Van Halen 1994 Charity Golf Tournament by Gerri Miller.

3/95: Extreme cover.

4/95: Van Halen cover.

5/95: Extreme cover.

8/95: Van Halen cover. "Van Halen Rocks L.A.": nine-page feature by Gerri Miller.

9/95: Eddie Van Halen on cover.

10/95: Van Halen cover.

11/95: Van Halen cover.

2/96: Van Halen cover. "Van Halen Live and Backstage": six-page photo and commentary feature by Gerri Miller.

5/96: "Metal Wire": short feature on New Year's Cabo Wabo gig. "Rockin' at the Hard Rock with Sammy Hagar and Michael Anthony": two-page feature on Los Tres Gusanos gig at Universal City, CA, Hard Rock Café. Edward pinup.

6/96: Van Halen cover.

11/86: Van Halen cover. "Van Halen Shakes Up!": five-page feature on breakup by Gerri Miller. "Ray Danniels: Counterpoint": one-page reprint of Ray Danniels interview with Pollstar.

12/96: Van Halen cover and feature.

1/97: Van Halen cover. "Van Halen Giveaway": one-page feature on *Best of Volume 1* giveaway. "MTV Video Music Awards": feature on Van

Halen with Dave at awards by Gerri Miller. "Voice of Metal": short features on Dave and Sammy by Gerri Miller.

2/97: Van Halen cover and feature.

3/97: Van Halen cover. "1996 Year in Review": one-page feature on reconciliation with David Lee Rot; one-page feature on breakup of Extreme. "Sammy Hagar Rockin' in Cabo and on the Record": three-page feature on Sammy in Cabo San Lucas, Mexico, and news about new solo album by Gerri Miller.

1997: Sammy Hagar's *Marching to Mars* reviewed.

1997: Sammy at Cabo Wabo feature.

1/98: Sammy Hagar cover and feature.

4/98: Van Halen cover. Three-page Gary interview by Gerri Miller and Paul Gargano. Van Halen centerfold. Short David Lee Roth write-up.

5/98: Eddie, Alex, and Mike interviewed.

2/99: David Lee Roth featured in the Rockin' Roundup section.

Address: Sterling/Macfadden Partnership, 233 Park Avenue S., New York, NY 10003.

Metal Hall of Fame-In 1986 Van Halen appeared on the cover of this magazine which included a five-page interview by Dave DiMartino entitled "Give Us Van Halen."

Metal Hammer-This German magazine's index of Van Halen-related issues:

4/92: "Van Halen & Baby Animals Road Report": four-page Van Halen and Baby Animals live feature. 5150 amplifier review.

2/93: "F.U.C.K.in' Live!": four-page Van Halen live feature. "Besucht Van Halen Im Proberaum!": one-page Van Halen giveaway.

3/93: Van Halen cover. "Live at Last!": four-page Van Halen feature. Van Halen tour dates. *Live: Right Here, Right Now* album and video reviewed.

1/95: Van Halen cover. "Back, Bearded, and Blastin'": Van Halen interview by Paul Suter. "Hittin' the Road": live report. "Van Video": short video report. "The James Brown Connection": short feature on James Brown opening for Van Halen on the *5150* tour.

3/98: Van Halen appeared on the cover of the Spanish version of Metal Hammer.

Metal Hotline-Van Halen appeared on the cover of the September 1986 issue of this magazine, which featured a three-page interview with the band by Jill Rosenberg entitled "Van Halen Back on Patrol." Address: Charlton Building, Derby, CT 06418.

Metal Letters-Van Halen appeared on a 1986 cover of this magazine, which published a collection of readers' letters about the band entitled "Van Halen: Old vs. New."

Me Wise Magic-(*Best of Volume 1* [6:05]) This was the first song that Dave recorded when he reunited with the band in 1996. At first Dave didn't want to sing it, but changed his mind after reviewing the rest of the prepared songs. Recording ran from 7/22/96 to 8/02/96, and mixing took place on 8/05/96.

Edward used a prototype Wolfgang on this song, outfitted with a Transtrem tremolo (a standard feature of the Steinberger guitar). He also used the Fernandes Sustainer on the end of the track.

The title was taken from a racehorse of the same name.

Though videos were scheduled for both new songs from *Best of Volume 1*, only the one for "Me Wise Magic" was actually started, but it was scrapped shortly thereafter. It was a concept video that involved voodoo rituals.

The song was leaked to radio stations on 10/03/96 and officially released to radio on 10/07/96, four days after David Lee Roth's open letter to the public condemning the reunion.

Midnight Special-Montrose performed "Paper Money" and "I Got the Fire" on this mid-1970s television show.

Might Just Take Your Life-This Edgar Winter cover was reportedly played by the band in their early years.

Mighty Morphin Power Rangers: The Movie-The Van Halen song "Dreams" appears in both this movie (20th Century Fox, 1995) and the movie's soundtrack (Fox Records/Atlantic 82777-2, 1995).

The soundtrack consisted almost entirely of prerecorded songs from various artists including the Red Hot Chili Peppers, Devo, and They Might Be Giants.

Mighty Van Halen Jr.-A New England Van Halen cover band.

Mine All Mine-(*OU812* [5:11]) This is an antidrug song and was the second song written for the album. It is about fulfilling your future without letting drugs get in the way.

The track was recorded on a Roland D-50 with a Yamaha TXC-816 rack through a Roland MC-500 sequencer. Ed sequenced the keyboard parts, and Alex overdubbed the drums to it. Mike then overdubbed bass to those tracks, and the guitar and vocals were overdubbed on top of that.

Mission to Mars-"Dance the Night Away" was featured prominently in this film (Touchtone, 2000).

Mississippi Queen-This Mountain cover was performed by Van Halen several times throughout the *F.U.C.K.* tour. On 5/21/92 the song was played at the 2nd anniversary of the Cabo Wabo Cantina. On 8/25/95 ex-Mountain guitarist/lead singer Leslie West joined the band on stage at Jones Beach Theater in Wantaugh, NY, to perform the tune.

Modern Drummer-Alex Van Halen appeared on the cover of the 10/83 issue of this magazine. A nine-page interview with Alex Van Halen by Adam Budowsky was featured in its July 1993 issue.

Monitor-This Peavey Electronics publication's index of Van Halen-related issues:

1991: Volume 10, Issue 4. Edward cover. Nine-page Ed interview by Renee Young titled "The Edward Van Halen Legacy," and a one-page interview with Matt Bruck titled "The Peavey EVH 5150."

1995: Volume 5, Issue 1. Edward cover. "The Peavey/Edward Van Halen Connection: a Question of Balance": ten-page Edward interview and guitar feature by Jimmy Phillips. "A Symbiotic Relationship": three-page look at Edward and the 5150 amplifier by Hartley Peavey. Wolfgang guitar poster. One-page look at Ed's live rig. Two-page look at the making of a Wolfgang. "Alan Fitzgerald Van Halen's Man behind the Curtain": three-page interview and look at Fitz's live setup.

Address: Peavey Electronics Corp., Meridian, MS 39302-2898; Telephone: 601-483-5365.

Monkey Hour-When David Lee Roth was in the second grade, he was diagnosed as hyperactive. "Monkey Hour" was the term coined by his parents to describe his after-dinner time ranting and raving. Roth is well known for bragging that he turned "Monkey Hour" into a career.

Montrose-1. Sammy Hagar was the lead singer in this band formed by Ronnie Montrose in 1972. Sammy remained the singer for three years, completing two albums with the band before pursuing a solo career in 1975.

2. The band's first album, *Montrose* (Warner Bros. BSK 2740, 1973), was produced by Ted Templeman. The album spent twelve weeks on the charts, starting on 5/11/74 and reaching its highest position at #133. Tracks: • Rock the Nation • Bad Motor Scooter • Space Station #5 • I Don't Want It • Good Rockin' Tonight • Rock Candy • One Thing on My Mind • Make It Last

Monty-The name of a springer spaniel owned by Edward in the early 1980s.

Monty, Gil-Hollywood tattoo artist who tattooed the banner "Valerie" over a heart on Edward Van Halen's left shoulder.

Moving Violations-(20th Century Fox, 1985) Sammy Hagar's "I Can't Drive 55" appeared in this movie about the pratfalls and perils of driving, traffic tickets, and the police in general, starring John Murray II (brother of comedian Bill Murray), Jennifer Tilley, and Sally Kellerman.

Mr. Bookworm-The part David Lee Roth played in his very first school play.

MTV-MTV's records of Van Halen appearances are not at all organized; therefore, at this time there can only be an incomplete record on the band's past specials, concert, and news segments. With MTV's help, the following index of appearances was pieced together.

MTV Concerts
1983: Sammy Hagar live in St. Louis, MO.
3/25/95: "Spring Break Rocks" Pensacola, FL. Hour-long broadcast taped at the first gig of the *Balance* tour on 3/11/95. The broadcast also includes interviews with the band by Jon Stewart. Songs shown: • The Seventh Seal • Big Fat Money • Finish What Ya Started • Guitar Solo • Why Can't This Be Love? • Feelin' • Right Now • Dreams (Only the last half of this song was aired.)
5/01/98: Live from the 10 Spot episode. A one-hour concert special filmed on 4/20/98 at the Sydney Entertainment Centre in Sydney, Australia. Songs shown: • Unchained • Without You • One I Want • Mean Street • Why Can't This Be Love • Year to the Day • Ain't Talkin' 'Bout Love • Panama

MTV Interviews, Rockumentaries, and Specials

10/14/82: Martha Quinn interviews Dave.

5/29/83: Mark Goodman interviews Dave backstage at the Us Festival.

3/21/84: Lost Weekend with Van Halen.

1984: Martha Quinn interviews Dave.

1985: Martha Quinn interviews Ed and Val at the New York Hard Rock Cafe grand opening.

5/25/85-5/26/85   : "David Lee Roth Weekend"

1986: "Unleashed" with Kurt Loder. A one-hour special similar to a rockumentary.

8/21/86: David Lee Roth interview with video outtakes.

4/16/88-4/17/88: David Lee Roth Weekend.

6/11/88-6/12/88: Monsters of Rock Weekend.

7/29/89: Van Halen Rockumentary 1.

1990: Viva Van Halen Saturday, Cabo Wabo grand opening. Van Halen performs and Van Halen videos are shown.

1991: Gary Cherone and Nuno Bettencourt featured in New York's Central Park.

8/13/91: Martha Quinn interviews Gary and Nuno Bettencourt.

8/20/91: "We're with the Band: Backstage with Van Halen" Filmed at the Lakewood Amphitheater in Atlanta, GA on 8/16/91.

9/91: Feature on Extreme's Monica Goretsky benefit.

10/19/91: Van Halen Rockumentary 2.

10/20/91: "Famous Last Words": Kurt Loder interviews Van Halen.

1991: Paulie Shore interviews Edward at *Bill and Ted's Bogus Journey* premiere party.

2/12/92: Extreme featured in "Day in Rock."

6/27/92: Lonn Friend interviews Gary about *Extreme III: III Sides to Every Story.*

6/29/92: "Hangin' with MTV": Extreme featured in the studio in Ft. Lauderdale, FL.

10/14/92: Extreme interviewed for "Day in Rock" segment.

6/22/94: Euro-MTV Headbanger's Ball interviews Sammy Hagar for 15 minutes at the Kerrang Awards.

4/05/95: Van Halen is interviewed backstage.

6/11/95: Van Halen featured on MTV Europe.

6/27/96: Welcome Back Dave! commercial: montage of clips taken from a David Lee Roth live performance and the following videos: "Goin' Crazy," "Stand Up," "Just Like Paradise," "Panama," "Hot for Teacher," "Yankee Rose," "California Girls," "Jump," and "That's Life." The commercial was designed to welcome Dave back into the fold of Van Halen after he reunited with the band to record new material for *Best of Volume 1*.

1996: "Year in Rock." Beck, Sheryl Crow, and Q-Tip of A Tribe Called Quest comment on Van Halen.

2/27/97: Dave appears at *Howard Stern Private Parts* after-movie party.

11/11/97: David Lee Roth is interviewed.

4/16/98: Van Halen interview on MTV Latino.

5/05/98: Rockumentary Remix episode featuring an updated version of last Van Halen rockumentary.

5/12/98: Australian MTV interviews Van Halen for their web site.

MTV News, 1515, and the Week in Rock

1988: Preview of "Finish What Ya Started" video.

9/04/91: Feature on EVH Music Man guitar.

3/07/92: Sammy at Bay Area Music Awards.

4/92: MTV tapes news clip from a Van Halen show at the Palace of Auburn Hills in Auburn Hills on 4/04/92.

1993: Report on the end of the *Right Here, Right Now* tour.

1/20/95: Report on "Don't Tell Me (What Love Can Do)" video shoot at National Studios in Hollywood, CA.

4/04/95: "Week in Rock" report about "Don't Tell Me (What Love Can Do)" video.

4/95: Ed's gun arrest report on "Week in Rock."

6/28/96: "Week in Rock" reports Sammy leaving the band.

191191191191191191

7/04/96: "Week in Rock": Sammy leaves, Lars Ulrich comments.

10/18/96: MTV News interviews Ed with Alex at 5150; also used for "Week in Rock."

10/19/96: "Week in Rock" interviews Sammy in the studio.

1997: Ed is honored at 1997 Gibson Awards.

3/27/97: Van Halen signs a petition, along with several bands, protesting Egypt's recent crackdown on CDs the country feels are satanic.

5/12/97: News on *Van Halen III* producer Mike Post.

5/23/97: Sammy feature and "Little White Lie" video clips.

5/30/97: Sammy interviewed. "Little White Lie" video clips featured.

3/06/98-3/08/98: Van Halen interviewed about *Van Halen III* on "1515."

3/13/98: Van Halen interviewed on MTV News on MTV Latino.

7/13/98: MTV News airs clips of an interview with David Lee Roth about his new album and *Van Halen III*.

MTV Programs

1990: House of Style featuring Sammy and his Red Rocker wear.

1990: Rock 'n' Jock Softball featuring Sammy as a coach.

12/26/92: David Lee Roth hosts Classic MTV from the Hit Factory in New York, NY.

1/29/95: Van Halen appears on Euro-MTV's Headbanger's Ball.

10/02/95: Road Rules episode featuring Van Halen.

5/12/97: Lovelines filmed on 4/25/97 with Sammy Hagar.

1/03/98: *Van Halen III* update on an episode of Mattrock.

3/14/98: Special Van Halen episode of Mattrock.

3/17/98: Van Halen makes an appearance on MTV Live to celebrate the debut of *Van Halen III*.

3/23/98: A Van Halen feature appears on Eruo-MTV's Superock.

4/16/98: The video and interviews for "Without You" appear on Artist's Cut.

5/10/98: Van Halen appears in the "Rock and Roll Feuds" episode of Ultrasound.

7/06/98: Van Halen appears in an episode of Fanatic.

8/03/98: Van Halen appears in an episode of Lunch with Jesse filmed at The Canyons in Park City, UT on 7/14/98

8/04/98: Van Halen appears on Lunch with Jesse to award a contest winner with a Wolfgang guitar and a lesson from Ed.

MTV Video Music Awards

9/06/86 : David Lee Roth and Van Halen present awards. Van Halen's performance of "Best of Both Worlds" from *Live Without a Net* set a still-standing record for the longest performance at the Awards show, 19 minutes.

9/05/91: Held at Radio City Music Hall, New York, NY. Van Halen performs "Poundcake" and a second untelevised song before the show starts. The band is also interviewed.

9/09/92: Van Halen attends the awards ceremony, held at the Pauley Pavillion at UCLA in Los Angeles, CA, and is interviewed before and after the ceremony. The band took home awards for Best Editing (Michael Sinaway), Best Direction (Mark Finske), and Video of the Year, all for the "Right Now" video.

9/04/96: Van Halen (with Dave) present an award and are interviewed afterwards.

MTV Contests

1987: Name Sammy's album contest.

1988: Monsters of Rock contest. Winner gets to play one song on stage with the band.

1990: Cabo Wabo contest. 10 winners get to attend the opening of the Cabo Wabo Cantina.

Much Music-Another music channel that offers Van Halen-related programming.

1/30/95: Van Halen at the Factory in Milan, Italy, broadcast on Euro-MuchMusic.

6/21/97: Sammy Hagar hosts a "Start Me Up" video segment.

3/08/98-3/09/98: Fax with Gary Cherone.

3/19/98: Van Halen interview.

5/06/98: Spotlight (part 1) Van Halen videos and interviews.

5/07/98: Spotlight (part 2) Van Halen videos and interviews.

7/27/98: Van Halen concert from Sydney, Australia. Same concert as MTV's Live from the 10 Spot, but with added songs.

Musical Chairs-(Capitol/EMI Records 11706, 1977) Sammy Hagar solo album that spent 11 weeks on the charts, starting on 1/21/78 and peaking at #100. The only single released was "You Make Me Crazy," which reached #62. The album was later rereleased with a cover version of Otis Redding's "Sittin' on the Dock of the Bay." Tracks: • Turn Up the Music • It's Gonna Be All Right • You Make Me Crazy • Reckless • Try (to Fall in Love) • Don't Stop Me Now • Straight from the Hip Kid • Hey Boys • Someone Out There • Crack in the World

Music Connection-Issue #22 (10/23/00-11/05/00) of this magazine featured an interview with Sammy Hagar.

Music Express-This magazine (now known as Rock Express) featured a three-page interview with David Lee Roth titled "Van Halen Is Watching You" in March 1984. David Lee Roth also appeared on the cover of the March 1985 issue.

Musician-This magazine's index of Van Halen-related issues:

9/82: Eddie Van Halen cover. "Eddie Van Halen": six-page Edward interview by J.D.Considine. "David Lee Roth": one-page Dave interview by Dan Forte.

9/83: Edward interview by J.D. Considine.

6/84: Eddie Van Halen/David Lee Roth cover. "Van Halen Is...": nine-page Edward and Dave interview by Charles M. Young.

2/86: Van Halen cover. "Van Halen All for One & Free for All": eight-page interview by J.D. Considine.

6/86: *5150* reviewed.

2/87: Eddie Van Halen cover. Van Halen interview excerpts originally published in 9/82, 9/84, and 2/86 issues.

9/88: Eddie Van Halen cover. "Monsters of Guitar": nine-page Monsters of Rock feature by Ted Drozdowski.

5/91: Eddie Van Halen cover. "Jamming with Edward": fourteen-page interview with Edward Van Halen, Steve Morse, and Albert Lee before and during NAMM jam by Matt Resnicoff.

3/95: Eddie Van Halen cover. "Twilight of the Guitar Gods?": nine-page Edward and Slash interview by Marc Rowland.

2/96: "Edward Van Halen": one-page Edward interview by Mac Randall. Edward interview by J.D. Considine from 9/83 excerpt reprinted. Edward quotations reprinted from past interviews.

Address: BPI Communications, Inc., 1515 Broadway, New York, NY 10036.

Music Life-This Japanese magazine devoted an entire issue to Van Halen in 1979. Van Halen appeared on the cover and the issue was titled "Van Halen Japan Tour '79." Address: Shinko Music Pub. Co., Ltd., 2-12 chrome, Toyko, Japan.

Musicosis-A term coined by David Lee Roth to describe when a song's chorus or first line of a verse gets embedded in your subconscious, causing you to hum it all day long.

Musper, Erwin-Erwin was the man originally responsible for mixing *Van Halen III*. In June 1997 he began to chronicle the mixing of the album in what was to be called the "5150 Diaries." However, a sickness in his family prevented him from continuing with his mixing duties, and only two posts were made to the Van Halen Internet Mailing List for the diaries. The posts explained the mixing process behind "Year to the Day," "Fire in the Hole," and "From Afar."

Erwin eagerly accepted suggestions from the fans on the list about how to mix the songs. For example, he searched for a way to incorporate more bass into "Year to the Day" upon hearing the fans cry for more Michael in the mix. The two posts Erwin made can be read at the official Van Halen Web site.

In addition, Musper engineered *Balance* and the two new Dave-era tracks on *Best of Volume 1*: "Can't Get This Stuff No More" and "Me Wise Magic."

My Generation-(2:40) Van Halen performed this The Who cover on 10/20/88 at the Richmond Coliseum in Richmond, VA.

N

Nash Bridges-Sammy Hagar played a bartender in an episode of this CBS television show that aired on 10/02/98.

National Association of Music Merchants (NAMM)-This is an annual convention in which music merchants showcase their latest offerings and celebrity endorsers. In 1985 the show was held at the Hilton Ballroom in New Orleans, LA. Eddie's appearance at this show was completely documented by Steven Rosen in an article that would appear in Guitar World (November 1985) and again in The Inside magazine (Issue #9, Fall 1997).

At the 1985 convention in a special jam sponsored by Schecter, Edward joined Brian May, Ted Nugent, Julian Lennon's Carlos Morales, Billy Idol's Thommy Price, Quiet Riot's Rudy Sarzo, and The Who's John Entwhistle for an evening of rock and blues. Edward was not scheduled to play the gig but was eventually coaxed onto the stage, where he jammed using Seymour Duncan's white Fender Esquire. The group performed "Wild Thing."

In 1986 the show was held at the Limelight in Chicago, IL. Edward took part in Kramer Guitars' All-Star Jam, teaming up with Journey's Neal Schon to crank out some tunes to the packed house. Other performers included harmonica player Sugar Blue and Kiss guitarist Bruce Kulick.

In 1987 the show was held in Anaheim, CA. Sponsored by Seymour Duncan and Kramer, the All-Star Jam at NAMM featured performances by Loverboy and a rousing rendition of "Superstition" by Edward and Billy Idol's main axester, Steve Stevens. That very same day, Stevens completed the recording of a guitar solo for Michael Jackson's "Dirty Diana" for his forthcoming album Bad.

In January 1998 the show was again held in Anaheim, CA. An all-star jam sponsored by Kramer featured Billy Idol, Edward Van Halen, Billy Sheehan, and Jon Bon Jovi.

Sheehan, sporting a Yamaha bass, was asked by Kramer to cover up the Yamaha logo on its headstock with tape.

On 1/17/91 at the Trancas Beach Club in Malibu, CA, Biff Baby's All-Stars, featuring Edward Van Halen, Albert Lee, and Steve Morse on guitar; John Ferraro on drums; and Jimmy Cox on keys, warmed up for their 1/19/91 NAMM performance in Anaheim, CA.

On 1/19/96 Sammy Hagar took part in Washburn's Monster Jam IV at Inn at the Park, in Anaheim CA. Hagar was featured as the leadoff performer (with fellow Los Tres Gusanos drummer David Lauser) on a bill that also included performances by Craig Chaquico, Pantera's Dimebag Darrell, the Allman Brothers, and teenage wonders Kenny Wayne Shepard and Josh Smith.

Sammy opened his six-song set with "High Hopes" followed by "Three Lock Box." Other songs included "Eagles Fly" and "Bad Motor Scooter," which also featured Brother Cane's Damon Johnson on rhythm guitar and the legendary Greg Allman on keys.

On 1/18/97 Michael Anthony took part in St. Louis Music's 75th Anniversary Birthday Jam at the Anaheim Hilton in Anaheim, CA. Sponsored by St. Louis Music and organized by Ken Hensley, the star-studded event was held in conjunction with the 1997 NAMM convention. The event featured a full roster of performances including appearances by Zakk Wylde, an all-star bass jam featuring Steve Bailey and Victor Wooten, and one-time Van Halen bass tech Craig DeFalco's band, Moonshine.

After quickly running through one song they were joined by former Uriah Heep songwriter/keyboardist/guitarist Hensley (who left the Heep in 1980 to pursue a solo career and who also did a stint with Blackfoot), Michael Anthony, and ex-Kiss guitarist Bruce Kulick.

The group then dazzled the packed ballroom with a five-song set of Uriah Heep classics including "Stealin'," "July Morning" (from the 1971 album *Look at Yourself*), "The Wizard" (from 1972's *Demons and Wizards*), and "Look at Yourself" (also from *Look at Yourself*), which featured Michael doing an extended solo spot. Hensley handled keys and lead vocals, switching to acoustic guitar for "The Wizard," while Michael handled all the bass lines and background harmonies. DeFalco, James, and Kulick shared guitar duties throughout the set. Bassist Billy Sheehan joined the group on their final number, "Easy Livin'" (also from Demons and Wizards), arguably Uriah Heep's most successful song. Sheehan and Michael not only laid down tandem bass lines, but shared background harmonies, with Anthony taking the high parts and Sheehan handling the lower registers.

National Enquirer-A one-page feature on Edward and Valerie's wedding appeared in this tabloid in 1983. An interview with Eddie appeared in the 6/03/99 issue.

Neil Young's Bridge School Benefit-On 10/28/89 at the San Francisco Civic Auditorium in San Francisco, CA, Sammy Hagar performed "Give to Live" and joined Neil Young, Tom Petty and the Heartbreakers, Tracy Chapman, and Crosby, Stills, Nash, and Young in the traditional all-star jam encore. The school itself caters to the education of handicapped children, and the benefit has been an annual event to raise money for this organization since 1986.

Other Bridge School Benefit appearances included:

11/01/92 San Francisco Civic Auditorium, San Francisco, CA. Sammy Hagar performed.

11/06/93 Shoreline Amphitheater, Mountain View, CA. Sammy Hagar and Edward joined Melissa Etheridge, Warren Zevon, Anne and Nancy Wilson, Bonnie Raitt, Simon and Garfunkel, and Neil Young at the 7th annual benefit.

Ed played a black Parker Fly guitar the entire evening, beginning by standing in with Simon and Garfunkel while performing "The Sound of Silence."

Sammy, sporting a goatee and mustache, traded vocals with Neil Young and several other artists when everyone gathered on stage and treated the crowd to a rousing rendition of Young's "Rockin' in the Free World." Ed played rhythm guitar and threw in a solo to boot.

The feature of the evening, however, was a short all-acoustic set by Ed and Sammy. The set began with a Hagar original known as "The Love." Ed later took the stage behind a black grand piano. "Love Walks In" and "Right Now" followed, with Sammy encouraging the crowd to join in on the chorus to "Right Now." Ed then switched back to the Parker Fly to rip through a mini version of "Spanish Fly" before launching into another tune from *5150*, "Best of Both Worlds."

Nerf Herder-A band who recorded the song "Van Halen" (from their 1997 release *Nerf Herder* [My Records 8052-2]). The accompanying video included many Van Halen references including posters and pictures of the band. Ed, Alex, and Michael all gave Nerf Herder their permission to use the pictures, but the band was unable to contact David Lee Roth and Sammy Hagar in time for the video's release, so their faces were blocked out on all the images.

New Halen-Australian-based Van Halen tribute band.

Neworld-(*Van Halen III* [1:45]) Mike Post performed on the piano for this track because he and Ed wanted to record it live. The song was recorded in one take at Mike Post's studio. Ed used his Musser guitar to record his part. The title was picked to reflect the new era of the band with singer Gary Cherone.

New York Post Online-This web site featured an Eddie Van Halen interview in March 1998. URL: http://www.nypostonline.com

Night at the Opera-Gary Cherone performed songs by The Who at this Boston Rock Opera concert with Pat Badger and Mike Mangini on 6/25/98 at The Middle East Downstairs in Cambridge, MA.

Night Shift-(Warner Bros., 1982) Directed by Ron Howard and starring Michael Keaton, Shelley Long, and Henry Winkler, this comedy about prostitution featured songs by Quarterflash, Rod Stewart, The Rolling Stones, and, of course, Van Halen.

"You Really Got Me" appears during a college frat party held at the city morgue where Keaton and Winkler pull late-night duty.

Night Tracks-Van Halen hosted a segment of this weekly music video program in 1986 featuring Alex with a newly shaven head.

Nightwatch-This NBC show featured an interview with David Lee Roth in 1984.

Nine on a Ten Scale-(Capitol/EMI Records 11489, 1976) Sammy Hagar solo album that featured the Van Morrison penned "Flamingos Fly." Tracks: • Keep on Rockin' • Urban Guerilla • Flamingos Fly • China • Silver Lights • All American • Confession (Please Come Back) • Young Girl Blues • Rock and Roll Romeo

1984-1. Van Halen's sixth album (Warner Bros. 23985 [33:18]) released on 1/09/84. It reached #2 on U.S. charts (entering U.S. charts on 1/28/84, and reaching #2 on 3/17/84) and #15 on U.K. charts (entering U.K. charts on 2/04/84). 10 million copies have been sold in the U.S. It was certified gold and platinum on 3/12/84, quadruple platinum on 10/24/84, platinum five times over on 1/23/85, platinum six times over on 7/01/87, seven times platinum on 7/11/94, platinum nine times over on 8/08/96, and platinum ten times over on 2/08/99. It was certified diamond on 3/16/99. The album was remastered and rereleased on 9/19/00. Errors were reported with this latest release. Some booklets had pages that were stapled upside down.

1984 was the first album recorded at the 5150 Studio, where every Van Halen album since *1984* has been recorded.

All of the lyrics on this album, with the exception of those for "I'll Wait" were written in the back of Dave's 1951 Mercury lowrider. As the music was recorded, Dave would send a tape to roadie Larry Hostler. Larry would show up at Dave's house after lunch and the pair would drive through the Hollywood Hills, up the coast highway, and throughout the San Fernando Valley with the songs blaring. As Dave would come up with lyrics, he would show them to Larry and get his opinion.

1984 was voted the #1 album of the eighties by Guitar World magazine's editors.

The album was banned from some U.K. stores because the artwork depicted a baby smoking. The artwork was designed by David Lee Roth, who borrowed the futuristic style from Moebius, a comic by Jean Giraud. The pod-looking things that appear on the inner sleeve photo are Par Cans, part of a tour lighting rig taken Gary Moderling. On the *1984* tour the entire lighting rig was chrome and the crew operating the lights wore chrome-colored jumpsuits to blend in.

Ed initially wrote around 16 songs for this record, and at one point the other band members got upset with him because he wouldn't stop writing.

Michael didn't use a pick on any of the bass lines.

2. The first song on the *1984* album, this instrumental (1:07) was recorded on an Oberheim synthesizer and was originally 45 minutes long. It was one of the many long instrumental recordings Ed had in his "vault," which also included another lengthy opus that later became "Strung Out."

This was the first song ever recorded in the 5150 Studio. According to Ed, he was playing around with the song and Donn Landee secretly recorded the session.

1984 singles/promos
"Jump," "Runnin' with the Devil," "House of Pain," WEA W9384T, 12" Vinyl, UK, 1983.

"Jump," "Jump" (promo), WB PRO-A-2105, 12" Vinyl, USA, 1983.

"Jump," "House of Pain," WB 7-29384, 7" Vinyl, USA, 1/14/84. Highest chart position: #1 in USA and #7 in UK.

"Jump," "House of Pain," WEA P-1817, 7" Vinyl, Japan, 1984.

"Jump," "House of Pain," EMI-Odeon 16-256, 7" Vinyl, Brazil, 1984.

"Jump," "I'll Wait," "Panama," "House of Pain," EMI-Odeon 96-078, 7" Vinyl, Brazil, 1984.

"Jump," "I'll Wait" (edit), Back Trax 2-489, CD, USA.

"Jump" "I'll Wait," WB GWB 0489, 7" Vinyl, USA.

"Panama," "Girl Gone Bad," WEA 929 273-7, 7" Vinyl, Germany, 1984.

"Panama," "Dance the Night Away," "Girl Gone Bad," WEA W9273T, 12" Vinyl, UK, 1984.

"I'll Wait" (edit), "Drop Dead Legs" (promo), WB PRO-A-2126, 12" Vinyl, USA, 1984.

"I'll Wait," "Girl Gone Bad," WEA P-1851, 7" Vinyl, Japan, 1984.

"I'll Wait" (edit), "I'll Wait" (edit) (promo), WB BCA 2784S, 7" Vinyl, USA, 1984.

"I'll Wait," "Girl Gone Bad," WB 7-29307, 7" Vinyl, USA, 4/14/84. Highest chart position: #13 in USA.

"Panama," "Drop Dead Legs," WB 7-29250, 7" Vinyl, USA, 6/23/84. Highest chart position: #13 in USA and #61 in UK.

"Hot for Teacher" (edit), "Hot for Teacher" (promo), WB 7-29199, 7" Vinyl, USA, 10/27/84. Highest chart position: #56 in USA.

"Hot for Teacher," "Hear about It Later," "Little Dreamer," WEA W9199T, 12" Vinyl, UK, 1984.

"Panama," "Panama," WB PRO-A-2162, 12" Vinyl, USA, 1984.

"I'll Wait," "Drop Dead Legs," "And The Cradle Will Rock," " (Oh) Pretty Woman," WEA W9213T, 12" Vinyl, UK, 1984.

"Hot for Teacher," "Hot for Teacher" (edit), WB PRO-A-2177, 12" Vinyl, USA, 1984.

"Hot for Teacher," "Little Dreamer," WB 29199-7, 7" Vinyl, USA, 1984. Includes poster.

"Panama," "Hot for Teacher," WB GWB 0523, 7" Vinyl, USA, 1984.

Nissan Commercial-This television commercial first aired on 9/09/96. Van Halen's classic Kinks cover "You Really Got Me" was used as the music for this 60-second commercial for the Nissan 300 ZX entitled "Toys."

The claymation commercial was an hilarious look at a day in the life of two dolls and the "prestige" and "glamour" of owning such an automobile. It featured a Ken look-alike (named Nick) hopping into a toy Nissan and speeding over to the house of a Barbie-like woman. He whisks her away as her boyfriend, Tad, watches in amazement from the house.

The commercial was later parodied on Mad TV (Fox network) and a behind-the-scenes look at its making was featured on the Oprah Winfrey Show entitled "How'd They Do That?" on 11/18/96.

In addition to the fee for purchasing the rights to "You Really Got Me," Edward, Alex, Michael, and Dave were each presented with a limited-edition, jet black 1996 300ZX with tan leather interior. All except Dave, gave them away.

Nobody's Fault but Mine-This Led Zeppelin cover was reportedly played by the band in their early years.

No More Waiting-This unreleased original was performed on 6/10/77 and 12/31/77 at the Whisky A GoGo in West Hollywood, CA, and on 2/25/78 in Hollywood, CA, at an unknown location. The intro riff of this song was reincarnated as the opening riff to "Take Me Back (Déjà Vu)" from the *Balance* album. This song is sometimes called "Get Off My Back" and "Show No Mercy."

Norwegian Wood-The band performed this Beatles cover throughout Europe in 1993.

Not Enough-(*Balance* [5:13]) On this song Michael Anthony played a Music Man Stingray fretless bass, the first time a fretless bass was used on a Van Halen recording.

The original title of this song was "To Love Somebody." It was changed because another artist had already recorded a song with that title.

Ed recorded this song through his Marshall into a Leslie provided by Matt Bruck, after he used it on the demo album for his band, Zen Boy.

The video for this song, parts of which were filmed atop a Los Angeles, CA, building, was produced by David Naylor and directed by Jeth Weinrich. Sammy considers it his favorite Van Halen video.

Now I'm Here-This Queen cover was reportedly played by the band in their early years.

NRG (Canada)-Sammy Hagar was interviewed on this show in November 1991. Performance footage from the band's show at the Saddledome on 11/11/91 was also shown.

Numb to the Touch-This unreleased original is a leftover song from the *Balance* sessions. It's one of only two completely recorded tunes left off *Balance*.

O

The Ocean-The band performed this Led Zeppelin cover on 5/21/92 at the Cabo Wabo Cantina in Cabo San Lucas, Mexico.

O'Connor, Jim-Jim began his association with Van Halen when he was asked to paint some faceplates for Edward's Steinberger guitars: the 1984 plate for the 12-string and the 5150 plate for the 6-string. Several months before the Monsters of Rock tour, Jim was contacted to paint a Jack Daniels bass for Michael (not the original, but a backup). Jim also painted the Tabasco bass for the Monsters of Rock tour and refurbished the original Jack Daniels bass, which has since been donated to the Hard Rock Café chain. The paint jobs on the basses were primarily lacquers and took three to four days for each bass.

Other basses/guitars painted included seven different basses for Gene Simmons; guitars for Paul Stanley, Bruce Kulick, and Don Dokken; and a very intricate clown guitar for Cheap Trick's Rick Nielsen.

Before painting guitars O'Connor built minute man missiles for Boeing in Utah. He began painting in 1978, doing custom work on motorcycle tanks and fenders.

Ode to Argentina-This song was a staple of the South American leg of the *Diver Down* tour. Performed solo by Dave on guitar, this tune usually served as a leadoff to "Ice Cream Man." Whether it is an original or a cover is not known.

Off the Record-Van Halen was featured on this radio program in 1981.

(Oh) Pretty Woman-(*Diver Down* [2:53]) This song was recorded in one day at Sunset Sound Recorders in Hollywood, CA, and was released prior to the completion of *Diver Down*. The song's demo was recorded in

Malibu, CA, in a 16-track studio owned by the brother of Daryl Dragon (one-half of the 1970s singing duo the Captain and Tennille).

It was David Lee Roth's idea to record and release a single just to keep the band's name in circulation. Initially, Roth wanted to cover "Dancing in the Streets," but Edward suggested covering Roy Orbison's "(Oh) Pretty Woman" instead. As the single raced up the charts, Warner Brothers demanded an album to back it up, more than likely forcing the band to hurriedly record. This may be the biggest reason why more than one-third of the *Diver Down* album is made up of cover songs.

During the rehearsal for "(Oh) Pretty Woman," Ed and Dave got into an argument. Ed wanted to know if Dave had learned all the lyrics, and Dave pressed Ed about whether he'd learned all the music. The pair got so caught up in the spat that neither noticed they'd left out part of the song. However, when the mistake was discovered, the band decided to leave it as it was.

When the single was initially released, it didn't include the word "(Oh)" in the title, though this was corrected in later releases.

Orbison's wife, Claudette, inspired the 1964 version of this song.

The video for "(Oh) Pretty Woman" marked the band's trying their hand at a spaghetti western of sorts. Filming took place at a movie set in Malibu, CA, and took approximately 40 hours. It was so cold during the day and a half of filming that between takes, Alex (dressed in only a loin-cloth) would wrap up in a robe and warm himself by one of the several space heaters in place throughout the set.

Michael Anthony did not use a stunt double during his horse-riding scene. Upon completion of the scene, bass tech Kevin Dugan said to him, "I didn't know you could ride like that." To which Anthony replied, "To tell you the truth, neither did I!"

"(Oh) Pretty Woman" was banned from MTV and elsewhere in the U.S. shortly after its debut after angry parents across the nation called to complain about the transvestite being fondled by midgets. It seems many viewers, including those in Australia and New Zealand, which also banned the video, felt the video victimized women. MTV's stance was that the scene made the video too controversial to be broadcast. Japan also gave the video the thumbs down because it felt the band was making fun of a highly respected figure in their culture: the Samurai warrior (portrayed by Michael Anthony). Unknowingly, Anthony's headband was worn upside down, adding to the insult. Probably the biggest downfall to the ban was the fact that it killed the initial support the song needed.

Originally, "Intruder" was not part of the video. After filming for "(Oh) Pretty Woman" was complete, it turned out that this mini-movie was longer than the song. So the band decided to add a musical introduction, and "Intruder" was the result. Though never confirmed, David Lee Roth once claimed to have written "Intruder," noting Edward later rerecorded it for the *Diver Down* album.

The Old Grey Whistle Test-This British BBC2 television program aired an Andy Kershaw interview with David Lee Roth and Alex Van Halen on 5/21/84.

Once-(*Van Halen III* [7:40]) Ed used a double-neck guitar with a 6-string bass to record the solo for this song.

A remixed single for this song was recorded during a break in the *Van Halen III* tour when Alex was injured. Warner Brothers asked for a new version of the song for the "adult contemporary" market and Eddie worked some serious overtime to get it right. He even invited a female friend of Gary's to sing background vocals on the remix. A copy of the remix was released on the Internet auction site Ebay (http://www.ebay.com) to the tune of $256. The band soon after released two videos for the song on van-halen.com made by David Bertinelli, which included one for the remixed version.

The working title for this song, while Sammy was still in the band, was "Returning of the Wish." That title was then used for a different song on Sammy's solo album, *Red Voodoo*.

One Crazy Summer-(A&M Films, 1986) David Lee Roth's song "Easy Street" appeared in this movie and on the soundtrack (WB 28173).

One Foot Out the Door-(*Fair Warning* [1:56]) Producer Ted Templeman suggested that the idea for this song was inspired by the pace at which Van Halen albums were being recorded at the time.

One I Want-(*Van Halen III* [5:31]) The working title for this song was "Candyman."
Wolfgang and Ed went searching for stones on the beach that resembled picks. Ed used one of these stones to record the solo for this song.
The parts of this song on which Ed and Gary shared vocals on were recorded with a Shure 57 microphone.
This was the third U.S. radio single to be released from the album debuting on 7/27/98.

One More Time-The band performed this unreleased original sometime in late 1977 or early 1978 at Magic Mountain in Valenica, CA.

On Fire-(*Van Halen* [3:01]) On early studio takes, Mike and Dave sang the verses in unison.
The solo in this song was Edward's attempt at sounding like John McLaughlin. He used his Ibanez Destroyer "Shark."

On the Street-This Australian publication featured a Sammy Hagar article in 1997.

OOR-This Netherlands magazine featured a Van Halen interview in its February 1998 issue.

Oprah Winfrey Show-Edward and Valerie were interviewed on this show for a Valentine's Day special broadcast on 2/14/97.

Orion Music, Style, & Automotive Audio Guide-This publication's first issue, in 1997, featured an interview with Michael Anthony.

OU812-(Warner Bros. 25732 [50:04]) Released on 5/24/88, this album entered the U.S. charts at # 5, reaching #1 on U.S. charts and #16 on the U.K. charts. 4.4 million copies have been sold in the U.S. It was certified gold, platinum, and double platinum on 7/26/88 and was certified triple platinum on 1/18/89.

Ed suggested naming this album Rock 'n' Roll, and Source of Infection (coined by Sammy Hagar). The latter was disliked by Al, who joked that the name sounded like a sore. It was also Ed's idea to have the band members on the album cover.

The song list on the CD, cassette, and vinyl releases was in alphabetical order rather than tracking order, undoubtedly causing confusion to some fans on the first listen as to what song they were actually hearing.

OU812 was the first Van Halen album to be dedicated to someone: Alex and Edward's father, Jan.

The monkey statue on the back of the album was a copy of Charles Darwin's The Evolution of Man. Many copies of the statue were given away as promo items and featured the Warner Brothers logo along with "OU812" written into the flat base.

The two-hand symbol in the liner notes has been a source of speculation and confusion for many years. Some contend that it is supposed to represent a vagina, others feel it is the sign language equivalent of "we love you." The symbol was originally introduced by Michael Anthony.

Toto's Jeff Porcaro and Private Life's Jennifer Blakeman helped Edward set up all the keyboard MIDI equipment for this album. Ted Templeman was brought in to sequence the tracks.

Whenever the band was stumped during the writing and recording of the album, they played a Jerky Boys-style tape of a prankster caller who complained to restaurants about becoming sick after eating at them. Some believe this is the meaning behind the title *OU812*.

The title *OU812* was honored/mocked by Mr. Bungle who released *OU818* that same year and performed Van Halen songs in concert.

Gang Green released an album titled *181B4U* as a spoof of *OU812*'s title.

OU812 singles/promos
"Black and Blue" (fade) (promo), "Black and Blue" (album version), WB PRO-CD-3085, CD, USA, 1988.

"Black and Blue" (fade), "A Apolitical Blues," WB 7-27891, 7" Vinyl, USA, 1988. Highest chart position: #34 in USA.

"When It's Love" (edit) (promo), "When It's Love" (album version), WB PRO-CD-3142, CD, USA, 1988.

"When It's Love," "Cabo Wabo," WB 7-27827, 7" Vinyl, USA, 1988. Highest chart position: #5 in USA and #28 in UK.

"When It's Love," "When It's Love" (promo), WB 966, 7" Vinyl, Spain, 1988.

"When It's Love," "A Apolitical Blues," "When It's Love" (edit), "Why Can't This Be Love?" WEA W7816, CD, France, 1988.

"When It's Love," WEA W7816T, 12" Vinyl, UK.

"When It's Love," "A Apolitical Blues," WEA, 12" Vinyl, UK, 1988.

"Feels So Good," WEA, 7" Vinyl, UK, 1989. Highest chart position: #35 in USA on 3/19/89.

"Feels So Good" (remix/edit), "Feels So Good" (album version), WB PRO-CD-3422, CD, USA, 1988.

"Feels So Good," "Sucker in a 3-piece" (promo), WB 7-27565, 7" Vinyl, USA, 1988.

"Feels So Good," "Sucker in a 3-Piece," "Best of Both Worlds" (live in New Haven), WEA W7565, 3" CD, France, 1988.

"Feels So Good," "Feels So Good" (edit), WEA, 7" Vinyl, Germany, 1988.

"Finish What Ya Started" (remix), "Sucker in a 3-Piece," WB 27746, 7" Vinyl, Cassette, and 3" CD, USA, 1988. Highest chart position: #11 in USA.

"Feels So Good," "Sucker in a 3-Piece," WEA W7565, 7" Vinyl and Cassette, UK, 1989. Fishnet t-shirt included.

"Feels So Good," "Finish What Ya Started" (remix), WB 7-21866, 7" Vinyl, USA.

"Finish What Ya Started" (promo), WB PRO CD 3240, CD, USA.

"Finish What Ya Started" (remix) (promo), WB PRO-CD-3240, CD, USA, 1988.

OUI-The 11/81 issue of this magazine featured a seven-page interview with David Lee Roth by Rusty Hamilton and Diana Clapton. Another article appeared in the same issue entitled "Valerie: The Ultimate Van Halen Groupie."

Out of the Ether-This unreleased original is a leftover song from the *F.U.C.K.* sessions. It was later planned for *Balance*, with a working title of "Hendrix Jam," but was not used.

Outside Woman Blues-The band performed this Cream cover on 12/12/91 at the Suncoast Dome in St. Petersburg, FL, and on 8/12/95 at the Polaris Amphitheater in Columbus, OH.

Outta Love Again-(*Van Halen II* [2:49]) Because Eddie dominated the mix in Van Halen, some of the second album was supposed to highlight Alex and Mike. This particular song showcased Alex's powerhouse drumming style.

This song was frequently on the band's set list in the backyard party days.

Over the Edge-(Orion Pictures Company, 1979) "You Really Got Me" appears in this film starring a very young Matt Dillion about a group of rebellious children in an upscale suburban neighborhood. The track also appears on the film's soundtrack (WB 3335).

Over the Top-(Cannon Group, 1987) The song "Winner Takes It All" (3:58) was written by Giorgio Moroder; performed by Sammy Hagar, Edward Van Halen, and Denny Carmassi; and produced by Sammy, Ed, and Giorgio. Sammy Hagar performed lead vocals and played guitar, while Eddie played bass and Denny Carmassi drums. Edward also played a portion of the guitar work on this track, though his contribution is unknown.

This film was Sylvester Stallone's ode to the sport of arm wrestling and, in addition to Sly, starred Robert Loggia and Susan Blakely.

This song was part of the film's soundtrack, released as a single, and made into a video. The video features Sammy barefoot and playing a red Performance guitar interspersed with clips from the movie. The video ends with Sammy and Stallone battling each other in an arm-wrestling match.

"Winner Takes It All" is heard in the movie while Stallone's character, Lincoln Hawk, is in Las Vegas taking part in an arm-wrestling tournament. In the movie the song features a longer intro than in the soundtrack and single versions.

The song was released as a single by Columbia (38-06647) with "The Fight" also written by Giorgio Moroder, as the B-side. It entered the charts on 3/14/87 and made it to #54.

Other artists on the soundtrack included Asia, Eddie Money, and Frank Stallone. Edgar Winter played saxophone on the Stallone cut "Bad Nite." The soundtrack was released on vinyl (CBS 40655, 1987) and CD (Columbia CK 40655) in the U.S. and on vinyl in Japan (28Ap-3290).

The Overture-This The Who cover was reportedly a staple of band's live sets from their backyard party days.

Oxby, Elmo-Famed billboard painter in the 1980s hired by David Lee Roth to paint a skull and crossbones in 24-carat gold leaf on the hood of the vocalist's then brand-new 1983 chrome black Mercedes Benz.

P

The Palomino Club-Eddie Van Halen, Steve Lukather, Sterling Ball, Dudley Gimple, and Jay Graydon performed together at this club in North Hollywood, CA, in October 1991.

Panama-1. (*1984*; *Best of Volume 1* [3:31]) According to Dave the lyrics to "Panama" were written after a day at the drag races in Fontana, CA, where he'd seen a car named the Panama Express. The lyrics are about a car referred to as a woman.

The "whooshing" sounds during the song's interlude were created by Edward's early 1970s black Lamborghini Countach S-5000 (the car has since been sold). The sports car was backed up to the studio, and microphones were attached to the exhaust pipes. The band then recorded the sound of the engine revving.

In concert Sammy sang slightly different lyrics to "Panama" than Dave did.

The video for this song was directed by Pete Angelus and produced by Jerry Kramer. The live portions of this video were filmed over a three-day period at the Spectrum in Philadelphia, PA, while the band was in the middle of the *1984* tour. The pickups and inserts were filmed during the second and third days of the same time frame.

Michael Anthony's infamous Jack Daniels bass had just been delivered, and this was the first time it had ever been used or seen. It featured a body carved by Wayne Charvel and a paint job by Chuck Wild Studios. Zeta pickups were used that were mounted in the saddles of the bridge. During filming the bass was dinged twice by careless gaffers as Anthony was being swung back and forth, suspended from the stage rigging.

This song makes an appearance on the compilation album *Slammin' Sports Jams Vol. 4* (Simitar, 2000).

Pat Boone covered this song on his 1997 release *In a Metal Mood-No More Mr. Nice Guy* (Hip-O Records HIPD-40025). The entire album consisted of hard rock and heavy metal songs covered in a Las Vegas, jazz-type style.

The band Grade covered this song on their EP *Truimph & Tragedy* (Victory 103, 1999).

2. A Toronto-based Van Halen tribute band.

Paper Money-(Warner Bros. BSK 2823, 1974) This was Sammy Hagar's last album with Montrose. It was produced by Ted Templeman and engineered by Donn Landee. It entered the charts on 11/16/74 and lasted for 14 weeks, topping out at #65. Tracks: • Underground • Connection • Dreamer • Starliner • I Got the Fire • Space Age Sacrifice • We're Going Home • Paper Money

The album features a cover version of The Rolling Stones 1967 classic "Connection" from their album *Between the Buttons* (Abkco 7499).

The track "I Got the Fire" was later covered by Iron Maiden and released as a B-side to their single "Sanctuary/Drifter" in 1980 and again as a B-side to the single "Flight of Icarus" in 1983. A live version of "I Got the Fire" was also included on Iron Maiden's greatest hits compilation, *Iron Maiden* (Castle Records 102-2).

Alan Fitzgerald played the bass synthesizer on this album.

Paradise Club-Edward joined Mick Fleetwood's Zoo at a gig at this Aspen, CO, club on 12/31/86.

Pay Per View Concert-Commonly referred to as the "Pay-Per-View concert," this show, filmed on 8/18/95 and 8/19/95 at the Molson Amphitheater in Canada, was broadcast on Canada's Viewer's Choice network on 11/10/95 and in the U.S. through Pay-Per-View on 12/08/95. Tracks: • Right Now • Big Fat Money • Top of the World • Not Enough • Mine All Mine • Amsterdam • Drum Solo • Can't Stop Lovin' You •

Feelin' • Eagles Fly • Guitar Solo • Why Can't This Be Love? • Dreams • Poundcake • Don't Tell Me (What Love Can Do) • Panama

Canada's showing of the concert also included Our Lady Peace's (the opening act's) set. Van Halen's performance was later rebroadcast on Canada's Much Music and included "Jump," and the "Runnin' with the Devil" teaser.

A very excited female fan, showing off her sequined Van Halen bikini top, is featured at the beginning and near the end of the concert. Known only as Bridget, she later went on to make infomercials in Canada and was featured in the March 1997 issue of Easy Rider magazine.

Penthouse-This magazine's January 1987 issue featured a five-page David Lee Roth interview by Gerard Van der Leun titled "David Lee Roth." The March 1998 issue had a small write-up on Dave. The September 1998 issue featured an article on Van Halen.

People-This magazine's 4/06/98 issue featured an article about Gary Cherone and *Van Halen III* titled "One Way Ticket to Ride."

People's Choice Awards-In 1990 Eddie Van Halen appeared briefly while Valerie Bertinelli presented an award.

People Weekly-This magazine's index of Van Halen-related issues:
11/09/81: "Valerie Bertinelli's Happily over the Deep End about Her Rocker Husband, Eddie Van Halen": Eddie and Val interviewed about their marriage.
2/11/85: David Lee Roth cover. "No Longer (for Now) Wailin' with Van Halen, David Lee Roth Jumps Out with a Sunny Solo Hit": four-page interview by Carl Arrington.
9/16/85: David Lee Roth cover. "Parents vs. Rock": six-page feature on rock music lyrics and the PMRC ("Hot For Teacher" video was among those targeted) by Roger Wolmuth.

6/23/86: "High-Jumping Hagar Helps Van Halen Fans Forget David Lee Roth": two-page Van Halen feature by Steve Dougherty.

12/18/95: "Star Tracks": photo and write-up on Sammy Hagar's wedding to Kari Karte.

Address: Time and Life Building, Rockefeller Center, New York, NY 10020.

Petschulat, Dave-A Nashville, TN, luthier who built Edward two miniature Les Paul copies, frequently used live on the Diver Down tour. He presented the first one to Ed while the band was in Nashville. The first miniature had Smith pickups and an amplifier built into it. Eddie liked the guitar so much that he had Petschulat build him a second, which was loaded with Gibson humbuckers. It also featured a thicker body and a wider neck than its predecessor.

Photograffitti-(A&M 75026 1740 3, 1991) This video featured the first six videos from Extreme including: • Decadence Dance (uncensored) • Get the Funk Out • More Than Words • Mutha (Don't Wanna Go to School Today) • Little Girls • Kid Ego (East Coast Version).

The video was released on 5/14/91 and certified gold on 12/13/91. The video includes interviews between songs conducted by former RIP magazine editor Lonn Friend.

Piece of Mind-(3:57) This unreleased original was recorded for the band's 1977 Warner Brothers demo. Recordings also exist of a performance of this song in 1976 at the Starwood in Hollywood, CA. The song is sometimes known as "Bad Women."

Pipeline-This Surfaris cover was reportedly played during the *5150* tour, though no known recordings exist of it.

Piper-The band S.I.R.'s Bill Aucoin chose to sign instead of Van Halen, stating that he didn't "see any commercial potential" in the band. Aucoin was Kiss's manager at the time Van Halen was discovered by Gene Simmons. After Van Halen was rejected, Gene Simmons actively pursued Eddie Van Halen for other projects; Edward declined on each occasion.

Playboy-*Van Halen III* was reviewed in this magazine's May 1998 issue. The German version of the magazine featured a Van Halen article in its February 1998 issue.
Eddie Van Halen was voted Best Rock Instrumentalist in a poll featured in the 2/09/99 issue of this magazine.

Player-Eddie Van Halen appeared on the cover of the 11/98 issue of this Japanese magazine. The article profiled Ed and Mike's gear on the *Van Halen III* tour.

Playgirl-*Crazy from the Heat* (the book) was reviewed in the December 1997 issue of this magazine.

Pleasure Dome-(*For Unlawful Carnal Knowledge* [6:57]; *Live: Right Here, Right Now* [9:38]) This song was pieced together from three different riffs, including a lick Ed had written on the *OU812* tour and an intro he had come up with a few years earlier. Arranging the pieces into a song was mostly the work of Alex Van Halen.
This track also features Ed "chickin' pickin'," a technique frequently used in country and bluegrass music. The guitarist had used this technique only once before, on "Finish What Ya Started." For this track Ed used a prototype wood-body Steinberger, and Mike used his 1964 Fender Jazz bass.

Pointer, Mark-Keyboardist who tried out for a keyboard position in the early days of the band, though he only lasted one show.

Politically Incorrect-Sammy Hagar made guest appearances on this television show on 8/29/97 and 11/25/97.

Pollan, Chris-Monsters of Rock and *OU812* tour manager. Went on to become tour manager for Sammy Hagar during his *Marching to Mars* tour.

Popsmear-David Lee Roth was interviewed in this magazine and appeared on its cover for a special collectors' issue released in 9/98.

Porcaro, Jeff-A drummer, formerly of Toto, whose death on 8/05/92 prompted Eddie Van Halen to perform at a benefit concert and record a few tracks on a tribute album. Eddie performed on two songs, Jimi Hendrix's "If Six Was Nine" and "It Takes a Lot to Laugh, It Takes a Train to Cry," for the album *Tribute to Jeff* (Zebra Records ZD 44005-2, 1997) by David Garfield and Friends.

This import CD was released in the U.S. on 8/19/97. "If Six Was Nine" features appearances by Edward, Michael Landau, Will Lee on bass, Simon Philips on drums, and David Garfield. "It Takes a Lot to Laugh, It Takes a Train to Cry" features Boz Scaggs, Jim Keltner, Neil Stubenhaus, Richie Hayward, Paul Barrere, Fred Tackett, Larry Klimas, Mike Finnigan, Eddie Van Halen, and David Garfield. Other artists on the album include Greg Bissonette, Larry Carlton, Don Henley, and Steve Lukather. (See also "Jeff Porcaro Benefit." entry)

Portrait in Platinum-David Lee Roth and Alex were interviewed on this radio program in 1983.

Poundcake-(*For Unlawful Carnal Knowledge*; *Best of Volume 1* [5:22]; *Live: Right Here, Right Now* [5:28]) Three main guitar tracks make up this song. They include two tracks of electric 12-string, a Roger Giffin custom guitar with Smith pickups. The prototype Peavey 5150 amplifier (designed by Edward and James Brown) was also used.

Had it not been for Alex Van Halen, this song would have never been made. Ed had recorded a 10 or 15-second riff while jamming one day, and while listening to it the next day, Alex picked up on it and brought it to Ed's attention. Ed then turned that riff into "Poundcake." Alex once insisted that the solo on this track is unfinished. Ed explained that the solo wasn't counted (in terms of bars) perfectly, but that it felt right.

Ed used a Makita drill, set at 60 cycles, for parts of this song, including the intro. His tech Matt Bruck left the drill on the recording console after replacing the tubes in Ed's Soldano amp. When he came back, Ed was using the drill in the solo for "Poundcake." While on tour the drill was stolen, but luckily Scott Smith, formerly of The Inside magazine, had a replica drill that Ed borrowed until the original was recovered.

This song is about Sammy's ideal woman, plain and simple.

The video for the song was a typical performance video interspersed with clips of scantily-clad women (it was banned from Canada's Much Music video channel shortly after its debut for this reason). It debuted on MTV on 6/15/91. It was produced by Warren Hewlett and directed by Andy Morahan, who also did the "Finish What Ya Started" video.

This is one of only two known videos featuring Edward performing on a red-, white-, and black-striped Ernie Ball Music Man guitar, the other being "Runaround."

MTV used scenes from the making of the video in a few news specials and in a rockumentary about the band.

The Power Hour-This British ITV television program aired a 25-minute interview with the band on 3/16/88.

The Pretenders-On 2/14/82 at the Pauley Pavilion at UCLA in Los Angeles, CA, Edward joined Chrissy Hynde and company on stage to perform "You Really Got Me" and "Wild Thing" in one of the last shows of the Pretenders' 1982 U.S. tour. Edward suffered amplifier troubles and ended up using one of Chrissy's guitars, a Fender Telecaster, along with one of her amplifiers.

Lead guitarist James Honeyman-Scott was found dead four months later on 6/16/82, having reportedly died in his sleep sometime after returning from a multiple sclerosis benefit at the Venue Club in London U.K.

Primary-(*Van Halen III* [1:27]) Originally, this was as bluesy guitar intro with mumbled words by Eddie. It was part of the next song on the album, "Ballot or the Bullet." Because Ed's word's were considered too "inside," the song was rerecorded as a purely instrumental song on an electric sitar. More than a minute in length, the band decided to give it a title of its own. At first Gary wanted to call it "Super Tuesday," but Ed suggested "Primary."

Prime Choice-This web site featured an Alex Van Halen interview and a review of *Van Halen III* on 7/31/98. URL: http://www.prime-choice.com

Private Life-Eddie Van Halen produced two albums for this band, *Shadows* (Warner Bros. 9 25803-2, 1988) (co-produced with Donn Landee) and *Private Life* (Warner Bros 9 26150-2, 1990) (co-produced with Ted Templeman).

Push Comes to Shove-(*Fair Warning* [3:48]) According to Edward this song came about partly because Dave wanted to cash in on the reggae craze that was sweeping the country in the very early 1980s.

Edward played the guitar solo at least 20 different times, but Ted Templeman wasn't happy with it. They called it a day, and Edward returned to the studio that night and played it again, the same way he had done earlier that day. The next day he showed it to Templeman and the producer loved it.

Put Out the Lights-(3:39) This unreleased original appeared on the band's 1977 Warner Brothers demo.

R

Randy Bachman Benefit-Sammy headlined and helped organize a tribute concert for Bay Area photographer Randy Bachman, who was killed in an automobile accident, to help raise money for the photographer's family. The concert was held on 1/28/88 at the Warfield in San Francisco, CA.

Rat Salad-Edward's choice for the band's name upon deciding to drop the moniker Mammoth. The name was based on a track of the same name from Black Sabbath's 1970 *Paranoid* album (WB 3104-2).

Raw-The 4/28/93-5/11/93 issue of this publication featured sixteen pages of Van Halen interviews, posters, and Van Halen, Sammy Hagar, and David Lee Roth discographies in an article titled "The Van Halen Story." Address: P.O. Box 3AU, London W1A 3AU.

Raw Power-This no-longer-in-print magazine featured a two-page David Lee Roth interview by Quick Draw entitled "Van Halen" in its 10/77-11/77 issue.

Real TV-This show featured a segment on the making of the Nissan commercial. (see "Nissan Commercial" entry.)

Record-This magazine featured two Van Halen-related issues. The first, in April 1984, featured David Lee Roth on the cover and a five-page interview by Deborah Frost titled "Rock 'n' Roll as a Contact Sport." The second, in April 1985, featured Dave on the cover and a four-page interview with Dave titled "What It Be, David Lee?" about *Crazy from the Heat* by David Gans. Address: 745 Fifth Avenue, New York, NY 10151.

Record Mirror-Sammy Hagar appeared on the cover of this magazine's 3/15/80 issue.

Record Review-This magazine's index of Van Halen-related issues:
4/79: Van Halen cover. "Record Review Interview: Van Halen": four-page Edward interview by Steven Rosen.
6/80: Van Halen cover. Van Halen feature (part 1).
8/80: Van Halen feature (part 2).
2/81: Van Halen cover.
6/81: 1981 Readers' Poll. Song #3 "And the Cradle Will Rock." Van Halen places #5 for Artist of the Year and #2 for Group of the Year. Eddie wins Best Guitarist.
8/82: Eddie Van Halen cover. "Diver Down Leaves No Sinking Feeling": four-page Edward interview by Steven Rosen.
10/83: Eddie Van Halen cover. Eight-page Edward and Alex interview by Steven Rosen entitled "Edward and Alex Speak Up."
4/84: *1984* reviewed by Carlo Wolff.
Address: 26 Harvard Road, Belmont, MA 02178.

Red Alert Dial Nine-(Capitol 26882, 1982) Sammy Hagar solo album. Tracks: • Red • Cruisin' and Boozin' • Turn Up the Music • Reckless • This Planet's on Fire (Burn in Hell) • Urban Guerilla • Trans Am (Highway Wonderland) • Miles from Boredom • Twentieth Century Man • Space Station #5 • I've Done Everything for You • Young Girl Blues

Red Ball Jets-David Lee Roth's last band before joining Mammoth. The band got its name from the tennis shoes of the same name. Mammoth used to rent Roth's Acoustic 850 PA system from him for $35 a gig. The PA was originally bought by Roth with a loan from his father.

Red Hot!-(Capitol CDL-57245, 1989; Pair 57245, 1992 [51:30]) Sammy Hagar solo album. Tracks: • I've Done Everything for You • Red •

Rock & Roll Weekend • Make It Last/Reckless • Turn Up the Music • Bad Motor Scooter • Love or Money • Plain Jane • Twentieth Century Man • The Danger Zone • Space Station #5

Red Rocker-1. Sammy Hagar's nickname. He explained in 1992 that there is no big mystery to the name. Red is simply his favorite color.

2. The name of Sammy Hagar's short-lived line of clothing. The 50-piece ensemble was unveiled at an Action Sports Retailer Convention in San Diego, CA, in 1990. The line consisted of moderately priced knits, denims, and loose and crazy Red Rocker clothes.

Red Voodoo-(MCA 11872, 1999) Sammy Hagar solo album released on 3/23/99. It debuted at #22 on the charts selling 48,043 copies in its first week. Tracks: • Mas Tequila • Shag • Sympathy for the Human • Red Voodoo • Lay Your Hand on Me • High and Dry Again • The Revival • Don't Fight It (Feel It) • The Love • Right on Right • Returning of the Wish

Regis and Kathy Lee-In 1993 Eddie Van Halen appeared in a promotional clip for Valerie Bertinelli's Café Americain.

Rematch-(Capitol SN-16336, 1982) Sammy Hagar solo album. Tracks: • Red • I've Done Everything for You • Rock and Roll Weekend • Cruisin' and Boozin' • Turn Up the Music • Trans Am (Highway Wonderland) • Love or Money • This Planet's on Fire (Burn in Hell) • In the Night (Entering the Danger Zone) • Space Station #5 • The Danger Zone

Rematch & More-(Capitol CDP 7 46471 2, 1987 (56:30)) Sammy Hagar solo album. Tracks: • Red • I've Done Everything for You • Rock and Roll Weekend • Cruisin' and Boozin' • Turn Up the Music • Keep on Rockin' • Fillmore Shuffle • Reckless • Don't Stop Me Now • Trans Am (Highway Wonderland) • Love or Money • This Planet's on Fire (Burn in Hell) • Plain Jane • Bad Reputation • Bad Motor Scooter

Revolver-A band Edward, Alex, and an unknown bassist belonged to sometime after the Broken Combs.

Respect the Wind-This song by Eddie and Alex Van Halen, which appeared on the soundtrack to the movie *Twister*, was written by Alex Van Halen. It represents the first time we hear Alex as a keyboard player. Two versions exist. The movie soundtrack's version (WB 9-46254) is timed at 5:49 while the movie score version (WB 82954) clocks in at 9:13. The score version is heard during the film's ending credits.

Right Now-(*For Unlawful Carnal Knowledge*; *Best of Volume 1* [5:21]; *Live: Right Here, Right Now* [6:13]) When Eddie first wrote this song, he envisioned Joe Cocker singing on it. "Right Now" was written before "Jump" and was inspired by "Feelin' Alright."

He recorded it using an acoustic Steinway piano and a Hammond organ. As for guitars, Sammy suggested the opening guitar parts that Ed played, and Ed used a 6-string bass and a Leslie amplifier for the rest. Mike used his 1964 Fender Jazz bass.

Portions of an early synthesizer version of this song can be heard in the 1984 movie *The Wild Life*.

The video for the song won Best Video, Best Direction, and Best Editing at the 1992 MTV Video Music Awards and was produced by Carolyn Mayer and directed by Mark Fenske. It debuted on MTV on 3/05/92.

Pepsi used this song in their commercials for their ill-fated product Crystal Pepsi. Saturday Night Live parodied this song and it's use by Pepsi in their commercial for "Crystal Gravy."

RIP-This magazine's May 1993 issue featured Van Halen on the cover and an interview about *Live: Right Here, Right Now* titled "Live At Last!"

Rip It Up-Alex Van Halen was interviewed in the March 1998 issue of this New Zealand magazine.

Ripley-This unreleased original is a leftover song from the *1984* sessions. It was written on a Ripley guitar, designed by Steve Ripley. Each string on the guitar can be sent to different sides of the speaker through the use of its individual string pan pots.

R 'n' R Popular 1-This Spanish magazine's 3/98 issue featured a Van Halen interview and an article about David Lee Roth's autobiography *Crazy from the Heat.*

The Road Concert Magazine-In 1997 this New York-based magazine featured a Sammy Hagar interview titled "Sammy Hagar: Unchained" by David Criblez. Address: P.O. Box 255, E. Norwich, NY 11732.

Rock!-This magazine's index of Van Halen-related issues:
Summer 1983: Van Halen feature.
4/84: David Lee Roth cover.
6/84: David Lee Roth cover and feature.
7/84: Van Halen feature.
10/84: David Lee Roth feature.
Address: 105 Union Avenue, Cresskill, NJ 07626.

Rockabilia-In 1996 this rock merchandise catalog (Volume 32) featured Eddie Van Halen on the cover. Address: P.O. Box 4206, Hopkins, MN 55343; 612-942-7895.

Rock and Roll-This Led Zeppelin cover was performed throughout the *5150* tour and can also be found on the video *Live without a Net.*

Rock and Roll All Night-This Kiss cover was performed by the band in their club days.

Rock Beat-This magazine featured Van Halen on the cover of its May 1986 issue as well as a two-page article. In the winter of 1987, the magazine put out a special all Van Halen/David Lee Roth issue. Address: 18455 Burbank Boulevard, Suite 309, Tarzana, CA 91356.

Rock Brigade-The November 1996 issue of this Brazilian magazine featured a Van Halen cover and a five-page interview titled "Van Halen: A Volta De David Lee Roth Ficou So No Sonho" by Daniel Oliveira. The band was again interview for the magazine's February 1998 issue. Address: Av. Paulista, 2073 Ed. Horsa I, Salas 821/822, Sao Paulo, Brazil 01311-940.

Rock Candy-1. This Montrose cover was performed by the band several times during the *5150* tour and once in 1992 at the Cabo Wabo Cantina.
2. An unofficial Sammy Hagar fan newsletter.

RockDaily.com-This web site featured a Van Halen trivia contest on 3/10/98 and an interview with the band on 4/11/98.

Rock Express-(formerly Music Express) This magazine's index of Van Halen-related issues:
1986: Van Halen cover and interview.
3/86: David Lee Roth cover. "Just a Gigolo": three-page Dave interview by Lenny Stoute.
4/86: Van Halen cover. "Van Halen's Revenge": two-page Van Halen interview by Sylvie Simmons.
8/86-9/86: David Lee Roth cover. "The Meaning of Life": three-page Dave interview about *Eat 'Em and Smile* by Ian Blair.

10/86: "Caught in the Act": Van Halen's live performance in Toronto reviewed by Keith Sharp.

1987: *Live without a Net* and David Lee Roth's home video compilation reviewed.

8/87-9/87: "Waving, Not Drowning": three-page Sammy Hagar interview by Brad Kruger.

3/88: David Lee Roth cover. "The Glamour Factory": five-page David Lee Roth interview by Brad Kruger. Roth's *Skyscraper* reviewed.

6/88: Van Halen cover. "How Big Is Big?": four-page Van Halen feature about the Monsters of Rock tour by Lain Blair. *OU812* reviewed by David Fricke.

Address: 37 Madison Avenue, Toronto, Ontario, Canada, M5R 2S2; Telephone: 416-964-6624.

Rock Fever-This magazine's index of Van Halen-related issues:

10/84: Van Halen cover.

12/84: Eddie Van Halen cover. "Hot Rock Scoops": short Eddie, Dave, and Sammy Hagar features. "Rockin' Off Our Pages!": three-page Van Halen feature. "Jerry Kramer: The Man Behind Today's Hot Rock Videos": short segment on "Panama" video. "Video Rock Reviews 'Panama'": video reviewed.

4/85: Van Halen cover. "On the Set: 'Hot For Teacher'": three-page feature on the making of the "Hot for Teacher" video.

Address: 1115 Broadway, New York, NY 10010.

Rock Hard-This German magazine's January 1997 issue featured Van Halen on the cover and a three-page article by Chris Leibundgut as well as a review of *Video Hits Volume 1*.

Rockin' in the Free World-(7:03) This Neil Young cover was a staple of the band's live set during the 1993 tour. Another version was performed by Eddie and Sammy at the 7th Annual Bridge School Benefit on

11/06/93 in Mountain View, CA, along with Neil Young, Bonnie Raitt, and Simon and Garfunkel, among others.

Rock It-Volume 2 of this publication featured a Michael Anthony interview.

Rockit Chicago-This magazine printed a story about possible replacements for Sammy Hagar in their 7/01/96 issue.

RockLine-1. This magazine's index of Van Halen-related issues:
Summer 1981: "David Lee Roth Still Rebelling after All Those Years!": article about Dave's youth.
Summer 1982: Van Halen cover.
Fall 1982: Van Halen cover.
Winter 1982: Van Halen cover.
Summer 1983: Van Halen cover.
3/84-4/84: Van Halen cover.
5/84-6/84: Van Halen cover. "Eddie Van Halen Speaks!": three-page Edward interview. "Sammy Hagar, Neal Schon, and Their San Francisco Rock Event": two-page HSAS feature.
7/84: Van Halen cover.
7/84-8/84: Van Halen cover.
9/84: Van Halen cover.
11/84: "Michael and the Jacksons: The Victory Tour Takes Off": short entry on Edward's one-time live appearance with the Jacksons."Van Halen Times-Dateline: 1984": two-page Van Halen feature. "The Sound and the Fury": two-page feature on Sammy Hagar.
3/85: Van Halen cover.
7/85: "Diamond Dave & Elusive Ed-Is the Van Halen Bust-Up for Real?": two-page feature on Van Halen breakup. Two-page feature on 27th Annual Grammy Awards where Sammy Hagar was a presenter.

2/86: "Van Halen Rocked by the Winds of Change, but Weathering the Storm": three-page feature on Van Halen breakup.

4/86: "Eddie Van Halen Gets Plastered…and the Rest of the Band Gets Crazy! (but not from the Heat!)": three-page feature on Edward's induction into Hollywood, CA's Rock Walk.

5/86: "Everybody Wants to Know…Just How Different Is the New Van Halen?": Three-page Van Halen feature.

6/86: Eddie Van Halen cover. "Van Halen's on the Road Again": two-page Van Halen feature.

9/86: David Lee Roth cover. "At Home with Eddie Van Halen": three-page feature on home of Edward and Valerie. "David Lee Roth's 'Ugly Divorce' Leads to a Brand New Band! (part 1)": four-page David Lee Roth interview.

12/86: One-page feature on 1986 NAMM convention featuring write-up on appearance by Edward with Neal Schon."Van Halen's Platinum Party!": three-page Van Halen concert and after-show party review. "The Things David Lee Roth Won't Say": two-page David Lee Roth feature.

Address: 157 W. 57th Street, New York, NY 10019.

2. Rockline is a 90-minute radio program that airs live every Monday night starting at 11:30 P.M. EST. You can call the guests on Rockline toll-free from anywhere in the continental U.S., Canada, Hawaii, Japan, and Puerto Rico at 800-344-7625.

Van Halen is the only band in Rockline's 16-year history to do back-to-back Rockline shows. Index of Van Halen's Rockline appearances:

2/15/82: Dave and Al appear.

8/09/82: Dave, Al, and Mike appear.

2/20/84: Dave, Al, and Mike appear.

1987: Sam and Ed appear (from San Francisco, CA). (Ed is Sam's surprise guest.)

4/05/88: Dave appears.

5/16/88: Mike and Al appear.

5/23/88: Sam and Ed appear.

4/22/91: Dave appears.

1/13/92: Al and Ed appear.

1/20/92: Mike and Sam appear.

3/14/94: Sammy appears.

2/20/95: Al and Ed appear.

2/27/95: Sammy and Mike appear.

Rock 'n' Roll Hoochie Koo-(7:52) The band performed this Rick Derringer cover in 1976 at the Hilton in Pasadena, CA and in April of 1975.

Rock Photo-The Fall 1984 issue of this publication featured a David Lee Roth cover and several Dave photos. Address: Modern Photography, 825 Seventh Avenue, New York, NY 100119.

Rockpop-Van Halen appeared on this German television show on 6/21/80 and lip-synced "And the Cradle Will Rock" and "You Really Got Me."

Rock Power-The August 1991 issue of this German magazine featured a Van Halen cover and a four-page article by Markus Ott. *F.U.C.K.* was also reviewed.

Rock Rap-The September 1986 issue of this magazine featured a Van Halen cover and a three-page article titled "The New Van Halen: It's Only Love!" by Lori Bernstein.

Rock Scene-The December 1988 issue of this magazine featured a Van Halen cover and a four-page interview with Eddie by Anne Leighton titled "A Visit to the Laboratory of Rock's Mad Scientist." Address: 475 Park Avenue South, Suite 2201, New York, NY 10016.

Rock Special-The Fall 1980 issue of this publication featured a Van Halen cover. David Lee Roth again appeared on the cover of the Winter 1981 issue along with a three-page Van Halen feature titled "Van Halen: Breaking All the Rules-the Right Way."

Rock Stars-The May 1980 issue of this magazine featured a David Lee cover and a four-page interview titled "David Lee Roth on Van Halen: The Best Parts of Our Songs Are Made Up on the Spot." Address: 2 Park Avenue, New York, NY 10016.

Rock Steady-(7:31) The band performed this Bad Company cover in 1976 at the Hilton in Pasadena, CA.

Rock World-Van Halen appeared on the cover of the November 1984 issue of this magazine.

Rod and Custom-The August 1998 issue of this magazine featured an article about Michael Anthony.

Rogers, Roy-Sammy Hagar provided background vocals for this artist's *Pleasure and Pain* (Virgin 45547, 1998) track "You Can't Stop Now. "

Rolling Stone-This magazine's index of Van Halen-related issues:
9/04/80: "The Endless Party": interviews backstage during the 1980 *Invasion* tour by Mikal Gilmore, plus a summary of band's career to 1980.
6/21/84: "Van Halen's Split Personality": four-page Van Halen interview by Debby Miller.
4/11/85: David Lee Roth cover. "David Lee Roth": five-page David Lee Roth interview by Nancy Collins. Sammy Hagar tour dates.
7/03/86: Van Halen cover. "Can This Be Love?": six-page Van Halen interview by David Fricke.

7/14/88: Van Halen cover. "Random Notes": one-page feature on Sammy Hagar's boxing experience. "Music in Brief": short write-up on Van Halen concert in Foxboro, MA. "Van Halen Feels the Burn": five-page Van Halen feature by Steve Pond. Monsters of Rock tour review by Doug Pullen.

12/15/88: Van Halen cover. Short feature on Monsters of Rock tour and *OU812*. *OU812* reviewed. Top 200 Albums of 1988: *OU812* at #16 and David Lee Roth's *Skyscraper* at #34.

11/16/89: The 100 greatest albums of the 80s. *1984* places #81.

4/06/95: Eddie Van Halen cover. "Balancing Act": eight-page Eddie interview by David Wild.

11/28/96: "Random Notes": write-up on the City of Hope Benefit.

4/17/97: Edward and Alex debut their milk advertisement.

7/10/97: Sammy Hagar feature.

10/16/97: *Crazy from the Heat* autobiography reviewed by Mark Coleman.

4/16/98: Eddie Van Halen interviewed.

8/98: Eddie Van Halen feature in the Australian version of this magazine.

Address: 1290 Avenue of the Americas, New York, NY 10104-0298; Telephone 212-484-1616.

Romeo Delight-(*Women and Children First* [4:19]) One of the lines from this song came from "Get the Show on the Road," a song the band used to use as a show opener in their club days. The clicking sound heard throughout the song was created by Ed's shaking the low E string against the pickup of his guitar.

The Rose-(20th Century Fox, 1979) Bette Midler covered "Keep on Rockin'" from Sammy Hagar's *Nine on a Ten Scale* album in this movie about the life of a female rock star.

Rosen, Steven-A writer whose Van Halen interviews led him to begin writing a book about the life of Eddie Van Halen. The book was to be the first authorized Edward biography, portions of which appeared in several issues of Guitar World as the book was being written. However, the project was scrapped before completion.

Roth, David Lee-Born to Nathan and Sybil Roth on 10/10/54 in Bloomington, IN, David Lee Roth would, a mere twenty-four years later, begin his reign as one of the world's most well-known entertainers.

His life story is a tale of unusual events that eventually molded a great performer. His contribution to Van Halen has often been described as that of an outside ear, recognizing when the band had become too cerebral and helping to make the music the more primal force that it was in the early years.

So what made him what he is? Until the age of five, Dave was forced to wear leg braces, and by the age of six he had visited his first psychiatrist. He jumped his way out of the braces and onto the stage. He taught the psychiatrists that there was nothing wrong with him that being a rock star couldn't cure.

The Roths, who included Dave's sisters, Lisa and Allison, moved around quite a bit, first to New Castle, IN, then to Swampscott, MA, then to Brookline, MA, before settling in the Los Angeles area in 1963. Dave was expelled from his junior high school for fighting and attended the Webb School for Boys for a semester. He then attended John Muir High School. It was at this time that he began his lifelong karate disciplines.

More than just living through the 60s and 70s, Dave embodied these decades. He took part in every possible facet by smoking pot, attending as many concerts as possible, reading as much counterculture literature as possible, and adhering to the fashion trends of the day. He put on a show even when he wasn't on stage.

Dave's first big band was the Red Ball Jets. It was in this band that he developed his stage persona known as "Diamond Dave." His influences at this time included the Beach Boys, The Beatles, and The Rolling Stones, among many others.

He attended Pasadena Community College for a while, where the Van Halen brothers were also studying music theory, and took to the piano and the saxophone.

His father was in the Air Force and later became an eye surgeon. It was his father's eventual success in his trade that allowed the rehearsal space in the Roth home that Van Halen used to write many of their first songs. Rumors about the Roths' funding of the band in their club days were unfounded. The band was never given anything they didn't earn. Dave learned the value of a dollar the hard way working in Pasadena stables. He held other jobs, including one as a janitor in a hospital.

When Dave joined Van Halen, he applied his philosophies about the danceability of rock music. Simply put, if a song didn't make you want to get up and dance, it was taken off the set list. Dave could be heard in bootlegs of the time encouraging people to get on the dance floor.

There's no doubt that the party attitude of the band through their first twelve years was mainly attributable to Dave. On the first few Van Halen albums, Dave concentrated on his vocals and kept the parties mostly on the stage and on the road. Beginning with *Women and Children First*, though, Dave brought the party to the albums. His philosophy here was to say and do anything on the albums to convey an attitude, whether it meant mumbling the lyrics or picking up the harmonica. During concerts he started to rely heavily on funny and provocative phrases and stories that always kept the crowd either laughing or cheering. It was pure entertainment.

In 1985 Dave struck out on his own. He recorded an EP and began work on a movie. His hopes for further entertaining the world were a bit too ambitious for the rest of Van Halen, and the group parted ways with the vocalist. The split was a shock for rock fans around the world.

Not missing a beat, Dave assembled an all-star band to make his first and second solo albums. At first music magazines made comparisons to Van Halen and chose to stick with Dave because he kept the party atmosphere of the old Van Halen in his new band. However, no matter how many great musicians Dave got to play on his albums, sales didn't keep up with Van Halen's, and the same press that stuck by Dave at the beginning of his solo career turned on him.

Dave returned to the band in 1996 to record two songs for *Best of Volume 1*. What resulted was an ugly sequence of events that continues to be disputed. Entire groups of people became devoted to the debate and remain so. The reason is partly due to the direct contradictions in the stories of Van Halen and Dave. What really happened is probably best left to the people involved. There's no doubting that the songs Dave performed with the band were some of the most important moments in the history of rock music.

For more about the life of David Lee Roth, read his autobiography, *Crazy from the Heat* (Hyperion, 1997).

The Rover-This Led Zeppelin cover was performed by the band at the Starwood in Hollywood, CA, in 1976 and on 9/18/76 at the Bogart in San Bernardino, CA.

The Roxy-Edward joined Allan Holdsworth and Jeff Berlin at this West Hollywood, CA, club on 4/23/82, where they performed a song Edward had written the night before with Allan's bass player, Jeff Berlin. In April 1985 Edward joined Scandal on stage here to perform the following songs: • Maybe We Went Too Far (5:05) • River Deep, Mountain High (5:45)

Rumpus-One of two instrumental tunes Ed remembers his first band, the Broken Combs, writing and performing.

Runaround-(*For Unlawful Carnal Knowledge* [4:21]; *Live: Right Here, Right Now* [5:21]) Ed used a 6-string bass and his custom-built Fender

Esquire (#232 of 300) on this track. The guitar was given to him by Fender in hopes of an endorsement deal.

The band made a typical performance video for this song that featured the band ripping through the song on a circular 40-foot platform, spinning at 12 miles per hour. Michael Anthony was almost thrown from it on more than one occasion when he got too close to the edge. The video was produced by Ben Dossett and directed by Meiert Avis.

This video also marks one of two rare occasions in which Edward performs part of the song on a red-, white-, and black-striped Ernie Ball Music Man guitar. The only other known video appearance of the guitar was in the "Poundcake" video.

Runnin' with the Devil-(*Van Halen*; *Best of Volume 1* [3:32]) 1. The noise at the beginning of this song is a collection of car horns. The horns were taken from the band's own cars, including Alex's Opel, Ed's Volvo, a Mercedes Benz, and a Volkswagen. The horns were mounted in a box and powered by two car batteries, with a foot switch to turn them on and off. Producer Ted Templeman slowed the horns down before adding them to the track. This same idea was first used during the band's club sets and appeared on their Simmons financed demo on "House of Pain" (which later appeared on *1984*), sounding after each verse. On the demo the automotive noisemakers also acted as a segue to "Runnin' with the Devil." Eddie recalled that the horns were detrimental to the songs on the demo and may have been partly responsible for its failure.

There was a mixing error when this song appeared on *Best of Volume 1*. The error was corrected in later pressings of the album.

The video for the song (filmed at the Whisky A GoGo in 1977) starts off in much the same way as the song had been performed live: Mike seemingly plucking the strings with his teeth. Dave provides one of his more glaring lip-sync errors in the first few seconds by missing half a scream. Ed and Mike launch into what would later be called a Kiss impersonation, rocking back and forth perfectly choreographed twice. Near the end of the video a crew member accidentally shares the stage during a shot; he flees, realizing his mistake.

Corporation of One's 1989 song "Guns of the Boogie Down" featured a sample of the song's intro riff.

A recording of Pearl Jam covering this song in concert is in circulation among Pearl Jam and Van Halen fans.

2. A Van Halen tribute album (Progressive Arts, 8/18/00) featuring the following tracks and bands: "Somebody Get Me a Doctor" by Project X, "Romeo Delight" by Aces Wild, "Everybody Wants Some" by Elephant Orange, "Feel Your Love Tonight" by Hear Here, "Little Dreamer" by Project X, "D.O.A." by Babt Jones, "Atomic Punk" by Wraith, "Unchained" by 5150, "IceCream Man" by Drop, "Eruption 2000" by Don Sullivan, "I'll Wait" by Klank, and "Mean Street" by 1984.

S

Sammy Hagar-(Capitol/EMI Records 11599, 1977) This Sammy Hagar solo album is also known as "The Red Album" and features a reunion of sorts with former Montrose bandmates Bill Church (bass) and Alan Fitzgerald (keyboards).

The album spent nine weeks on the charts, starting on 2/26/77 and reaching a high point of #167.

Bette Midler covered "Red," which was included on her 1977 release, *Broken Blossom* (Atlantic, 82780-2). Tracks: • Red • Catch the Wind • Cruizin' & Boozin' • Free Money • Rock 'n' Roll Weekend • Fillmore Shuffle • Hungry • The Pits • Love Has Found Me • Little Star/Eclipse

Sammy Hagar Birthday Celebration Video-This video is a Los Tres Gusanos performance taped on 10/19/95 at the Cabo Wabo Cantina. Sammy wanted to make a video of one of his birthday performances so that customers of the Cabo Wabo Cantina could at least buy a video of a Los Tres Gusanos performance if they couldn't see them in person. The set list: • Boy's Night Out • I'll Fall in Love Again • Good Rockin' Tonight • Make It Last • Red • Baby's on Fire • High Hopes • Rock Me Baby (Blues Jam) • I Don't Need Love • Three Lock Box/I'm Goin' Down • Roadhouse Blues • Bad Motor Scooter • Plain Jane • Your Love Is Driving Me Crazy • Heavy Metal • Rock Candy • Rock 'n' Roll Weekend • There's Only One Way to Rock • Wild Thing • I Can't Drive 55 • Baby Please Don't Go

San Francisco Chronicle-This newspaper's web site featured an interview with Eddie Van Halen on 3/22/98.

Satisfaction-This Rolling Stones cover was performed by the band on 5/21/92 at the Cabo Wabo Cantina.

Saturday Night Live-Eddie Van Halen and Valerie Bertinelli appeared on this show on 2/28/87. Eddie accompanied Valerie Bertinelli to the taping of this particular episode and wound up not only jamming a song with G.E. Smith, Tom "T-Bone" Wolk (both of Hall and Oates fame), and the Saturday Night Live band, but performing in a skit as well. The show was filmed at the GE building in Rockefeller Plaza, New York, NY.

When Valerie introduced Ed just before his jam with G.E. Smith, she was wearing a button on her jacket that read 91X. 91X is a radio station in San Diego, CA. Reportedly they were running a contest in which you had to get the radio station logo exposed in any way possible, with the booty being a prize of $20,000. One listener convinced Valerie to wear the sticker during the show and earned second place in the contest.

The bluesy, instrumental jam Ed played was titled "Stompin' 8H" (2:53) after the name of the studio the show was filmed in. Smith handled rhythm guitar on his beaten up Fender Telecaster, while Edward shot his patented licks from his Kramer 5150 Strat over the top.

The jam resurfaced in 1989 when Ed played bass on the Steve Lukather cut "Twist the Knife," albeit in a slightly different form. The main riff was used a third time on *Van Halen III* for the song "Dirty Water Dog."

The skit, entitled "Dinner at the Van Halens," was a humorous poke at a typical evening meal at the Van Halen household, complete with roadies frisking the guests, screening phone calls, and causing more chaos than order.

Since that episode there have been several references to Van Halen on Saturday Night Live, the most blatant being a parody of David Lee Roth that appeared on 4/19/97 in which the actor portraying Dave fought with a "goatboy" for food. In yet another episode, the late Chris Farley and Adam Sandler both took part in the commercial parody "Schmitt's Gay Beer," which was set to "Beautiful Girls."

Secrets-(*Diver Down* [3:25]) The original title for this track was "Lookin' Good." Dave was inspired to write the lyrics to "Secrets" after reading several greeting and get-well cards while in Albuquerque, NM, in late 1980 or very early1981. The cards were written in the style of American Indian poetry, with lines like "May your moccasins leave happy tracks in the summer snows."

Ed originally wanted to put this track on *Fair Warning*, but the rest of the band didn't like the song at the time. Ed used a Gibson 12-string/6-string doubleneck to record this track. Live he used a custom Kramer doubleneck.

The Seduction of Gina-(CBS, 1983) Eddie wrote three synthesizer songs (one of which included a guitar solo) for this made-for-television movie, which starred Valerie Bertinelli as a compulsive gambler who cheats on her husband to earn money to gamble. The remainder of the music was done by Tom Neuman.

Eddie wrote the opening composition without ever seeing any footage from the film. The other songs were written based on scene descriptions from Valerie, though he and Donn Landee were shown a rough cut of the film. The director liked Ed's work so much that he asked the guitarist to score the entire film, but Van Halen was unable to dedicate any more time to the project due to the recording of *1984*, which was already in progress.

Originally, the title of the movie was going to be Another High Roller, but CBS changed it to *The Seduction of Gina*, hoping the sexually suggestive title would attract more viewers. Tracks: • Opening Theme (2:40) • Car Chase Sequence (3:30) • End Credits Theme (0:30)

The Seventh Seal-(*Balance* [5:18]) This song was named after the 1957 Ingmar Bergman film of the same name.

The Buddhist harmonic chanting that opens this track was performed by the Monks of Gyuto Tantric University, courtesy of Gyuto Wheel of Dharma Monastery. The monk's introduction to the song was taken from their album *The Gyoto Monks Tibetan Tantric Choir* (Windham Hill, 1987) produced by the Grateful Dead's Mickey Hart. The monks appeared in concert with the Grateful Dead several times.

Ed used his infamous MXR Flanger on this track.

On 1/04/96 it was announced that this song had earned a Grammy nomination in the category of Best Hard Rock Performance; it didn't win.

"I threw everything that I've ever thought about the beginning and the end of earth and mankind in there. It's really a prayer. It's a prayer to not destroy and not to reach the point of Armageddon, to where there's no return."-Sammy Hagar on Rockline, 2/27/95.

79th and Sunset-Two versions of this unaccompanied acoustic Humble Pie cover song by David Lee Roth are known to exist: the full song and a shortened version, both taken from the same recording and used for many bootlegs. The song was recorded during an interview with Jim Ladd on KMET, Los Angeles, CA, in 1982. At the end of the song, Dave did a plug for KMET, which is not available on any known recordings. The song is sometimes known as "Real Go Getter" or "Cookie Box."

Sgt. Bilko-(Universal Pictures/Imagine Entertainment, 1996) David Lee Roth performed a song for this film titled "Bad Habits," written by Billy Field.

In addition to "Bad Habits," a second song titled "Ain't That Peculiar" was included on a test pressing for the soundtrack. Both tracks were recorded in September 1994. Mysteriously, though, the soundtrack was never released. Dave also performed this song live on more than one occasion during his nightclub tour with the Blues Bustin' Mambo Slammers.

"Bad Habits" was originally written and recorded by Australian Billy Field in 1980 and went to #1 on the Australian singles charts, where it stayed for 24 weeks.

The movie is a humorous look at a gambling Army platoon, led by Steve Martin as MSgt. Bilko. The film also stars Dan Akroyd and Phil Hartman. "Bad Habits" appears during a troop inspection by Martin's nemesis, Major Thorn (played by Hartman).

Shaker-This unreleased original is a leftover from the *Balance* recording sessions.

Shape You're In-(4:24) This unreleased original was performed by the band on 6/10/77 at the Whisky A GoGo in West Hollywood, CA.

Sherman-Eddie's Dalmatian. The dog can be heard on "Baluchitherium" from *Balance*.

She's the Woman-(3:00) This unreleased original was recorded for the band's 1977 Warner Brothers demo. It was also performed on 6/03/76 at The Starwood in Hollywood, CA. The song contains riffs later found in "Mean Street."

Showbizz-The January 1998 issue of this Brazilian magazine featured an interview with Eddie Van Halen by José Emílio Rondeau titled "Eleven Questions: Eddie Van Halen."

Show Your Love-The original title for "I'm the One." It was under the name "Show Your Love" that this song appeared on the band's 1977 Warner Brothers demo.

The Simpsons-Van Halen made an appearance, in animated form, on this television show on 5/21/00. In the episode Willie Nelson remarks that he's trying get the band and Sammy Hagar back together.

Sinatra, Frank-Released in 1984, the video for Sinatra's "L.A. Is My Lady" featured Dave and Ed walking through a crowd of fans into a limo equipped with a VCR. Dave inserts a videocassette, which then plays the video by Frank.

Sinner's Swing!-(*Fair Warning* [3:08]) In the 4/96 issue of Guitar World Billy Corgan of the Smashing Pumpkins used this song as a summary of the entire *Fair Warning* album-dark and aggressive. Almost nothing is known about the song's history. However, it is believed the lyrics may have been inspired by Hunter Thompson's book "Hell's Angels."

Sitting on Top of the World-An instrumental version of this Cream cover was performed by Ed, Al, and Mike at several shows on the *5150* tour.

16 Magazine-This magazine's index of Van Halen-related issues:
5/81: "An Intimate Interview with Eddie Van Halen.": Two-page Edward interview.
6/81: "David Lee Roth Squeals on Van Halen!": Two-page David Lee Roth interview.
6/82: "Eddie Van Halen & Valerie Bertinelli-On the Town!": Two-page Edward and Valerie feature.

Skyscraper-(Warner Bros. 9 25671-2, 1988) David Lee Roth's second full-length solo album. The album was released in February 1988, beginning a 27-week run on the charts on 2/13/88, reaching U.S. #6 and U.K. #11. Billy Sheehan was at a very low point with this album-it was the beginning of the end of his involvement with the band. He felt it had too many overdubs and that none of the songs were really taken apart and looked at properly, the way a piece of music should be. Both "Just Like Paradise" and "Stand Up" featured sequenced, synthesized bass lines.

All of the songs were planned to be played slightly faster on the supporting tour. The day Sheehan left the band, he, Brett Tuggle, Pat Torpey, and an unknown guitarist went into the studio to lay down background vocals at a faster tempo, with Tuggle later loading them into a sampler. So, even though Sheehan was no longer in the band when the tour rolled around, he was still providing background vocals, albeit in a digital capacity.

As part of a promotional gig for the album, Dave scaled a plaster mountainside erected atop Tower Records in West Hollywood, CA. Drummer Greg Bissonette's brother, Matt, stepped in to replace Sheehan for the accompanying tour.

"Damn Good" features Billy Sheehan on fretless bass. "Hot Dog and a Shake" came about after hearing Dave wisecrack, "Hey baby, can I get a hot dog to go along with that shake?"

After Sheehan left the band, he planned on starting a band with Steve Stevens. That fell through for unknown reasons, and Sheehan went on to form Mr. Big with Paul Gilbert, Eric Martin, and Pat Torpey. Tracks: • Knucklebones • Just Like • The Bottom Line • Skyscraper • Damn Good • Hot Dog and a Shake • Stand Up • Hina • Perfect Timing • Two Fools a Minute

The Australian release also includes "California Girls" and "Just a Gigolo/I Ain't Got Nobody."

The mountain-climbing sequences in the video for the song "Just Like Paradise" were filmed at Yosemite National Park's Half Dome. The only other video made for this album was "Stand Up."

Skyscraper singles/promos
"Just Like Paradise," "The Bottom Line," WB 7-28119, 7" Vinyl, USA, 1988. Highest chart position: #6 in USA and #27 in UK.

"Stand Up," "Damn Good," WB, USA, 1988. Highest chart position: #64 in USA.

"Just Like Paradise," "The Bottom Line," "Yankee Rose," WEA W8119, CD, France, 1988.

Sleepwalkers-(a.k.a. Stephen King's Sleepwalkers) (Columbia Pictures/Ion Pictures, 1992) "It('s a Monster)," originally from Extreme's *Pornograffitti* album, appeared in this Stephen King horror film. The song is featured during a scene when Charles Brady (played by Brian Krause) is driving down the road in a blue Trans Am and is motioned to the side of the road by a suspicious teacher.

Slow Ride-This Foghat cover was reportedly played in the band's early years.

Smash Hits-Van Halen appeared on the cover of the March 1985 issue of this magazine.

Snake-Michael Anthony's last band before joining Mammoth. He played bass and sang lead vocals. Snake opened for Mammoth on occasion and even lent Mammoth their PA system for a gig once because Mammoth had blown up theirs.

Somebody Get Me a Doctor-(*Van Halen II* [2:51]) This song was on the band's 25-song demo tape for Warner Brothers in 1977. The solo on the demo version is much longer than the album version, lasting more than a minute. The intro chords are also played in reverse order on the demo.

This song is considered a favorite of the members of Pantera.

Someday-This unreleased original was written by Sammy Hagar and performed during his solo on 7/29/95 at Alpine Valley in East Troy, WI, during the *Balance* tour.

Song Hits-This magazine's index of Van Halen-related issues:

2/83: David Lee Roth cover. "Exclusive Interview: Van Halen's David Lee Roth""Van Halen Concert Review": concert review from 1982 New Haven, CT, performance.

6/84: Eddie Van Halen/David Lee Roth cover. "Van Halen Pop Star of the Month": two-page Dave interview. Lyrics to Sammy Hagar's "The Girl Gets Around."

9/84: David Lee Roth cover. "Van Halen": three-page Van Halen feature. Lyrics to HSAS' "Missing You" and "Top of the Rock."
Address: Charlton Building, Derby, CT 06418.

Sonrisa Salvaje-(Warner Bros. LWB-6550, 1986) This is the Spanish version of David Lee Roth's *Eat 'Em and Smile* album. It was Billy Sheehan's idea to record *Eat 'Em and Smile* in Spanish. He came up with this idea during a plane trip. He was reading an article in Time magazine that mentioned that almost half of the Spanish-speaking population was under the age of 20. Knowing that Roth spoke some Spanish, Sheehan suggested recording the album over again, entirely in Spanish. Ultimately, if the album did well, the band planned on doing the same thing with further releases, but sales were poor and the idea ended with this album. Sheehan attributes this to the fact that the album was considered "Gringo Spanish," not "True Spanish."

He and Dave rerecorded all the vocals (none of the music was rerecorded) in the same studio being used by Missing Persons, who were recording an album of their own. Roth had a Spanish tutor in the studio to help him with some of the lines, and a few words and phrases had to be changed due to the differences in the two languages and the lack of translatable slang terms (like "bump and grind," for example). A more few lines were changed because Roth was concerned that some of them might have been a little too sexually suggestive for the more conservative Mexican culture.

Roth was invited to Mazatlan shortly after the album's release to be the halftime entertainment at the Miss Mexico pageant. The pageant was broadcast on a show called Siempre en Domingo. Tracks: • Yankee Rose • Timido • Soy Facil • Noche De Ronda En La Ciudad • Loco Del Calor! • La Calle Del Tabaco • Arma De Caza Mayor • En Busca De Pleito • Cuanto Frenesi • Asi Es La Vida

So This Is Love?-(*Fair Warning* [3:05]) The solo on this track was a compilation of about four solos put together by Ed and recorded on the first attempt. The video for the song appeared in the compilation of *Fair Warning* videos filmed in Oakland, CA, sometime between 6/11/81 and 6/13/81.

Sounds-Van Halen appeared on the cover of this magazine in the following issues: 4/79, 7/79, 6/81, 6/82, 8/84.

The Sounds of Las Vegas-One of the first bands Eddie and Alex Van Halen formed in approximately 1967. Performing pop tunes of the 1960s, like "I'm a Believer," the fledgling band also featured a bass player named James Wright. Alex performed lead vocals for a time, until the band took on a singer named Daniel.

Source of Infection-(*OU812* [3:58]) Alternate titles for this track included "Source." The entire *OU812* album was almost named after this song.

Spaceballs-(Brooksfilms/MGM-UA, 1987) The Van Halen track "Good Enough," taken from *5150*, is featured in this Mel Brooks Star Wars parody starring Mel Brooks, John Candy, Bill Pullman, and Rick Moranis. The track is played during a scene when Barf (Candy's character) and Lone Star (Pullman's character) enter an intergalactic diner.

The song is also included on the movie's soundtrack (Atlantic 81770-1, 1987).

Spanish Fly-(*Van Halen II* [:58]) Ed got the idea for this instrumental after playing on an acoustic guitar during a New Year's Eve party at Ted Templeman's house on 12/31/78. Templeman was surprised that Eddie could play an acoustic guitar just as well as an electric and suggested the guitarist write an acoustic instrumental for *Van Halen II*. He recorded it on a nylon-string Ovation.

The song became a regular part of Eddie's solo spot on tour.

Spanked-(*For Unlawful Carnal Knowledge* [4:53]; *Live: Right Here, Right Now* [5:08]) Producer/Engineer Andy Johns used the term "spanked" to describe the monitor speakers in the 5150 Studio the first time he saw them, and the band quickly adopted the term into their vocabulary.

Ed played a Danelectro 6-string bass through his Marshall on this track. He also used his custom-built Fender Esquire. He used an Ebow (an electronic device that bows the guitar strings with an energy field) to open this song, a suggestion from Al.

Mike used a 5-string Music Man, 4-string Music Man, and a Heartfield 6-string bass for this track. He had Sterling Ball shave the necks down on the Music Man basses to give them more of a Fender Jazz bass feel.

In concert Ed had a doubleneck guitar/bass that he played for this song. However, there were problems with delay time between the guitar, the wireless system, and the amps, which made this song increasingly difficult to play live, so it was eventually dropped from the set list.

SPIN-David Lee Roth appeared on the cover of this magazine's April 1986 issue, which featured a five-page interview by Scott Cohen titled "It's Only Roth 'n' Roll" about the band's split with Dave.

The magazine featured Dave on the cover again in their 10/00 issue for a feature titled "The 100 Sleaziest Moments in Rock." Dave's bonus system for getting the right women backstage, detailed in "The Tours" chapter, came in at #10.

Spooch-Sammy Hagar's pet cockatoo.

Spoonful-This Cream cover was reportedly a staple of the band's live set during their backyard party days.

Standin' at the Same Old Crossroads-Van Halen performed this Sammy Hagar track from his *I Never Said Goodbye* album on 11/07/88 at the Peoria Civic Center in Peoria, IL.

Standing Hampton-(Geffen 2006-2, 1982) Sammy Hagar solo album released on 1/13/82, certified gold on 1/28/83, and certified platinum on 4/03/92. Its 32-week run on the charts began on 1/30/82. The album eventually reached #28. The title of this album was reportedly derived from an English slang term for a man's erection: "Hampton Wick." Tracks: • I'll Fall in Love Again • There's Only One Way to Rock • Baby's on Fire • Can't Get Loose • Heavy Metal • Baby It's You • Surrender • Inside Lookin' In • Sweet Hitchhiker • Piece of My Heart

Standing Hampton singles/promos
"I'll Fall in Love Again," "Satisfied," Geffen, 7" Vinyl, USA, 1982. Highest chart position: #43 in USA.

"Heavy Metal," "Satisfied," "Don't Get Hooked," Geffen, 12" Vinyl, USA, 1982.

"Piece of My Heart," Geffen, USA, 1982. Highest chart position: #73 in USA.

Star-This publication's index of Van Halen-related issues:
7/28/87: Cover and two-page feature on Edward and Valerie.
11/10/87: One-page feature on Edward's reported drunk driving arrest by Geoff Richards.
4/22/97: "Wild and Wacky Demands of Hollywood' Biggest Names": one-page feature on strange demands, included Van Halen's brown M&Ms ban from their early tour rider.
6/24/97: "Valerie to Be Mom Again to Save Marriage": one-page feature by Steve Tinney on Edward and Valerie supposedly having another child.

Star Hits-This magazine's index of Van Halen-related issues:
3/84: "Personal File: David Lee Roth": one-page background feature on David Lee Roth.

6/84: Cover and two-page Edward and David interview titled "Crazy Eddie."

Address: 150 East 58th Street, New York, NY 10022.

Steinberger-In 1985 this guitar company's brochure featured a one-page article on Eddie. Address: Steinberger Sound Corporation, 122 South Robinson Avenue, Newburgh, NY 12550; Telephone: 914-565-4005.

Steve Vissard Show-On 3/04/93 Extreme performed "Stop the World" on this Australian program.

Sticks-This German magazine's July 1993 issue included a nine-page Alex Van Halen interview by Adam Budowsky reprinted from the July 1993 issue of Modern Drummer titled "Alex Van Halen Right Here, Right Now!"

Still Alive and Well-(2:22) The band performed this Rick Derringer cover on 9/18/76 at the Bogart in San Bernardino, CA. This song was written by Derringer as sort of a "comeback" tune for Johnny Winter, who had just returned from rehabilitation. Derringer later recorded his own version of the song, which is available on both his *Spring Fever* and *Derringer Live* albums.

Stone Cold Sober Again-This David Bowie cover was reportedly played by the band in their early years.

The Stoned Age-(Trimark Pictures, 1993) The Montrose classic "Rock Candy" makes an appearance in this movie.

Street Machine-(Capitol Records 11983, 1979) Sammy Hagar solo album that entered the charts on 9/18/79, lasting 13 weeks and reaching #71. Only one single was released: "Plain Jane," which reached its highest chart position at #77. Boston's Tom Scholz was originally set to produce this album, but that fell through for unknown reasons. "Wounded in Love" was written by Sammy's ex-wife, Betsy. Tracks: • Growing Pains • Child to Man • Trans Am (Highway Wonderland) • Feels Like Love • Plain Jane • Never Say Die • This Planet's on Fire (Burn in Hell) • Wounded in Love • Falling in Love • Straight to the Top

Strung Out-(*Balance* [1:29]) This track was recorded in the spring/summer of 1983. While renting Marvin Hamlish's beach house in Malibu, CA, Eddie trashed Hamlish's white Yamaha grand piano. He threw everything he could find into the piano and raked various items across the strings, including ping-pong balls, D-cell batteries, and even silverware. The small 1-minute, 29-second piece actually comes from hours of tape Eddie made while destroying the piano.

Ed had the piano fixed and once claimed that Hamlish might not have known about the incident until the song came out.

Sucker in a 3-Piece-(*OU812* [5:52]) An alternate title for this track was "Sucker."

This song was given special attention by Good Morning America. During the Monsters of Rock Tour, surprised parents were read the lyrics as they were asked about their feelings toward the tour.

Summer Nights-(*5150* [5:04]) This was the first song Ed, Al, and Mike jammed to with Sammy Hagar. Rumor has it that an alternate version of this song exists with Roth-written lyrics.

Ed recorded the track on a Steinberger GL-2T.

Summertime Blues-(5:01) The band performed this Eddie Cochran cover on 5/10/78 in Paris, France; again in 1978 in Osaka, Japan; in 1983 throughout the South American tour; in 1984 in Quebec City, Quebec;

and on 8/18/86 at the Capitol Centre in Largo, MD. It was also performed in their club days.

Sunday Afternoon in the Park-(*Fair Warning* [2:00]) Ed used a cheap
Electro-Harmonix Micro-Sythesizer to create this unusual instrumental.
The song later became a part of Mike's bass solo during the *For
Unlawful Carnal Knowledge* tour.

Super Chevy-This magazine featured an Eddie Van Halen interview in
its 6/99 issue.

Super Mario Brothers-(Lightmotive/Allied Filmmakers, 1993)
(Capitol, 1993) Extreme performed their song "Where Are You Going?"
for the soundtrack to this movie.

Superstition-(5:07) The band performed this Stevie Wonder cover on
9/18/76 at the Bogart in San Bernardino, CA. The song was also performed several times throughout the 1988 Monsters of Rock tour.

Suzy Q-This Creedence Clearwater Revival cover has reportedly been
played live by the band.

Sweet Emotion-(5:35) The band performed this Aerosmith cover on
9/18/76 at the Bogart in San Bernardino, CA.

Sydney-"Finish What Ya Started" was the song played during the opening credits to this 1990 sitcom for which Valerie Bertinelli served as executive producer and in which she starred as a private investigator. Other
actors on the show included Matthew Perry (of Friends) playing a cop and
Barney Martin (of Sienfeld) playing a bartender.

T

Take Me Back (Déjà Vu)-(*Balance* [4:43]) The music for this song was originally written for *For Unlawful Carnal Knowledge*. The intro for this song was the same intro used for "No More Waiting," an unreleased Van Halen song dating back to the band's club days.

The acoustic guitar used on this track is a "Musser," a South American guitar Ed bought at Norm's Rare Guitars in Los Angeles. Edward also plays some slide guitar on this track.

Two complete sets of lyrics were rejected by producer Bruce Fairburn before a final third set from Sammy was accepted. This may be one of the reasons Sammy wanted this song dropped from the album and replaced with "Crossing Over."

This song was remixed in February 1995, but no one has yet reported hearing a difference on any official releases.

Take Your Whiskey Home-(*Women and Children First* [3:09]) This was a song from the band's club days that Edward didn't care for anymore but that the rest of the band insisted be on the album.

Teen-A two-page Van Halen feature, "Van Halen: Still Rockin' Strong," by B.J. Hoffman appeared in this magazine's September 1985 issue.

TeenAge-David Lee Roth and Eddie Van Halen appeared on the cover of the October 1983 issue of this magazine. The five-page Edward and David Lee Roth interview by David Rensin was titled "Interview: Van Halen." Address: 217 Jackson Street, P.O. Box 948, Lowell, MA 01853.

Teen Bag-In the Fall 1985 issue of this magazine, a two-page Edward and Valerie feature titled "We'll Be Married for 60 Years" appeared.

Teen Stars-This magazine's index of Van Halen-related issues:
1985: Rock Special 1 Eddie Van Halen/David Lee Roth cover.
1985: Rock Special 2 "Van Halen Hotline": two-page Van Halen feature and cover.

Tennessee Squires-An elite club created by the Jack Daniels company. Michael Anthony is a member and even owns a piece of land at the distillery.

Ten 13-(BMG/Beyond 78110, 2000) Sammy Hagar solo album released on 10/24/00. The album debuted at #52 with 25,061 copies sold in the first week. Tracks: • Shaka Doobie (The Limit) • Let Sally Drive • Serious Juju • The Message • Deeper Kinda Love • Little Bit More • Ten 13 • Protection • 3 in the Middle • The Real Deal • Tropic of Capricorn

That's Why I Love You-This unreleased original was planned for inclusion on *Van Halen III* but was replaced by "Josephina." Since the song was on test pressings of *Van Halen III* at Warner Brothers, it wasn't long before it became available in the bootlegging community. This was the first unreleased studio track since the Dave-era to make it into public circulation. This was also the first song Dave worked on with the band when he returned to 5150 in 1996.
Gary and Ed wrote the song at least partially over the phone disagreeing on a proper style for the vocals on the track.

Thelonius Monster-This band recorded a song titled "Sammy Hagar Weekend" for their 1989 *Stormy Weather* album (Combat/Relativity).

There's Only One Way to Rock-The band regularly played this Sammy Hagar original throughout their tours with Sammy.

30 Days in the Hole-(2:26) Van Halen performed this Humble Pie cover song on 9/18/76 at The Bogart in San Bernardino, CA.

Three Lock Box-(Geffen 2021, 1982) Sammy Hagar solo album featuring background keyboard tracks by Giant's Alan Pasqua and Journey's Jonathan Cain. The album entered the charts on 12/25/82, lasting 34-weeks and reaching #17. It was certified gold on 5/25/83. Tracks: • Growing Up • I Don't Need Love • I Wouldn't Change a Thing • In the Room • Never Give Up • Remember the Heroes • Remote Love • Rise of the Animal • Three Lock Box • Your Love Is Amazin' • Your Love Is Driving Me Crazy

"Your Love Is Driving Me Crazy" was released as a single, reaching #13 on the charts. "Never Give Up" was also released as a single, reaching #46.

One video was made for this album, for the song "Three Lock Box."

316-1. (*For Unlawful Carnal Knowledge* [1:29]) This song derived its name from the birthday of Wolfgang William Van Halen, son of Eddie and Valerie, born 3/16/91. During Valerie's pregnancy Ed would lay a guitar next to her stomach and play this song, which had a calming effect on the then-unborn Wolfgang.

Ed used to play this song as an introduction to his live solo as early as the *5150* tour.

For the album version, Ed used a Chet Atkins steel-string acoustic solid-body guitar and an Eventide H3000 harmonizer.

2. (*Live: Right Here, Right Now* [11:37]) The live solo Eddie performed for the *Live: Right Here, Right Now* album was also given the name "316" because the solo began with a rendition of the *For Unlawful Carnal Knowledge* version of the song.

Through the Fire-(Geffen GHS 4023, 1984) This was a one-time project album by HSAS featuring Sammy on vocals, Journey's Neil Schon on guitar, ex-Billy Squier bassist Kenny Aaronson, and Santana drummer Michael Shrieve.

The quartet spent two weeks writing the songs and two weeks rehearsing them. They then went out on the road for a special 8-gig minitour through the Bay Area of California, doing shows in San Francisco, San Jose, and San Rafael. The album was recorded live by the Westwood One Mobile Facility. Refinements and overdubs were done at Fantasy Studios (built by the members of Creedence Clearwater Revival) in Berkeley, CA, in December 1983. "Missing You" features 22 guitar parts. The album was released on 3/31/84. It spent 18 weeks on the charts, reaching #42. Tracks: • Top of the Rock • Missing You • Animation • Valley of the Kings • Giza • Whiter Shade of Pale • Hot & Dirty • He Will Understand • My Hometown

A second album was initially planned but never materialized. All profits from the live gigs were donated to area schools' arts and sports departments.

"Whiter Shade of Pale" was released as a promotional 12" (Geffen PRO-A-2142) and featured each band member's autograph etched into the back side of this one-sided vinyl release. The single reached #94 on the charts.

Time Life Gold and Platinum-The Van Halen song "Why Can't This Be Love?" appeared in this CD compilation of hits from 1985 to 1988.

Toad-This Cream cover was reportedly Al's signature drum solo during the band's backyard party days.

The Today Show-In 1986 this show interviewed Van Halen in a two-part series. Eddie was also interviewed on this show with Valerie Bertinelli in the same year. On 7/05/88 the band was interviewed on the show in Malibu, CA, about the Monsters of Rock tour. On 3/07/94 David Lee Roth appeared on the show and on 11/05/98 he appeared briefly in a piece about Puff-Daddy's birthday party, on 11/04/98, at which he made an appearance.

Today Tonight-Van Halen was interviewed on this Australian television show on 4/15/98. The show included footage of the rehearsal, back stage, and concert at the Silverdome in Launceston, Australia on 4/14/98.

The Tonight Show-On 10/31/85 David Lee Roth was interviewed on this program by Joan Rivers. Dave appeared on the show again on 11/13/95. He was interviewed by Jay Leno and performed his Vegas version of "California Girls."

On 3/30/99 Sammy Hagar made an appearance on the show. He cut is hair on camera for charity and performed "Mas Tequila."

Sammy appeared again on 12/29/00 to perform "Let Sally Drive."

Too Hot for Teachers-Canadian-based Van Halen tribute band.

Top Jimmy-(*1984* [2:59]) The track was recorded using a Ripley stereo guitar (only the fourth in existence at the time). Each string was assigned to either the right or the left (6th string = left, 5th string = right, 4th string = left, 3rd string = right, 2nd string = left, 1st string = right). The song is in an unknown tuning. Ed had a melody in his head and simply tuned the guitar to the melody he was hearing.

The lyrics were inspired by a musician named Top Jimmy. Top Jimmy got his name from Top's Tacos where he worked until he decided to become a blues singer. He was known for playing outrageous shows at the Whisky A GoGo, where Van Halen also played. Top Jimmy lived up to his name by giving out tacos to starving musicians. He later went on to perform at Café de Grande with his band the Rhythm Pigs. Together as Top Jimmy and the Rhythm Pigs, they released an album in 1987 titled *Pigus Drunkus Maximus* (Restless 72221).

Top of the World-(*For Unlawful Carnal Knowledge* [3:55]; *Live: Right Here, Right Now* [4:59]) Ed didn't want this track on the album. He had five other songs he wanted on the album rather than this track, but producer Andy Johns loved the song and insisted it be on the album.

The intro riff was first heard as the "outro" riff on *1984*'s "Jump." It is believed that originally this lick was actually written for another song and that it was Ted Templeman's idea, upon hearing it, to tag it onto the end of

"Jump." Ed recorded the song using the same 1958 Gibson "Flying V" used in "Hot for Teacher" and his faithful 100-watt Marshall Super Lead amplifier. The solo was played through a Soldano.

This was the first official single off the album, though not the first song released-that distinction belongs to "Poundcake."

Three different videos for this song were released: a concept video that debuted on MTV on 10/14/91 and two different live videos-one recorded in Sacramento, CA, and the other recorded at the Dallas "Free Concert" on 12/04/91.

Tora! Tora!-1. (*Women and Children First* [:57]) This instrumental was actually recorded to tape backwards. It was first played with a wind sound effect fading in, followed by a dive bomb on the open E string. Ed then proceeded to shake the slackened string against the pickup of his guitar, pluck on the tremolo springs, and pluck on the strings above the nut.

Ed originally wanted to name this song "Act Like It Hurts."

2. A short-lived Van Halen fanzine.

Total Guitar-Eddie Van Halen was interviewed in this magazine's March 1998 issue.

Toys 'R' Bus-The nickname of one of the band's tour busses on the *5150* tour. The name was coined because of the fact that the children of both Michael Anthony and Sammy Hagar often accompanied the band on tour.

Trampled under Foot-This Led Zeppelin (*Physical Graffiti* [Swan Song SS-200-2, 1975) cover was reportedly played by the band in the early years.

Tribe of Judah-This eclectic Gary Cherone project, managed by Paul Geary, was recording their first album as this book went to press.

Tribute to Van Halen 2000-See *Little Guitars* tribute album.

The Tube-This British Channel 4 television program aired a Paula Yates interview with David Lee Roth, from a rooftop in Los Angeles, on 5/18/86.

Turn Up the Music-(1987) Sammy Hagar solo album. Tracks: • Trans Am (Highway Wonderland) • Plain Jane • Iceman • Run for Your Life • I've Done Everything for You • Rock 'n' Roll Weekend • Turn Up the Music • Urban Guerrilla • Love or Money • Reckless

Tush-The band reportedly included this ZZ Top cover in their club-days sets.

Tuxedo-The name of Edward's cat from the early 1980s.

Twist and Shout-(2:10) The band performed this Isley Brothers cover on 9/18/76 at the Bogart in San Bernardino, CA.

Twister-(Universal Pictures, 1996) Two Van Halen songs appear in this movie and on the soundtrack (Warner Sunset/Warner Bros. 9-46254-2, 1996, with "Respect the Wind" edit version) and the movie score (Atlantic 82954-2, 1996, with "Respect the Wind" movie score version).
The first song, "Humans Being," appears in a tornado chase sequence and "Respect the Wind," written and performed solely by Alex and Edward, appears in the ending credits.
The band's involvement with the movie fueled insurmountable problems within the band, and Sammy Hagar left the band soon after. Sammy was completely against recording and releasing the tunes on a soundtrack that featured virtually no other band that was in Van Halen's particular rock genre. (Any singles that include the tracks from *Twister* are listed

under the singles for *Best of Volume 1*, because "Humans Being" was also released on that album.)

The movie opened on 5/10/96 and was released on video on 10/01/96.

A *Twister* pinball machine with Van Halen background music was also released.

U

Ultra Bass-(*Live: Right Here, Right Now* [5:15]) This was the title of Mike's bass solo as it was heard on this album. The solo included parts of the "Star Spangled Banner" and "Sunday Afternoon in the Park."

Unboxed-(Geffen 2064 24702 4, 1994) This was a greatest hits collection of sorts from Sammy Hagar that included two new songs: "High Hopes" and "Buying My Way into Heaven." The album strained relations within Van Halen because the entire band was trying to recuperate from the death of manager Ed Leffler. Even though Leffler had been a very close friend to Sammy, it was Eddie Van Halen that felt it was inappropriate for Sammy to release another solo album at this time. Eventually differences were ironed out enough so that the band could begin work on the Balance album. Unboxed was released on 3/15/94 and certified gold on 9/21/95. Tracks: • High Hopes • Buying My Way into Heaven • I'll Fall in Love Again • There's Only One Way to Rock • Heavy Metal • Eagles Fly • Baby's on Fire • Three Lock Box • Two Sides of Love • I Can't Drive 55 • Give to Live • I Don't Need Love
A promotional CD single for "High Hopes" (Geffen PRO-CD-4616, U.S.) was released in 1994. The song was originally presented by Hagar for use on a Van Halen album, but the band wasn't interested in the song, so he included it on this compilation.

Unchained-(*Fair Warning; Best of Volume 1* [3:27]) This classic has long been considered the favorite song of many Van Halen fans. It was voted favorite song by the fans in the Winter 1997 issue of The Inside magazine, easily beating its closest competitor, "Dreams."
Like "Hear about It Later," this song was originally written on keyboards.

Ted Templeman is the man behind the line, "Come on, Dave, Gimme a break!" Ted reportedly felt that Dave was getting a little too obnoxious during the song's interlude, so he interjected, asking Dave to give it a rest. But, the band liked how it sounded, and the tongue-lashing was left in.

The video is also a fan favorite and is part of the *Fair Warning* set of live videos filmed between 6/11/81 and 6/13/81 in Oakland, CA.

Up the Academy-(Warner Bros., 1980) The Sammy Hagar song "Bad Reputation" (from the *Danger Zone* album) was featured in this film starring Ralph Macchio, Robert Downey, Jr., and Barbara Bach. The movie about military school was Mad magazine's first-known foray into celluloid satire.

Other artists contributing to the film included Blondie, Cheap Trick, the Boomtown Rats, and Pat Benatar.

Urquidez, Benny-David Lee Roth's trainer and teacher of Ukidokan, a personal system of kickboxing devised from nine different styles of karate, for which Benny holds black belts. Benny also taught Dave how to do a back flip for the "Jump" video.

For Ukidokan, Dave trained every day, twice a day, running, stretching, and learning fighting techniques at Uruqidez' now-defunct Van Nuys, CA, gym, the Jet Center. Benny holds 6 titles in 5 weight divisions in kickboxing. He started acting in 1972, getting involved as a stuntman and in choreographing fights. He retired from competition in 1995. He has choreographed fight sequences for Con Air, Gross Point Blank, The Crow, and The Gladiators and has worked with Chuck Norris, Steven Segal, Jean Claude Van Damme, Patrick Swayze, Michael Keaton, and Michelle Phieffer. He now owns a small gym in North Hollywood, CA, called Jet's Gym where he teaches while he awaits the opening of a new combination gym/acting school in Santa Monica, CA.

In the beginning of his training, Benny described Roth as very aggressive. At one point Roth wanted to go into competition, so Benny put together a 3-round full-contact fight, which Dave won.

Us-This magazine's index of Van Halen-related issues:

5/09/87: "The Secret Struggle of Mrs. Eddie Van Halen": five-page Edward and Valerie interview by Merle Ginsberg.

8/22/88: "Eddie Gets Steady": three-page Edward interview by Kevin Connal.

Address: 10202 West Washington Boulevard, Culver City, CA 90232; Telephone: 213-558-6630.

Us Festival (2nd Annual)-This was a music festival held on 5/28/83 through 5/30/83 at Glen Helen Regional Park in San Bernardino, CA, that is often referred to as the "Disgust Festival." Van Halen performed on "Heavy Metal Day" (5/29/83) as headliners for the record-setting fee of $1.5 million. Originally that amount was to be paid to David Bowie, with Van Halen getting only $1 million, but their contract stated that their fee must equal or exceed that of the other highest paid group at the show. So Van Halen ended up with the bigger amount. The 1984 *Guiness Book of World Records* created a new category based upon the price of this performance. The band's own expenses for the show totaled around $500,000, which included a full line of merchandise for fans attending the event.

The performance began with a 3-minute peek at Van Halen backstage just prior to the show and was broadcast on a big-screen monitor placed high above the stage.

It fades in to a giant party, hosted by Los Angeles disc jockey Paraquat Kelly. Kelly wanders throughout the ruckus, which includes revelers of all ages, a midget leading a saddled sheep around, a nurse, bodyguards, photographers, and several scantily-clad women. Each of the band members is interviewed for several moments with the highlight being Kelly "accidentally" walking in on David Lee Roth and a female fan in a comprising position on a piano in a room known as the Love Dungeon.

An announcement is made just seconds prior to show time as the band and fellow partygoers gather for a final toast in which Dave dedicates his bottle of whiskey to "alcoholics unanimously."

The band kicked off the show with "Romeo Delight," and it soon became apparent that the band had perhaps had a bit too much to drink before the show. Dave mumbled the words to the first two songs and invented an entirely new set of lyrics to "The Full Bug." It wasn't the best Van Halen performance, but it was a wild performance that has earned a place alongside the best Van Halen videos on collectors' shelves. The set list: • Romeo Delight • Unchained • Drum Solo • The Full Bug • Runnin' with the Devil • Jamie's Cryin' • So This Is Love? • Little Guitars • Bass Solo • Dancing in the Street • Somebody Get Me a Doctor/Girl Gone Bad/I'm So Glad • Dance the Night Away • Cathedral • Secrets • Dave's Tai Chi Solo • Everybody Wants Some!! • Ice Cream Man • Intruder • (Oh) Pretty Woman • Guitar Solo • Ain't Talkin' 'Bout Love • Growth • Bottom's Up • You Really Got Me/Happy Trails

Four of the songs performed were included in a special Showtime presentation of the three-day event: "Runnin' with the Devil," "(Oh) Pretty Woman," "You Really Got Me," and "Happy Trails." The film was done by Pacific Video and was produced by Robert Lombard and Noel Monk. Donn Landee was in charge of the audio. All three tunes were touched up with numerous vocal overdubs prior to being shown.

Two deaths occurred on Heavy Metal Day.

V

Van Halen-(Warner Bros. 3075, 1978 [35:03]) It took three weeks to record this album (at a cost of $40,000), which was released on 2/10/78. The album spent 169 weeks on the charts, reaching #19 on the U.S. charts (3/11/78) and #34 on the U.K. charts (5/27/78). 10.3 million copies of this album have been sold in the U.S., making it Van Halen's bestseller. It was certified gold on 5/24/78, platinum on 10/10/78, platinum five times over on 10/22/84, platinum six times over on 2/01/89, seven times platinum on 9/29/93, platinum eight times over on 7/11/94, and ten times platinum on 8/07/96. It was certified diamond on 3/16/99. The album was remastered and rereleased in a Gold Edition on 9/29/98. It was rereleased again in remastered form on 9/19/00.

Interestingly, the cassette version of this album ends with "Ice Cream Man," while the CD and vinyl versions end with "On Fire."

Production had to be rushed on Van Halen because Ed had mistakenly let the band Angel hear "You Really Got Me" at drummer Barry Brandt's house before the album was finished. Both bands raced to put out the song.

25 songs were brought into consideration during the *Van Halen* sessions.

This was the only album for which the band handed complete control over to the producer, Ted Templeman.

Sometime in late 1977 or early 1978, four videos were filmed for this album at the Whisky A GoGo in West Hollywood, CA: "You Really Got Me," "Runnin' with the Devil," "Jamie's Cryin'," and one unknown, which may have been "Eruption." Warner Brothers paid for the sessions in an effort to decide which song to promote as the first single. The videos were planned for release as a promotional set, but for unknown reasons, the set never materialized.

Overall, the band's performance was quite humorous and provided a rare glimpse at their performance persona in its developmental stages.

Smoke machines, star filters, and other cheap camera and lighting techniques were used. The band's overexaggerated moves and slightly off lip-syncing combined with the leather and disco-shirt clothing combinations add even more amusement.

Van Halen singles/promos
"You Really Got Me," "Atomic Punk," WB WBS 8515, 7" Vinyl, USA and UK, 1/28/78. Highest chart position: #36 in USA and #34 in UK.

"You Really Got Me," "Atomic Punk," WB Pioneer, P-226W, 7" Vinyl, Japan, 1978.

"Runnin' with the Devil," "Eruption," WB WBS 8556, 7" Vinyl, USA, 5/06/78. Highest chart position: #84 in USA on 5/20/78 and #52 in UK.

"Jamie's Cryin'," "I'm the One," WB WBS 8631, 7" Vinyl, USA, 5/16/78.

"Ain't Talkin' 'Bout Love," "Feel Your Love Tonight," WB WBS 8707, 7" Vinyl, USA, 10/25/78.

"Runnin' with the Devil," "You Really Got Me," WB WB 17.604, Holland.

Van Halen II-(Warner Bros. 3312 [31:14]) This album was recorded in six days and released on 3/23/79. It reached #6 on the U.S. charts (4/14/79) and #23 on the U.K. charts (4/14/79). 5.7 million copies have been sold in the U.S. It was certified gold on 4/03/79, platinum on 5/08/79, triple platinum on 10/22/84, and quadruple platinum on 7/05/90. The album was remastered and rereleased on 9/19/00.

The album was recorded about a week after the first world tour ended. The band felt that the tour made them better prepared for recording than they would ever be after a rest.

The Sheraton Inn of Madison, WI, is thanked in the album's liner notes. During Van Halen's first tour, they destroyed the seventh floor of the hotel, throwing televisions out the windows and having fire extinguisher fights in the hallways-blaming the incident on their tour-mates, Journey.

David Lee Roth broke his foot during a photo shoot for the back cover. He did three 12-foot leaps, landing incorrectly on the third jump, subsequently breaking his right foot. When the inner sleeve photos were shot at a later date, the foot was still bandaged and is clearly evident on the final sleeve included with the album. Incidentally, the third jump was the best, and it was used for the shot.

Mysteriously, Alex Van Halen is absent from the songwriting credits on side two of the cassette version of this album, more than likely due to a printing error.

Michael Anthony used a small bass amp for his parts on the album, and for the guitar overdubs, Ed used only one cabinet and head as opposed to his usual wall of amplifiers.

Three live videos were filmed after the album was released, and these were later televised on a Don Kirshner's Rock Concert broadcast: "Dance the Night Away," "You're No Good," and "Bottoms Up!"

Van Halen II singles/promos
"Dance the Night Away," "Outta Love Again," WB WBS 8823, 7" Vinyl, USA, 4/02/79. Highest chart position: #15 in USA on 7/04/79.

"Beautiful Girls" (edit), "D.O.A.," WB WBS 49035, 7" Vinyl, USA, 9/15/79. Highest chart position: #84 in USA on 10/06/79.

"You Really Got Me," "Dance the Night Away," WB GWB 0383, 7" Vinyl, USA, 1979.

"You Really Got Me," "Dance the Night Away," WB 7-21974, 7"
Vinyl (reissue), 1980s.

Van Halen III-This album was fans' first look at Van Halen with Gary
Cherone at the vocal helm. The album was released in the U.S. on
3/17/98 and in Japan about a week earlier. It was certified gold on
8/19/98. 550,000 copies have been sold in the U.S. A limited edition version, limited to 15,000 copies, was made available in a tin box, with 11
connectable cards, Van Halen logo decal, and a guitar pick.

A German promotional version of the album was released on 2/20/98.
To make sure these promos wouldn't fall into the wrong hands, almost a
full month before the official release of the album, each disc was numbered.

An even earlier version of the album that included "That's Why I
Love You" was released in November 1997 for Warner Brothers use
only. Some copies of this release leaked to the public and are now in the
hands of collectors.

The cover was picked by Alex, who considered it extremely funny.

Mike Post was picked by Gary to produce the album. He was
brought in to oversee recording in April 1997, and on 9/30/97 the
album was done.

Ed used dozens of guitars on this album, testing hundreds of ways
to record them. He also tried out his new 5150 II prototype amps for
the album.

Van Halen III singles/promos

"Without You" (edit), "Without You" (album version), WB PRO-CD-
9200, CD (in clear pink case), USA, 2/19/98.

"Without You" (edit), "Without You" (album version), "Ballot or the
Bullet," WB 9362439892, CD, Australia, 2/23/98.

"Without You" (edit), "Without You" (album version), WB PRO 6351/PRCD 1008, CD, Germany.

"Fire in the Hole" (edit), "Fire in the Hole" (album version), WB PRO-CD-9309, CD, USA, 4/16/98.

"You Really Got Me," "Fire in the Hole," WB WPDR-3085, 3" CD, Japan, 6/05/98.

"Fire in the Hole" (edit), "Fire in the Hole" (album version), "One I Want," WB 9362445312, CD, Australia, 6/11/98.

"Fire in the Hole," CD, Japan, 6/14/98.

"Fire in the Hole," WB PRCD 1192/PRO 6399, CD, Germany. Actually includes entire *Van Halen III* album.

"Dirty Water Dog" (album version), "Dirty Water Dog" (edit), WB WPCR-2073, CD, Japan, 7/24/98.

"One I Want," WB PRO-CD-9407-R, CD, USA, 7/27/98.

Van Halen, Alex-On 5/08/53 Alexander Arthur Van Halen was born in Amsterdam, Netherlands. He was raised, in Nijmegen, a town just outside Amsterdam. Through a government-incentive program to reunite families, the Van Halens moved to the U.S. when Alex was about 9.

Because the family spoke little English, Alex and Eddie formed a bond during this time that has lasted their entire lives. Together they adapted to a new country, a new language, and new ideas about music. The brothers still keep a picture of their old Dutch home in the 5150 Studio and revisited the house after the recording of *Balance*.

Early on, Jan and Eugenia Van Halen impressed upon their sons a love of music that originally meant classical training. In Alex's case this meant playing classical guitar. He didn't take to it, though, and preferred playing his brother's drums. When Eddie took a job as a paperboy to pay for the $125 Japanese St. George drum kit, Alex played the drums instead of the guitar. The practice paid off, and Alex learned to play the drums very quickly. When he learned "Wipe Out," the two knew it was time to switch instruments.

Having found their musical niches, the brothers began to play at intermissions of their father's gigs. The audience loved them. Eddie recalled that once his father passed a hat around to collect money from the audience while the brothers were playing. More than $22 was collected. Jan gave each of his sons $5. When they asked about the rest of the money, his father responded, "Welcome to the music business."

One of Alex's first jobs was delivering chicken for a restaurant called Chicken Delight. Their ads stated, "Don't cook at home tonight, order Chicken Delight!"

Alex was the real rocker in the family, partying like a rock star well before Mammoth formed. However, Alex has always remained the most silent member of the band. Not much is known about his personal life.

No other drummer in his generation has a technique that is as distinctive. As early as his late teens, Alex was baffling the other musicians with his skill, including in his music theory class at Pasadena Community College. Alex is a strict composer as well, making arrangements and arguing with his brother over theory.

In the early days of Van Halen, Alex had a signature bushy hairstyle and a stage presence rivaled only by David Lee Roth. Though he never changed his stage persona, he did shave his head bald in 1986. When asked about this, Alex explained that the entire band was going to shave their heads, but chickened-out after seeing what the barber had done to him.

Alex almost lost a finger working in a machine shop before the band got signed. Luckily he kept the finger and pounded out the grooves that made Van Halen the revolutionary debut it was. *Van Halen II* was fans' first real exposure to the gifted playing of this drummer, though. "Outta Love Again" showcased the previously lesser-known Van Halen brother.

Since then Alex's beat has inspired new songs like "Poundcake" and "Without You." His arrangements are evident in songs like "Pleasure Dome" and "Doin' Time," and every tour has introduced a new and improved drum solo.

He has had his own signature series of sticks by Calato. In the early days he used a 3S wood-tip model. He doesn't keep his equipment. Though some of his old drum sets are being restored, he wants everything to be given away. There's no need to cling to the past in a band with a bright future.

While not much may be known about the man himself, fans can deduce all they really need to know by listening to his music.

Van Halen, Edward-Ed has given the world a gift, three decades of musical genius. His approach to the guitar has given birth to an entire generation of guitar players who look at the guitar as an instrument with unlimited possibilities. He introduced a myriad of new styles and sounds that will be scrutinized for decades.

It all started in Amsterdam, Holland, on 1/26/55. Edward Lodewijk van Halen ("Lodewijk" is pronounced "Load-ah-vike") was born. From the age of six until the age of twelve he was trained in classical piano by his father and a Russian teacher, Stass Kalvitis.

By the age of twelve Ed had discovered rock and roll. Inspired by the Dave Clark Five's "Glad All Over" and "Bits and Pieces," he decided to become a drummer. After switching instruments with Alex, the first song Eddie played on his brother's guitar was the Ventures' "Walk, Don't Run" (BLP 2031, 1964). He also took up the violin and cello at this time.

A friend of Jan Van Halen built an amp for Ed, and for the first time he was plugged in. One of the first songs played through this amp was the Arrow's "Blues Theme." The amp was short-lived, though, and in 1969

Ed bought his Marshall amp, which has since become the most famous amp in rock history.

Eddie's favorite band was Cream. A Clapton fanatic to this day, he took it upon himself to memorized and perform Cream songs note-for-note. He became locally famous for it. Clapton wasn't his only influence, though. Jimmy Page seemed to embody more of what Ed was really about, feeling over accuracy. It was Page who inspired Eddie to develop his tapping technique. Jimi Hendrix seemed to perplex Edward, however. Although he liked Hendrix's whammy bar techniques enough to build on them within his own style, Ed was never comfortable playing Hendrix's songs.

In these early years Ed was both a guitar player and a lead singer for his band Mammoth, nicknamed Junior Cream. Ed hated singing lead, though, and the lineup of Mammoth changed to include David Lee Roth.

"I never technically learned how to sing," Ed remembered on the Drew and Mike show on Detroit's WRIF in 1996. "So, I would kind of do a Kurt Cobain, after five songs and three beers my voice would be gone. You know, I would just scream it out and kind of waste my voice."

The band transformed from a high concept technical band to a hard pounding party band. By 1974 Mammoth was an established band on the local scene and Eddie had developed his tapping technique into a recognizable, unique style. This is not to say that Eddie was the only one tapping at this time. Several musicians had been doing similar techniques for decades. Tapping was not new, but Eddie didn't know that. He developed his own style independent of outside tapping influences. It was this style that brought the technique to the forefront of rock guitar in the late 1970s.

Rather than helping the band, Ed was actually keeping the band from getting the best gigs. When they became known as Van Halen, they tried to get gigs at the popular Los Angeles clubs, but Eddie was too loud. He had to be. In order for his Marshall to sound its best, it had to be turned up to 10 at all times. To rectify this Ed would turn his amp around or put padding in front to muffle the sound. Later, Ed used a Variac to adjust the voltage instead of the volume, so the amp would always sound its best.

Eventually it all paid off and the band was accepted into Gazzari's. Other prestigious gigs followed as the band spent about three years working the club circuit.

During the club years the band recognized the talent they had in Eddie. Alex, the closest thing the band had to a manager the early club days, suggested that Eddie should probably conceal some of his more innovative techniques from the audiences, which at times included guitarists from all over the L.A. scene including Randy Rhodes.

"Yeah, that is kinda like Alex telling me, 'Hey, wait until we have it on a record; their gonna rip it.'" Ed recalled. "Ya know, when I started doing the two-hand technique, as soon as the record came out, everyone did it." (WRIF, 1996)

It wasn't long before there was a buzz around town about this band and their amazing guitar player. It wasn't until after the band had been discovered that "Eruption" was unveiled to producer Ted Templeman. Ted saw the potential of the ground-breaking instrumental and soon guitarists from around the world, in their studios and in their garages, would be spending countless hours trying to copy it. Ed was just getting started. His talent has never lied in any one technique, but in his ability to translate the sounds in his heads to the guitar. If that means coming up with a new innovative technique to achieve that sound, so be it.

While on tour in support of *Van Halen*, Ed added another innovation to his repertoire. It was a combination of tapping and harmonics that came to be known as "False Harmonics." Again, this was a technique Eddie developed independently, though it had been used by Jazz guitarists since the 1950s. The technique can be heard most prominently on the track "Dance the Night Away."

At the end of 1979 Ed was voted Guitar Player's Best Rock Guitarist. He had enough money to retire his father and buy him a boat. Eddie resurrected "And the Cradle Will Rock," a song he and Alex struggled with in 1974, with keyboards for the band's 1980 album *Women and Children*

First. Though the keyboards were subtle, it marked a new beginning for Eddie. He refused to be confined to the guitar to express his musical ideas.

The band embarked on the *World Invasion* tour. It was on this tour that Eddie met Valerie Bertinelli backstage at the Hirsh Memorial Arena in Shreveport, Louisiana, on 8/29/80. Seven months later they were married. Rumors starting spreading that Roth was unhappy with Ed's new lifestyle. Ed wasn't exactly the member of Van Halen expected to marry a famous actress or hang out with Hollywood's A-list.

Eddie's personal life was going well, but his life in Van Halen was getting worse. He was frustrated that he hadn't been expressing himself fully on the last few Van Halen albums. The party was over. After recording three albums and going on three tours in three years the band was set to do the same thing for the fourth album *Fair Warning*. Ed was admittedly depressed and made it clear to some that he no longer wanted to be in the band. During the recording of *Fair Warning*, he would often sneak into the recording studio late at night and rerecord his guitar parts the way he wanted them. He feared that the rest of the band wouldn't approve of some the musical risks he was taking in his solos. He even included a haunted growling keyboard instrumental called "Sunday Afternoon in the Park," that truly made this Ed's album.

What came out of the recordings was a dark, heavy guitar album that many die-hard Van Halen fans consider the best written of the Dave-era albums. However, it was the least popular in terms of sales. Ed was more reluctant to step out and take control for the next album and instead concentrated more on making guitars and refining his own position in the band.

There were excuses now to set aside Eddie's style on the next album and go back to the formula that sold albums: covers plus lots of Dave equals record sales. To a certain extent they were correct, but the band suffered musically. They were determined to get back the legions of adoring pop fans and the result was 1982's *Diver Down*, Ed's least favorite album. He rarely liked cover tunes and this album was loaded with them. Ted wanted to use an original composition written by Ed for a cover, "Dancing in the Street," something Ed would later regret terribly.

Tensions in the band between Eddie and Dave that began when *Fair Warning* was released were now coming to a head. The building of the 5150 Studio marked the beginning of the end of the power struggle between Ed and Dave. Constructed in March of 1983, 5150 has been the recording studio every Van Halen album has been recorded in since. It lies just down the road from Ed's house.

The result of the struggle within the band for freedom of expression was *1984*.

The next few years would hold many changes for the band as a whole, but for Ed it meant more freedom to explore different styles of music and to stray a bit from his expected position atop the heap of '80s speedster guitar heroes. Even with those changes, Eddie only got more and more popular.

The next big change for Eddie didn't occur until 1990. In January he entered rehab. He said in many subsequent interviews that he drank to take away his inhibitions, whether they were in the studio or on stage. It didn't work out and Ed continued to drink, but other changes managed to take hold on his life over the next few years.

During the recording of the *F.U.C.K.* album Valerie Bertinelli gave birth to Wolfgang William Van Halen on 3/16/91, "Wolfie" as his parent's call him. At the same time, the 5150 Studio was remodeled and Ed began work on a line of guitars and a new amp.

The result of all of these changes was 1991's *For Unlawful Carnal Knowledge*. The album exhibited a new style and sound that was embraced by both the press and the fans.

Years of touring followed which included the release of a live album as an excuse to tour even more.

Ed's drinking was still a problem though. Before he could give it up, he had to want to give up. That hadn't been the case until 1994. One night in 1994, while drunk, Eddie cut off his hair. It was an act of frustration that Ed would confuse reporters with by saying he did it on a bet. Actually he enjoyed the way his new look protected him from fan recognition on the streets. Shortly after this, Eddie sponsored a charity golf tournament and concert, the only public Van Halen performance that year. Ed's love of golf is no secret. In fact, the whole Van Halen family loves sports. Their favorite football team is the New Orleans Saints. They once even threw a party in honor of the Saints, when the football team went 8-8.

When Eddie stopped drinking he began to become more aware of a pain in his hips. All the years of jumping on stage had deteriorated his hips and the alcohol had only helped to cover up the pain. After losing some weight, the pain subsided and a hip operation was postponed until November of 1999.

Sammy left the band in 1996, putting Ed in the spotlight as the primary spokesman for the band. Ed wasn't comfortable with any of it.

This new era of Van Halen would prove to be Eddie's most diverse and prolific, though, and he has a lot more to offer.

Although Eddie has given Van Halen fans and guitar players more than enough to ponder over and copy, it must be remembered, as he has often stated, his music is all about sounds, not notes.

Ed's Gear

Eddie's first guitar was his brother's acoustic. He then borrowed a Sears Silvertone guitar before buying his first electric guitar. He would buy 2 Silvertones years later from Dan Martin, Ed's guitar hunter.

In either 1967 or 1968, he got bored with his brother's acoustic guitar and bought a Teisco Del Ray guitar at Sears for around $110. He bought it because it had four pickups, the most of any other guitar in the store. In the late 1980s he would buy another Teisco Del Ray from Dan Martin. This was a stereo guitar with six pickups that can be seen in the "Finish What Ya Started" video.

Ed's next guitar was a Gibson 12-string hollowbody. He took off half the strings to play it as a regular 6-string guitar. This guitar was eventually broken due to Ed's lack of a guitar case. This was the beginning of Ed's devotion to Gibson guitars, which was probably also prompted by one of his guitar heroes, Jimmy Page. Around this time he bought his first really valuable guitar, a 1968 Gibson Les Paul gold top with soap bar pickups. He destroyed the original paint job by painting it black. The neck warped because Ed used very heavy gauge string for the low E, A, and D strings. He later changed this practice. Ed would use Les Pauls throughout his early career, but was disappointed that he couldn't get one that sounded good in both neck and bridge pickups. He drew from this frustration when designing the pickups for his signature series guitars several years later.

In these early days, Ed used Ernie Ball strings, later switching to Fender 150XLs. He stuck with the Fenders through at least half of the 1980s. As is usual while touring or playing outside the studio, Ed boils the strings to loosen them up. While recording Ed doesn't change strings unless they break.

After playing a homemade amp for a few years, Ed bought his infamous Marshall in 1969. It's a 1959-model 100-watt Marshall Super Lead amp circa 1966-67. It began its life at the Pasadena Rose Palace, where it was used as the house amp until Ed bought it. While in his first interviews after the release of *Van Halen*, he claimed that this amp was modified in some secret ways, the truth was that the amp was stock with little modification. The one modification everyone knows about was the Ohmite variac that Ed used in conjunction with the amp. It was an autotransformer that allowed one to take the voltage from 0 to 160 volts. The idea was to get the effect of having the amp turned all the way up without the high volume. The Variac adjusted the voltage which overrides the master volume of the amp. However, fooling around with electricity in these ways is very dangerous, and he caused some damage with this combination.

Due partly to his love for Led Zepplin and partly to the guitar's sound, Ed started buying more Gibsons. He particularly loved the sound of his Gibson 335, which was a little too cumbersome to use in a rock band. He destroyed this guitar in an effort to learn how to repair other guitars. With this guitar he learned how to refret, refinish, and do just about anything else you can do to a guitar. When the band started making money in the late 1970s Ed bought more Gibsons as investments. Of course this included a 335.

Eddie was using a Gibson Flying V in the early seventies at around the same time he was destroying his 335. It was reportedly stolen.

He also bought a 1955 Gibson Les Paul, Jr., around this time. He found that it went out of tune a lot and had to be retuned between songs. To modify the look of this guitar, Ed used paint remover on the body and swirled the dissolving paint to give it a finger-painted look. He then inflicted a multitude of cigarette burns on the guitar.

Among his first well-known guitars was an Ibanez Destroyer named "Shark." This guitar played a major role in the early recording of the band. Ed was often seen pictured with this guitar in flyers during the band's club days. This mid-1970s guitar was made of Korina wood and fitted with two Gibson PAF humbuckers, one black and one white. Its final paint job was red with silver stripes. The neck was made of rosewood.

Shark was used in the recording of about half the songs on *Van Halen*. Ed used a hacksaw to cut a large piece out of the body early in the life of the guitar. In this effort to change the aesthetic value of the guitar, Ed ruined its distinctive sound. Shark can be seen in the videos for "You Really Got Me," "Runnin' with the Devil," in photos from the *Van Halen II* sessions, and on the cover of *Women and Children First*. Ed did eventually get nostalgic for the original sound of the guitar, so he borrowed another Destroyer from Chris Holmes of W.A.S.P. to record parts of *Women and Children First*.

Eddie started getting into Charvel guitars at around the same time he became known for playing Shark. It has been suggested that Ed changed to strat-style bodies after seeing the Jimmy Hendrix movie *Jimmy Plays Berkeley* with one of his techs, Tom Broderick. He wanted a guitar with a whammy bar.

His most famous guitar from this time, known to most as the "Frankenstrat" and to Ed as "Franky," was bought from Wayne Charvel and built by Linn Ellsworth. The guitar had a $50 Boogie ash unfinished strat-style body, serial number 61071. Ed found the body in a box of cast-offs. It had been routed only for the middle-and neck-position pickups. The third, bridge-position pickup had to be routed by Ed using a chisel and fitted with a Gibson PAF humbucker taken from a 1961 Gibson 335.

This approach of using a single humbucker was adopted from Ed's previous experience with a 1961 Fender Stratocaster.

After Ed played this strat and another, possibly a 1959 strat, the band concluded that the sound of the Fenders was too thin compared to that of the Gibsons. To make up for the thin sound, Ed replaced the 1961 Fender bridge pickup with a Gibson PAF. Not knowing how to rewire the guitar for all three pickups, Ed wired the guitar for only the PAF, thus creating the notion of a single-humbucker guitar. Ed used the same technique for the building of the Frankenstrat. He slanted the humbucker because the poles were made for Gibson string positions, which are slightly closer together than Fenders. The main problem was aligning the E and B poles. He then potted the humbucker using paraffin wax, a practice that melted many pickups before it was successful. This design became so popular that by the mid-1980s most guitar makers had made this a standard design in their new guitars. Even by 1979 Ed had seen his guitar copied by so many companies that he added two pickups to the Frankenstrat. The new neck pickup was a deactivated single-coil. The manufacturer is unknown, and the pickup has never been used or even connected.

The trademark striped design came together after the body was first painted completely black. Ed then taped stripes all over it and repainted it in white. When the tape was removed, the black stripes remained. He used several coats of Schwinn bicycle acrylic lacquer and hung the body on a coat hanger in his parents' garage to dry. His parents were concerned because he painted it with little to no ventilation in the garage. His mom felt he should've painted it outside and was worried about his health. He tried to dry a guitar in the house once, placing it over a small floor heater, thinking the heat would speed up the drying process. However, this caused paint to run and drip onto the heater. He and Alex painted another guitar using the tires of their Yamaha bike. Ed also had a pair of shoes with tire tread on the bottom that he once painted and wore while stepping all over another body.

The back of the Frankenstrat body was adorned with reflectors from various bicycles. The volume pot was taken from an old Les Paul Junior. Originally, there was a white tone knob. The brass nut and tailpiece were taken from a 1961 strat.

The pickguard was cut by Edward himself, but later removed after he painted the guitar red in 1979. The strap was a combination of chains, leather with studs, and electrical tape that had to be replaced later because of the interference it caused when using wireless systems. One night the strap locks were pulled out during a leap on stage. Ed replaced them using eyelets.

Originally, the guitar had a typical Fender tremolo taken from either a 1962 or 1963 strat. It was replaced with a Floyd Rose prototype. To prevent the Floyd Rose from becoming a floating tremolo, Ed attached a 1971 quarter under the trem, probably in 1983.

The neck was bought on the same day as the body, also built by Ellsworth, and sold by Charvel for $30. In an attempt to fret the neck himself, Ed got some Gibson jumbo fret wire from Ellsworth and used super glue to bond the frets to the neck. Ed liked the Ellsworth necks so much that he used them up until the early 1980s when he started using Kramer necks. The original and replacement necks had Schaller tuners. Edward also widened the nut grooves and frequently oiled them with 3-in-1 oil to keep the strings from grabbing.

When the guitar was initially completed, Ed took it to the basement of Roth's parents' home where the band frequently practiced. The rest of the band was shocked by how it looked. He put the guitar through its paces, and they were amazed at how well it stayed in tune. They had seen him experimenting many times with whammy bars and tuning, including once sawing the whammy bar of a Gibson 335 in half.

He used to wash the necks from time to time to clean them but stopped because he didn't like the brand new feel of it. He later developed a body-cleansing technique in which he sanded the body with .600 sandpaper, applying steel wool, then using Ivory soap and a toothbrush to remove the dirt.

Ed's involvement with Charvel guitars continued when he used a Charvel Explorer and a Charvel Star Guitar in the 1980s.

On the day of the photo shoot for *Van Halen II*, Ed put together a new black guitar with yellow stripes that he'd use throughout the next tour. The idea behind this guitar was to have something made of the same things as the Frankenstrat without its drawbacks. The body was a Charvel, just like Franky's, and made of ash wood. He had Charvel route the body in the bridge position for a humbucker. He put a temporary humbucker in the guitar during the photo shoot for show. The real humbucker was hand-built by Ed using Gibson PAF and DiMarzio parts. The pickup was probably modified, as Ed modified all his pickups through the early eighties, by dipping it in wax. The wax prevented excessive feedback. Ed didn't really like the way the guitar sounded, mostly just the way it looked.

When he was on tour in support of *Van Halen II*, Eddie met a person who would change the face of guitars forever, Floyd Rose. It seemed like the perfect union. Here was a guitarist doing everything to his guitars to keep them in tune while performing, and here was a tremolo maker determined to create a better way to keep guitars in tune. It wasn't love at first sight for Eddie, though. The early prototypes of the Floyd Rose tremolo were more trouble than help. Nevertheless, Ed believed in the system and he helped improve it over the next three years, using it on just about all his guitars. As with everything else, the guitar industry followed by including the Floyd Rose system on just about every high-end guitar made in the 1980s. But Eddie never really got the credit he was due.

After having met him in 1979, Ed was interested enough in Floyd's new type of tremolo that he had Boogie Bodies make a new Strat style guitar specifically centered around the new system. The guitar had a Gibson PAF humbucker but still sounded thin because of the new type of tremolo. To compensate for this, the body was made much thicker and with mahogany wood.

It was around this time that Ed had a Pasadena furniture maker named John Sterry carve two snakes and a dragon into the body of a Gibson Explorer. Both the body and neck were made of Korina wood and the guitar was outfitted with a single humbucker in the bridge position. Ed used it for a cover of Guitar World magazine and took it out on the *Van Halen II* tour, but didn't use it.

Ed was able to invest in several Gibsons at this time. He bought two 1958 Les Paul Jr.'s, one a single cut-away and another a double cut-away. Ed also acquired a '58 bookmatched goldtop Les Paul and a '59 flametop Les Paul. The '58 was later used on the 1980 *Invasion* tour. He also bought a '58 and a '59 sunburst Les Paul.

While on the *Fair Warning* tour in Memphis, a fan named Dave Petschulat gave Eddie a mini replica of a Les Paul. Ed played around with it while on tour and used it later to record "Little Guitars." He also used the guitar to play this song live. To string the guitar he used a heavy .010 to .050 gauge made by Ernie Ball. A set of custom designed heavy strings were in the making, but that was abandoned because they caused the neck to bow.

In 1982 Ed purchased a Gibson Flying V, serial number 582849, from Dan Martin. The guitar would be used to record some of the band's best songs including "Hot for Teacher," "Drop Dead Legs," "Girl Gone Bad," and "Top of the World." The body was made of Korina wood, naturally finished with two humbuckers. The neck is rosewood with a black headstock. He refretted the guitar after he bought it.

Dennis Bernardi, president of Kramer guitars, contacted Ed shortly after the 1982 National Association of Music Merchants show. They discussed Kramer's future and he became interested. Ed endorsed Kramer guitars and began visiting the factory, a practice he would repeat for every guitar he endorsed after this. He regularly inspected the assembly line and took an active role in business decisions.

Ed took full advantage of his new alliance with Kramer guitars on the *Diver Down* tour. He switched to Kramer necks on some of his guitars and used two Kramer custom-made double neck guitars. Both featured an aluminum neck with a split headstock (12-string) and a 6-string maple neck. His main double neck when he performed "Secrets" live was painted in yellow with thin black stripes and a small black Van Halen logo.

The second Kramer double neck was primarily used as his backup for the yellow and black double neck and was rarely, if ever, seen live. It was painted with Edward's infamous red, white, and black striped design.

Ed had taken a liking to Ripley guitars around this time. These are stereo guitars, built by Steve Ripley, which send the sound from each string to either the left or right channel. Using switches Ed could change the channel for each string whenever he wanted. By 1985 Eddie could be seen using several Kramer built Ripley models, including one he calls "Bowling Ball." This one was pictured in a 1986 issue of Guitar World magazine and gets its name from the bowling-ball paint finish on the body and headstock. The numbers "5150" appear at the bottom of the fretboard. Ed's first Ripley was used to record "Top Jimmy" and was one of only a few original Ripley's.

During the *1984* tour, Ed began using Kramers extensively. The 5150 Kramer was a guitar assembled by Ed from a Kramer Baretta body and Kramer neck. It featured a Seymour Duncan 59 humbucker at the bridge. It was painted with Van Halen's classic stripes and a star on the headstock. Its name comes from the numbers "5150" written in reflective tape under the chrome bridge. Another Kramer that was very similar was his 1984 Kramer. This guitar was almost identical to the 5150 Kramer, but had "1984" written in reflective tape under a black bridge. There were also differences in the headstocks. Ed also changed his amp and effects setup for the *1984* tour.

Dan Martin first introduced Edward to the Steinberger Transtrem GL2T in December of 1984. It was outfitted with EMG humbucking pickups and a graphite neck and body.

A removable plate on the body of the guitar was painted with the classic Van Halen stripes by Jim O'Connor, with the numbers "5150" running along the bottom edge of the plate. Two more were purchased one year later. Eddie continued acquiring Steinbergers including a double neck custom built by Ned Steinberger and a 12-string nearly identical in appearance to the GL2Ts. The face plate was hand-painted by Jim O'Connor and featured the letters "OU812" painted along the bottom of the plate.

In 1990 fans were treated to a peak at a new guitar in Eddie's collection during MTV's "Viva Van Halen Saturday," the opening of the Cabo Wabo Cantina. Ed played this guitar, in the shape of the Cabo Wabo logo, briefly at the beginning of the show.

At this point Kramer had folded and Ed was in need of a new guitar company. Fender and Steinberger made bids for his endorsement with a prototype guitars that he used to record parts of *For Unlawful Carnal Knowledge*.

Ed chose to go with Ernie Ball because of their previous work with his custom strings, the proximity of the company (San Luis Obispo, California), and the persistence of Sterling Ball, or "Biff," as Eddie knew him. The strings were called 5150s and were gauged at .009, .011, .015, .024, .032, and .040. He used these sizes through at least the Right Here, Right Now tour before working extensively with Peavey.

The guitar they collaborated on was prototyped as the "Axis." Twenty-one prototypes were made starting in the second week of January 1990. The guitars were delivered to Eddie in April for the recording of *F.U.C.K.* The final product was called the Eddie Van Halen Ernie Ball Music Man. Most refer to it by the initials EBMM.

The body design is Ed's idea of what a combination Les Paul/Telecaster would look like. It was designed by Ed, Sterling Ball, and Dudley Gimple. The flat-top body was made of basswood topped with maple and the neck was made of unfinished bird's-eye maple. The pickups were DiMarzios, custom designed by Ed and Steve Blucher and screwed directly into the body for better sustain. The tremolo was a slightly recessed Floyd Rose style

Gotoh that didn't allow for any backward movement. The neck was a digitally measured reproduction of the Frankenstrat neck. It was already worn in right off the assembly line. The neck was connected to the body with five bolts and a rounded heel, bolted into a sculptured neck joint that allowed for easy access to the upper frets. The frets were made small to contrast Ed's years of playing with big frets. Another interesting feature was that the truss rod was exposed at the body end, allowing for easy access. The volume knob was labeled "Tone." The headstock design was patented.

To make it possible to inspect almost all the guitars coming off the line, Ed restricted production to only 1000 guitars per year. It has been suggested that the production was increased to meet demand. Production ended on this version of the guitar on 9/30/95.

In concert he had a purple double neck guitar/bass version of the Music Man, which he used for "Spanked." The bass was a hollow six-string that sat above a solid body EBMM.

Ed wanted to use his famous Marshall amp to record the *F.U.C.K.* album, but he felt it had lost some of its sustain. This brought Matt Bruck to 5150 as Ed's new tech in 1990. He brought some other vintage Marshalls to help in the recording of *F.U.C.K.* The original was restored and used for *Balance.*

One of the amps Ed relied on while his Marshall was being fixed was the Soldano. He used this amp on all but four tracks on *For Unlawful Carnal Knowledge.* He recorded dry, adding touches from an AMS Echo and his Evantide H3000 Harmonizer afterwards.

Another amp he used was the prototype Peavey 5150. Ed had started working with Peavey to create a signature amp at around the same time he was looking for a new guitar maker. Peavey wanted to make the guitars too, but Ed decided it would be best if they worked on the amp alone. A prototype designed by Edward, Matt Bruck, and Peavey technician James Brown was used sporadically throughout *For Unlawful Carnal Knowledge.* The amp wasn't used extensively until *Balance.* It's a 120-watt amp with 4 6L6 power tubes and 5 12AX7 preamp tubes. Ed now uses NOS GE 6L6,

Chinese 6L6, Russian 5881, and Phillips 6L6 tubes in his 5150 amps. The speaker design was a collaborated effort between the above mentioned people and Mike O'Neill. The Peavey 5150 began what would be a great relationship with the Peavey company that would lead to the "Wolfgang."

For the recording of *Balance*, Ed used his old Marshall amp and new Peavey 5150. In all, eight prototype Peavey 5150 heads were made. Ed used one, which is identical to the consumer model.

After *Balance* debuted, complaints began to reach Ed about his signature series EBMM guitar. The guitar had been sought after by so many that the waiting period for the guitar was now stretching beyond a year and the price kept rising. Even though the guitar was considered one of the best in the business, Ed knew that Ernie Ball could no longer cope with the demand. Ernie Ball refused to change to meet the new demand. They continued producing slightly different versions of the guitar under its previous name "Axis."

Eddie began working with Peavey on a new and improved signature series guitar named "Wolfgang."

The Wolfgang features slightly hotter pickups than the EBMM, sleeker body design, new headstock and the new, Eddie Van Halen-invented, Drop-D tuner. A cheaper version under the name "Wolfgang Special" is a scaled down version of the Wolfgang without the maple carved-top. Ed employed numerous new versions of the Wolfgang and Wolfgang Special on *Van Halen III*. A new version of the 5150 amp was also used, named the 5150 II.

Peavey took full advantage of their new arrangement with Eddie by releasing a line of EVH Wolfgang merchandise including T-shirts, hats, jackets, guitar straps, and strings. The strings are gauged at: .009, .011, .016, .024, .032, and .042.

Work on *Van Halen III* also resurrected the Coral Electric Sitar, similar to what was used on *Van Halen*.

Just like the other members of the band, Ed enjoys car collecting. His collection consists of: '56 Chevy pro street, '56 Chevy nomad, lam 4x4, lam muira, a Ferrari, '59 Chevy pro street, a Mercedes (porsche-model), '92 Chevy pickup with Corvette running gear, Porsche turbo and several Lamborghinis, including a rare red 1971 Miura (only 860 were produced) and a 4X4 12-cylinder LM2 pickup truck.

More About Ed's Gear…

Besides the gear already mentioned, Ed owns:

Guitars: A Gibson Les Paul Lite, serial number 82187816; a custom red, white, and black striped guitar outfitted with a Steinberger Transtrem given to Edward by Paul Jernigan and Dan Martin; a 1968 Gibson Les Paul gold top; a 1957 Les Paul Jr.; a 1959 Gibson ES 345 given to Ed by Dan Martin; a 1962 Gibson SG re-issue given to Ed by Gibson; two Gibson J-180 Everly Brothers Model Acoustics given to Ed by Paul Jernigan, two Gibson Chet Atkins Model Acoustic/Electrics, one white and one black, one of which was used to record "316;" a prototype Gibson Alecto, a cross between a Gibson Firebird and a Gibson Victory, given to Ed by Gibson (only three exist); two 1957 Fender strats; a 1959 strat, which Ed traded a one-of-a-kind custom Van Halen logo shaped guitar built by Grover Jackson for; a 1957 strat, serial number 19827, with heavily battered tabacco sunburst finish, white pickguard and standard maple strat neck. Ed later replaced this neck with a maple telecaster neck sometime after 1990; Seymour Duncan sold Eddie a Fender Esquire with a sunburst finish, white pickguard and maple neck. The only noticeable flaw is a small chunk missing from the binding edge on the lower top left side of the body; a Hamer 12-string with translucent gold finish; a Vox Phantom 12-string; a custom Giffin 12-string electric with Smith pickups; a Mighty Mite Megazone; a Dean Flying V; a 1959 Gretch 6120; a 1953 white Supro Dual Tone with two humbuckers and graduating rectangle inlays; a Mid-60's Supro with a single pickup; a Belmont and a Guild F-50 given to Ed by Guild; two 1961 Silvertones: one a red sunburst and the other black. The red sunburst had a white pickguard, rosewood neck, and two pickups. It included a guitar case with a built-in amplifier. Edward installed a new bridge on the guitar shortly after adding it to his collection. The black Silvertone had two pickups. Like its red sunburst relative, this axe also came with a guitar case with a built-in amplifier and had a new bridge installed shortly after Edward acquired it; Les Paul gave Eddie an autographed mid-1980s Les Paul guitar with sunburst finish, Floyd Rose trem, and rosewood neck.

Bass guitars: An Apostrophe purchased from Dan Martin after Ed had heard Michael Anthony's. Ed used his on 5150; a blue Danelectro copy custom built by Jerry Jones featuring a Floyd Rose tremolo; two Fender P-Basses, one fretless with bright orange finish and rosewood neck and one 1963 P-Bass sold by Dan Martin; a 1963 Jazzmaster purchased from Dan Martin; a 1958 EB1 Gibson Violin Bass sold by Dan Martin; a 1964 Fender Bass VI with sunburst finish and rosewood neck purchased from Dan Martin; a 1965 Fender Jazz purchased from Dan Martin; two Steinberger XL2A Basses purchased from Dan Martin; two Spector NS-2 maple basses hand made by Stuart Spector for the NAMM convention-one of which was purchased from Dan Martin, the other is white and was purchased three weeks later.

Amplifiers: Ed used a little white Fender Bandmaster practice amp before there was a 5150 Studio to practice in.

Keyboards: Roland JX-8P, Sequential Circuits Prophet-10, E-mu Systems Emulator, Oberheim Matrix 12, and a Kurzweil 250.

Effects: A Roland DC30; an original Jimi Hendrix Fuzz Face purchased from Dan Martin sometimes between 1982 and 1984; a Roland Echo box used during live performances of "Hot for Teacher;" a Roland SDE-3000 Delay; a Rockman Smart Gate used for recording; a Boss OC-2 Octave; Boss SD-1 Overdrive; a Lexicon PCM-70 used for live performances of "Cathedral."

Other Equipment: While in the studio and during live performances, Ed prefers light to medium picks. In the earlier years, he used D'Andrea picks and later switched to D'Addario.

Ed rarely uses tuners, but when he did in early recordings it was a Peterson Strobe Tuner 420.

He uses Shure 57 and 58 microphones.

Ed's first wireless system was a Schaffer Vega that had a built in compressor, he used it through the first few tours. However, this system made his humbuckers sound much thinner than usual as well as adding an irritable crispness and brilliance to the signal. To rectify this Ed ran a forty-foot cable between the receiver and his amp, which acted as a buffer. Later, in the early 1980s Ed used a Nady FM system. In the early 1990s Sony made a special prototype wireless, the WRR-840 UHF, which Ed started using on the *F.U.C.K.* tour.

He also used a Bradshaw Switcher, which is an 8-loop effects switcher without MIDI capabilities that Eddie used even though better technology existed for years. It simply worked for Ed's purposes and that's all that was needed.

Van Halen, Eugenia-The mother of Eddie and Alex, Eugenia was the one who brought musical discipline into the Van Halen home. She made Ed practice the piano until he got so good he was winning competitions. According to interviews with the brothers, Eugenia was employed cleaning houses, in the family's typical hard working way, when the family came to America.

Van Halen, Jan-The father of Edward and Alex. Jan spent time in the Dutch Air Force band playing marches. He met Eugenia van Beers while in Indonesia and married her. After the Van Halen family emigrated to the U.S., he earned money washing dishes at Arcadia Methodist Hospital and as a janitor at a Masonic Temple. To continue making money with his true occupation in music, he went gigging on weekends playing proms, bar mitzvahs, etc.

The Van Halen Internet Mailing List-This a group of a hard core Van Halen fans and band insiders that converse through e-mail. An Internet mailing list is like a discussion group, but instead of people talking to each other in real time, e-mail is used. Several different lists are available. They vary in content and frequency.

Information is exchanged quickly and in high volume making this one of the best places to get information on Van Halen. If you have a question about the band chances are one of these people has the answer. Hundreds of messages are exchanged every day on the most detailed or the most general Van Halen topics. It is the closest thing to a world-wide Van Halen fan club.

The list doesn't just exchange information, though. There have been several list projects in its history, which dates back years.

Among the lists' past projects is the first known Van Halen tribute album titled *Fan Halen: Mustard on Our Legs Tribute Album*, named after a famous Eddie Van Halen quote. The list organized the first world-wide Van Halen conventions held annually in a major city (voted upon annually by the lists). The conventions include live performances by Van Halen tribute bands, member jam sessions, T-shirts, memorabilia, and contests for band-related merchandise including an autographed guitar. Several regional mini-conventions are also held throughout the year.

The lists have also archived the band's rare and unreleased songs in a series of eleven compilation audio cassettes. Similar tapes were made of David Lee Roth's and Sammy Hagar's rare and unreleased songs. In 1996 the list compiled 78 of these songs in a four CD set entitled *Looney Tunes: The Unreleased*.

New projects are always springing up and this book is just one of them.

For more information about joining the list please visit some of the many web sites devoted to Van Halen. (See "Web Sites" entry)

Van Halen Productions-The band's private business office that was used throughout the 1980s. The office was located at Rudolph Valentino's former Hollywood, CA, gymnasium, located on a 7th floor building on Sunset Boulevard. The building is still in existence and is now known as the Hollywood Athletic Club. It offers a restaurant, bar, billiards, dancing and live music.

Van Inkels Choice-Van Halen appeared on this Dutch television show on 4/20/93.

Van Wailin'-Canadian-based Van Halen tribute band.

Van Wheelden, Peter-Amplifier repairman from Holland who restored Ed's original Marshall 100-watt Super Lead in 1995. He is also the lead guitarist in Holland's Van Halen tribute band, Hot for Teacher.

Varsity Blues-"Hot for Teacher" appears on the soundtrack (PGD/Hollywood 162177, 1/12/99) to this movie (Paramount, 1999).

Veronica-1. A two-page feature on the addition of Gary Cherone titled "Van Halen Ziek Van Zefurende Zangers" appears in the 11/96 issue of this Dutch television guide. Address: Vaartweg 89, 1217 SM Hilversum, Holland 035-6723 723.
2. On 2/12/98 Veronica Television aired a tribute concert for Alfred La Garde entitled "Farewell to Big All." Snippets from a recent interview with Ed and Alex were aired throughout the broadcast.

The Very Best of Montrose-(Rhino 79982, 2000) Compilation album that includes some of Sammy Hagar's greatest hits. Tracks: Rock the Nation • Bad Motor Scooter • Space Station #5 • Rock Candy • I Got the Fire • Spaceage Sacrifice • We're Going Home • Paper Money • All I Need • Twenty Flight Rock • Clown Woman • Dancin' Feet • Let's Go • Jump on It • Music Man • M for Machine • Stand • Ready, Willing, and Able

VH1-This network's index of Van Halen-related televised specials:

6/26/94: VH1 Honors Sammy joins Melissa Etheridge to perform "Honky Tonk Woman."

7/20/95: Naked Café: Van Halen featured.

1995: The cast of Frasier reviews the video for "Can't Stop Lovin' You."

Fall 1995: Michael Anthony appears on "Fairway to Heaven" golf tournament

3/08/97: "All-Star Garage Band-City of Hope Benefit" at Universal City, CA. Ed performed at this benefit, which took place on 10/16/96 and was only broadcast on this one day.

8/12/97: "Fistful of Alice": Sammy plays lead guitar on "School's Out" with Alice Cooper at the Cabo Wabo Cantina.

2/28/98: Eddie Van Halen's high school yearbook photo appears on a program titled "Before They Were Rock Stars."

3/08/98: Van Halen is featured on European VH1 on Talk Music.

4/98: Sammy Hagar is interviewed in a Behind the Music episode about Ted Nugent.

6/15/98: David Lee Roth interview clip featured in an episode of Sex Appeal.

3/13/99: Van Halen episode of Rock Candy.

9/01/99: Van Halen episode of Video Timeline.

10/02/99: Sammy Hagar and the Waboritas appear on Hard Rock Live.

11/16/00: Van Halen places #7 on VH1's 100 Greatest Artists of Hard Rock.

Video Hits Volume 1-(Warner Home Video 38428, 1996) This collection of past Van Halen videos was released on 10/28/96 in the U.K. and on 10/29/96 in the U.S. It was certified gold on 2/14/97. Videos included: • Jump • Panama • Hot for Teacher • When It's Love • Finish What Ya Started • Poundcake • Runaround • Right Now • Dreams • Don't Tell Me (What Love Can Do) • Can't Stop Lovin' You • Not Enough • Humans Being

The band is still considering putting out a second volume of this video to include some of the older videos they've done. "Amsterdam" is conspicuously missing from volume one, probably due to Ed and Al's dislike of the song's portrayal of their hometown. "Top of the World" is also missing possibly because there were three official videos made for the song.

The video is also available on laserdisc with the same track listing. On 11/09/99 the DVD version was released with the extra video, "Without You."

Video Rock Stars-This magazine's index of Van Halen-related issues:
8/84-9/84: Eddie Van Halen/David Lee Roth cover.
3/85: David Lee Roth cover.
5/85: David Lee Roth cover.
9/85: David Lee Roth cover.
3/86: Van Halen cover. "This Year's Model": two-page Van Halen feature by Marc Shapiro. "Behind the Scenes with...": four-page feature on the *Crazy from the Heat* movie casting call by Sharon Liveten.
Summer 1986: "Van Halen Revs Its Motor with Power Thrusting Porsche": two-page Van Halen interview by Marc Shapiro.
Address: Ideal Publishing Corporation, 215 Lexington Avenue, New York, NY 10016.

VidGrid-A multi-media CD-ROM game featuring videos from Van Halen, Jimi Hendrix, Aerosmith, Peter Gabriel, the Red Hot Chili Peppers, and Guns 'n' Roses.

The respective artist's music video was displayed and broken into six equal squares that randomly changed position. Your objective was to put the puzzle together before the video ended. The Van Halen video was "Right Now."

The CD is no longer in print and is fairly hard to find.

Virtual Halen-An Ohio-based Dave-era Van Halen tribute band, formerly known as Valerie's Revenge.

Virus-One of the names Gene Simmons wanted to rename Van Halen with after discovering them in 1976.

Vision Quest-(Warner Bros., 1985) Two Sammy Hagar songs appear in this drama about a high school wrestler who falls in love with an older woman starring Matthew Modine and Linda Fiorentino with a special appearance by Madonna. "I'll Fall in Love Again" and "Two Sides of Love" appear in the film. "I'll Fall in Love Again" was also included on the movie's soundtrack. The soundtrack was also available for a short time on vinyl in Japan (28AP-3000).

VOA-(Geffen 24043, 1984) Sammy Hagar solo album produced by Ted Templeman that hit the charts on 8/11/84. It was certified gold on 11/13/84 and platinum on 11/19/85. The album spent 36-weeks on the charts reaching its highest position at #32. Tracks: • Burnin' Down the City • Dick in the Dirt • Don't Make Me Wait • I Can't Drive 55 • Rock Is in My Blood • Swept Away • Two Sides of Love • V.O.A.

Reportedly, Sammy had a personal acupuncturist visit him twice a day during this album's recording sessions.

"Two Sides of Love" (Geffen, 29446) was the album's first single, initially charting at #76 on 7/14/84 and peaking at #38 on 9/08/84 (10 weeks on chart).

Sammy got the inspiration for "I Can't Drive 55" (Geffen, 7-29173) after being pulled over for speeding while on a trip to Lake Placid, NY. It charted on 9/29/84 at #77 and reached #26.

"V.O.A." was Hagar's response to Russia after they pulled out of the 1984 Olympics.

"Don't Make Me Wait" was co-written with Jesse Harms, who also played keys and sang background vocals on this album.

Videos from this album include "I Can't Drive 55," with a cameo by Claudio Zampolli, "V.O.A.," and "Two Sides of Love."

Vogue-The April 1992 issue of this magazine included a photo shoot of Gary Cherone and Nuno Bettencourt with Claudia Mason and Spanish actress Rossy de Palma. The layout was titled "Gypsy Soul."

Von Halen-Tokyo-based Van Halen tribute band.

Voodoo Queen-(3:33) This unreleased original is basically an early version of "Mean Street," with completely different lyrics. Four different recordings of this song are known to exist. In 1977 the song was recorded for the band's Warner Brothers demo. Live recordings exist from 1976 in an unknown location, 1978 in Paris, France, and 1979 in Osaka, Japan.

W

Waitin' for the Bus-(3:50) The band performed this ZZ Top cover on 9/18/76 at the Bogart in San Bernardino, CA, on 5/12/92 at the Great Western Forum in Inglewood, CA and on 5/21/92 at the Cabo Wabo Cantina.

Waiting for the Punchline-(A&M 31454 0327, 1995) This Extreme album, released in February 1995, is Extreme in the rough. Very few effects, just down and dirty rock. Drummer Paul Geary left after recording the album to pursue a management career (Godsmack is among his clients) and was replaced by Mike Mangini, who went on to perform with Steve Vai during the G3 tour. The album was recorded at Criteria in Miami, FL, and Sound Techniques in Boston, MA.

Videos from this album included "Hip Today," "Cynical," and "Unconditionally."

The Japanese CD release of this album contained a bonus track, "Fair Weather Faith." (4:49) Tracks: • There Is No God • Cynical • Tell Me Something I Don't Know • Hip Today • Naked • Midnight Express • Leave Me Alone • No Respect • Evilangelist • Shadow Boxing • Unconditionally • Waiting for the Punchline

Waiting for the Punchline singles/promos
"Cynical" (edit), "Cynical" (album version)(promo), A&M 31458 8418 2, CD, USA, 1995.

"There Is No God," "Never Been Funked," A&M 31458 8015 2, CD, UK 1995.

"There Is No God" (edit), "Never Been Funked," "Better Off Dead," A&M 580 609-2, CD, Germany, 1995.

Hip Today (disk 1): "Hip Today" (edit), "Better Off Dead," "Never Been Funked," "Kid Ego" (live), (disk 2): "Hip Today" (edit), "There Is No God" (edit), "When I'm President" (live), "Strutter," A&M 580 993-2, CD, UK, 1995.

"Hip Today" (edit), "No Respect," "Strutter," "Kid Ego" (live), A&M 580 929-2, CD, USA.

"Hip Today" (edit), "Hip Today" (album version) (promo), A&M 31458 8371 2, CD, USA, 1995.

"Cynical" (edit), "Am I Ever Gonna Change" (live), "Tell Me Something I Don't Know" (live), A&M 581 099-2, CD, Germany, 1995.

"Unconditionally" (Nuno edit), "Get The Funk Out" (7" What the funk? Mix), "Rest in Peace" (edit), "Hole Hearted" (horn mix), A&M 581 121-2, CD, 1995.

"Unconditionally" (edit), "Am I Ever Gonna Change" (live), "Tell Me Something I Don't Know" (live), "Naked" (live), "When Will It Rain?" A&M POCM-1130, CD, Japan, 1995.

"Unconditionally" (Nuno edit), "Am I Ever Gonna Change" (live), "When Will It Rain?" "Naked" (live), A&M, CD, UK, 1995.

Walk Away-(3:58) The band performed this James Gang cover in their club days.

Walk This Way-(3:01) The band performed this Aerosmith cover on 9/18/76 at the Bogart in San Bernardino, CA.

Wall of Sound-The music news web site's index of Van Halen-related articles:
12/24/97: Eddie Van Halen interview.
5/13/98: Eddie Van Halen interview
5/14/98: Eddie Van Halen feature.
8/19/98: Van Halen featured in Top 100 Albums of the 70s Vote
URL: http://www.wallofsound.com

War Pigs-The band reportedly played this Black Sabbath cover in their early years.

Watson, Jeff-Sammy Hagar performed on the Jeff Watson album *Lone Ranger* (Shrapnel 1055, 1992) for the song "Cement Shoes" (4:20). Sammy is credited with "Vocal Scatts" on this track, which begins with some nasty growling compliments of a dog named Zeus. In addition it features Watson's Night Ranger guitar counterpart, Brad Gillis, as guest soloist. Hagar's lines are the only vocals on the track and comprise a fairly decent-sized portion of the song, serving as an intro verse and chorus of sorts, with plenty of soloing by Watson and Gillis rounding out the tune.

WCCO-TV-Van Halen was interviewed and a live performance of "Why Can't This Be Love?" from an unknown concert was played on this Japanese station in 1986.

W.D.F.A.-Abbreviation for "We Don't Fuck Around." The acronym appears on the last page of the *Women and Children First* tour program, on the cover of the Us Festival tour program (on the banner in the eagle's mouth), on various *Fair Warning* tour backstage passes, and on a white Gibson Explorer-style bass owned by Michael Anthony. The front of the bass was splattered with red paint to resemble blood and W.D.F.A. is written in red on the back. David Lee Roth was also known to write the acronym on his shirt during the *Women and Children First* tour.

We All Had a Real Good Time-The band performed this Edgar Winter cover, from the album *They Only Come Out at Night* (Epic EQ-31584, 1972), in their club days. A bootleg of a 1974 performance of this song is in circulation.

Web Sites-Van Halen enjoys a huge web presence. So many sites exist that an accurate list could never been listed here. However, below you'll find the most popular and authoritative resources for the band on the web. Many of these sites include constantly updated lists of Van Halen-related web sites.

The Official Van Halen Web Site: www.van-halen.com
The Van Halen News Desk: www.vhnd.com
The Van Halen Store: www.vanhalenstore.com
The Van Halen Encyclopedia: www.vanhalenencyclopedia.com
Van Halen Bootlegs: www.vhboots.com
Van Halen Links: www.vhlinks.com
The Van Halen FAQ: www.vh-faq.com
Van Halen IRC: www.vanhalen-irc.com
The Official Sammy Hagar Site: www.redrocker.com
The Official David Lee Roth Site: www.davidleeroth.com
The David Lee Roth Army: www.dlrarmy.com
Gary Cherone Site: www.cherone.com

We Die Young-(3:01) This unreleased original was recorded for the Warner Brothers demo. A live version surfaced in late 1997 from a 1976 performance at the Golden West Ballroom in Norwalk, CA. The song is sometimes known as "We Die Bold."

The Weekender Online-This web site featured an Alex Van Halen interview and contest on 7/16/98. URL: http://www.theweekender.com

We Gotta Get Out of This Place-The band performed this Animals cover several times throughout the *F.U.C.K.* tour.

Weird Science-(MCA/Universal, 1985) A short portion of David Lee Roth's "Just a Gigolo/I Ain't Got Nobody" video appears in this comedy about two teenagers who create the "perfect woman" with their computer. The movie starred Anthony Michael Hall, Bill Paxton, and Keely LeBrock.

Western Exterminator Co.-Since companies often sponsored tours, to be different Van Halen decided to sponsor a company on their huge *1984* tour. The Western Exterminator Company was their choice. It is the largest family owned pest control company in the western U.S. The company was created in 1921 on Fremont Avenue in Los Angeles, CA, and founded by Carol Strom, a Swedish immigrant.

Their corporate headquarters are now in Irvine, CA. Offices are spread throughout California, Arizona, and Nevada, with over 750 employees. In 1931 their hammer man mascot was born. It was created by Vaughn Kaufman of the telephone company after they approached Western Exterminator Company about advertising in the yellow pages. "The Little Man with the Hammer" was first known as "Kernel Kleenup." In June 1964 a television contest was held to rename the Kernel. The winning entry was "Inspector Holmes." Neither name caught on and mascot is still referred to as "The Little Man." He was used by the band (prominently) as a mascot of sorts on the *1984* tour, showing up on T-shirts, backstage passes, posters, and as the backdrop for the stage.

What They Gonna Say Now-Van Halen performed this Sammy Hagar song from his album *I Never Said Goodbye* on 2/08/92 at Freedom Hall in Louisville, KY.

When It's Love-(*OU812*; *Best of Volume 1* [5:36]; *Live: Right Here, Right Now* [5:22]) "When It's Love" was almost named "How Do You Know When It's Love?" This was the first track written for *OU812* and the second single released.

The track was recorded using a Roland D-50, an Oberheim OB-8, a Roland TXC-816 rack, a digital DX7 synthesizer, and a six-foot 1920 Steinway grand piano. Both pianos were outfitted with a Forte MIDI modification by Jim Wilson. The hammers were treated with lacquer to make them sound brighter during recording. For the solo, Ed used a Fender Stratocaster through a Marshall amplifier.

The video for the song was filmed during a three-day break on the *Monsters of Rock/OU812* tour. The band flew to California to spend some time with their families, and spent 1½ days shooting this video at a small bar in Southern California. Alex's old drum technician was contacted and he made all the equipment arrangements for the band prior to their arrival. The video was produced by Anthony Payne and Kim Dempster and directed by Jeremiah Chechik.

Where Have All the Good Times Gone?-(*Diver Down* [3:02]) A riff from this version of this Kinks' cover was taken from the unreleased Van Halen version of the song "Young and Wild."

Whisky A GoGo Anniversary Gig-Van Halen celebrated their fifteenth anniversary on 3/03/93 by performing at one of the clubs they performed in before they were signed, the Whisky A GoGo in Hollywood, CA. 250 tickets were available for sale for $20. It sold out in fifteen minutes. Thousands of fans were left in the streets. Police riot squads were called. A live video for "Dreams" was made at the event. The complete set list: • Dreams • Poundcake • Judgement Day • Runaround • When It's Love • Panama • There's Only One Way to Rock • Right Now • Why Can't This Be Love? • Finish What Ya Started • You Really Got Me • Best of Both

Worlds • Ain't Talkin' 'Bout Love • Top of the World • Won't Get Fooled Again • Jump

White Room-The band performed this Cream cover on 8/05/95 at the Blockbuster Entertainment Center in Camden, NJ.

Whole Lotta Love-The band performed this Led Zeppelin cover in 1992 at the Cabo Wabo Cantina.

Whoopi-Sammy Hagar was interviewed on this show by host Whoopi Goldberg in 1992.

Why? Because Why-This unreleased original is a leftover from the *Van Halen III* sessions that included vocals by Wolfgang Van Halen.

Why Can't This Be Love?-(*5150*; *Best of Volume 1* [3:45]; *Live: Right Here, Right Now* [5:21]) This track was the first single with Sammy Hagar as lead singer. It was recorded on an Oberheim OB-8.

Wilbur-One of two Burmese cats owned by Edward and Valerie in the late 1980s.

Wild Fire-This Spooky Tooth cover, from *You Broke My Heart, So I Busted Your Jaw* (A&M 4385, 1973), was performed by the band in their club days as a set opener. A live recording of the song was recorded at a February 1975 performance.

Wild Thing-(5:00) The band played this Troggs cover on 5/10/86 at Joe Louis Arena in Detroit, MI, and on 8/27/86 at Veterans Memorial Coliseum in New Haven, CT, during the filming of *Live without a Net*. The song was not included on the video.

The Wild Life-(Universal Pictures, 1984) (Video release: MCA Home Video, 80145) Eddie Van Halen wrote the score for this movie. Sharp-eared listeners will recognize portions of early versions of "Right Now," "Good Enough," "Feels So Good," "A.F.U. (Naturally Wired)," and "Strung Out" interspersed throughout the film. In addition, the synthe-sized backdrop music for David Lee Roth's "Tai Chi Solo" on the *1984* tour also made its debut in this film.

"Donut City" (3:57), is the only complete track for the movie written by Edward that appears on the film's soundtrack (MCA MCA-5523, 1984). The songs were recorded and mixed at 5150 by Donn Landee and Ken Deane. Ed played all the instruments on the songs.

Williams, Jr., Hank-Sammy Hagar played guitar on "Almost Persuaded," a song from Willams' *Lone Wolf* album (Warner Bros./Curb 26090, 1990). The album spent 18 weeks on the charts beginning on 2/24/90. It reached #71.

Van Halen appeared in the video for the Williams' song "My Name Is Bocephus." Filmed at an American Legion Hall in Van Nuys, CA, Van Halen portrayed Williams' backup bar band in the video, which won the Video of the Year award at a Country Music Association ceremony.

In the video Edward appears with an almost military-style haircut and Alex is completely bald. Both Edward and Sammy are on guitar. Ed used his main striped Kramer and Hagar played a white Fender Stratocaster. Other celebrity appearances included Gallagher, Bobcat Goldthwaite, and Dan Haggerty.

Winchell-Sammy Hagar's black and white rat terrier, named after the donut maker.

Wipeout-The band performed this Surfaris cover throughout their early years and on 9/01/86 at the Silver Stadium in Rochester, NY. The 1986 version was performed during a soundcheck with Sammy on the drums.

The Wish-This unreleased original is a leftover keyboard-oriented song from the *F.U.C.K.* sessions. It was kept off of *F.U.C.K.* because Ed felt it wouldn't have fit in the grand scheme of the album. (Similar to the reason "Angel Eyes" was not included on *Van Halen II*) Thomas Dolby lent a hand on this song, sequencing the notes into a MAC computer using Opcode Vision software.

Without You-(*Van Halen III* [6:28]) Edward employed the use of a quarter on this track, raking it back and forth across the strings to produce a strange scratching effect. He later had some metal picks made up to use when playing the song live. Ed used a prototype Wolfgang with P-90 pick-ups to record the song. This same guitar appeared in the video for "Without You."

The "Without You" video premiered on MTV's MTV Live at 6:00pm EST on Monday 3/02/98. Segments of the video were filmed in Los Angeles on 1/29/98. The Ice Hotel was filmed in Sweden at the actual Ice Hotel. The structure is made completely of ice and is rebuilt every year. The Los Angeles soundstage was structured to look like the Ice Hotel with real ice. The ice was trucked in and kept at low temperatures during the shoot making some of the scenes very uncomfortable for the band. The total cost of the video was approximately $1 million. A short segment of the video went on to be used in the opening of VH1's Rock Show.

This was the first song from Van Halen mach III to be aired on radio. It set a record by being the first single to debut at #1 on the Billboard Mainstream Rock Chart. It was also the first song written for the album. It was written on the day Gary and Ed met.

Ed wrote most of the lyrics to this song as nod to his new philosophies on life that began to take shape after he quit drinking. The song itself was written about 45 minutes after Gary first showed up at 5150. Ed did the engineering and the final product heard on the album is actually the original demo of the song.

Woman in Love-(4:38) This unreleased original was performed by the band in 1976 at the Hilton in Pasadena, CA. It does not resemble "Women in Love" from *Van Halen II*. A bootleg studio performance of this song, believed to have been recorded in the mid-1970s, was leaked to the public in early 1999.

Woman in Tokyo-The band performed this Deep Purple cover on 2/01/89 at the Tokyo Super Dome.

Women and Children First-(Warner Bros. 3415, 1980 (33:13)) This album was recorded in seventeen days and released on 3/26/80. 4.3 million copies have been sold in the U.S. It reached #6 on the U.S. charts (4/19/80) and #15 on the U.K. charts (4/06/80). It was certified gold on 5/29/80, platinum on 6/02/80, double platinum on 10/22/84, and triple platinum on 8/04/94. The album was remastered and rereleased on 9/19/00.

Parts of this album were recorded on an Ibanez Destroyer borrowed from Chris Holmes of W.A.S.P.

One version of the album was released on a special cassette form along with *Fair Warning*.

Included in the album (reportedly only the first million pressings) was a three-foot black and white poster of David Lee Roth, bound to a chain-link fence. The photograph was taken by famed fashion photographer Helmut Newton. It was used for shock value. Dave didn't want fans to think they had a handle on the band. Surprisingly Newton did not charge Roth for the photo session, only for the supplies used by Newton's assistants.

This was the first album Van Halen went into the studio to record for unprepared, prompting the band to revive songs from their early demo tapes which was something Edward wasn't happy doing.

In 1995 a collection of unused material from this album was leaked to the public in the form of a bootleg recording titled Women and Children

First Studio Sessions. These recordings revealed an instrumental with a strong bass line that was not used on this or any other Van Halen album.

The album's title came from Dave. One morning, after a typical Van Halen-style rampage, Dave awoke to distant screams of, "The ship is sinking!" Dave replied, "Women and Children First!" The phrase stuck.

Women and Children First singles/promos
"And the Cradle Will Rock," "Could This Be Magic?" WB, USA, WB 45-1980, Spain, WB P-555W, Japan, WB 17.630, Holland, 7" Vinyl, 5/24/80. Highest chart position: #55 in USA on 6/28/80.

"And the Cradle Will Rock" (mono), "And the Cradle Will Rock" (promo), WB WBS 49501, 7" Vinyl, USA, 1980.

"And the Cradle Will Rock," "Could This Be Magic?" WEA W 17630, 7"Vinyl, Italy, 1980.

"And the Cradle Will Rock," "Everybody Wants Some!!" "Loss of Control," WEA K17645, 7" Vinyl, UK, 1980. Logo sticker included.

Women in Love…-(*Van Halen II* [4:05]) This song is about a guy who loses his girlfriend to another girl. The title also is also the name of a book by D.H. Lawrence and David Lee Roth is known to be an avid reader.

Ed used a strat with a telecaster pickup, doubling the track, for the intro. He recreated the technique live by using a Harmonizer. The intro showcased Ed's new technique of false-harmonics.

Won't Get Fooled Again-(*Live: Right Here, Right Now* [5:49]) The band performed this The Who cover on 4/01/93 at Palaghaccio in Rome, Italy and on 3/03/93 at the Whisky A GoGo in West Hollywood, CA. It also appears on the 5150 promotional video included in the first pressings of the *Live: Right Here, Right No*w video.

Word-Sammy's nickname for Edward around 1987.

Wyman, Rich-Eddie Van Halen performed on Wyman's album *Fatherless Child* (Apricot Records 53162-0, 1996). Originally, Edward's involvement was to be limited to producing. "The Little Things" (3:43), a bluesy rocker, features a guitar solo by Edward. While the "Right Now"-ish feel of "Blinded by Pain" (4:37) features Edward on rhythm guitar, guitar solo, and bass (during the song's chorus). Ed helped write the chorus to the song. Finally, the majestic instrumental "The Water Sings" (3:21) features Edward on acoustic and electric guitar and Andy Johns on bass.

All three tracks, along with a fourth track, "Even the Dog Knows" (5:00), were produced by Edward and Johns and were recorded at the 5150 Studio.

The cover photographs were done by David Bertinelli, Valerie's brother, who also did the cover photography for Rich's first effort, Just Might Make It. Wyman was best man at David's wedding.

Wyman, based in Park City, UT, met Edward and Valerie on a ski trip in Park City. The guitarist was eager to lend Wyman a hand after witnessing a performance at a local bar later that evening.

Y

Yamaha All Access-This magazine, for users of Yahama music gear, interviewed Michael Anthony in its launch issue of July 2000.

Year to the Day-(*Van Halen III* [8:32]) The working title for this track was "365."
This song was a struggle to mix taking two days, 6/06/97 and 6/07/97. Special attention was paid by Erwin Musper to boost the bass in the mix.
Ed used a Wolfgang Special on this track equipped with a Fernandes Sustainer.

You Never Know-This unreleased original is a leftover keyboard-oriented song from the *F.U.C.K.* sessions. Like "The Wish," Thomas Dolby also lent a hand on this song.

Young and Wild-(2:35) This unreleased Kim Fowley & Stephen Tetsch cover (recorded by Cherie Currie and The Runaways [Raven RVCD-60]) was recorded for Van Halen's 1977 Warner Brothers demo.
Steven Tetsch was also known as Venus of Venus and the Razorblades, a band that Van Halen opened for in their Whisky A GoGo days. The song was written in 1975 and the band most likely heard this song at one of these shows and decided to come up with their own version. Venus and the Razorblades never released their own version of the song.

Young Guitar-Eddie Van Halen appeared on the cover of this Japanese guitar magazine's February 1993 issue. The issue featured "Top of the Guitars," a 16-page interview and axe profile. The magazine also featured an Eddie poster and a transcription to "316." In their January 1996 issue, an eleven-page, four-part feature with an Edward interview titled "Van

Halen Special" appeared with a Wolfgang guitar feature, an Eddie poster and live-rig feature. A four-page Sammy interview also appears.

Young Man's Blues-The band performed this Mose J. Allison cover on 8/22/93 at the Cal Expo Amphitheater in Sacramento, CA, and on 8/28/93 at the Pacific Amphitheater in Costa Mesa, CA.

Young Miss-The March 1983 issue of this magazine featured a three-page Van Halen interview by Vicki Jo Radovsky titled "The One, the Only Supergroup Van Halen."

Young Players-A trivia board game that contains two Van Halen-related questions, both with the same answer: "Who did Valerie Bertinelli marry?" and "Who played the guitar solo on Michael Jackson's 'Beat It'?"

You Really Got Me-(*Van Halen*; *Best of Volume 1* [2:37]) Initially released to only 35 radio stations, this song was added to 26 more the very next week. Within one month it was getting airplay on 140 stations across the country.

The lurching, staccato sound at he end of the guitar solo was performed by Edward bending the G string at the 7th fret and turning his pickup toggle switch back and forth on his Ibanez Destroyer "Shark." His neck pickup was disengaged and when he toggled back and forth it allowed the note to sound as if it was being turned off and on. Ed demonstrated this technique in the video for the song.

The original version of this song, written by the Kinks, reached #7 on the U.S. charts and #1 on the U.K. charts in 1964.

When the band recorded the demo for this song Dave missed his cue on the second verse and the band covered for him extending the song a little. Nevertheless, the song was picked for the album.

You're No Good-(*Van Halen II* [3:12]) The band used to play a completely different version of this song during their club days.

On the cassette version of the *Van Halen II* album, this song was incorrectly credited to Holland-Dozier-Holland (the trio responsible for writing many of the Supremes hits).

"You're No Good" was originally recorded by Betty Everett for Vee Jay in 1963 and was covered shortly thereafter by the Swingin' Blue Jeans. In 1974 Andrew Gold added strings to the arrangement and Linda Ronstadt had her first #1 single with the song in 1975.

The bass intro for this song was originally meant to be a complete bass solo. Later it was determined that it would be better as an intro.

It was Ted Templeman's idea to record this tune. Edward came up with his version after Templeman hummed him the main riff.

Your Filthy Little Mouth-(Reprise 9 45391, 1994) David Lee Roth solo album released on 3/08/94. He went for diversity on this album covering Willie Nelson's "Night Life," enlisting the talents of country star Travis Tritt for a duet on "Cheatin' Heart Café," and adding a taste of Jamaica with "No Big 'Ting." The only video made for the album was for "She's My Machine," which according to Roth, was a love song to his car. Tracks: • She's My Machine • Everybody's Got the Monkey • Big Train • Experience • A Little Luck • Cheatin' Heart Cafe • Hey, You Never Know • No Big 'Ting • You're Breathin' It • Your Filthy Little Mouth • Land's Edge • Night Life • Sunburn • You're Breathin' It (Urban NYC Mix)

The supporting tour was originally scheduled to span the globe, but shows in Puerto Rico, Japan, Ireland, England, Germany, Norway, Finland, Sweden, Denmark, France, Belgium, Holland, Austria, and Italy were cancelled, most likely based on poor ticket sales in the United States.

Your Filthy Little Mouth singles/promos
"She's My Machine," WB PRO-CD-6744, CD, USA, 1994.

"She's My Machine," "Mississippi Power" (non-album track), "Land's Edge," "You're Breathin' It," WEA WO229CDX, CD, UK, 1994.

"She's My Machine," "Hey, You Never Know," WEA WP DP-6350, 3" CD, UK, 1994.

Limited Edition CD Set #1: "Night Life," "Jump" (live), "She's My Machine" (live), WEA WO249CDX 9362-41586-2, CD, UK, 1994.

Limited Edition CD Set #2: "Night Life," "Panama" (live), "Big Train" (live), "Experience" (live), WEA WO249CD 9362-41585-2, CD, UK, 1994.

Yule-Eddie's nickname for Sammy around 1987.

Z

Zampolli, Claudio-Owner a foreign auto shop in Van Nuys, CA. Edward called Sammy to jam with the then Roth-less Van Halen at Zampolli's suggestion.

Zap Mag-(a.k.a. Max Mag) Two issues of this magazine featured Van Halen interviews and posters in 1984. One of the issues featured Dave on the cover and the other featured Eddie with Dave.

Zappa, Dweezil-Eddie Van Halen and Don Landee produced the single "My Mother Is a Space Cadet" for the Zappa kids on the album *Dweezil* (Barking Pumpkin AS 1579, 1982) though both are uncredited. Lyrics were by Dweezil and Moon Zappa and Steve Vai. The music is by Steve Vai and Dweezil Zappa. Eddie did the intro to the track. Dweezil was 12 at the time, according to Edward. The flip side is "Crunchy Water."

Gary Cherone, Nuno Bettencourt, and Pat Badger provided background vocals on Dweezil's album *Confessions* (Barking Pumpkin D2 74232, 1991) for the songs "Gotta Get to You" (5:38), "Bad Girl" (5:30), and "Vanity" (3:40). The album was recorded in April and May 1990 at Paramount Studios in Devonshire, U.K. and at Preferred Sound and Courtlen Studio in Hanson, MA. Bettencourt co-produced the album with Zappa.

Eddie also contributed to Dweezil's *What the Hell Was I Thinking?* album, which at press time had not been released.

Zero One-A Los Angeles after-hours nightclub/gallery once co-owned by David Lee Roth.

Zink, Paulie-International Pek Kwar champion who helped David Lee Roth develop his sword dance routine for the *1984* tour. Pek Kwar is a Northern Chinese style of kung fu, also known as monkey-style kung fu.

The Tours

Club Days (1974-1977)

Van Halen began their assault on the world in the very early 1970s, playing high school gigs, backyard parties, weddings, wet t-shirt contests, and
everywhere in between. As the band's popularity spread, they became *the*
party band. The police were a regular fixture at many an outdoor gig,
often resorting to bringing in helicopters to breakup gigs as kids from
every corner came to catch a show much to the dismay of the hosting
neighborhood. Known then as Mammoth, the band was reputed to have a
repertoire in excess of 200 songs. They often rehearsed in the basement of
David's parents' home.

In 1974 they changed their name to Van Halen (due in part to the fact
that the name Mammoth was already in use by another band) and hit the
club circuit. Bill Gazzari, owner of Gazzari's on Sunset Boulevard in West
Hollywood, CA, was the first club owner to give Van Halen a shot after
turning them down the first three or four times they auditioned. Known
back then as the Godfather, the oft-fedora-endowed Gazzari was a staunch
advocate of hosting unsigned talent.

Opening in 1963 Gazzari's was a spawning ground for several unsigned
acts including the Byrds, the Walker Brothers, and Buffalo Springfield.
Many popular 1980s bands including Metallica, Guns 'n' Roses, Warrant,
and Motley Crue all cut their teeth here as well. Unfortunately the venue
was closed shortly after Gazzari's death in the early 1990s. Another club,
Billboard Live, now stands in its place.

According to Gazzari in a 1979 letter to the Los Angeles Times, David
Lee Roth had informed him upon being hired that the band had auditioned at 19 area clubs and were turned down every time. The band

317

earned $75 per gig at Gazzari's and sometimes after a good night Gazzari would slip Roth an additional $20.

By 1976 Van Halen had begun their move towards superstardom, playing the Starwood, the Whisky A GoGo, the Pasadena Hilton, and Walter Mitty's Rock & Roll Emporium. Their sets consisted mostly of cover tunes at first and they would sneak in originals as often as they could.

At Walter Mitty's in Pomona, CA, which had a capacity of 300 (Van Halen was said have squeezed 1000 people into the place on some nights) the band witnessed a man die from stab wounds during an argument between two bikers about whose bike was faster while the band played "You Really Got Me." After this particular incident the band decided to move their amplifiers roughly one-and-a-half feet away from the wall so they could hide behind them when fights broke out. The club was reportedly closed a short time later due to an increase in violence.

In addition to Van Halen, the Whisky A GoGo featured a bevy of now-well-known acts in the mid-to-late 1970s, including the Ramones, Tom Petty, AC DC, Devo, Blondie, the Runaways, and Pat Travers. Buffalo Springfield and The Doors were two of the club's house bands in the mid-1960s. Owned by former Chicago policeman Elmer Valentine, the Whisky opened on 1/11/64 in an old bank. It featured a female DJ who played records and danced in a suspended cage near the stage. The Whisky is still in existence today hosting bands such as Cellophane Flowers, Native Tongue, Brave New World, and I, Mother Earth.

The Starwood, which was managed by Eddie Choran and Ray Stayer, also frequently featured several pre-big-name bands including Quiet Riot (then with Randy Rhoads on guitar), Yesterday and Today (now knows as Y&T), and The Quick. Randy Rhodes was often in attendance during Van Halen shows and would later admit to copping many of Ed's moves. Rodney Bingenheimer, a disc jockey on Los Angeles' KROQ who was known at one time as the Mayor of Sunset Strip, played a large part in the band's club success.

Reportedly it was Bingenheimer (who MCed at the Whisky from time to time) that got them their first gig at the Starwood. The disc jockey ran his own club on Sunset Boulevard, called Rodney Bingenheimer's English Disco. Opening in 1972, the now defunct club was the home of glam rock and featured acts ranging from Slade and T Rex to David Bowie and Sweet. The Starwood was closed sometime in 1980 or 1981 after owner Eddie Nash was involved in a murder that reportedly involved drugs and the late porn star John Holmes.

To advertise themselves, the band would often make flyers for upcoming gigs and paper them everywhere. They would even scour the parking lots at big-time concert events, jamming flyers under the windshield wipers of every car they could.

In between club gigs Edward and Alex would earn extra money by dressing up in blue coveralls, going door-to-door in their neighborhood, posing as city employees. They told residents that they were there to repaint the address numbers on the curb, charging anywhere from $4 to $8 per house.

It was at the Starwood that the band caught the attention of Kiss bassist Gene Simmons, who produced a demo tape for them. Though the demo was turned down by every major label, it eventually wound up in the hands of Marshall Berle who later went on to become the band's first manager. On a rainy Monday night in May 1977, Berle brought Warner Brothers Chairman Mo Ostin and producer Ted Templeman to see Van Halen perform. Unbeknownst to the band, Templeman had also been there the previous night as well, probably scoping them out in preparation for the following night's visit. Van Halen was offered a contract on the spot. They accepted it 24 hours later.

Prior to being signed, Van Halen opened for several national acts including Sparks, UFO, Santana, and Nils Lofgrin at venues such as the Santa Monica Civic Center, Long Beach Arena, and the Golden West Ballroom.

4/04/74: Gazzari's, West Hollywood, CA
4/05/74: Gazzari's, West Hollywood, CA
4/06/74: Gazzari's, West Hollywood, CA
4/07/74: Gazzari's, West Hollywood, CA
4/11/74: Gazzari's, West Hollywood, CA
4/12/74: Gazzari's, West Hollywood, CA
4/13/74: Gazzari's, West Hollywood, CA
4/14/74: Gazzari's, West Hollywood, CA
5/16/74: Gazzari's, West Hollywood, CA
5/17/74: Gazzari's, West Hollywood, CA
5/18/74: Gazzari's, West Hollywood, CA
5/19/74: Gazzari's, West Hollywood, CA
5/29/74: Gazzari's, West Hollywood, CA
5/30/74: Gazzari's, West Hollywood, CA
5/31/74: Gazzari's, West Hollywood, CA
6/01/74: Gazzari's, West Hollywood, CA
6/02/74: Gazzari's, West Hollywood, CA
6/06/74: Gazzari's, West Hollywood, CA
6/07/74: Gazzari's, West Hollywood, CA
6/08/74: Gazzari's, West Hollywood, CA
6/09/74: Gazzari's, West Hollywood, CA
6/20/74: Gazzari's, West Hollywood, CA
6/21/74: Gazzari's, West Hollywood, CA
6/22/74: Gazzari's, West Hollywood, CA
6/23/74: Gazzari's, West Hollywood, CA
6/27/74: Gazzari's, West Hollywood, CA
6/28/74: Gazzari's, West Hollywood, CA
6/29/74: Gazzari's, West Hollywood, CA
6/30/74: Gazzari's, West Hollywood, CA
8/01/74: Gazzari's, West Hollywood, CA
8/02/74: Gazzari's, West Hollywood, CA
8/03/74: Gazzari's, West Hollywood, CA

8/04/74: Gazzari's, West Hollywood, CA
8/08/74: Gazzari's, West Hollywood, CA
8/09/74: Gazzari's, West Hollywood, CA
8/10/74: Gazzari's, West Hollywood, CA
8/11/74: Gazzari's, West Hollywood, CA
8/15/74: Gazzari's, West Hollywood, CA
8/16/74: Gazzari's, West Hollywood, CA
8/17/74: Gazzari's, West Hollywood, CA
8/18/74: Gazzari's, West Hollywood, CA
9/12/74: Gazzari's, West Hollywood, CA
9/13/74: Gazzari's, West Hollywood, CA
9/14/74: Gazzari's, West Hollywood, CA
9/15/74: Gazzari's, West Hollywood, CA
9/19/74: Gazzari's, West Hollywood, CA
9/20/74: Gazzari's, West Hollywood, CA
9/21/74: Gazzari's, West Hollywood, CA
9/22/74: Gazzari's, West Hollywood, CA
9/26/74: Gazzari's, West Hollywood, CA
9/27/74: Gazzari's, West Hollywood, CA
9/28/74: Gazzari's, West Hollywood, CA
9/29/74: Gazzari's, West Hollywood, CA
11/14/74: Gazzari's, West Hollywood, CA
11/15/74: Gazzari's, West Hollywood, CA
11/16/74: Gazzari's, West Hollywood, CA
11/17/74: Gazzari's, West Hollywood, CA
1/10/75: Gazzari's, West Hollywood, CA
1/11/75: Gazzari's, West Hollywood, CA
1/17/75: Gazzari's, West Hollywood, CA
1/18/75: Gazzari's, West Hollywood, CA
2/75: Pasadena High School, Pasadena, CA. Partial set list: I Wanna Be Your Lover • In For The Kill • Take Your Whiskey Home • Wildfire. Audio recording exists.

2/07/75: Gazzari's, West Hollywood, CA
2/08/75: Gazzari's, West Hollywood, CA
2/09/75: Gazzari's, West Hollywood, CA
2/14/75: Gazzari's, West Hollywood, CA
2/15/75: Gazzari's, West Hollywood, CA
2/16/75: Gazzari's, West Hollywood, CA
3/28/75: Gazzari's, West Hollywood, CA
3/29/75: Gazzari's, West Hollywood, CA
3/30/75: Gazzari's, West Hollywood, CA
4/75: Pasadena High School, Pasadena, CA. The set list: Chevrolet •
Maybe I'm A Leo • Brown Sugar • We All Had A Real Good Time • Walk
Away • Rock and Roll Hochie Koo • Don't Call Us, We'll Call You • I Live
with Fools • Audio recording exists.
4/04/75: Gazzari's, West Hollywood, CA
4/05/75: Gazzari's, West Hollywood, CA
4/06/75: Gazzari's, West Hollywood, CA
5/16/75: Gazzari's, West Hollywood, CA
5/17/75: Gazzari's, West Hollywood, CA
5/18/75: Gazzari's, West Hollywood, CA
5/23/75: Gazzari's, West Hollywood, CA
5/24/75: Gazzari's, West Hollywood, CA
5/25/75: Gazzari's, West Hollywood, CA
6/13/75: Pasadena Hilton Hotel, Pasadena, CA. Opening act:
Sundance.
7/04/75: Gazzari's, West Hollywood, CA
7/05/75: Gazzari's, West Hollywood, CA
7/06/75: Gazzari's, West Hollywood, CA
7/11/75: Gazzari's, West Hollywood, CA
7/12/75: Gazzari's, West Hollywood, CA
7/13/75: Gazzari's, West Hollywood, CA
9/05/75: Gazzari's, West Hollywood, CA
9/06/75: Gazzari's, West Hollywood, CA

9/09/75: Gazzari's, West Hollywood, CA
9/12/75: Gazzari's, West Hollywood, CA
9/13/75: Gazzari's, West Hollywood, CA
9/14/75: Gazzari's, West Hollywood, CA
10/31/75: Gazzari's, West Hollywood, CA
11/01/75: Gazzari's, West Hollywood, CA
11/02/75: Gazzari's, West Hollywood, CA
11/07/75: Gazzari's, West Hollywood, CA
11/08/75: Gazzari's, West Hollywood, CA
11/09/75: Gazzari's, West Hollywood, CA
1/09/76: Gazzari's, West Hollywood, CA
1/10/76: Gazzari's, West Hollywood, CA
1/11/76: Gazzari's, West Hollywood, CA
1/16/76: Gazzari's, West Hollywood, CA
1/17/76: Gazzari's, West Hollywood, CA
1/18/76: Gazzari's, West Hollywood, CA
3/24/76: Walter Mitty's Rock & Roll Emporium, Pomona, CA
3/25/76: Walter Mitty's Rock & Roll Emporium, Pomona, CA
3/26/76: Gazzari's, West Hollywood, CA
3/27/76: Gazzari's, West Hollywood, CA
3/28/76: Gazzari's, West Hollywood, CA
4/07/76: Walter Mitty's Rock & Roll Emporium, Pomona, CA
4/08/76: Walter Mitty's Rock & Roll Emporium, Pomona, CA
4/09/76: Walter Mitty's Rock & Roll Emporium, Pomona, CA
4/10/76: Walter Mitty's Rock & Roll Emporium, Pomona, CA
5/01/76: Gazzari's, West Hollywood, CA
5/02/76: Gazzari's, West Hollywood, CA
5/09/76: Golden West Ballroom, Norwalk, CA. Van Halen opened this show for UFO. This was the first show that the band ever played where the set list was made up of mostly original songs. The set list: • On Fire • Show Your Love • Last Child • Tush • The Rover • Let's Get Rockin' • Ice Cream Man • Last Night • Eruption • We Die Young • Somebody

Get Me a Doctor • Babe Don't Leave Me Alone • Let Me Swim • She's the Woman. Audio recording exists.

5/30/76: Pasadena Community College, Pasadena, CA. The set list for this show included: • Show Your Love • Runnin' with the Devil • Eyes of the Night • In a Simple Rhyme • La Grange • Eruption • House of Pain • I Live with Fools. Audio recording exists. "Walk Away" appears on bootlegs of this show, but was not played at this performance.

6/01/76: The Starwood, Hollywood, CA. Audio recording exists.

6/03/76: Gazzari's, West Hollywood, CA

6/04/76: Gazzari's, West Hollywood, CA

6/05/76: Gazzari's, West Hollywood, CA

6/10/76: Gazzari's, West Hollywood, CA

6/11/76: Gazzari's, West Hollywood, CA

6/12/76: Gazzari's, West Hollywood, CA. Audio recording exists.

6/13/76: Gazzari's, West Hollywood, CA

6/28/76: The Starwood, Hollywood, CA. Audio recording exists.

6/29/76: The Starwood, Hollywood, CA. The set list for this show was: • Let's Get Rockin' • Somebody Get Me a Doctor • Babe Don't Leave Me Alone • Show Your Love • D.O.A. • Runnin' with the Devil • Let Me Swim • She's the Woman • Believe Me • Ice Cream Man • Honolulu Baby • Simple Rhyme • Guitar Solo • Eyes of Night • House of Pain • I Live with Fools. Audio recording exists.

6/30/76: The Starwood, Hollywood, CA. The set for this show was the same as the previous night. Audio recording exists.

7/31/76: Sexson Auditorium, Pasadena City College, Pasadena, CA. Opening act: Stormer

8/05/76: Gazzari's, West Hollywood, CA

8/06/76: Gazzari's, West Hollywood, CA

8/07/76: Gazzari's, West Hollywood, CA

8/08/76: Gazzari's, West Hollywood, CA

8/12/76: Gazzari's, West Hollywood, CA

8/13/76: Gazzari's, West Hollywood, CA

8/14/76: Gazzari's, West Hollywood, CA

8/15/76: Gazzari's, West Hollywood, CA

9/18/76: The Bogart, San Bernardino, CA. The set list for this show was: • Believe Me • Show Your Love • You Really Got Me • Last Child • Live for the Music • Runnin' with the Devil • The Rover • Sweet Emotion • Waitin' for the Bus • Walk This Way • Superstition • Still Alive and Well • Firehouse • Beer Drinkers and Hell Raisers • Keep Playing that Rock and Roll • Twist and Shout • 30 Days in the Hole • Francine • Gudbuy T' Jane • Fuck Off Chorus/Happy Trails • Rock and Roll Hoochie Koo • D.O.A. • Don't Call Us, We'll Call You. Audio recording exists.

9/21/76: The Bogart, San Bernardino, CA. Audio recording exists.

10/01/76: Pasadena Center Exhibit Hall, Pasadena, CA. Opening acts: Headwinds and Eulogy. Eulogy frequently opened for Quiet Riot, who were one of Van Halen's most-advertised rivals at the time.

10/06/76: Gazzari's, West Hollywood, CA

10/07/76: Gazzari's, West Hollywood, CA

10/08/76: Gazzari's, West Hollywood, CA

10/09/76: Gazzari's, West Hollywood, CA

10/10/76: Gazzari's, West Hollywood, CA

10/14/76: Gazzari's, West Hollywood, CA

10/15/76: Gazzari's, West Hollywood, CA

10/16/76: Gazzari's, West Hollywood, CA

10/17/76: Gazzari's, West Hollywood, CA

11/19/76: Pasadena Civic Center, Pasadena, CA. Opeing acts: Stormer and Smile.

12/03/76: Whisky A GoGo, West Hollywood, CA. Opening act: Venus & the Razorblades.

12/04/76: Whisky A GoGo, West Hollywood, CA. Opening act: Venus & the Razorblades.

12/05/76: Whisky A GoGo, West Hollywood, CA. Opening act: Venus & the Razorblades.

12/21/76: Whisky A GoGo, West Hollywood, CA

12/22/76: Whisky A GoGo, West Hollywood, CA

12/23/76: Whisky A GoGo, West Hollywood, CA

12/25/76: Whisky A GoGo, West Hollywood, CA

1/77: The Golden Bear, Huntington Beach, CA. This was Van Halen's only known appearance at the Golden Bear. The club normally featured already-signed acts such as Rick Derringer, Captain Beefheart, Spirit, and Tower of Power.

1/14/77: Whisky A GoGo, West Hollywood, CA

1/15/77: Whisky A GoGo, West Hollywood, CA. Opening acts: Randy California and The Motels.

1/18/77: The Starwood, Hollywood, CA. Van Halen opened this show for Yesterday & Today. The set list was: • Show Your Love • Runnin' with the Devil • Somebody Get Me a Doctor • In a Simple Rhyme • I Wanna Be Your Lover • Last Night • Bad Women (Peace of Mind) • Eruption • House of Pain • D.O.A. • You Really Got Me. Audio recording exists.

1/19/77: The Starwood, Hollywood, CA. Van Halen opened this show for Yesterday & Today.

1/27/77: Whisky A GoGo, West Hollywood, CA. Opening act: Berlin Brats.

1/28/77: Whisky A GoGo, West Hollywood, CA. Opening acts: Berlin Brats and Orange.

1/29/77: Whisky A GoGo, West Hollywood, CA. Opening act: Berlin Brats.

2/18/77: Pasadena Civic Center, Pasadena, CA. The bill for this show included Smile and Smokehouse.

2/25/77: Whisky A GoGo, West Hollywood, CA. Opening act: The Motels.

2/26/77: Whisky A GoGo, West Hollywood, CA. Opening act: The Motels.

3/13/77: Golden West Ballroom, Norwalk, CA. The bill for this show included The Dogs and The Ramones.

4/23/77: Glendale College Auditorium, Glendale, CA. Quiet Riot also performs at this show.

5/27/77: Whisky A GoGo, West Hollywood, CA. Opening acts: Lance Loud and The Mumps.

6/10/77: Whisky A GoGo, West Hollywood, CA. The set list for this show was: • Get the Show on the Road • Feel Your Love Tonight • Runnin' with the Devil • Atomic Punk • Little Dreamer • Voodoo Queen • Show No Mercy • Guitar Solo • Somebody Get Me a Doctor • Show Your Love • Bottoms Up! • On Fire • Feel Your Love Tonight • Young and Wild • Shape You're In • Ice Cream Man • Last Night • D.O.A. • Gudbuy T' Jane. Audio recording exists.

6/11/77: Whisky A GoGo, West Hollywood, CA

7/14/77: Whisky A GoGo, West Hollywood, CA. Opening act: Emerald City.

7/15/77: Whisky A GoGo, West Hollywood, CA. Opening act: Emerald City.

7/16/77: Whisky A GoGo, West Hollywood, CA. Opening act: Emerald City.

8/19/77: Whisky A GoGo, West Hollywood, CA

8/20/77: Whisky A GoGo, West Hollywood, CA

9/16/77: Whisky A GoGo, West Hollywood, CA. Opengin act: The Weasels.

9/17/77: Whisky A GoGo, West Hollywood, CA. Opeing act: The Weasels.

10/15/77: Pasadena Civic Center, Pasadena, CA. The soundcheck for this show was recorded and circulated. It included "Ain't Talkin' 'Bout Love" and "On Fire' as well as instrumental versions of "On Fire," "Voodoo Queen," and "Atomic Punk." This bootleg has been circulated under many different dates.

10/22/77: Whisky A GoGo, West Hollywood, CA

12/20/77: Pasadena Civic Center, Pasadena, CA. The set list for show was: • On Fire • Feel Your Love Tonight • Runnin' with the Devil •

Atomic Punk • Drum Solo • Little Dreamer • Somebody Get Me a Doctor • Ice Cream Man • Ain't Talkin' 'Bout Love • Eruption • D.O.A. • You Really Got Me. Audio recording exists.

12/30/77: Whisky A GoGo, West Hollywood, CA

12/31/77: Whisky A GoGo, West Hollywood, CA. Despite what some bootlegs suggest, the set list for this show was: • On Fire • Show Your Love • Runnin' with the Devil • Atomic Punk • Down in Flames • Bullethead • Little Dreamer • Somebody Get Me a Doctor • Ice Cream Man • Ain't Talkin' 'Bout Love • Eruption • D.O.A. • Happy Trails • You Really Got Me. Audio recording exists.

1/28/78: Fresno, CA

2/08/78: Pasadena Civic Auditorium, Pasadena, CA

2/18/78: Pasadena Civic Auditorium, Pasadena, CA. Audio recording exists.

2/25/78: Whisky A GoGo, West Hollywood, CA. Audio recording exists.

Sometime in late 1977 or early 1978 Van Halen played at Magic Mountain, an amusement park located in Valenica, CA. They were introduced as Warner Brothers recording artists, Van Halen. The set list for this show was: • On Fire • One More Time • Runnin' with the Devil • Atomic Punk • Ain't Talkin' 'Bout Love • Loss of Control • Show No Mercy • Eruption • Feel Your Love Tonight • Show Your Love • Summertime Blues • Unknown Jam. Audio recording exists.

Van Halen Tour (1978)

Van Halen spent most of their first world tour as an opening act for Journey, Montrose, and later Black Sabbath. The tour was initially supposed to last only three weeks. Due to their enormous success, the band ended up touring roughly eight months. Jack Boyle of Cellar Door Productions advised the band to play smaller venues rather than the full-scale coliseums that Warner Brothers wanted them to tackle. The reasoning behind this approach was that Van Halen could sell out each performance and learn how to work the crowd to hone their overall stage presence.

Edward relied heavily on his white and black striped Charvel "Franky" for this tour, and all of his guitars were strung with Fender strings. His rig consisted of 16 Marshall heads (six were for backup) running through 10 Marshall cabinets, outfitted with a combination of Marshall and JBL speakers. Guitar tech Rudy Leiren was kept busy replacing blown transformers at an average of two per week. Ed's Marshall arsenal was made up primarily of Mach II's and also included his now legendary 100-watt Super Lead, which was temporarily lost by an airline when the band was returning to the states from Japan to play the first ever Texxas Jam. His effects setup included a Univox echo unit, two Echoplexes, an MXR Phaser, and an MXR flanger. All were duct-taped to a piece of unfinished plywood. He also used an echoplex that he housed inside an old World War II practice bomb, an idea originally conceived during the latter part of the band's club days.

While in Madison, WI, the band destroyed the entire 7th floor of the Sheraton Inn. Alex and David removed the screen from Edward's window and threw his table and chairs outside to the ground below. Edward retaliated by going to the front desk and telling the clerk he was David Lee Roth and had lost his room keys. He then slipped into Roth's room and took Roth's table and chairs and put them in his own room. The police were confused, as Edward's screen was missing but he had a table and chairs, while Roth had a screen but was missing his furniture. This incident was just one of many such tales of pillage and destruction over the years. By 1980 Van Halen was racking up damages on almost every stop, ranging from the seemingly harmless act of smashing a hotel lamp to punching holes into the walls of hotel room after hotel room.

Upon completion of the tour the band took a five day break vacationing off the Caribbean coast on the island of Balise before heading back into the studio to record *Van Halen II*.

A typical setlist consisted of: • On Fire • I'm the One • Bass Solo • Runnin' with the Devil • Feel Your Love Tonight • Atomic Punk • Drum Solo • Little Dreamer • Ain't Talkin' 'Bout Love • Ice Cream Man • Guitar Solo • You Really Got Me • D.O.A. • Bottoms Up!

3/03/78: Aargon Ballroom, Chicago, IL
3/04/78: Nelson Center, Springfield, IL
3/05/78: Indianapolis Convention Center, Indianapolis, IN
3/07/88: Shuffle Inn, Madison, WI
3/08/78: The Orpheum, Madison, WI
3/09/78: Riverside Theater, Milwaukee, WI. Attendance: 2,106
3/10/78: Masonic Auditorium, Detroit, MI
3/11/78: Hara Arena, Dayton, OH. Attendance: 6,060
3/12/78: Leona Theater, Pittsburgh, PA
3/14/78: Massey Hall, Toronto, ON
3/15/78: Cleveland Convention Center, Cleveland, OH
3/16/78: Fairgrounds Coliseum, Columbus, OH
3/17/78: Commonwealth Convention Center, Louisville, KY
3/18/78: Evansville Coliseum, Evansville, IN
3/19/78: Morris Civic Center, South Bend, IN
3/21/78: Memorial Coliseum, Utica, NY
3/22/78: Palace Theater, Albany, NY
3/23/78: Century Theater, Buffalo, NY
3/24/78: Tower Theater, Philadelphia, PA. Audio recording exists.
3/25/78: The Palladium, New York, NY. Audio recording exists.
3/26/78: Calderone Theater, Hampstead, NY
3/28/78: The Palladium, New York, NY
3/29/78: Duluth Auditorium, Duluth, MN
3/30/78: St. Paul Civic Center, St. Paul, MN
3/31/78: Municipal Auditorium, Kansas City, MO
4/01/78: Kiel Opera House, St. Louis, MO. Attendance: 3,557
4/02/78: Omaha Music Hall, Omaha, NE. Attendance: 2,572

4/06/78: IMA Auditorium, Flint, MI

4/07/78: War Memorial, Nashville, TN

4/08/78: Murray State University, Murray, KY

4/09/78: Boutwell Auditorium, Birmingham, AL

4/11/78: Corpus Christi Memorial Coliseum, Corpus Christi, TX

4/12/78: Austin Municipal Auditorium, Austin, TX

4/13/78: Shreveport Municipal Auditorium, Shreveport, LA

4/14/78: Will Rogers Theater, Ft. Worth, TX

4/15/78: Houston Music Hall, Houston, TX

4/16/78: The Warehouse, New Orleans, LA

4/18/78: Ellis Auditorium, Memphis, TN

4/20/78: Ruby Diamond Auditorium, Tallahassee, FL

4/21/78: Sportatorium, Hollywood, FL

4/22/78: Curtis Hickson Hall, Tampa, FL

4/23/78: Fox Theater, Atlanta, GA

4/25/78: Rogues, Virginia Beach, VA

4/26/78: Rogues, Virginia Beach, VA

4/28/78: The Palladium, New York, NY. Audio recording exists.

5/04/78: Poperinge, Belgium

5/05/78: Stads Opelen, Delft, Holland

5/06/78: The Paradiso, Amsterdam, NL. "Summertime Blues" added to set list for this show. Audio recording exists.

5/08/78: Hamburg, GE

5/09/78: Hamburg, GE

5/10/78: Le Theater Mogador, Paris, France. "Voodoo Queen" and "Summertime Blues" added to set list for this show. Audio recording exists.

5/16/78: Sheffield City Hall, Sheffield, UK. Opened for: Black Sabbath

5/17/78: Liverpool Empire, Liverpool, UK. Opened for: Black Sabbath

5/18/78: Apollo Theatre, Glasgow, Scotland. Opened for: Black Sabbath. Audio recording exists.

5/19/78: Abderdeen Capitol, Abderdeen, Scotland. Opened for: Black Sabbath

5/21/78: Newcastle City Hall, New Castle, UK. Opened for: Black Sabbath. Audio recording exists.

5/22/78: Manchester Apollo, Manchester, UK. Opened for: Black Sabbath.

5/23/78: Victoria Hall, Hanley, England. Opened for: Black Sabbath.

5/25/78: Guild Hall, Portsmouth, UK. Opened for: Black Sabbath.

5/26/78: Bristol Hippoorome, Bristol, UK. Opened for: Black Sabbath.

5/27/78: Lewisham Odeon, Lewisham, UK. Opened for: Black Sabbath. Audio recording exists.

5/28/78: Ipswich Gaumont, Ipswich, UK. Opened for: Black Sabbath.

5/30/78: Coventry Theatre, Coventry, UK. Opened for: Black Sabbath.

5/31/78: Leicester De Montfort Hall, Leicester, UK. Opened for: Black Sabbath.

6/01/78: Hammersmith Odeon, London, UK. Opened for: Black Sabbath. Audio recording exists.

6/02/78: Oxford New Theatre, Oxford, UK. Opened for: Black Sabbath.

6/03/78: Southampton Gaumont, Southampton, UK. Opened for: Black Sabbath.

6/05/78: Birmingham Odeon, Birmingham, UK. Opened for: Black Sabbath.

6/06/78: Birmingham Odeon, Birmingham, UK. Opened for: Black Sabbath.

6/07/78: St. George Hall, Bradford, UK. Opened for: Black Sabbath.

6/08/78: Preston Guild Hall, Preston, UK. Opened for: Black Sabbath.

6/10/78: Hammersmith Odeon, London, UK. Opened for: Black Sabbath.

6/11/78: Hammersmith Odeon, London, UK. Opened for: Black Sabbath.

6/12/78: Hammersmith Odeon, London, UK. Opened for: Black Sabbath.

6/14/78: Manchester Apollo, Manchester, UK. Opened for: Black Sabbath.

6/15/78: Manchester Apollo, Manchester, UK. Opened for: Black Sabbath.

6/16/78: Bridlington Spa, Bridlington, UK. Opened for: Black Sabbath.

6/17/78: The Sun Palace, Tokyo, Japan. "Down in Flames," "Somebody Get Me a Doctor," and "Last Night" added to the set list for this show. "Down in Flames" continued to be played throughout the Japanese tour. Audio recording exists.

6/19/78: The Sun Palace, Tokyo, Japan. Audio recording exists.

6/22/78: The Sun Palace, Tokyo, Japan. "Somebody Get Me a Doctor" added to set list. Audio recording exists.

6/24/78: Nagoya-Shi Kokaido, Nagoya, Japan. "Somebody Get Me a Doctor" and "Summertime Blues" added to set list. Audio recording exists.

6/25/78: Festival Hall, Osaka, Japan. Audio recording exists.

6/26/78: Kyoto Kaikan Hall, Kyoto, Japan. Audio recording exists.

6/27/78: Kosei Nenkin Hall, Osaka, Japan. "Somebody Get Me a Doctor" added to set list. Audio recording exists.

7/01/78: The Cotton Bowl, Dallas, TX. The Bill for this show included Walter Egan, Van Halen, Eddie Money, Mahogany Rush, Heart, Ted Nugent, Cheech and Chong, Atlanta Rhythm Section, Head East, and Aerosmith. 80,000 fans paid $12.50 per ticket to cram themselves into the Cotton Bowl for a weekend-long gathering of some of the world's top rock and roll acts at the first annual Texxas Jam Day in Dallas Texas on the weekend of 7/01/78. Van Halen was one of the first acts to hit the stage, just after Walter Egan. Having just returned from Japan and playing on rented equipment, Van Halen ripped through a spirited, high-voltage set. It was reportedly so hot at the Texxas Jam, that the stage crewmembers repeatedly sprayed down the crowd with water from a fire hose. Movies like The Beatles' *Magical Mystery Tour*, The Who's *Tommy*, and *Monterey Pop* were being screened continually. By promoters' standards, the first annual Texxas Jam Day was a success. It ended with no births, no deaths, and very few injuries.

7/03/78: Armadillo World Headquarters, (AWHQ) Austin, TX. Opening act: Bugs Henderson Group.

7/09/78: Long Beach Arena, Long Beach, CA. Attendance: 8,614. Audio recording exists.

7/13/78: Superdome, New Orleans, LA. Opened for: The Doobie Brothers and The Rolling Stones. Attendance: 80, 173.

7/15/78: Fairgrounds, Oklahoma City, OK (The Oklahoma Jam). Audio recording exists.

7/16/78: Credit Island, Davenport, IA. Known as the Mississippi River Jam 1978 and sometimes the Iowa Jam, the bill included: Journey, Atlanta Rhythm Section, and The Doobie Brothers. This outdoor festival took place in a sweltering Iowa July heat and was plagued with delays. David Lee Roth told the nearly 35,000 fans in attendance to "Get your minds off the heat and put it in the beat." Almost 50 people were treated for heat exhaustion throughout the festival. The intense temperature also created havoc for the bands. It took over an hour for the sound crew to set up Journey's equipment, which was longer than their 45-minute set. In addition, at the end of the Atlanta Rhythm Section's 50-minute set a piece of their stage equipment caught fire, sending up flames from a nearby electronic panel. After waiting for nearly two hours close to 4,000 over-zealous fans crashed a fence before the venue opened (authorities had attempted to keep the concert-goers away from the performance area until the stage was completely erected) and almost as many left the performance early due to all of the delays.

7/18/78: Outagamic County Fairgrounds, Seymour, WI. Opened for: Journey

7/23/78: Oakland Coliseum, Oakland, CA. Known as Bill Graham's Day on the Green Festival, the bill included: AC/DC, Pat Travers, Foreigner, and Aerosmith. Eddie gives his first interview for a guitar magazine on this day. Attendance: 57,512

8/03/78: Lubbock Municipal Auditorium, Lubbock, TX. Opened for: Rick Derringer. Attendance: 3,032

8/04/78: Hollywood Bowl, Amarillo, TX (West Texxas Jam)

8/09/78: Second Chance, Peoria, IL. Opeing act: Bigfoot

8/19/78: Engle Stadium, Bay City Central High School, Bay City, MI. Known as the Summer Celebration '78, the bill included two local bands and Bob Seger. Attendance: 22,572

8/22/78: Milwaukee Arena, Milwaukee, WI. Opened for: Black Sabbath. Attendance: 10,424

8/27/78: Madison Square Garden, New York, NY. Opened for: Black Sabbath.

8/29/78: The Spectrum, Philadelphia, PA. Opened for: Black Sabbath. Audio recording exists.

9/02/78: Pittsburgh Civic Arena (The Igloo), Pittsburgh, PA. Opened for: Black Sabbath.

9/04/78: Cape Cod Coliseum, S. Yarmouth, MA. Opened for: Black Sabbath.

9/05/78: Portland Civic Center, Portland, NH. Opened for: Black Sabbath. Attendance: 7,744.

9/07/78: Niagra Falls Civic Center, Niagra Falls, NY. Opened for: Black Sabbath.

9/08/78: Niagra Falls Civic Center, Niagara Falls, NY. Opened for: Black Sabbath. Attendance: 8,186. Audio recording exists.

9/09/78: Baltimore Civic Center, Baltimore, MD. Opened for: Black Sabbath. Attendance: 9,253.

9/10/78: New Haven Coliseum, New Haven, CT. Opened for: Black Sabbath. Attendance: 7,438.

9/12/78: Indianapolis Convention Center, Indianapolis, IN. Opened for: Black Sabbath. Attendance: 7,653.

9/14/78: Cobo Hall, Detroit, MI. Opened for: Black Sabbath.

9/15/78: Cleveland Convention Center, Cleveland, OH. Opened for: Black Sabbath.

9/16/78: Checkerdome, St. Louis, MO. Opened for: Black Sabbath. Attendance: 13,133.

9/17/78: Municipal Auditorium, Kansas City, MO. Opened for: Black Sabbath. Attendance: 11,000.

9/22/78: Selland Arena, Fresno, CA. Audio and Video recordings exist.

9/23/78: Anaheim Stadium, Anaheim, CA. The bill for this show included Richie Lecea, Sammy Hagar, Black Sabbath, and Boston. Attendance: 56,000. Van Halen stold the show by hiring look-a-likes to parachute from an airplane into the stadium (David Lee Roth's idea). An announcer frantically declared, "From out of the sky, Van Halen is coming into the stadium!" Looking as though they would land right on the stage, the four parachutists maneuvered to an area just outside the stadium gates at the last minute. Moments later, Van Halen, dressed in parachute gear, took the stage arm-in-arm to a thunderous ovation (though Alex Van Halen twisted his ankle while waiting for the parachuters to land). The event set a new one-day gross record with receipts totaling $710,000. Unadvertised Lecea, fresh from opening the California Jam 2 at Ontario Motor Speedway, opened the 9-hour extravaganza, followed by Hagar, who relied heavily on his then newly released live album, *All Night Long*. Van Halen followed with a 10-song set made up of nine songs from *Van Halen* and "Bottoms Up!" Audio recording exists.

9/26/78: Portland Memorial Coliseum, Portland, OR. Opened for: Black Sabbath. Attendance: 11,000.

9/27/78: Vancouver Coliseum, Vancouver, BC. Opened for: Black Sabbath.

9/28/78: Spokane Coliseum, Spokane, WA. Opened for: Black Sabbath.

9/29/78: Seattle Coliseum, Seattle, WA. Opened for: Black Sabbath. Attendance: 12,000.

9/30/78: Seattle Coliseum, Seattle, WA. Opened for: Black Sabbath.

10/09/78: Musikhalle, Hamburg, GER. Opened for: Black Sabbath.

10/10/78: Cambrais, Palais des Grottes, Valenciennes, FRA. Opened for: Black Sabbath. Audio recording exists.

10/11/78: Stadthalle, Offenbach, GER. Opened for: Black Sabbath. Audio recording exists.

10/13/78: Haldenberghalle, Goppingen, GER. Opened for: Black Sabbath.

10/14/78: Friedrich-Ebert-Halle, Ludwigshafgen, GER. Opened for: Black Sabbath. Audio recording exists.

10/15/78: Kurnachthalle, Wurzburg, GER

10/17/78: Hemmerleinhalle, Wurzburg, GER. Opened for: Black Sabbath.

10/18/78: Sporthalle, Heilbronn, GER

10/22/78: Rainbow Theater Ballroom, London, UK. "Down in Flames" is added to set list for this show. Audio recording exists.

10/27/78: Sporthal, Koekeiaere, Belgium

11/05/78: Sportatorium, Hollywood, FL. Opened for: Black Sabbath. Attendance: 12,631.

11/08/78: Boutwell Auditorium, Birmingham, AL. Opened for: Black Sabbath.

11/13/78: Nashville Municipal Auditorium, Nashville, TN. Attendance: 9,082. Audio recording exist.

11/14/78: Mobile Municipal Auditorium, Mobile, AL. Attendance: 9,690.

11/20/78: The Myriad, Oklahoma City, OK. Attendance: 10,176.

11/23/78: Sam Houston Coliseum, Houston, TX (Thanksgiving). Opened for: Black Sabbath.

11/28/78: McNichols Arena, Denver, CO. Attendance: 15,354.

12/02/78: Oakland Coliseum, Oakland, CA

12/03/78: San Diego Sports Arena, San Diego, CA

Van Halen II "World Vacation" Tour (1979)

Van Halen II was released on the same day the band began its tour in Fresno, CA. The stage setup boasted 33 tons of equipment including a 22 ton 10,000 watt sound system and 10 tons and 444,000 watts of lighting. The road crew consisted of a 24-person technical team and a personal security team. The band used two custom coaches, a Lear jet, and three 44-foot semi-trucks to move the production from city to city.

Rabid Van Halen fans rivaled the band's own tales of destruction demolishing eight stage barricades in the first six weeks of the tour.

Alex was now regularly lighting his drum kit on fire. Just before the final encore each night, lighter fluid was applied to all of his drumheads. His drum tech would then hand him a pair of mallets soaked in fluid and lit. The effect was nothing short of spectacular. One night, however, a little too much fluid was used and Alex lit himself fire. The effect was retired by tour's end.

During the Japanese leg of the tour David Lee Roth had an idea: he wanted to have the band photographed chopping down a huge stack of hamburgers with a Samauri sword in front of a Tokyo McDonald's. The restaurant wouldn't allow the photo shoot, so the food was purchased and taken to a local studio. Once there, the band went crazy splashing beer everywhere, pouring ketchup all over each other and creating a huge mess of hamburgers, french fries, and beer.

Typical Set List: • Light Up the Sky • Somebody Get Me a Doctor • Runnin' with the Devil • Beautiful Girls • On Fire • Bass Solo • Feel Your Love Tonight • Drum Solo (at times featuring Dave and Mike on drums along with Alex) • Outta Love Again • Ice Cream Man • Ain't Talkin' 'Bout Love • Guitar Solo • D.O.A. • You Really Got Me • Bottoms Up!

3/25/79: Selland Arena, Fresno, CA. Audio recording exists.

3/27/79: Armory, Medford, OR

3/29/79: University of Montana, Missoula, MT

3/30/79: Fieldhouse, Caldwell, ID

3/31/79: University of Utah, Logan, UT

4/03/79: University of Puget Sound, Tacoma, WA. Opening act: Big Horn. Attendance: 4,200.

4/05/79: Veterans Memorial Auditorium, Marin, CA. Opening act: Barooga Bandit. Attendance: 2,028.

4/06/79: San Jose Center for the Performing Arts, San Jose, CA. Opening act: Barooga Bandit. Attendance: 5,189.

4/07/79: San Jose Center for the Performing Arts, San Jose, CA. Opening act: Barooga Bandit.

4/08/79: Memorial Coliseum, Los Angeles, CA. This was known as the Califfornia World Music Festival. The bill on 4/07/79 included the Fabulous Poodles, Cheech and Chong, Head East, Mahogany Rush, the Outlaws, REO Speedwagon, Toto, Cheap Trick, and Ted Nugent. The bill on 4/08/79 included April Wine, Boomtown Rats, Brownsville, Cheech and Chong, Eddie Money, Mother's Finest, Toto, UFO, and Aerosmith. Van Halen invited more than 300 people to the show as their personal guests. The band and crew arrived in a fleet of 16 white limousines. A chimpanzee dressed up like David Lee Roth and accompanied by two little person bodyguards greeted the guests at the gate. Attendance: 106,000. Audio recording exists.

4/10/79: Coliseum, Reno, NV

4/12/79: Arena, Seattle, WA

4/13/79: Arena, Seattle, WA. David Lee Roth collapses on stage, due to a stomach virus and exhaustion.

4/16/79: Jantzen Beach, Portland, OR. Attendance: 8,000.

4/17/79: Jantzen Beach, Portland, OR

4/18/79: Vancouver Coliseum, Vancouver, BC. Opening act: Eddie Money. Attendance: 13,200.

4/19/79: Center Coliseum, Seattle, WA. Opening act: Robert Fleischman. Attendance: 7,457. Audio recording exists.

4/21/79: Boulder, CO. Opening act: Robert Fleischman. Attendance: 10,898.

4/22/79: Boulder, CO. Opening act: Robert Fleischman. Attendance: 8,420.

4/24/79: Municipal Auditorium, Kansas City, MO

4/26/79: Aragon Ballroom, Chicago, IL

4/27/79: Aragon Ballroom, Chicago, IL

4/28/79: Checkerdome, St. Louis, MO. Opening act: Robert Fleischman. Attendance: 8,420.

4/29/79: Market Square Arena, IN

5/01/79: Masonic Auditorium, Detroit, MI. Audio recording exists.

5/02/79: Masonic Auditorium, Detroit, MI

5/03/79: Wings Stadium, Kalamazoo MI

5/05/79: Cincinnatti, OH

5/06/79: Gardens, Louisville, KY

5/07/79: Stanley Theatre, Pittsburgh, PA

5/08/79: Toledo Sports Arena, Toledo, OH

5/09/79: Memorial Auditorium, Buffalo, NY

5/11/79: Warner Theatre, Washington, DC

5/12/79: The Palladium, New York, NY

5/13/79: Orpheum Theater, Boston, MA

5/14/79: Orpheum Theater, Boston, MA. Video recording exists.

5/15/79: Maple Leaf Gardens, Toronto, ON

5/16/79: London Gardens, London, ON

5/17/79: Manley Fieldhouse, Syracuse, NY

5/18/79: War Memorial, Rochester, NY. Audio recording exists.

5/19/79: The Spectrum, Philadelphia, PA

5/30/79: Fox Theater, Atlanta, GA. Opening act: G-Force. Attendance: 3,812.

5/31/79: Coliseum, Charlotte, NC

6/01/79: Norfolk Arena, Norfolk, VA

6/02/79: Carter Stadium, Raleigh, NC. The bill for this show included Poco, the Outlaws, and Boston.

6/04/79: Coliseum, Knoxville, TN

6/05/79: Boutwell Auditorium, Birmingham, AL

6/07/79: Mid-So. Coliseum, Memphis, TN

6/08/79: Barton Coliseum, Little Rock, AR. Audio recording exists.

6/09/79: Louis Messina Cotton Bowl, Dallas, TX. Also known as the Texxas Jam, the bill for this show included Sammy Hagar, Heart, and Boston. Attendance: 81,000.

6/10/79: The Superdome, New Orleans, LA. Attendace: 62,000.

6/14/79: Forest National Brussels, Belgium

6/15/79: Jaap Edenhal, Amsterdam, NL. Audio recording exists.

6/17/79: Philipshalle, Dusseldorf, GER

6/18/79: Stadthalle, Offenbach, GER

6/19/79: Circus Krone, Munchen, GER

6/20/79: Paris, France

6/21/79: Palais Des Sports, Lyon, France. Audio recording exists.

6/22/79: Porte de Pantin, Paris, France

6/23/79: Palais Des Sports, Lille, Framce

6/25/79: Birmingham Odeon, Birmingham, UK

6/26/79: New Castle City Hall, Newcastle, UK. Opening act: St. Paradise.

6/27/79: Apollo Theatre, Manchester, England. Opening act: St. Paradise. Audio recording exists.

6/28/79: Rainbow Theater, Ballroom London, UK. Audio recording exists.

6/29/79: Rainbow Theater, Ballroom London, UK. Audio recording exists.

6/30/79: Pacific Coliseum, Vancouver, BC, Canada. Audio recording exists.

7/01/79: Seattle, WA. Audio recording exists.

7/05/79: Auditorium, Jacksonville, FL

7/06/79: Auditorium, West palm Beach, FL

7/07/79: Jai Alai, Miami, FL. Audio recording exists.

7/08/79: Civic Center, Lakeland, FL. Audio recording exists.

7/10/79: Corpus Christi Memorial Coliseum, Corpus Christi, TX. Attendance: 6,113.

7/11/79: The Music Hall, Houston, TX. Audio recording exists.

7/12/79: The Music Hall, Houston, TX

7/15/79: Chaparral Center, Midland, TX. Attendance: 4,076.

7/16/79: Municipal Auditorium, Austin, TX

7/17/79: Convention Center, San Antonio, TX

7/19/79: Century II Convention Center, Wichita, KS. Opening act: Screams. "Everybody Wants Some!!" is added to the set list for this show.

7/20/79: Assembly Center, Tulsa, OK

7/21/79: Music Hall, Oklahoma City, OK

7/22/79: Pershing Auditorium, Lincoln, NE

7/24/79: St. Paul Theatre, St. Paul, MN

7/25/79: St. Paul Theatre, St. Paul, MN

7/26/79: Five Flags Civic Center, Dubuque, IA. Opening act: Screams.

7/27/79: Illinois State Armory, Springfield, IL

7/28/79: Dayton, OH

8/10/79: Cumberland County Civic Center, Portland, ME. Opening act: Screams.

8/11/79: Convention Hall, Asbury Park, NJ. Audio recording exists.

8/12/79: Coliseum, New Haven, CT

8/14/79: Music Hall, Cleveland, OH

8/15/79: Music Hall, Cleveland, OH

8/17/79: Springfield Civic Center, Springfield, MA

8/18/79: Cape Cod Coliseum, Hyannis, MA

8/20/79: Dane County Memorial Coliseum, Madison, WI

8/21/79: Milwaukee Auditorium, Milwaukee, WI. Audio recording exists.

8/22/79: Hara Arena, Dayton, OH

8/25/79: Oakland Coliseum, Oakland, CA. David Lee Roth claims that he first started his practice of jumping around on stage at one of these shows at the Oakland Coliseum.

8/26/79: Oakland Coliseum, Oakland, CA

9/03/79: Kaikan Hall, Kyoto, Japan. Audio recording exists.

9/05/79: Kyoden-Taiiku-Kan, Fukuoka, JAP

9/07/79: Shi Kokaido, Nagoya, JAP

9/08/79: Shimin Kaikan, Kurashiki, JAP

9/10/79: Furitsu Taiiku-Kan, Osaka, JAP. Audio recording exists.

9/11/79: Furitsu Taiiku-Kan, Osaka, JAP

9/13/79: Budokan, Tokyo, JAP. Audio recording exists.

9/18/79: Coliseum, Edmonton, AB

9/19/79: Corral, Calgary, AB

9/22/79: Agridome, Regina, Saskatchewan

9/23/79: Convention Center, Winnipeg, MB

9/25/79: Arena, Duluth, MN

9/27/79: Civic Center, Bismark, ND

9/28/79: Civic center, Rapid City, SD

9/29/79: Metra, Billings, MT

10/02/79: Tucson Community Center, Arena Tucson, AZ. Opening act: Screams.

10/03/79: Civic Plaza, Phoenix, AZ

10/06/79: San Diego Sports Arena, San Diego, CA

10/07/79: Great Western Forum, Inglewood, CA. Opening act: Screams. Audio recording exists.

Women and Children First "World Invasion" Tour (1980)

Kicking off in Spokane, WA, the World Invasion tour (also dubbed the Party 'Til You Die tour) featured an impressive sound system once belonging to the Bee Gees. The stage boasted more than 800 lights on a 64-foot tress, which according to David Lee Roth, was a Guinness world record at the time.

A Dutch cinematographer (reportedly named Snade Krellmans) was hired to document the tour on film and the band intended to release a documentary that would rival The Who's *The Kids Are Alright* and Led Zeppelin's *The Song Remains the Same*. Unfortunately the footage was never released.

The band got creative when checking into hotels, using all kinds of silly names. Dave liked "Hugh Jazz," Ed used "Justin Time," Al followed with "Justin Kase," and Mike used the moniker still associated with him by diehard fans, "Biff Malibu."

The offstage carnage continued. The band routinely caused hundreds of dollars in damage to their hotel rooms, dressing rooms, and everywhere in between, including an incident believed to have taken place in Edward's room in Fresno, CA, dubbed by management as "The Famous Ketchup Kaper."

The World Invasion tour also saw the birth of the legendary brown M&M contract rider. The band demanded M&M candies backstage with all of the brown ones removed. Only one documented case exists where the rider wasn't adhered to, a show at the University of Colorado in Pueblo, CO. They paid dearly for their error. The band demolished their backstage dressing room causing thousands of dollars of damage.

The rider itself was genius. Its sole purpose was to ensure that venue and promoter personnel read the entire contract before each performance, and brown M&Ms backstage was an instant indicator they hadn't. If the venue couldn't perform a task as simple as removing a specified color of M&Ms, how could they be trusted to fulfill lighting, sound, and other technical requirements?

Another new idea ended up becoming the precursor to the Grid System, which was later introduced in full force on the *Diver Down* tour. This early version of the Grid System involved several roadies being loaded with backstage passes marked with the letter "Q." The band would point out a particular female fan in the audience to invite backstage and the roadie would hunt her down and grace her with the pass.

A host of bands filled the opening slot throughout the tour, which had become a very tough gig. The openers were frequently targets for whatever the audience had handy, and were normally heavily booed and otherwise verbally abused by the Van Halen-hungry crowd. Some bands cracked under the pressure while others fared pretty well. Rail, the Fabulous Poodles, the Cats, and Talas (featuring Billy Sheehan on bass) were the opening bands for this tour, with Talas actually doing quite well. They weren't booed and Van Halen's production manager Patrick Whitley even let them perform encores on more than one occasion.

Reflecting back on Van Halen during Talas' stint as an opening band, Sheehan remarked, "Every night they [Van Halen] were totally awesome. On their worst night they were incredible. Every night I went out front and watched. It was an incredible education on how you perform live. How you do an arena. I'd been a club player my whole life and I was pretty good at that if I do say so myself. I knew how to do the club thing. But I learned so much more about entertainment and how it works from watching that band play night after night. Just sitting and really studying what was goin' on; it was an incredible experience. Dare I say a lot of my success, I think, eventually came from some of the inspiration that I acquired right there."

Typical set list: • Romeo Delight • Bottoms Up! • Runnin' with the Devil • Loss of Control • Take Your Whiskey Home • Dance the Night Away • Women in Love • Jamie's Cryin' • Everybody Wants Some!! • And the Cradle Will Rock • Light Up the Sky • Ain't Talkin' 'Bout Love • Ice Cream Man • You Really Got Me

3/22/80: Lane County Fairgrounds, Eugene, OR. Opening act: Rail.

3/24/80: Spokane, WA. Opening act: Rail. The song "Bright Lights, Big City" is added to the set list for this show. Audio recording exists.

3/25/80: Four Seasons Arena, Great Falls, MT

4/02/80: Vancouver, BC

4/03/80: Portland Memorial Coliseum, Portland, OR. Opening act: Rail.

4/04/80: Seattle Coliseum, Seattle, WA. Opening act: Rail.

4/05/80: Seattle Coliseum, Seattle, WA. Opening act: Rail.

4/07/80: Calgary, AB

4/08/80: Edmonton, AB

4/14/80: Milwaukee Arena, Milwaukee, WI. Audio recording exists.

4/24/80: Cincinnati, OH. During "Light Up the Sky," Dave tells the audience to "Light 'em up!" Thinking that Roth is inciting the crowd to smoke where smoking isn't allowed, he is charged with a misdemeanor for complicity in inciting others to violate the fire code. Dave makes great use of the publicity by dressing as a bandit. The charges were later dropped due to a "lack of evidence."

4/30/80: Pittsburgh Civic Arena, Pittsburgh, PA. Opening act: Rail.

5/01/80: Capitol Center, Largo, MD. Audio recording exists.

5/05/80: Buffalo Memorial Auditorium, Buffalo, NY. Opening act: Rail. Audio recording exists.

5/06/80: War Memorial, Rochester, NY. Opening act: Rail.

5/09/80: The Spectrum, Philadelphia, PA. Audio recording exists.

5/23/80: Fakloner Centre, Copenhagen, DE

5/24/80: Stadthalle, Bremen, GER

5/26/80: Burg. Damen Sportpark, Geleen, NL. Known as the Pinkpop Festival, the bill for this show included Garland Jefferys, Raymond van het Groenewoud, Joe Jackson, the Specials, J. Geils, and The Jam. This was Van Halen's first European outdoor festival. It was originally canceled after

Dave broke his nose filming a special on Italian television. The night before the gig on 5/25, probably some time after rehearsals, Edward and Alex appeared on Dutch radio announcing they would still play the festival, quoting Dave's remark, "Fuck the doctor!" Attendance: 50,000. Audio recording exists.

5/27/80: Eberthalle, Ludwigshafen, GER

5/29/80: Grugahalle, Essen, GER

5/30/80: Ernst-Merckhalle, Hamburg, GER

5/31/80: Cambrais, Palais des Grottes, Valenciennes, FRA

6/01/80: Hall Central (Parc des Exposition), Rouen, FRA

6/03/80: Palais des Sports, Paris, FRA

6/04/80: Palais des Sport, Lyon, FRA

6/06/80: Maison des Sport, Reims, FRA

6/07/80: Kuernachthalle, Nurnberg, GER

6/08/80: Nurnberg Hemmerleinhalle, Nurnberg, GER

6/10/80: Phillipshalle, Dusselforf, GER

6/11/80: Messehallen Sindelfingen, Stuttgard, GER

6/14/80: Rudi-Sedlmayerhalle, Munich, GER

6/17/80: Newcastle City Hall, Newcastle, UK

6/18/80: Apollo Theatre, Glasgow, Scotland

6/19/80: Apollo Theatre, Manchester, UK. Audio recording exists.

6/20/80: DeMont Fort Hall, Leicester, UK. Audio recording exists. Van Halen and Rush stay at the same hotel. Geddy Lee plays a tape for Edward and whispers something into the guitarist's ear. Ed in turn pours his beer, glass and all, into Lee's tape recorder. As payback, Van Halen is banned from Rush's show when the two bands performed in Las Vegas, NV, one year later.

6/21/80: ZDF Rockpop, GER

6/22/80: Odeon Theatre, Birmingham, UK

6/23/80: Rainbow Theatre, Ballroom London, UK. Audio recording exists.

6/24/80: Rainbow Theatre, Ballroom London, UK. Audio recording exists.

7/10/80: Wings Stadium, Kalamazoo MI

7/12/80: Charleston Civic Center, Charleston, WV

7/13/80: Toledo Sport Arena, Toledo, OH

7/15/80: Montreal Forum, Montreal, QE

7/16/80: Ottawa Civic Center, Ottawa, ON

7/17/80: London Treasure Island Gardens, London, ON. Opening act: Teenage Head.

7/18/80: C.N.E. Coliseum, Toronto, ON. Opening act: Teenage Head. Audio recording exists.

7/21/80: Hampton Coliseum, Hampton, VA

7/22/80: Baltimore Civic Center, Baltimore, MD. Audio recording exists.

7/25/80: Boston Garden, Boston, MA. Opening act: The Cats. Audio recording exists.

7/26/80: Nassau Veterans Memorial Coliseum, Uniondale, NY. Audio recording exists.

7/27/80: Nassau Veterans Memorial Coliseum, Uniondale, NY. Audio recording exists.

7/28/80: Freedom Hall, Louisville, KY. Opening act: Fabulous Poodles.

7/29/80: Chicago International Amphitheater, Chicago, IL. Opening act: Rail.

7/30/80: Market Square Arena, Indianapolis, IN. Opening act: The Cats.

8/02/80: Barton Coliseum, Little Rock, AR. Opening act: The Cats.

8/08/80: Ft. Myers, FL. Audio recording exists.

8/09/80: Sportatorium, Hollywood, FL. Audio recording exists.

8/10/80: Jacksonville Coliseum, Jacksonville, FL

8/12/80: Bayfront Center, St. Petersburg, FL

8/15/80: Roberto Clemente Coliseum, San Juan, Puerto Rico

8/16/80: Roberto Clemente Coliseum, San Juan, Puerto Rico

8/22/80: Kemper Arena, Kansas City, MO

8/23/80: Omaha Civic Auditorium, Omaha, NE

8/24/80: Bicentennial Center, Salina, KS

8/26/80: Corpus Christi Memorial Coliseum, Corpus Cristi, TX

8/27/80: San Antonio Convention Center, San Antonio, TX

8/28/80: Sam Houston Coliseum, Houston, TX. Opening act: The Cats.

8/29/80: Hirsh Memorial Arena, Shreveport, LA. Edward meets Valerie (accompanied by her brother Patrick) for the first time, backstage after the show. As a joke, Valerie presents each of the band members with a bag of M&Ms with brown ones included. Patrick snapped a photo of the pair together with Ed clenching his bag between his teeth. The photo rests comfortably on the couple's fireplace to this very day.

8/30/80: Centroplex, Baton Rouge, LA. Opening act: The Cats. Valerie, with Patrick in tow, attends her second Van Halen concert.

9/01/80: Mobile Municipal Auditorium, Mobile, AL. Edward telephones Valerie for the first time after meeting her backstage on 8/29/80.

9/02/80: Jackson Coliseum, Jackson, MS

9/03/80: Fairpark Coliseum, Beaumont, TX

9/04/80: Reunion Arena, Dallas, TX

9/06/80: University of Oklahoma (Owen Field), Norman, OK

9/07/80: Municipal Coliseum, Amarillo, TX

9/08/80: Municipal Coliseum, Amarillo, TX

9/09/80: El Paso Civic Center Coliseum, El Paso, TX. Opening act: The Cats.

9/10/80: University of New Mexico Arena, Albuquerque, NM. Audio recording exists.

9/12/80: McNichols Arena, Denver, CO

9/13/80: McNichols Arena, Denver, CO

9/15/80: Veterans Memorial Coliseum, Phoenix, AZ

9/16/80: Tucson Community Center Arena, Tucson, AZ

9/18/80: Selland Arena, Fresno, CA

9/19/80: Sports Arena, Los Angeles, CA. Opening act: The Cats.

9/20/80: Sports Arena, Los Angeles, CA. Opening act: The Cats. At least one of these L.A. shows was filmed. Dave even invited the camera crew out on stage to film the audience.

9/27/80: Toronto, ON

10/03/80: Rushmore Plaza, Rapid City, SD

10/04/80: Bismarck Civic Center, Bismarck, ND

10/06/80: Salt Palace, Salt Lake City, UT. Audio recording exists.

10/09/80: Oakland Coliseum, Oakland, CA. Opening act: Talas. Audio recording exists.

10/10/80: Oakland Coliseum, Oakland, CA. Opening act: Talas. Dave celebrates his birthday on stage with a woman who jumps out of a 5-foot tall cake. Audio recording exists.

10/12/80: San Diego Sports Arena, San Diego, CA. Opening act: The Cats.

10/15/80: Sioux Falls Arena, Sioux Falls, SD

10/16/80: Veterans Memorial Auditorium, Des Moines, IA

10/17/80: Pershing Auditorium, Lincoln, NE

10/19/80: Western Hall, Macomb, IL (Western Illinois University). Opening act: Talas.

10/21/80: Hulman Center, Terre Haute, IN

10/22/80: Rupp Arena, Lexington, KY

10/26/80: Fayetteville, NC. This show was canceled.

11/07/80: Roberts Stadium, Evansville, IN. Opening act: Talas.

11/08/80: Von Braun Civic Center Arena, Huntsville, AL

Fair Warning Tour (1981)

Kicking off in Nova Scotia, this 10-month opus (also dubbed the W.D.F.A. Tour) was then considered the largest continental tour in rock and roll history and grossed more than $10 million. The 75-man crew was made up of a large number of Vietnam veterans who managed 175,000 tons of equipment. The stage show featured 90,000 watts of sound and over 1.5 million watts of lighting. The band frequently trashed the stage routinely covering it with amazing amounts of confetti, trash, streamers, and even blow-up sex dolls.

Once again the band got creative with their hotel check-in identities. Dave was known as "Ray Dio," Mike as "Captain Crash," and Al as "Bigus Dickus."

One interesting feature of this tour (which may have also been in effect on earlier tours) was the "Bounty System." The "Bounty System" was yet another creative backstage pass idea concocted by Roth. For every show, each roadie was given a number of passes with his initials marked on them. The overall concept was quite simple: every female fan who spent "time" with the vocalist that evening wearing a pass with initials on it, earned the appropriate roadie a monetary reward, normally in the amount of $25 per pass.

Rumors of Billy Sheehan replacing Michael Anthony had surfaced some time during the album's production and the start of the tour though obviously nothing ever became of them.

The band's stage attire this tour was quite interesting. Alex normally wore a zebra-striped karate-like gui (his drums were painted in the same manner). Michael wore a fatigue-green jumpsuit, Dave regularly donned a pair of white skin-tight pants with red fringe up the legs, and Edward looked like a rock and roll version of Raggedy Andy in his white knickers and red and white-striped knee-high socks.

Typical set list: • On Fire • Sinner's Swing • Drum Solo • Hear about It Later • So This Is Love? • Jamie's Cryin' • Bass Solo • Runnin' with the Devil • Dance the Night Away • Sunday Afternoon in the Park • Romeo Delight • Everybody Wants Some!! • Mean Street • Ice Cream Man • Guitar Solo (sometimes including an early version of "Cathedral") • You Really Got Me

5/12/81: Halifax Metro Center, Halifax, Nova Scotia, Canada. Opening act: The Fools.

5/13/81: Moncton Coliseum, Moncton, New Brunswick, Canada. This show was reportedly canceled.

5/15/81: Providence Civic Center, Providence, RI. "Lucille" is added to the set list for this show. Audio recording exists.

5/16/81: Cumberland County Civic Center, Portland, ME. Opening act: The Fools.

5/17/81: Glen Falls Civic Center, Glen Falls, NY. Opening act: The Fools.

5/18/81: Rochester War Memorial, Rochester, NY

5/20/81: Charleston Civic Center Coliseum, Charleston, WV

5/22/81: Freedom Hall, Louisville, KY

5/23/81: Hara Arena, Dayton, OH

5/24/81: Wings Stadium, Kalamazoo, MI. Opening act: The Fools.

5/27/81: Edmonton Coliseum, Edmonton, AB

5/28/81: The Corral, Calgary, AB

5/29/81: The Corral, Calgary, AB

5/31/81: Spokane Coliseum, Spokane, WA

6/02/81: P.N.E Coliseum, Vancouver, BC

6/04/81: Seattle Coliseum, Seattle, WA

6/05/81: Seattle Coliseum, Seattle, WA. Audio recording exists.

6/06/81: Seattle Civic Center, Seattle, WA. Audio recording exists.

6/08/81: Portland Memorial Coliseum, Portland, OR. Opening act: 3 Out of 5 Doctors.

6/09/81: Portland Memorial Coliseum, Portland, OR. Opening act: 3 Out of 5 Doctors.

6/11/81: Oakland Coliseum, Oakland, CA. Opening act: The Fools. Audio recording exists.

6/12/81: Oakland Coliseum, Oakland, CA. Opening act: The Fools.

6/13/81: Oakland Coliseum, Oakland, CA. Opening act: The Fools. According to Dave, all three of these Oakland shows were filmed, but only the third night was a keeper. According to Warner Brothers, special attention was paid to the first show. Three songs ended up being picked as videos to promote the *Fair Warning* album: "Hear about It Later," "So This Is Love?" and "Unchained." There remains some confusion about exactly which show was used for the videos.

6/16/81: Aladdin Hotel, Las Vegas, NV. Van Halen is banned from Rush's show when the two bands perform in Las Vegas, NV, together on separate bills as a payback from an earlier altercation on 6/20/80. To further heighten tensions, Geddy Lee and Eddie Van Halen cross paths in a casino later that evening and an unwitting bodyguard gives the boot to Lee when the bassist attempts to mend ways with Edward.

6/18/81: Selland Arena, Fresno, CA

6/19/81: Los Angeles Sports Arena, Los Angeles, CA. Opening act: The Fools. Audio recording exists.

6/20/81: Great Western Forum, Inglewood, CA. Audio recording exists.

6/21/81: Great Western Forum, Inglewood, CA. Opening act: The Fools. Audio recording exists.

7/02/81: Milwaukee Arena, Milwaukee, WI

7/03/81: Cobo Hall, Detroit, MI

7/04/81: Cobo Hall, Detroit, MI. Audio recording exists.

7/05/81: Cobo Hall, Detroit, MI. Opening act: The Fools.

7/07/81: St. Paul Civic Center, St. Paul, MN

7/09/81: Market Square Arena, Indianapolis, IN. Opening act: The Fools

7/10/81: International Amphitheater, Chicago, IL. Opening act: The Fools. Audio and Video recordings exist.

7/11/81: International Amphitheater, Chicago, IL. Opening act: The Fools.

7/12/81: Chicago Stadium, Chicago, IL. Opening act: The Fools.

7/14/81: Pittsburgh Civic Arena, Pittsburgh, PA

7/16/81: Cross Country Coliseum, New Haven, CT

7/17/81: Madison Square Garden, New York, NY. Audio recording exists.

7/18/81: Nassau Veterans Memorial Coliseum, Uniondale, NY. Opening act: The Fools. Audio recording exists.

7/20/81: The Spectrum, Philadelphia, PA. Audio recording exists.

7/21/81: The Spectrum, Philadelphia, PA. Audio recording exists.

7/22/81: The Spectrum, Philadelphia, PA

7/24/81: Boston Garden, Boston, MA. Opening act: G-Force.

7/25/81: Boston Garden, Boston, MA. Audio recording exists.

7/26/81: Cumberland County Civic Center, Portland, ME

7/28/81: Capitol Centre, Largo, MD. Audio recording exists. Warner Brothers films this show.

7/29/81: Capitol Centre, Largo, MD. Audio recording exists.

7/30/81: Capitol Centre, Largo, MD

7/31/81: Buffalo Memorial Auditorium, Buffalo, NY. Opening act: G-Force.

8/02/81: Richfield Coliseum, Cleveland, OH. Audio recording exists.

8/03/81: Richfield Coliseum, Cleveland, OH

8/04/81: Maple Leaf Gardens, Toronto, ON. Opening act: G-Force.

8/05/81: Montreal Forum, Montreal, QE. Audio recording exists.

8/18/81: Sportatorium, Hollywood, FL

8/19/81: Civic Center, Lakeland, FL. Opening act: G-Force.

8/22/81: The Omni, Atlanta, GA. Audio recording exists.

8/23/81: Knoxville Coliseum, Knoxville, TN

8/24/81: Charlotte Coliseum, Charlotte, NC

8/25/81: Greensboro Coliseum, Greensboro, NC. Audio recording exists.

8/27/81: Hampton Coliseum, Hampton, VA

8/29/81: Riverfront Coliseum, Cincinnati, OH. Audio recording exists.

8/30/81: Nashville Municipal Auditorium, Nashville, TN

8/31/81: Birmingham-Jefferson Civic Center, Birmingham, AL. Audio recording exists.
9/01/81: Mid-South Coliseum, Memphis, TN
9/03/81: Von Braun Civic Center Arena, Huntsville, AL
9/04/81: Jackson Coliseum, Jackson, MS
9/05/81: Mississippi Coast Highway Coliseum, Biloxi, MS
9/06/81: Riverside Centraplex, Baton Rouge, LA
9/08/81: Hirsch Memorial Coliseum, Shreveport, LA
9/10/81: Reuninon Arena, Dallas, TX
9/12/81: Sam Houston Coliseum, Houston, TX
9/13/81: Sam Houston Coliseum, Houston, TX. Opening act: G-Force.
9/28/81: Arizona Veterans Memorial Coliseum, Phoenix, AZ. Audio recording exists.
9/29/81: San Diego Sports Arena, San Diego, CA
10/02/81: Austin Special Events Center, Austin, TX
10/03/81: Lloyd Noble Center, Norman, OK. Opening act: G-Force
10/06/81: Tingley Coliseum, Albuquerque, NM
10/07/81: El Paso County Coliseum, El Paso, TX. Audio recording exists.
10/09/81: San Antonio Convention Center Arena, San Antonio, TX
10/15/81: Tulsa Assembly Center, Tulsa, OK
10/16/81: Kansas Coliseum, Wichita, KS. Opening act: G-Force.
10/17/81: Kemper Arena, Kansas City, MO
10/18/81: Checkerdome, St. Louis, MO. Opening act: G-Force.
10/21/81: Five Seasons Center, Cedar Rapids, IA. Opening act: G-Force.
10/24/81: Tangerine Bowl, Orlando, FL. The bill for this performance included the Henry Paul Band and The Rolling Stones. A photo taken at this show appears in the artwork for the *Diver Down* album.

Diver Down "Hide Your Sheep" Tour (1982-83)

Beginning in Augusta, GA, the Hide Your Sheep tour (also known as the K.A.T.N. [Kicking Ass and Taking Names tour]) sold out all 80 of its U.S. concerts while grossing $10 million during an industry-wide slump in concert ticket sales. As in previous tours, this tour was the largest ever with 170 tons of equipment including 1.4 million-watts of light, 70,000 watts of sound and a road crew of 70.

With this tour we saw the birth of the infamous "Grid System." Mostly Dave's idea, it began when the band was planning the tour in the late spring/early summer of 1982. A small-scale model of the stage was designed and housed at their Hollywood, CA, business office. Each of the stage barricades was marked with a number and each number corresponded to specific security guards, located at various points around the stage. If Roth spotted a female fan that he wanted to party with after the show at say, section 24, the appropriate guard was sent to hunt her down and provide her with a backstage pass. Should the guard be unable to locate the specified person or if he found others en route who were good enough or better than the selected recipient, it was his call whether or not to provide them with a pass.

This tour introduced Jimmy Briscoe and Danny Rodgers, Dave's personal little person bodyguards, who remained with the band through the *1984* tour. They were frequently seen dressed in all kinds of outfits, including S.W.A.T. uniforms, karate guis, and tuxedos.

Michael's live rig was made up of four or five basses, each strung with Rotosound Swing Bass Roundwound strings. This collection included Fender Precisions with Yamaha pickups and Badass bridges along with his main bass-a prototype Yamaha Broad Bass 2000, given to him when the band was in Japan a few years earlier. For amplification he used SVT amplifiers fed through Flagg System cabinets with 18-inch Gauss bottoms and 12-inch Gauss tops. His solo routinely featured the Bonanza theme.

Alex's Ludwig setup consisted of one kick drum, one 14-inch-by-10-inch rack tom, one 18-inch-by-20-inch floor tom, one rosewood 6 ¼-inch-by-14-inch snare drum with a Black-Dot CS head, three tomtoms measuring 12-inch, 13-inch, and 20-inch respectively, a high-hat, and various other Paiste cymbals, including a 24-inch heavy ride and a 20-inch crash. His hardware was a hybrid mixture of sorts and everything was welded together to keep from breaking when Roth would climb on his kit during the show.

The band had planned a European leg for the tour, with stops in the Netherlands, but it was canceled by Warner Brothers who reportedly demanded Van Halen back to the studio to begin work on a new album.

In January 1983, as a substitute for the canceled leg of the U.K. tour, the band made a short run through South America (dubbed the No Problem tour). Stops included Argentina, Venezuela, Brazil, and Uruguay. At one Venezuelan show, Edward played the entire evening from stage right (the spot normally held by Michael Anthony) for the first and only time in the band's history. During this leg of the tour, Dave played a song entitled "Ode to Argentina," unaccompanied on an acoustic/electric guitar.

Typical set list: • Romeo Delight • Unchained • Drum Solo • The Full Bug • Runnin' with the Devil • Jamie's Cryin' • Little Guitars • Where Have All the Good Times Gone? • Bass Solo • Hang 'Em High • Cathedral • Secrets • Everybody Wants Some!! (with Ed and Al on drum intro) • Dance the Night Away • Somebody Get Me a Doctor/I'm So Glad • Dave's Solo • Ice Cream Man • Intruder • (Oh) Pretty Woman • Guitar Solo • Ain't Talkin' 'Bout Love • Bottoms Up! • You Really Got Me/Happy Trails

7/14/82: Augusta-Richmond County Civic Center, Augusta, GA. Opening act: After the Fire.

7/16/82: Greensboro Coliseum, Greensboro, NC. Audio recording exists. Warner Brothers films this show and some backstage footage.

7/17/82: Charlotte Coliseum, Charlotte, NC. Audio recording exists.

7/18/82: Carolina Coliseum, Columbia, SC

7/20/82: Knoxville Coliseum, Knoxville, TN. Opening act: After the Fire.

7/22/82: Birmingham Jefferson Civic Center, Birmingham, AL. Opening act: After the Fire. Audio recording exists.

7/23/82: Jackson Coliseum, Jackson, MS

7/24/82: Biloxi Coliseum, Biloxi, MS

7/27/82: Nashville Memorial Coliseum, Nashville, TN

7/29/82: Hara Arena, Dayton, OH

7/30/82: Freedom Hall, Louisville, KY. Opening act: After the Fire. Audio recording exists.

7/31/82: Allen County Memorial Coliseum, Ft. Wayne, IN

8/03/82: Rockford Metro Centre, Rockford, IL

8/04/82: Veterans Memorial Coliseum, Des Moines, IA. Opening act: After the Fire.

8/06/82: Checkerdome, St. Louis, MO. Edward meets Dan Martin and by 5:30 the following morning, purchases a mint condition 1958 Gibson Flying V.

8/07/82: Kemper Arena, Kansas City, MO

8/08/82: Omaha Civic Auditorium, Omaha, NE

8/10/82: St. Paul Civic Center, St. Paul, MN. Opening act: After the Fire. Attendance: 15,207.

8/11/82: Dane County Memorial Coliseum, Madison, WI. Audio recording exists.

8/13/82: Cobo Hall, Detroit, MI. Audio recording exists.

8/14/82: Cobo Hall, Detroit, MI. Opening act: After the Fire. Audio recording exists.

8/16/82: Mecca Auditorium, Milwaukee, WI. Opening act: After the Fire.

8/18/82: Brown County Veterans Memorial Arena, Green Bay, WI

8/19/82: The Pavilion, Chicago, IL. Opening act: After the Fire. Audio recording exists.

8/20/82: The Pavilion, Chicago, IL
8/21/82: Richfield Coliseum, Cleveland, OH
9/01/82: Portland Memorial Coliseum, Portland, OR
9/02/82: Seattle Coliseum, Seattle, WA. Audio recording exists.
9/03/82: Vancouver Coliseum, Vancouver, BC
9/05/82: Selland Arena, Fresno, CA. Audio recording exists.
9/07/82: Veterans Memorial Coliseum, Phoenix, AZ. Opening act: After the Fire.
9/08/82: Omaha Civic Auditorium, Omaha, NE
9/10/82: Great Western Forum, Inglewood, CA. Opening act: After The Fire. Audio recording exists.
9/11/82: Great Western Forum, Inglewood, CA
9/12/82: Great Western Forum, Inglewood, CA
9/14/82: Cow Palace, San Francisco, CA. Opening act: Kix. Audio recording exists.
9/15/82: Cow Palace, San Francisco, CA. Opening act: After The Fire. Audio recording exists.
9/17/82: Aladdin Hotel, Las Vegas, NV
9/18/82: Aladdin Hotel, Las Vegas, NV
9/19/82: El Paso County Coliseum, El Paso, TX
9/21/82: The Myriad, Oklahoma City, OK. Opening act: After the Fire.
9/22/82: Assembly Hall, Tulsa, OK
9/23/82: Kansas Coliseum, Wichita, KS
9/24/82: The Summit, Houston, TX
9/25/82: Hirsch Memorial Coliseum, Shreveport, LA
9/26/82: Casper, WY
10/07/82: New Haven Coliseum, New Haven, CT. Opening act: After the Fire. Audio recording exists.
10/08/82: Madison Square Garden, New York, NY. Opening act: After the Fire. Audio recording exists.

10/09/82: The Carrier Dome, Syracuse, NY. Opening act: After the Fire. Attendance: 32,000. Audio recording exists.

10/11/82: Capitol Centre, Largo, MD. Opening act: After the Fire. Audio and video recordings exist. Warner Brothers films this show.

10/12/82: Capitol Centre, Largo, MD. Opeing act: After the Fire. Audio recording exists. Warner Brothers films this show.

10/13/82: Nassau Veterans Memorial Coliseum, Uniondale, NY

10/14/82: Pittsburgh Civic Arena, Pittsburgh, PA

10/15/82: Brendan Byrne Arena, East Rutherford, NJ. Canceled due to Eddie's wrist fracture.

10/16/82: Brendan Byrne Arena, East Rutherford, NJ. Canceled due to Eddie's wrist fracture.

10/18/82: Nassau Veterans Memorial Coliseum, Uniondale, NY. Canceled due to Eddie's wrist fracture.

10/19/82: The Spectrum, Philadelphia, PA. Audio recording exists.

10/20/82: The Spectrum, Philadelphia, PA. Audio recording exists.

10/22/82: The Centrum, Worcester, MA. Opening act: Joe Whiting & the Bandit Band. A third show at this venue was added to the tour schedule and Van Halen Day is declared due to a 25,000-signature petition headed by radio's WAAF program director, Rob Barnett.

10/23/82: The Centrum, Worcester, MA. Opening act: Joe Whiting & the Bandit Band.

10/24/82: The Centrum, Worcester, MA. Opening act: Joe Whiting & the Bandit Band.

10/26/82: Maple Leaf Gardens, Toronto, ON. Opening act: Joe Whiting & the Bandit Band. Audio recording exists.

10/27/82: Montreal Forum, Montreal, QC. Audio and video recordings exist.

10/30/82: Roanoke Civic Center, Roanoke, VA

10/31/82: Hampton Coliseum, Hampton, VA. Opening act: Accept. Audio recording exists.

11/01/82: Pittsburgh Civic Arena, Pittsburgh, PA

11/03/82: The Omni, Atlanta, GA

11/05/82: Riverfront Coliseum, Cincinnati, OH

11/06/82: Rupp Arena, Lexington, KY

11/07/82: University of Tennessee Arena, Chattanooga, TN

11/13/82: Nassau Veterans Memorial Coliseum, Uniondale, NY. Makeup for canceled 10/18/82 show. Audio and video recordings exist.

11/14/82: Brendan Byrne Arena, East Rutherford, NJ. Makeup for canceled 10/15/82 show. Audio recording exists.

11/15/82: Brendan Byrne Arena, East Rutherford, NJ. Makeup for canceled 10/16/82 show. Audio recording exists.

11/18/82: Reunion Arena, Dallas, TX. Audio recording exists.

11/19/82: Reunion Arena, Dallas, TX. Audio recording exists.

11/20/82: Frank C. Irwin, Jr. Special Events Center, Austin, TX

11/22/82: San Antonio Convention Center Arena, San Antonio, TX

11/24/82: Kansas Coliseum, Wichita, KS

11/26/82: Riverside Centroplex, Baton Rouge, LA

11/28/82: Mobile Municipal Auditorium, Mobile, AL

11/29/82: Von Braun Civic Center, Huntsville, AL

11/30/82: Asheville Civic Center, Asheville, NC

12/02/82: Mid-South Coliseum, Memphis, TN

12/04/82: Freedom Hall, Johnson City, TN

12/05/82: Reynolds Coliseum, Raleigh, NC

12/07/82: Lakeland Civic Center, Lakeland, FL

12/08/82: Lakeland Civic Center, Lakeland, FL

12/09/82: Sportatorium, Hollywood, FL

12/10/82: Sportatorium, Hollywood, FL. Audio recording exists.

12/11/82: Jacksonville Coliseum, Jacksonville, FL

1/14/83: Paliebro, Caracas, VENEZUELA. May have been canceled.

1/15/83: Paliebro, Caracas, VENEZUELA. May have been canceled.

1/16/83: Paliebro, Caracas, VENEZUELA. "Beer Drinkers and Hell Raisers" is added to the set list for this show. Audio and video recordings exist.

1/21/83: Ibirapuera Gymnasium, Sao Paulo, BRAZIL. Opening act: Patrulha do Espaco. Video recording exists.

1/22/83: Ibirapuera Gymnasium, Sao Paulo, BRAZIL. Opening act: Patrulha do Espaco.

1/23/83: Ibirapuera Gymnasium, Sao Paulo, BRAZIL. Opening act: Patrulha do Espaco

1/26/83: Maracanãzinho Gymnasium, Rio De Janeiro, BRAZIL

1/27/83: Maracanãzinho Gymnasium, Rio De Janeiro, BRAZIL. "Beer Drinkers and Hell Raisers" and "Heartbreak Hotel" added to set list for this show. Audio recording exists.

1/28/83: Gigantinho Gymnasium, Porto Alegre, BRAZIL

1/29/83: Gigantinho Gymnasium, Porto Alegre, BRAZIL

2/05/83: Auditorio El Cilandro, Montevideo, URUGUAY. "Heartbreak Hotel" added to set list for this show. Audio recording exists.

2/07/83: Auditorio Obras, Buenos Aires, ARGENTINA

2/08/83: Newell's Old Boys, Rosario, ARGENTINA. May have been canceled.

2/09/83: Newell's Old Boys, Rosario, ARGENTINA. May have been canceled.

2/11/83: Auditorio Obras, Buenos Aires, ARGENTINA. "Summertime Blues" added to set list for this show. Audio and video recordings exist.

2/12/83: Auditorio Obras, Buenos Aires, ARGENTINA. May have been canceled.

2/13/83: Auditorio Obras, Buenos Aires, ARGENTINA. May have been canceled.

1984 Tour (1984)

According to legend, when the band was shopping for an opening band for this tour, one requirement was that the lead singer couldn't have blonde hair, dyed or natural. It was rumored that Twisted Sister's lead vocalist Dee Snider offered to change his hair color to anything but blonde if his band got the slot. They never got the opportunity.

Van Halen also claimed that rather than have the tour sponsored by some corporation, they would be the first band to sponsor a company for a tour. Western Exterminator, based in Los Angeles, CA, got the nod and the band used their mallet-bearing mascot in a top hat and tuxedo everywhere they could, including on the stage backdrop, backstage passes, and a full line of tour clothing and accessories.

The "Grid System" was once again in effect with some slight modifications. The guards behind the barricades were now fitted with headsets that connected them to more guards in the pits. Using a secret code like, "Red right, red T-shirt, out of sight, six feet back," Dave would alert one of the pit crew, who would then radio the appropriate barricade guard. The guard would then enter the floor and slap a pass on the selected woman.

The band unveiled several new aspects to their live show on this tour. Eddie was playing keyboards for "I'll Wait" and "Jump," with the latter featuring a guitar solo entirely on keys. David Lee Roth took his turn in the solo spotlight too, doing a kung fu-style sword dance. The dance, known as "Dave's Tai Chi Solo" was developed by Roth and kung fu master Paulie Zink and performed against a rousing synthesizer backdrop from Edward. That same instrumental piece also appeared in the 1984 movie scored by Edward, *The Wild Life*.

Another new aspect to the show was featured in Edward's unaccompanied guitar solo. His guitar had been outfitted with a clear, plexiglass tray table that allowed him to lay the guitar flat, perpendicular to his body. He would then hammer out chords with both hands on the neck. The technique first began taking shape in 1982, but didn't surface until this tour. He patented the tray table, thinking that slide players might get use out of it, though it has never been marketed. The technique later resurfaced on the *F.U.C.K.* album on "Judgement Day."

Michael's solo was mostly for show and at one point, featured the bassist hurling his bass down onto the stage from the rigging, then rushing down and stomping on it repeatedly before picking it up and taking off again.

Autograph got the nod to fill the opening act slot without even having a record deal or an album out. Apparently, a demo tape of theirs made it to David Lee Roth, who gave the young band a shot at opening the tour. They were signed partway through their stint.

On stage Edward had three sets of Marshall cabinets with eight in each set. Two sets were for backup. Each cabinet housed four Celestion speakers. In all, twelve Marshall tops and eight H&H V800 power amps were used.

He was also sporting a new effects system co-designed by Flagg Systems. Three identical pedal boards were in use: one in front of his microphone; one on Alex's drum riser; and one in a quick-change booth. Rudy Leiren manned a switcher at the main booth so he could add effects if need be.

Michael's live rig consisted of his tried-and-true Yamaha Broadbass 2000, outfitted with Schecter pickups and a neck he had narrowed for better access to the high frets, his custom Jack Daniels bass, and a beat up Kramer bass. His amplifiers were made by SVT.

The band's PA system on this tour was monstrous. Built by Audio Analysts, it consisted of 60 S-4 cabinets with 1,000-watts and ten JBL speakers in each (two 18-inch, four 10-inch, two horns, and two high frequency units). The monitor system (consisting of two 15-inch wedges, two horns and a high frequency unit) was buried under grates all over the stage in strategic areas, adding another 16,000-watts. The band's onstage volume reached a staggering 134 dB.

The band's road crew on this tour was one of the most numerous in existence at the time. Consisting of approximately 75 members and 175,000 tons of equipment (including 1.5 million watts of light) loaded onto nine trucks and five busses. The massive white and black-striped stage featured a giant catwalk system and an outdoor roof, which was used as a secondary grid to hang all 55 of the setup's lighting points. During the final encore each night a massive light setup spelling out "1984" would swing down onto the stage behind the band, as they sang "Happy Trails" a cappella.

A live album was considered for recording during this tour but never materialized.

Typical set list: • Unchained • Hot for Teacher • Drum Solo • On Fire • Runnin' with the Devil • Little Guitars • Cathedral • House of Pain • Bass Solo • Jamie's Cryin' • I'll Wait • Dave's Tai Chi Solo • Everybody Wants Some!! • Girl Gone Bad • 1984 • Jump • Guitar Solo • (Oh) Pretty Woman • Panama • You Really Got Me • Ain't Talkin' 'Bout Love • Happy Trails

1/18/84: Jacksonville Coliseum, Jacksonville, FL. Opening act: Autograph. Attendance: 11,628.

1/20/84: Sportatorium, Hollywood, FL. Attendance: 11,508.

1/21/84: Sportatorium, Hollywood, FL. Attendance: 11,508. Audio recording exists.

1/22/84: Lakeland Civic Center, Lakeland, FL. Attendance: 10,000.

1/24/84: Barton Coliseum, Little Rock, AR. Opening act: Autograph.

1/25/84: Mid-South Coliseum, Memphis, TN. Attendance. 10,020. During "You Really Got Me," a lighting operator falls from the tresses, hanging upside-down in his chair over the stage.

1/26/84: Jackson Coliseum, Jackson, MS. Attendance: 10,000.

1/28/84: Gulfcoast Coliseum, Biloxi, MS. Attendance: 14,517.

1/29/84: Birmingham Jefferson Civic Center, Birmingham, AL. Opening act: Autograph. Attendance: 15,842. Audio recording exists.

1/31/84: Savannah Civic Center, Savannah, GA

2/01/84: Charlotte Coliseum, Charlotte, NC

2/03/84: Greensboro Coliseum, Greensboro, NC. Audio recording exists.

2/04/84: Roanoke Civic Center, Roanoke, VA. Opening act: Autograph. Audio recording exists.

2/05/84: Charleston Civic Center, Charleston, WV. Opening act: Autograph. Attendance: 10,195.

2/07/84: Hara Arena, Dayton, OH. Opening act: Autograph. Attendance: 7,900.

2/09/84: Freedom Hall, Louisville, KY. Opening act: Autograph. Attendance: 18,500.

2/10/84: Knoxville Civic Center Coliseum, Knoxville, TN. Attendance: 10,000. Audio recording exists.

2/11/84: Nashville Municipal Auditorium, Nashville, TN. Opening act: Autograph. Attendance: 9,900.

2/12/84: Richmond Coliseum, Richmond, VA. Attendance: 12,500.

2/14/84: Charlotte Coliseum, Charlotte, NC. Opening act: Autograph. Attendance: 12,468. Audio recording exists.

2/15/84: Hampton Coliseum, Hampton, VA. Attendance: 13,800.

2/17/84: Carolina Coliseum, Columbia, SC. Attendance: 10,354.

2/18/84: Reynolds Coliseum, Raleigh, NC. Attendance: 9,109.

2/19/84: Atlanta-Richmond County Civic Center, Augusta, GA. Attendance: 8,508. Audio recording exists.

2/22/84: The Omni, Atlanta, GA. Attendance: 13,642.

2/23/84: The Omni, Atlanta, GA. Attendance: 13,642.

3/07/84: Pittsburgh Civic Arena, Pittsburgh, PA. Attendance: Autograph. Attendance: 14,559. Audio recording exists.

3/08/84: Cincinnati Gardens, Cincinnati, OH

3/09/84: Cincinnati Gardens, Cincinnati, OH. Opening act: Autograph.

3/11/84: St. Paul Civic Center, St. Paul, MN. Opening act: Autograph. Attendance: 15,957.

3/13/84: Rosemont Horizon, Rosemont, IL. Opening act: Autograph. Audio recording exists.

3/14/84: Richfield Coliseum, Cleveland, OH. Opening act: Autograph.

3/16/84: The Centrum, Worchester, MA. Opening act: Autograph. Attendance: 11,170. Audio recording exists.

3/17/84: Providence Civic Center, Providence, RI. Opening act: Autograph. Attendance: 10,970.

3/18/84: Providence Civic Center, Providence, RI. Opening act: Autograph. Attendance: 10,970. Audio recording exists.

3/19/84: The Spectrum, Philadelphia, PA

3/20/84: The Spectrum, Philadelphia, PA. Attendance: 15,655. Audio recording exists.

3/21/84: The Spectrum, Philadelphia, PA. Attendance: 15,655. Audio recording exists.

3/22/84: Buffalo Memorial Auditorium, Buffalo, NY. Opening act: Autograph. Audio recording exists.

3/24/84: Veteran's Memorial Coliseum, New Haven, CT. Opening act: Autograph. Attendance: 9,956. Audio recording exists.

3/25/84: Capital Centre, Largo, MD. Warner Brothers films this show.

3/26/84: Capital Centre, Largo, MD. Opening act: Autograph. Warner Brothers films this show.

3/29/84: Hartford Civic Center, Hartford, CT. Opening act: Autograph. Attendance: 14,287.

3/30/84: Madison Square Garden, New York City, NY. Opening act: Autograph. Audio recording exists.

3/31/84: Madison Square Garden, New York City, NY. Opening acts: Loudness and Autograph. Audio recording exists. Autograph landed a record deal after playing these two gigs at Madison Square Garden. Thousands of balloons adorned with the Van Halen logo were dropped from the ceiling during both performances.

4/01/84: Brendan Byrne Arena, East Rutherford, NJ. Attendance: 18,157.

4/02/84: Brendan Byrne Arena, East Rutherford, NJ. Attendance: 18,157. Audio recording exists.

4/03/84: Brendan Byrne Arena, East Rutherford, NJ. Attendance: 18,157. Audio recording exists.

4/05/84: Cobo Hall, Detroit, MI. Opening act: Autograph. Attendance: 11,879. Audio recording exists.

4/06/84: Cobo Hall, Detroit, MI. Attendance: 11,879. Audio recording exists.

4/14/84: Uniondale, NY

4/17/84: Maple Leaf Gardens, Toronto, ON. Opening act: The Velcros. Attendance: 16,072. Audio recording exists.

4/19/84: Montreal Forum, Montreal, QE. Opening act: The Velcros. Audio and video recordings exist.

4/21/84: Le Colisee de Quebec, Quebec City, QE. Opening act: The Velcros. Attendance: 12,373. "Summertime Blues" is added to the set list for this show. Audio recording exists.

4/25/84: The Arena, Winnipeg, MB. Opening act: The Velcros. Attendance: 13,878. Audio recording exists.

4/27/84: The Olympic Saddledome, Calgary, AB. Opening act: The Velcros. Andy Taylor canceled as the opener and was replaced by the Velcros. Attendance: 15,500. Audio recording exists.

4/28/84: Northlands Coliseum, Edmonton, AB: Opening act: The Velcros. Attendance: 16,327.

4/30/84: Seattle Coliseum, Seattle, WA. Opening act: The Velcros. Attendance: 14,150.

5/01/84: Dive Coliseum, Vancouver, BC. Opening act: The Velcros. Attendance: 14,463.

5/02/84: Portland Coliseum, Portland, OR. Opening act: The Velcros. Attendance: 11,115.

5/04/84: BSU Pavilion, Boise, ID. Opening act: The Velcros. Attendance: 8,393.

5/05/84: The Mini Dome, Pocatello, ID. Opening act: The Velcros. Attendance: 11,626.

5/07/84: Lawlor Events Center, Reno, NV. Opening act: The Velcros. Attendance: 10,293. Audio recording exists.

5/09/84: The Cow Palace, San Francisco, CA. Opening act: The Velcros. Attendance: 14,500. Audio recording exists.

5/10/84: The Cow Palace, San Francisco, CA. Opening act: The Velcros. Attendance: 14,500. Audio recording exists.

5/11/84: The Cow Palace, San Francisco, CA. Opening act: The Velcros. Attendance: 14,500. Audio recording exists.

5/13/84: Great Western Forum, Inglewood, CA. Opening act: The Velcros. Audio recording exists.

5/14/84: Great Western Forum, Inglewood, CA. Opening act: The Velcros. Audio recording exists.

5/15/84: Thomas and Mack Center, Las Vegas, NV. Opening act: The Velcros. Attendance: 14,523.

5/17/84: Veterans Memorial Coliseum, Phoenix, AZ. Opening act: The Velcros.

5/19/84: Veterans Memororial Coliseum, Phoenix, AZ. Opening act: The Velcros. Audio recording exists.

5/20/84: San Diego Sports Arena, San Diego, CA. Opening act: The Velcros. Audio recording exists.

5/21/84: San Diego Sports Arena, San Diego, CA. Opening act: The Velcros. Audio recording exists.

5/22/84: San Diego Sports Arena, San Diego, CA. Opening act: The Velcros.

6/02/84: McNichols Arena, Denver, CO. Opening act: The Velcros. Attendance: 15,303. Audio recording exists.

6/03/84: McNichols Arena, Denver, CO. Opening act: The Velcros. Attendance: 15,303.

6/05/84: Salt Palace, Salt Lake City, UT. Opening act: The Velcros.

6/07/84: Tingley Auditorium, Albequerque, NM. Opening act: The Velcros. Attendance: 10,548.

6/08/84: Tingley Auditorium, Albequerque, NM. Opening act: The Velcros. Attendance: 10,548.

6/10/84: Frank C. Erwin, Jr. Special Events Center, Austin, TX. Opening act: The Velcros. Attendance: 14,872.

6/11/84: Hemisfair Arena, San Antonio, TX. Opening act: The Velcros.

6/13/84: The Centraplex, Baton Rouge, LA. Opening act: The Velcros. Attendance: 11,721.

6/15/84: The Myriad, Oklahoma City, OK. Opening act: The Velcros. Attendance: 12,805.

6/16/84: The Myriad, Oklahoma City, OK. Opening act: The Velcros. Attendance: 12,805.

6/17/84: Kansas Coliseum, Witchita, KS. Opening act: The Velcros. Attendance: 12,148.

6/20/84: Kemper Arena, Kansas City, MO. Opening act: The Velcros.

6/21/84: Kemper Arena, Kansas City, MO. Opening act: The Velcros.

6/23/84: Omaha Civic Auditorium, Omaha, NE. Opening act: The Velcros.

6/24/84: Omaha Civic Auditorium, Omaha, NE. Opening act: The Velcros.

6/26/84: Checkerdome, St. Louis, MO. Opening act: The Velcros.

6/27/84: Checkerdome, St. Louis, MO. Opening act: The Velcros.

6/29/84: Peoria Civic Center, Peoria, IL. Opening act: The Velcros. Audio recording exists.

6/30/84: Allen County Memorial Coliseum, Ft. Wayne, IN. Opening act: The Velcros.

7/01/84: Rockford Metro Centre, Rockford, IL. Opening act: The Velcros.

7/03/84: Dane County Memorial Coliseum, Madison, WI. Opening act: The Velcros. Attendance: 10,000. Audio recording exists.

7/05/84: Market Square Arena, Indianapolis, IN. Opening act: The Velcros. Audio recording exists.

7/06/84: Market Square Arena, Indianapolis, IN. Opening act: The Velcros. Audio recording exists.

7/07/84: Roberts Stadium, Evansville, IN. Opening act: The Velcros. Audio recording exists.

7/10/84: Frank C. Erwin, Jr. Special Events Center, Austin, TX. Opening act: The Velcros. Audio recording exists.

7/11/84: The Summit, Houston, TX. Opening act: The Velcros. Attendance: 14,130.

7/12/84: The Summit, Houston, TX. Opening act: The Velcros. Attendance: 14,130.

7/13/84: The Summit, Houston, TX. Opening act: The Velcros.

7/14/84: Reunion Arena, Dallas, TX. Opening act: The Velcros. Attendance: 16,505.

7/15/84: Reunion Arena, Dallas, TX. Opening act: The Velcros. Attendance: 16,505.

7/16/84: Reunion Arena, Dallas, TX. Opening act: The Velcros. Attendance: 16,505. Audio recording exists.

8/18/84: Donington Park Castle, Donington, Leicestershire UK. Attendance: 80,000. Audio and video recordings exist. This show was the first Monsters of Rock show out of five the band played to wrap up the *1984* tour. This was also Van Halen's first U.K. appearance since 1981. The bill for this day included Motley Crue, Y&T, Accept, Gary Moore, Ozzy Osborne, and AC/DC. This Van Halen show was filmed and the performance of "Hot for Teacher" was used by European MTV.

8/25/84: Rasunda Stadium, Stockholm, Sweden. Audio recording exists.

8/31/84: Schuetzenwiese, Winterthur, Switzerland. Audio recording exists.

9/01/84: Wildparkstadion, Karlsruhe, Germany. Audio recording exists.

9/02/84: Zeppelinfeld, Nuremburg, Germany. Audio recording exists.

5150 Tour (1986)

The *5150* tour was Van Halen's first tour with newly appointed front-man, Sammy Hagar. The Red Rocker had some mighty big shoes to fill, stepping in for David Lee Roth, and with the first of four #1 albums fronting Van Halen, it looked like Hagar was filling the order quite nicely.

The opening band, Bachman Turner Overdrive, was attempting a comeback and Van Halen gave them the shot at opening the entire tour. Labeled as "1/2 a Ton of Rock and Roll," BTO was one of the few acts to survive the opening act slot. James Brown, fresh from a jail stint and rid-ing the success of "Living in America," was initially offered the opening slot, but both bands' management were unable to come to a suitable mon-etary agreement. Reportedly, Brown's camp was asking $25,000 per show and naturally Van Halen's management passed on the idea.

The tri-level stage consisted of over 1,000 lights, 20,000-watts of sound, 55 audio cabinets, and a 50-man road crew. According to legend, the stage was outfitted with a specially constructed truss that was to hoist Hagar out over the audience.

Sammy added guitar to several songs while on stage, including "You Really Got Me," "Ain't Talkin' 'Bout Love," "Why Cant This Be Love?" "Love Walks In," "There Only One Way to Rock," and "I Can't Drive 55." His live setup included Dean, Kramer, and Jackson guitars and a "mongrel" amp setup featuring Randall 4-by-12 cabinets with Electro-Voice speakers.

Edward's stage rig consisted of his main 5150 Kramer guitar outfitted with Seymour Duncan pickups, and a Steinberger GL-2T for "Get Up" and "Good Enough." Amplifier-wise he used one Marshall head powered by four H&H 800-watt power amps.

Also in use was a prototype Sony wireless transmitter. For the keyboard songs, Ed used a Kurzweil MIDIed to four Obenheimer OB-8s, one for "Why Can't This Be Love?" one for "Love Walks In," a third for "Dreams," and the fourth for backup.

His solo consisted of a short piece by Debussy, his own version of "Fur Elise," and his standards of "Spanish Fly," "Eruption," "Mean Street" (the funky, two-handed intro), and an early version of "316."

Michael's live rig consisted of a Mesa Boogie Bass 400 amplifier with a Mesa Boogie cabinet housing a 15-inch Mesa Boogie E-V speaker wound especially for the bassist. He also used Flagg Systems cabinets loaded with Gauss drivers. Effects-wise Anthony used an Electro-Harmonix Micro Bass synthesizer during his solo, along with a pair of Lexicon's, MXR and ADA flangers, a pair of Colorado Sound Tone Benders, and a Roland DC-30 Chorus Echo unit. His Aria, Schecter, and Jack Daniels basses were all outfitted with Roto Sound Round Wound strings, changed religiously after every three shows. For the keyboard-based tracks in the set, he used an Apostrophe five string bass with a low B string. He also used the same Schaeffer-Vega wireless unit he'd been using on every tour since 1978.

Alex's kit featured Ludwig shells housing Simmons electronic drums with two bass drums, three rack toms mounted in front, and two lower toms on his right. It also contained two acoustic toms measuring 13-inch and 14-inch respectively along with an acoustic 20-inch Ludwig floor tom. His snare drum was a rosewood Tama measuring 6½-inch deep. He used Paiste 2002 series cymbals including a 20-inch China, three 20-inch crashes, a 24-inch ride, a 15-inch Sound Edge hi-hat, and a 40-inch gong. All the hardware was made by Ludwig, to which he added Ghost pedals. His sticks were Pro-Mark 5As.

In an effort to be able to get both a double-headed and single-headed bass drum sound, a large orange-colored vacuum hose was run between two of the bass drums. The idea was for the soundman at each venue to have the option of picking the kind of bass drum sound that he wanted. It didn't quite work as planned though as there really wasn't enough air flowing around to make the second bass drum sound.

During the band's four-day run at the Centrum in Worcester, MA, the band was presented with the key to the city of Boston.

Two warm-up shows in Anchorage, AK, and a third in Hawaii were canceled because *5150* was still being mixed by Edward, Donn Landee, and Mick Jones in-between rehearsals. They were later rescheduled for the end of the tour, but for unknown reasons were again canceled.

Typical set list: • You Really Got Me • There's Only One Way to Rock • Summer Nights • Get Up • Drum Solo • Why Can't This Be Love? • "5150" • Bass Solo • Panama • Best of Both Worlds • Love Walks In • Good Enough • Guitar Solo • I Can't Drive 55 • Ain't Talkin' 'Bout Love • Jump • Wild Thing • Rock and Roll

3/27/86: Hirsch Memorial Coliseum, Shreveport, LA. Opening act: BTO.

3/28/86: Barton Coliseum, Little Rock, AR. Opening act: BTO. Audio recording exists.

3/29/86: Mid-South Coliseum, Memphis, TN. Opening act: BTO.

3/31/86: Birmingham-Jefferson Civic Center, Birmingham, AL. Opening act: BTO.

4/01/86: Von Braun Civic Center, Huntsville, AL. Opening act: BTO.

4/03/86: Jackson Coliseum, Jackson, MS. Opening act: BTO.

4/04/86: The Centraplex, Baton Rouge, LA. Opening act: BTO.

4/05/86: Gulf High Coliseum, Biloxi, MI. Opening act: BTO.

4/07/86: The Sportatorium, Hollywood, FL. Opening act: BTO. Miami Dolphins five-time Pro Bowler Bob Baumhower takes the stage to sing "Jump."

4/08/86: Lee Civic Center, Ft. Myers, FL. Opening act: BTO.

4/10/86: Lakeland Civic Center, Lakeland, FL. Opening act: BTO. Audio recording exists.

4/11/86: Lakeland Civic Center, Lakeland, FL. Opening act: BTO.

4/12/86: Jacksonville Coliseum, Jacksonville, FL. Opening act: BTO.

4/14/86: The Omni, Atlanta, GA. Opening act: BTO. The band is informed that *5150* is #1 on the Billboard charts, and a celebration party is held just before show time. Audio recording exists.

4/15/86: Carolina Coliseum, Columbia, SC. Opening act: BTO. Audio recording exists.

4/19/86: Roberts Stadium, Evansville, IN. Opening act: BTO.

4/20/86: Municipal Auditorium, Nashville, TN. Opening act: BTO.

4/22/86: Rosemont Horizon, Rosemont, IL. Opening act: BTO.

4/23/86: Rosemont Horizon, Rosemont, IL. Opening act: BTO. "Rock Candy" is added to the set list for this show. Audio recording exists.

4/24/86: Rockford Metro Centre, Rockford, IL

4/26/86: SIU Arena, Carbondale, IL. Opening act: BTO.

4/27/86: Peoria Civic Center, Peoria, IL. Opening act: BTO. "Wild Thing" and "Make It Last" are added to the set list for this show. Audio recording exists.

4/29/86: St. Paul Civic Center, St. Paul, MN. Opening act: BTO. Audio recording exists.

4/30/86: Five Seasons Center, Cedar Rapids, IA. Opening act: BTO.

5/02/86: Allen County Memorial Coliseum, Ft. Wayne, IN. Opening act: BTO. Audio recording exists.

5/03/86: Market Square Arena, Indianapolis, IN. Opening act: BTO. Audio recording exists.

5/06/86: Cincinnati Gardens, Cincinnati, OH. Opening act: BTO.

5/07/86: Cincinnati Gardens, Cincinnati, OH. Opening act: BTO. Audio recording exists.

5/09/86: Joe Louis Arena, Detroit, MI. Opening act: BTO. "Wild Thing" and "Make It Last" added to set list for this show.

5/10/86: Joe Louis Arena, Detroit, MI. Opening act: BTO. "Rock Candy" and "Wild Thing" added to set list for this show. Audio and video recordings exist.

5/11/86: Joe Louis Arena, Detroit, MI. Opening act: BTO. Audio recording exists.

5/13/86: Pittsburgh Civic Arena, Pittsburgh, PA. Opening act: BTO. Van Halen grosses $235,265. Attendance: 15,899.

5/14/86: Charleston Civic Center, Charleston, WV. Opening act: BTO.

5/16/86: Greensboro Coliseum, Greensboro, NC. Opening act: BTO. Audio recording exists.

5/17/86: Hampton Coliseum, Hampton, VA. Opening act: BTO.

5/18/86: Roanoke Coliseum, Roanoke, VA. Opening act: BTO.

5/20/86: The Omni, Atlanta, GA. Opening act: BTO. Makeup date for a previously canceled show. Sammy publicly slams a reporter over an article written about the canceled concert.

5/21/86: Thompson Boling Arena, Knoxville, TN. Opening act: BTO. Audio recording exists.

5/23/86: Alpine Valley Music Theater, East Troy, WI. Opening act: BTO. A short version of "Black and Blue" is performed at this show. Audio recording exists.

5/24/86: Alpine Valley Music Theater, East Troy, WI. Opening act: BTO.

5/26/86: Memorial Auditorium, Des Moine, IA. Opening act: BTO. "Make It Last" is added to the set list for the show. Audio and video recordings exist.

5/27/86: Omaha Civic Auditorium, Omaha, NE. Opening act: BTO.

5/28/86: Kansas Coliseum, Witchita, KS. Opening act: BTO.

5/30/86: Kemper Auditorium, Kansas City, MO. Opening act: BTO. Audio recording exists.

5/31/86: Kemper Auditorium, Kansas City, MO. Opening act: BTO. "Crossroads" and "Make It Last" added to set list for this show. Audio and video recordings exist.

6/02/86: Market Square Arena, Indianapolis, IN. Opening act: BTO. Audio recordings exist.

6/11/86: Oakland Coliseum, Oakland, CA. Opening act: BTO.

6/26/86: San Diego Sports Arena, San Diego, CA. Opening act: BTO.

6/28/86: San Diego Sports Arena, San Diego, CA. Opening act: BTO. Audio recording exists.

6/29/86: San Diego Sports Arena, San Diego, CA. Opening act: BTO.
7/02/86: Great Western Forum, Inglewood, CA. Opening act: BTO. Van Halen's first Los Angeles show with Sammy Hagar. Numerous celebrities joined the band backstage including Tommy Lee and Heather Locklear, John Stamos, Dweezil and Moon Zappa, Ratt's Stephen Pearcy, and Paul Stanley. After the show, the band was presented with platinum sales awards for *5150* at a Los Angeles Hard Rock Café.
7/03/86: Great Western Forum, Inglewood, CA. Opening act: BTO. Audio recording exists.
7/05/86: Great Western Forum, Inglewood, CA. Opening act: BTO.
7/08/86: Compton Terrace, Phoenix, AZ. Opening act: BTO.
7/12/86: Folsom Field, Boulder, CO. Known as the Colorado Sun Day, the bill for this show included Loverboy, Dio, and BTO.
7/14/86: Tingley Coliseum, Albuquerque, NM. Opening act: BTO.
7/16/86: The Myriad, Oklahoma City, OK. Opening act: BTO. "Make It Last" is added to the set list for this show. Audio recording exist.
7/19/86: Cotton Bowl, Dallas, TX. This was the 9th annual Texxas Jam. The bill included BTO, Keel, Krokus, Dio, and Loverboy. Attendance: 72,000.
7/21/86: St. Louis Arena, St. Louis, MO. Opening act: BTO.
7/22/86: St. Louis Arena, St. Louis, MO. Opening act: BTO.
7/23/86: St. Louis Arena, St. Louis, MO. Opening act: BTO.
7/25/86: Richfield Coliseum, Cleveland, OH. Opening act: BTO.
7/26/86: Richfield Coliseum, Cleveland, OH. Opening act: BTO. Leslie West joined BTO on stage to perform "Mississippi Queen."
7/28/86: The Meadowlands, East Rutherford, NJ. Opening act: BTO. "Make It Last" is added to the set list for this show.
7/29/86: The Meadowlands, East Rutherford, NJ. Opening act: BTO with Leslie West.
7/31/86: The Meadowlands, East Rutherford, NJ. Opening act: BTO with Leslie West. An unknown quantity of tickets for this show were

printed with the following date: "7-2-30-86." "Foxey Lady" is added to the set list for this show. Audio recording exists.

8/01/86: The Meadowlands, East Rutherford, NJ. Opening act: BTO with Leslie West. "Make It Last" is added to the set list for this show. Audio recording exists.

8/02/86: Nassau Veterans Memorial Coliseum, Uniondale, NY. Opening act: BTO.

8/04/86: The Spectrum, Philadelphia, PA. Opening act: BTO. Audio recording exists.

8/05/86: The Spectrum, Philadelphia, PA. Opening act: BTO. Audio recording exists.

8/06/86: The Spectrum, Philadelphia, PA. Opening act: BTO. "Rock Candy" is added to the set list for this show.

8/08/86: Capital Centre, Largo, MD   . Opening act: BTO. "Summertime Blues" is added to the set list for this show. Audio recording exists.

8/09/86: Capital Centre, Largo, MD. Opening act: BTO. Audio recording exists.

8/11/86: The Centrum, Worcester, MA. Opening act: BTO. Audio recording exists.

8/12/86: The Centrum, Worcester, MA. Opening act: BTO. Audio recording exists.

8/14/86: The Centrum, Worcester, MA. Opening act: BTO. Audio recording exists.

8/15/86: The Centrum, Worcester, MA. Opening act: BTO. "Growth" and "Outside Woman Blues" added to the set list for this show. Audio recording exists.

8/18/86: Canadian National Exhibition Stadium, Toronto, ON. Opening act: BTO and Loverboy. "Summertime Blues" added to the set list for this show. Audio recording exists.

8/19/86: Manitoba, Canada. Opening act: BTO.

8/20/86: Montreal Forum, Montreal, QE. Opening act: BTO. Sammy and Alex switch places for a short time during this concert. Alex takes the microphone while Sammy pounds Al's drums. Audio and video recordings exist.

8/22/86: Providence Civic Center, Providence, RI. Opening act: BTO. "Make It Last" added to set list for this show. Audio recording exists.

8/23/86: Providence Civic Center, Providence, RI. Opening act: BTO.

8/24/86: Portland Memorial Coliseum, Portland, ME. Opening act: BTO.

8/25/86: Portland Memorial Coliseum, Portland, ME. Opening act: BTO. Audio recording exists.

8/26/86: Veterans Memorial Coliseum, New Haven, CT. Opening act: BTO. *Live without a Net* footage is supposed to be filmed, but isn't due to an equipment malfunction. Audio recording exists.

8/27/86: Veterans Memorial Coliseum, New Haven, CT. Opening act: BTO. *Live without a Net* footage is filmed. Audio and video recordings exist.

8/29/86: Niagra Falls Convention Center, Niagra Falls, NY. Opening act: BTO.

8/30/86: Niagra Falls Convention Center, Niagra Falls, NY. Opening act: BTO.

9/01/86: Silver Stadium, Rochester, NY. Opening act: BTO and Kim Mitchell. Audio and video recordings exist.

9/27/86: Cajundome, Lafayette, LA. Opening act: BTO.

9/29/86: The Summit, Houston, TX. Opening act: BTO.

9/30/86: TCCC Arena, Ft. Worth, TX. Opening act: BTO. "Sunshine of Your Love" added to set list for this show.

10/01/86: TCCC Arena, Ft. Worth, TX. Opening act: BTO.

10/03/86: San Antonio Convention Center, San Antonio, TX. Opening act: BTO.

10/04/86: Frank C. Erwin, Jr. Special Events Center, Austin, TX. Opening act: BTO. "Sunshine of Your Love" added to set list for this show.

10/06/86: Pan American Center, Las Cruces, NM. Opening act: BTO.

10/08/86: Salt Palace, Salt Lake City, UT. Opening act: BTO.

10/10/86: Casper Events Center, Casper WY. Opening act: BTO.

10/11/86: Rushmore Plaza Civic Center, Rapid City, SD. Opening act: BTO.

10/14/86: The Metra, Billings, MT. Opening act: BTO.

10/16/86: BSU Pavilion, Boise, ID. Opening act: BTO. A bomb threat after the opening act caused the Pavilion to be evacuated and the show to be delayed by approximately one hour. Upon restarting, Sammy Hagar remarked, "Who in their right mind would want to blow up a Van Halen concert?"

10/18/86: ISU Minidome, Pocatello, WA. Opening act: BTO.

10/19/86: BSU Pavilion, Boise, ID. Opening act: BTO.

10/21/86: Seattle Center, Seattle, WA. Opening act: BTO.

10/22/86: Seattle Center, Seattle, WA. Opening act: BTO. Heart's Ann Wilson joins the band onstage to perform "Rock and Roll."

10/23/86: BC Place Stadium, Vancouver, British Columbia. Opening act: BTO and Tom Cochrane.

10/25/86: Portland Memorial Coliseum, Portland, OR. Opening act: BTO.

10/26/86: Portland Memorial Coliseum, Portland, OR. Opening act: BTO.

10/29/86: Lawlor Events Center, Reno, NV. Opening act: BTO.

10/31/86: Cow Palace, San Francisco, CA. Opening act: BTO. Attendance: 15,000.

11/01/86: Cow Palace, San Francisco, CA. Opening act: BTO. Attendance: 15,000.

11/02/86: Cow Palace, San Francisco, CA. Opening act: BTO. Attendance: 15,000.

11/03/86: Cow Palace, San Francisco, CA. Opening act: BTO. "Pipeline" added to the set list for this show. Audio recording exists. Attendance: 15,000.

Monsters of Rock / OU812 Tour (1988-89)

From 5/27/88 to 7/30/88 Van Halen toured the country with four other acts in a massive outdoor-only, stadium tour. Announced at Universal Studios in Universal City, CA, the Monsters of Rock tour (based on an idea by co-promoter Sharon Osbourne) was to be the first traveling festival of its kind in the United States. As part of the promotion, the band was joined by Frankenstein, Dracula, the Mummy, King Kong, and the Phantom of the Opera at the press conference.

An additional promotion consisted of 100 autographed guitars, specially designed for the tour, which were given away in various markets throughout the United States. Each guitar, signed by all four members of the band, was painted with a Godzilla-like creature in sunglasses destroying a stadium.

With 250,000-watts of power, supplied by two sound systems weighing 440,000 pounds, suspended over a huge 168-by-60-foot stage, weighing 971 tons and transported by 51 48-foot trucks and two 50-person crews in six busses, this nearly 10-hour Monsters of Rock extravaganza was no small affair. Two jumbo lighting systems weighing 100,000 pounds and generating 850,000-watts were augmented by 20 automated lights supplying one million candle-power units per bulb. All of this was held in place by 15 automated truss structures weighing 24 tons and powered by two generators weighing 52,000 pounds.

Each show kicked off with Kingdom Come, followed by Metallica, Dokken, the Scorpions (who also played with Van Halen during the 2nd Annual Us Festival on 5/29/83), and Van Halen.

Reportedly, Van Halen added a contract rider calling for a fluffer to be present backstage for each gig on this tour. A fluffer is a woman found on adult film sets and her job is to ensure the male actors remain "at attention." Metallica's James Hetfield and Kirk Hammett flew back and forth between gigs and the studio as they put the finishing touches on their new album, *And Justice for All*.

Michael's live solo added a new touch to showmanship. Prior to the tour starting, he had a bass made that was outfitted with the mechanism from a shotgun that opens the barrels (allowing the loading of the shells). During the solo, he would run around and flick the switch, "breaking" the bass over his head while the soundman blasted samples of cracking trees through the PA. Another nifty bass was painted up to look just like a bottle of Tabasco sauce. The paint job was done by Jim O'Connor, who also painted Michael's backup Jack Daniel's bass and Edward's Steinberger faceplates.

Edward's live rig had his signal going from his guitar to a Sony wireless, then into a 100-watt Marshall amplifier fed through a Rane mixer. From there it went through two Roland SDE 3000s, a Lexicon PCM-70, a pair of Eventide Harmonizers, and a Rocktron Exciter/Imager and compressor. Next, the guitar signal went to an H&H V800 power amp and out to a bank of Marshall cabinets, outfitted with 30-watt Celestion speakers wired at 16 ohms.

Alex's drum kit was designed to his specifications by Ludwig. It included two bass drums: one 24-inch-by-32-inch and a second at 26-inch-by-32-inch. A single felt strip was stretched across each of the heads as padding (or muffling). His pedals of choice were the now obsolete Ghost bass drum pedals outfitted with wood beaters, which required him to glue leather pads at the point of impact on the bass heads. This technique was required because Alex had a tendency to split the beaters almost immediately without the pads. His snare measured 14-inch-by-6½-inch and he used five power tom-toms measuring 13, 14, 15, 18, and 20-inches respectively. Ludwig Rockers heads were used on all of his drums. His cymbal setup consisted of one 24-inch Paiste crash cymbal, seven 20-inch cymbals, and a 15-inch hi-hat. All of the kit's hardware was Ludwig and the joints and tension mountings were welded, due to the fact that the other band members had a tendency to jump on his kit during the show.

During his solo, the kit was raised into the air above the stage, spinning and shooting off fireworks.

Although the Monsters of Rock tour lost money, the tour was the second highest grossing event of 1988, earning $26.7 million. The top-grossing act of the year was Pink Floyd with $27.6 million. Other big money makers included Aerosmith with $21.2 million, AC/DC with $20.1 million, and George Michael with $17.7 million.

Typical set list: • Summer Nights • A.F.U. (Naturally Wired) • Black and Blue • Panama • Bass Solo • Runnin' with the Devil • Why Can't This Be Love? • Mine All Mine • Drum Solo • You Really Got Me • Sucker in a 3-Piece • When It's Love • Eagles Fly • I Can't Drive 55 • Best of Both Worlds • Guitar Solo • There's Only One Way to Rock • Ain't Talkin' 'Bout Love • Cabo Wabo • Rock and Roll

On 9/30/88 the band embarked on a regular headlining tour in support of the *OU812* album. Typical Set List: • A.F.U. (Naturally Wired) • There's Only One Way to Rock • Summer Nights • Panama • Bass Solo • Runnin' with the Devil • Why Can't This Be Love? • Mine all Mine • Drum Solo • Cabo Wabo • Finish What Ya Started • "5150" • When It's Love • Eagles Fly • I Can't Drive 55 • Best of Both Worlds • Guitar Solo • Black and Blue • Ain't Talkin' 'Bout Love • You Really Got Me • Rock and Roll

5/27/88: Alpine Valley Music Theater, East Troy, WI. Sammy Hagar slips on a stage ramp, fracturing his tailbone. He sits on ice between songs and the wound requires 10 stitches. Van Halen earns the distinction of performing the top grossing concert of 1988 by earning $2.89 million during their 3-day stint at Alpine Valley Music Theater. "Source of Infection" was included in the set list for this show. Audio recording exists.

5/28/88: Alpine Valley Music Theater, East Troy, WI. Audio recording exists.

5/29/88: Alpine Valley Music Theater, East Troy, WI

6/04/88: Orange Bowl, Miami, FL. Attendance: 27,000. Audio and video recordings exist.

6/05/88: Hall of Fame Bowl, Tampa, FL. "Superstition" is added to the set list for this show. Attendance: 35,000. Audio recording exists.

6/10/88: RFK Stadium, Washington DC. Attendance: 40,000.

6/11/88: JFK Stadium, Philadelphia, PA. This gig was also the site of MTV's Monsters of Rock contest, where one person was to jam with the band on stage for one song. The winner didn't know how to play an instrument, so she danced with Sammy to "You Really Got Me." "Superstition" is added to the set list for this show. Audio recording exists.

6/12/88: Sullivan Stadium, Foxboro, MA. Initially the Board of Selectmen in Foxboro voted to deny the Monsters of Rock Tour a permit to play in Foxboro (a motion they had carried out before when they denied a permit to the Jacksons on 1984's *Victory* tour). Van Halen counter-attacked, threatening a lawsuit, and the board gave in, allowing the tour to play at Sullivan Stadium. Attendance: 33,000. Audio recording exists.

6/15/88: Three Rivers Stadium, Pittsburgh, PA. "Superstition" is added to the set list for this show. Attendance: 30,000. Audio recording exists.

6/16/88: Pontiac Silverdome, Pontiac, MI. Attendance: 50,000.

6/17/88: Pontiac Silverdome, Pontiac, MI. Attendance: 35,000. Audio recording exists.

6/18/88: Pontiac Silverdome, Pontiac, MI. Audio recording exists.

6/19/88: Rich Stadium, Buffalo, NY. Audio and video recordings exist.

6/22/88: The Rubber Bowl, Akron, OH. "Superstition" is added to the set list for this show. Audio and video recordings exist.

6/23/88: The Rubber Bowl, Akron, OH

6/24/88: Oxford Speedway, Oxford, ME. There most likely was not a concert on 6/24/88.

6/25/88: Oxford Speedway, Oxford, ME. A severe thunderstorm created havoc at this show. A close thunder clap scared The Scorpions off the stage for while. According to Sammy Hagar, fans in the audience were struck by lightning. The storm cleared up for Van Halen's performance, but it grew very cold. The band, dressed in jackets and all performing through chords, played a shortened set dropping "Why Can't This Be Love?" and

"Summer Nights" as well as the solo spots, with the exception of Eddie who played a quick version of "Eruption." Audio recording exists.

6/26/88: Giants Stadium, East Rutherford, NJ. Audio and video recordings exist.

6/27/88: Giants Stadium, East Rutherford, NJ. Canceled due to poor ticket sales.

7/02/88: Rice Stadium, Houston, TX

7/03/88: Cotton Bowl, Dallas, TX. This Texxas Jam was one of the shortest Van Halen headliner shows on record, their performance clocked in at just a little more than an hour due to the fact that Sammy was suffering from a cold. To make it up to the fans, he promised the crowd that Van Halen would return to Dallas and put on a free show, which they did on 12/04/91. "Superstition" was added to the shortened set list for this show. Audio and video recordings exist.

7/06/88: The Hoosier Dome, Indianapolis, IN

7/08/88: Liberty Bowl Memorial Stadium, Memphis, TN

7/09/88: Liberty Bowl Memorial Stadium, Memphis, TN. Audio recording exists.

7/10/88: Arrowhead Stadium, Kansas City, MO. Audio recording exists.

7/13/88: The Metrodome, Minneapolis, MN. "A Apolitical Blues" is added to the set list for this show. Audio recording exists.

7/16/88: Candlestick Park, San Francisco, CA. Audio and video recordings exist.

7/17/88: Candlestick Park, San Francisco, CA

7/20/88: Joseph A. Albi Stadium, Spokane, WA. Audio recording exists.

7/23/88: Memorial Coliseum, Los Angeles, CA

7/24/88: Memorial Coliseum, Los Angeles, CA. According to reports, the audience at one of these Los Angeles shows tried to rush the stage and over 200 police officers were used to control the crowd. Audio recording exists.

7/27/88: The Kingdome, Seattle, WA. "My Generation" is added to the set list for this show. Audio recording exists.

7/30/88: Mile High Stadium, Denver, CO

9/30/88: Rupp Arena, Lexington, KY. Opening act: Private Life.

10/01/88: Riverfront Coliseum, Cincinnati, OH. Opening act: Private Life.

10/03/88: The Omni, Atlanta, GA. Opening act: Private Life.

10/04/88: Starwood Amphitheater, Nashville, TN. Opening act: Private Life.

10/06/88: Greensboro Coliseum, Greensboro, NC. Opening act: Private Life.

10/07/88: Charlotte Coliseum, Charlotte, NC. Opening act: Private Life. Audio recording exists.

10/08/88: Thompson-Boling Assembly Center and Arena, Knoxville, TN. Opening act: Private Life. Audio recording exists.

10/11/88: Madison Square Garden, New York, NY. Opening act: Private Life. Van Halen receives the Gold Ticket award for playing to over 100,000 fans. Audio recording exists.

10/12/88: Nassau Veterans Memorial, Coliseum, Nassau, NY. Opening act: Private Life.

10/14/88: Hartford Civic Center, Hartford, CT. Opening act: Private Life.

10/15/88: The Carrier Dome, Syracuse, NY. Opening act: Private Life. A "Girl Gone Bad" jam was added to the set list for this show. Audio recording exists.

10/17/88: Providence Civic Center, Providence, RI. Opening act: Private Life.

10/18/88: Worcester Centrum, Worcester, MA. Opening act: Private Life.

10/20/88: Richmond Coliseum, Richmond, VA. Opening act: Private Life. Alex incorporates "Los Endos" into his unaccompanied solo. "My Generation" is added to the set list for this show.

10/21/88: Scope Arena, Norfolk, VA. Opening act: Private Life.

10/22/88: The Spectrum, Philadelphia, PA. Opening act: Private Life. A "Girl Gone Bad" jam is added to the set list for this show. Audio recording exists.

10/25/88: Rosemont Horizon, Rosemont, IL. Opening act: Private Life.

10/26/88: Allen County Memorial Coliseum, Ft. Wayne, IN. Opening act: Private Life. Originally scheduled for 10/27/88.

10/27/88: Allen County Memorial Coliseum, Ft. Wayne, IN. Opening act: Private Life. Rescheduled for 10/26/88.

10/28/88: Bradley Center, Milwaukee, WI. Opening act: Private Life. Audio recording exists.

10/30/88: Notre Dame Acc., South Bend, IN. Opening act: Private Life.

10/31/88: Five Seasons Center, Cedar Rapids, IA. Opening act: Private Life.

11/01/88: Hilton Coliseum, Ames, IA. Opening act: Private Life.

11/03/88: The Myriad, Oklahoma City, OK. Opening act: Private Life.

11/04/88: Kansas Coliseum, Witchita, KS. Opening act: Private Life.

11/05/88: Devanny Sports Center, Lincoln, NE. Opening act: Private Life.

11/07/88: Peoria Civic Center, Peoria, IL. Opening act: Private Life. Warner Brothers records this show for a possible live album. "Standin' at the Same Old Crossroads" and "My Generation" are added to the set list for this show. Audio recording exists.

11/08/88: St. Louis Arena, St. Louis, MO. Opening act: Private Life.

11/09/88: St. Louis Arena, St. Louis, MO. Opening act: Private Life.

11/11/88: New Orleans, LA. Opening act: Private Life.

11/13/88: Frank C. Irwin, Jr. Special Events Center, Austin, TX. Opening act: Private Life.

11/15/88: El Paso Special Events Center, El Paso, TX. Opening act: Private Life.

11/16/88: Tucson, AZ. Opening act: Private Life.

11/17/88: Veterans Memorial Coliseum, Phoenix, AZ. Opening act: Private Life.

11/19/88: San Diego Sports Arena, San Diego, CA. Opening act: Private Life. Audio recording exists.

11/21/88: Arco Arena, Sacramento, CA. Opening act: Private Life. Audio recording exists.

11/22/88: Lawlor Events Center, Reno, NV. Opening act: Private Life.

11/24/88: Portland Memorial Coliseum, Portland, OR. Opening act: Private Life.

11/26/88: Salt Palace, Salt Lake City, UT. Opening act: Private Life.

1/19/89: Tokyo, Japan. Opening act: Private Life. Video recording exists.

1/23/89: Kyoto, Japan. Opening act: Private Life.

1/24/89: Osaka, Japan. Opening act: Private Life.

1/25/89: Castle Hall, Osaka, Japan. Opening act: Private Life. Audio recording exists.

1/27/89: Hiroshima, Japan. Opening act: Private Life.

1/29/89: Pulse Plaza, Kyoto, Japan. Opening act: Private Life. Audio recording exists.

1/30/89: Nagoya, Japan. Opening act: Private Life.

2/01/89: The Super Dome, Tokyo, Japan. Opening act: Private Life. This show was broadcast on Japanese television. Audio and video recordings exist.

2/02/89: The Super Dome, Tokyo, Japan. Opening act: Private Life. "A Apolitical Blues" is added to the set list for this show. Audio recording exists.

2/26/89: Blaisdell Arena, Honolulu, HI. Opening act: Private Life.

For Unlawful Carnal Knowledge Tour (1991-92)

For the first time, Edward did not play keyboards live on stage at all during the tour. He recorded the keyboard parts into a sequencer during initial rehearsals before the start of the tour, then re-recorded them every few days.

Edward's live rig consisted of three Peavey 5150 cabinets, each housing four 12-inch speakers at 75-watts. One cabinet amplified a dry signal and the other two ran stereo effects. The speakers in the dry cabinet differed from the two effected cabinets in that they featured a lower efficiency coil form, which promoted a natural breakup and a more desirable tone. This cabinet fed a Palmer Speaker Simulator with a line level out to a Bradshaw switching system that controlled an Eventide H-3000 Harmonizer, two Roland SDE-3000s, a Lexicon PCM-70, an MXR Phase 90, a Boss SD-1, a Cry Baby Wah Wah, and a Boss OC-2.

The effected speakers featured a higher efficiency coil form and a cleaner tone. Four 5150 heads sat in guitar tech Matt Bruck's pit: two for backup, one to Edward's rig and the fourth was used as a direct feed to Alex (powering a pair of 2-by-12 cabinets on each side of his kit). He used a Sony wireless.

Michael's setup consisted of mostly Music Man basses and a standard Ampeg SVT 2 bass head (used as a preamp) in conjunction with three custom Ampeg 300-watt power amps. He also had Ampeg design a custom cabinet that housed two different speaker configurations, one for the high end bass sound and one for the low end. The high end was handled by eight 10-inch speakers and a horn. The low frequencies were handled by four 12-inch speakers. Added to the mix was a Rane crossover and four 12-inch port enclosures running at 80 or 90 cycles down for a "sub bass feel." The cabinets were interestingly striped with Ed's trademark red, white, and black design.

His effects included an ADA flanger, an Electro-Harmonix Micro-Synth, a Digitech harmonizer, a Roland delay, a ColorSound Fuzz Bender, and an old, analog Roland DC-30 chorus, all run through a Bradshaw switcher. He used Samson and Vega wireless systems.

Newly appointed bass tech Craig DeFalco handled effects activation during Michael's bass solo. DeFalco came on board, replacing his then-roommate, Kevin Dugan (who had been with the band since 1980), who took a self-imposed hiatus. Dugan, who remained in regular contact with

Michael (doing some pre-production on various projects among other things) returned to his hometown of Cleveland, OH, and started his own production company. Dugan returned to the road crew after the Right Here, Right Now tour.

Al's live Ludwig Super Classic Chrome setup consisted of one 6½-inch-by-14-inch snare drum, one 20-inch-by-22-inch bass drum, one 8-inch-by-10-inch mounted tomtom, a second mounted tomtom measuring 8-inch-by-12-inch, and two floor toms measuring 16-inch-by-16-inch and 16-inch-by-18-inch respectively. Cymbal-wise, he used one 20-inch power crash, 15-inch high hats, one 20-inch full crash, one 22-inch prototype large-bell ride, one 20-inch china and a 40-inch gong (all from the Paiste Signature Series). He also used some Simmons pads and an LP cowbell. His entire rig was held together with a custom Voelker drum rack and PureCussion RIMS. Add to that a Yamaha chain-drive double pedal (with felt beaters), Ludwig Silver-Dot Rocker heads (batter side), Ludwig Heavy Clear Rockers (bottom side), Remo Muff'ls (batter and front bass drum heads), a Simmons TMI trigger-to-MIDI interface, and a Peavey V3 synthesizer module. His sticks were Calato/Regal Tip "Alex Van Halen" sticks and his microphones were May EA/AKG internal microphones.

Typical set list: • Poundcake • Judgement Day • Spanked • Runaround • When It's Love • There's Only One Way to Rock • Bass/Drum Solo (with Pleasure Dome) • A.F.U. (Naturally Wired) • Panama • Why Can't This Be Love? • Finish What Ya Started • Eagles Fly • Guitar Solo • Best of Both Worlds • I Can't Drive 55 • The Dream Is Over • In 'n' Out • Jump • You Really Got Me • Top of the World

8/16/91: Lakewood Amphitheater, Atlanta, GA. Opening act: Alice In Chains. MTV films "We're with the Band: Backstage with Van Halen." 45 U.S. Sailors from the aircraft carrier USS Saratoga attend soundcheck. Audio and video recordings exist.

8/17/91: Starwood Amphitheater, Antioch, TN. Opening act: Alice in Chains.

8/20/91: Starlake Amphitheater, Burgettstown, PA. Opening act: Alice in Chains. Audio recording exists.

8/21/91: Blossom Music Center, Cuyahoga Falls, OH. Opening act: Alice in Chains. Audio recording exists.

8/24/91: Deer Creek Music Center, Noblesville, IN. Opening act: Alice in Chains. Audio recording exists.

8/25/91: Riverport Amphitheater, Maryland Heights, MO. Opening act: Alice in Chains. Audio recording exists.

8/26/91: Sandstone Amphitheater, Bonner Springs, MO. Opening act: Alice in Chains. Audio and video recordings exist.

8/29/91: New Pine Knob Music Center, Clarkston, MI. Opening act: Alice in Chains. Audio recording exists.

8/31/91: Marcus Amphitheater, Milwaukee, WI. Opening act: Alice in Chains. Audio recording exists.

9/01/91: World Music Theater, Tinley Park, IL. Opening act: Alice in Chains. Audio recording exists.

9/05/91: Universal Amphitheater, Universal City, CA. Opening act: Alice in Chains.

9/06/91: Fiddler's Green Amphitheater, Englewood, CO. Opening act: Alice in Chains.

9/08/91: Blockbuster Desert Sky Arena, Phoenix, AZ. Opening act: Alice in Chains.

9/09/91: Cal Expo Amphitheatre, Sacramento, CA. Opening act: Alice in Chains. Video recording exists. "Top of the World" (live) video is filmed.

9/10/91: Pacific Amphitheater, Costa Mesa, CA. Opening act: Alice in Chains. Audio recording exists.

9/11/91: Pacific Amphitheater, Costa Mesa, CA. Opening act: Alice in Chains. Audio recording exists.

9/13/91: Shoreline Amphitheater, Mountainview, CA. Opening act: Alice in Chains. Audio recording exists.

9/14/91: Shorline Amphitheater, Mountainview, CA. Opening act: Alice in Chains. Audio and video recordings exist.

9/15/91: Cal Expo, Sacramento, CA. Opening act: Alice in Chains.

9/23/91: Knickerbocker Arena, Albany, NY. Opening act: Alice in Chains.

10/08/91: Cumberland County Civic Center, Portland, ME. Opening act: Alice in Chains. Audio recording exists.

10/09/91: Providence Civic Center, Providence, RI. Opening act: Alice in Chains. "Time's a Waste" is added to the set list for this show. Audio recording exists.

10/11/91: Hampton Coliseum, Hampton, VA. Opening act: Alice in Chains.

10/12/91: Walnut Creek Amphitheater, Raleigh, NC. Opening act: Alice in Chains. Audio recording exists.

10/15/91: The Spectrum, Philadelphia, PA. Opening act: Alice in Chains. Audio and video recordings exists.

10/16/91: The Spectrum, Philadelphia, PA. Opening act: Alice in Chains. A "Jamie's Cryin'" jam is added to the set list for this show. Audio recording exists.

10/17/91: Capital Center, Columbia, MD. Opening act: Alice in Chains. Audio recording exists.

10/20/91: Buffalo War Memorial, Buffalo, NY. Opening act: Alice in Chains. Audio and video recordings exist.

10/23/91: Knickerbocker Arena, Albany, NY. Opening act: Alice in Chains. Audio and video recordings exist.

10/24/91: Meadowlands Arena, East Rutherford, NJ. Opening act: Alice in Chains. Audio recording exists.

10/25/91: Meadowlands Arena, East Rutherford, NJ. Opening act: Alice in Chains. Audio recording exists.

10/27/91: Nassau Veterans Memorial Coliseum, Uniondale, NY. Opening act: Alice in Chains. Ed briefly plays a black and white EBMM belonging to Matt Bruck, painted like the Asian Ying/Yang symbol. Video recording exists.

10/29/91: Hartford Civic Center, Hartford, CT. Opening act: Alice in Chains. Audio recording exists.

10/30/91: The Centrum, Worchester, MA. Opening act: Alice in Chains. Audio recording exists.

10/31/91: The Centrum, Worchester, MA. Opening act: Alice in Chains. Audio recording exists.

11/03/91: Montreal Forum, Montreal, QE. Opening act: Alice in Chains. Audio recording exists.

11/04/91: The Skydome, Toronto, ON. Opening act: Alice in Chains. Audio recording exists.

11/07/91: The Arena, Winnipeg, MB. Opening act: Alice in Chains. Audio recording exists.

11/09/91: Northlands Coliseum, Edmonton, AB. Opening act: Alice in Chains.

11/10/91: Saskatchewan Place, Saskatoon, SK. Opening act: Alice in Chains.

11/11/91: Olympic Saddledome, Calgary, AB. Opening act: Alice in Chains.

11/13/91: B.C. Place Stadium, Vancouver, BC. Opening act: Alice in Chains. For unknown reasons, Alice in Chains bassist Mike Starr stands in for Michael Anthony for one song. Starr told a friend after the show, "It was the most terrifying gig I'd ever done!"

11/14/91: Tacoma Dome, Tacoma WA. Canceled due to Sammy being sick.

11/15/91: Cal-Expo Amphitheater, Sacramento, CA. Opening act: Alice in Chains.

12/02/91: The Pyramid, Memphis, TN. Opening act: THC.

12/03/91: Hirsch Memorial Coliseum, Shreveport, LA. Opening act: Alice in Chains. Audio recording exists.

12/04/91: West End Market Place (Dallas Alley), Dallas, TX. This became known as the "Dallas Free Show." After having lost his voice at a previous Texxas Jam, Sammy promised to return to the Dallas area and make up for the concert. An undetermined mass of thousands gathered in the streets for the free concert announced at approximately 12:30 A.M. the day of the show. Several national news shows covered the event and a video was released for "Top of the World" made up of clips from the show and the soundtrack from the "Top of the World" (live) video shot on 9/09/91.Set list: • Poundcake • Judgement Day • There's Only One Way to Rock • Runaround • Why Can't This Be Love? • Panama • A Apolitical Blues • Finish What Ya Started • I Can't Drive 55 • Best of Both Worlds • Top of the World. Audio and video recordings exist.

   12/06/91: Gulf Coast Coliseum, Biloxi, MS. Opening act: Alice in Chains. Audio recording exists.

   12/07/91: The Centraplex, Baton Rouge, LA. Opening act: Alice in Chains. Audio recording exists.

   12/09/91: Tallahassee Civic Center, Tallahassee, FL. Opening act: Alice in Chains. "Born on the Bayou" and "We Gotta Get Outta This Place" added to the set list for this show. Audio and video recordings exist.

   12/10/91: Jacksonville Coliseum, Jacksonvile, FL. Opening act: Alice in Chains. Audio recording exists.

   12/12/91: Suncoast Dome, St. Petersburg, FL. Opening act: Alice in Chains. Attendance: 21,000. "A Apolitical Blues" is added to the set list for this show. Video recording exists.

   12/13/91: Miami Arena, Miami, FL. Opening act: Alice in Chains. "Outside Woman Blues" and a "Dick in the Dirt" jam added to the set list for this show. Audio and video recordings exist.

   12/14/91: Orlando Arena, Orlando, FL. Opening act: Alice in Chains.

   1/22/92: Tacoma Dome, Tacoma, WA. Opening act: Alice in Chains. Makeup for canceled 11/14/91 show. Audio and video recordings exist.

   1/23/92: Portland Memorial Coliseum, Portland, OR. Opening act: Alice in Chains.

   1/28/92: Reunion Arena, Dallas, TX. Opening act: Baby Animals. "Born on the Bayou" and "We Gotta Get Outta This Place" added to the set list for this show. Audio and video recordings exist.

1/29/92: Frank C. Irwin, Jr. Special Events Center, Austin, TX. Opening act: Baby Animals.

1/31/92: The Summit, Houston, TX. Opening act: Baby Animals. "Born on the Bayou" is added to the set list for this show. Audio and video recordings exist.

2/02/92: The Myriad, Oklahoma City, OK. Opening act: Baby Animals.

2/03/92: Kansas Coliseum, Witchita, KS. Opening act: Baby Animals.

2/05/92: S.I.U. Arena, Carbondale, IL. Opening act: Baby Animals. "We Gotta Get Outta This Place" added to the set list for this show. Audio recording exists.

2/07/92: Riverfront Coliseum, Cincinnati, OH. Opening act: Baby Animals. "Outside Woman Blues" and "We Gotta Get Outta This Place" added to the set list for this show. Audio recording exists.

2/08/92: Freedom Hall, Louisville, KY. Opening act: Baby Animals. "What They Gonna Say Now" is added to the set list for this show. Audio recording exists.

2/09/92: Roberts Stadium, Evansville, IN. Opening act: Baby Animals. Audio recording exists.

2/12/92: UTC Arena, Chattanooga, TN. Opening act: Baby Animals.

2/14/92: Birmingham-Jefferson Civic Center, Birmingham, AL. Opening act: Baby Animals. "Born on the Bayou" is added to the set list for this show. Video recording exists.

2/15/92: Von Braun Civic Center, Huntsville, AL. Opening act: Baby Animals. "Make It Last" is added to the set list for this show. Audio and video recordings exist.

2/16/92: Thompson Boling Arena, Knoxville, TN. Opening act: Baby Animals. "Make It Last" is added to the set list for this show. Audio and video recordings exist.

2/19/92: Wings Stadium, Kalamazoo, MI. Opening act: Baby Animals.

2/21/92: Palace of Auburn Hills, Auburn Hills, MI. Opening act: Baby Animals.

2/22/92: Palace of Auburn Hills, Auburn Hills, MI. Opening act: Baby Animals.

2/24/92: Ft. Wayne Coliseum, Ft. Wayne, IN. Opening act: Baby Animals.

2/26/92: Roanoke Civic Center Coliseum, Roanoke, VA. Opening act: Baby Animals.

2/28/92: Charlotte Coliseum, Charlotte, NC. Opening act: Baby Animals. Audio recording exists.

2/29/92: Carolina Coliseum, Columbia, SC. Opening act: Baby Animals. Audio recording exists.

3/02/92: Wings Stadium, Kalamazoo, MI. Opening act: Baby Animals. "Born on the Bayou" is added to the set list for this show. Audio recording exists.

3/03/92: Allen County Memorial Coliseum, Ft. Wayne, IN. Opening act: Baby Animals. Baby Animals joins Van Halen on stage to perform "Rock and Roll." Audio recording exists.

4/03/92: Palace of Auburn Hills, Auburn Hills, MI. Opening act: Hardline. "Suzy Q" and "Rock Candy" added to the set list for this show. Audio recording exists.

4/04/92: Palace of Auburn Hills, Auburn Hills, MI. Opening act: Hardline. Audio recording exists.

4/06/92: Bramlage Coliseum, Manhatten, KS. Opening act: Hardline.

4/07/92: Omaha Civic Auditorium, Omaha, NE. Opening act: Baby Animals.

4/08/92: Barton Coliseum, Little Rock, AR. Opening act: Baby Animals.

4/10/92: Five Seasons Center, Cedar Rapids, IA. Opening act: Baby Animals. Video recording exists.

4/11/92: Peoria Civic Center, Peoria, IL. Opening act: Baby Animals. Audio recording exists.

4/12/92: Hearns Center, Columbia, MO. Opening act: Baby Animals.

4/15/92: St. Louis Arena, St. Louis, MO. Opening act: Baby Animals. "Rock Candy," "Mississippi Queen," and "Crossroads" added to the set list for this show. Audio and video recordings exist.

4/17/92: Target Center, Minneapolis, MN. Opening act: Baby Animals. Audio recording exists.

4/18/92: Hilton Coliseum, Ames, IA. Opening act: Baby Animals. "Crossroads" is added to the set list for this show. Audio and video recordings exist.

4/19/92: Omaha Civic Auditorium, Omaha, NE. Opening act: Baby Animals. "We Gotta Get Outta This Place" is added to the set list for this show. Audio and video recordings exist.

4/22/92: Rushmore Plaza Civic Center, Rapid City, SD. Opening act: Baby Animals.

4/23/92: Metrapark Arena, Billings, MT. Opening act: Baby Animals.

4/25/92: McNichols Arena, Denver, CO. Opening act: Baby Animals.

4/27/92: Tingley Coliseum, Albuquerque, NM. Opening act: Baby Animals.

4/28/92: El Paso Special Events Center, El Paso, TX. Opening act: Baby Animals.

5/01/92: Great Western Forum, Inglewood, CA. Canceled due to Portland Trailblazers/Los Angeles Lakers playoff series.

5/02/92: Arco Arena, Sacramento, CA. Re-scheduled for 5/10/92.

5/02/92: Great Western Forum, Inglewood, CA. Opening act: Baby Animals. Makeup for canceled 5/01/92 show.

5/03/92: Great Western Forum, Inglewood, CA. Opening act: Baby Animals.

5/06/92: Thomas and Mack Arena, Las Vegas, NV. Opening act: Baby Animals.

5/08/92: Cow Palace, San Francisco, CA. Opening act: Baby Animals. Audio and video recordings exist.

5/09/92: Lawlor Events Center, Reno, NV. Opening act: Baby Animals. "Mississippi Queen" is added to the set list for this show. Audio recording exists.

5/10/92: Arco Arena, Sacramento, CA. Opening act: Baby Animals. Make-up for re-scheduled 5/02/92 show. Audio recording exists.

5/12/92: Great Western Forum, Inglewood, CA. Opening act: Baby Animals. "Waiting for the Bus" and "Mississippi Queen" added to the set list for this show. Audio recording exists.

5/14/92: Selland Arena, Fresno, CA. Opening act: Baby Animals. Audio recording exists.

5/15/92: Selland Arena, Fresno, CA. Opening act: Baby Animals. Audio recording exists.

5/16/92: Great Western Forum, Inglewood, CA. Opening act: Baby Animals. Audio recording exists.

5/17/92: McHale Center (University of Arizona), Tuscon, AZ. Opening act: Baby Animals. This show was originally booked at the Tucson Convention Center, but the band's stage was too wide to fit inside the venue, so the show was moved to the McHale center.

5/23/92: Palacio de los Deportes, Mexico City, Mexico. Opening act: Baby Animals.

5/24/92: Palacio de los Deportes, Mexico City, Mexico. Opening act: Baby Animals.

5/29/92: Blaisdell Arena, Honolulu, HI. Opening act: Baby Animals.

5/30/92: Blaisdell Arena, Honolulu, HI. Opening act: Baby Animals.

5/31/92: Blaisdell Arena, Honolulu, HI. Opening act: Baby Animals. Audio recording exists.

Right Here, Right Now Tour (1993)

This would mark Van Halen's first U.K. appearance with Sammy Hagar as lead singer. Prior to this tour, the last show performed here was at the Monsters of Rock gig at Castle Donington on 8/18/84.

Before an outdoor show in Boston, a Junebug managed to lodge itself in one of Eddie's ears, nearly damaging his eardrum. While staying at the Four Seasons Hotel, the guitarist awoke several times throughout the night experiencing excruciating pain. Not knowing just what may be in his ear, Ed sprayed saline solution into the ear canal, and after whacking himself in the head several times, the one-inch insect fell out into the sink.

Edward's live rig consisted of three Peavey 4-by-12 cabinets: one dry and two with effects. Each effected cabinet was paired with an SDE-3000 digital delay, with the delay time on one set to one-half the delay time on the other to created a layered echo. An Evantide H3000 fed both effected cabinets along with a Lexicon PCM-70 digital reverb, which was used during his unaccompanied solo for "Cathedral." All remaining effects were handled with effects pedals patched in via a Bob Bradshaw footswitching system. The Bradshaw unit featured four presets: one was a SDE-3000/H3000 combination, a second added a BOSS OC-2 octave divider, the third featured an MXR Phase 90 phaser, and the fourth added a Dunlop Crybaby Wah-Wah, which was always kept in the ON position. On stages that required extra-long cable runs, Edward added a BOSS SD-1 Super Overdrive pedal to boost the signal to the wah (which occurred at approximately 10 shows throughout the tour). A Rockman noise gate was used with Ed's Sony wireless unit which sent a clean signal to his Peavey 5150 head. The signal was fed through a Palmer speaker simulator and an H&H power amp before hitting the speaker cabinets. The entire rig was capped off with Furman power conditioners keeping control of the AC voltage.

Michael added the "Star Spangled Banner" to his bass solo, now named "Ultra Bass." As in past tours, he used an Electro Harmonix Micro-Bass Synthesizer and an Evantide Harmonizer. He used three Music Man Stingray basses as his workhorses, using a 5-string for "Runaround" and "Spanked."

Alex's live Ludwig kit consisted of one 14-inch-by-8-inch snare drum, one 10-inch-by-8-inch tom, one 12-inch-by-8-inch tom, two floor toms measuring 16-inch-by-16-inch and 18-inch-by-16-inch respectively and two 22-inch-by-20-inch bass drums. Cymbal-wise, he used Paiste: one 15-inch Sound-edge hi-hat, five 20-inch crash cymbals, one 22-inch ride cymbal, and one 20-inch china cymbal. His sticks of choice were the Alex Van Halen signature model Calato/Regal tips.

The band designated the U.S. leg of their tour as the National Hunger Relief tour for USA Harvest, the largest all-volunteer food distribution organization in the United States. Fans were asked to donate canned goods, which were collected at the doors of each show and distributed to local missions and shelters in those cities.

Extreme was one band considered for the opening act slot.

Typical set list: • Poundcake • Judgement Day • Runaround • When It's Love • There's Only One Way to Rock • Bass Solo • Pleasure Dome • Drum Solo • Panama • Right Now • Why Can't This Be Love? • Finish What Ya Started • Eagles Fly • Guitar Solo • Unchained • "5150" • Best of Both Worlds • Top of the World • Ain't Talkin' 'Bout Love • Jump • You Really Got Me • All Right Now • Rockin' in the Free World

3/30/93: Olympiahalle, Munchen, GER. Opening act: Little Angels. Audio recording exists.

4/01/93: Palaghaccio, Rome, Italy. Opening act: Little Angels. "Won't Get Fooled Again" is added to the set list for this show. Audio recording exists.

4/02/93: Palatrussardi, Milan, Italy. Opening act: Little Angels. "We Gotta Get Outta This Place" added to the set list for this show. Audio recording exists.

4/04/93: Festhalle, Frankfurt, GER. Opening act: Little Angels. Audio and video recordings exist.

4/05/93: Frankenhalle, Nurnburg, GER. Opening act: Little Angels.

4/07/93: Alsterdorfer Sporthalle, Hamburg, GER. Opening act: Little Angels. Video recording exists.

4/09/93: Globe Arena Stockholm, Sweden. Opening act: Little Angels. Audio and video recordings exists.

4/10/93: Spektrum, Oslo, Norway. Opening act: Little Angels. "Norwegian Wood" and "Waitin' for the Bus" added to the set list for this show. Audio recording exists.

4/11/93: The Forum, Copenhagen, Denmark. Opening act: Little Angels. Audio recording exists. "Born on the Bayou" and "Crossroads" added to the set list for this show.

4/13/93: S.P. Ahoy, Rotterdam, Netherlands. Opening act: Little Angels. Audio and video recordings exist.

4/14/93: Flanders Expo, Gent, Belgium. Opening act: Little Angels. Audio and video recordings exist.

4/16/93: Hallenstadion, Zurich, Switzerland. Opening act: Little Angels. Audio recording exists.

4/17/93: Hans-Martin-Schleyerhalle, Stuttgart, GER. Opening act: Little Angels. Audio recording exists.

4/19/93: Grugahalle, Essen, GER. Opening act: Little Angels. Audio and video recordings exist.

4/21/93: Le Zenith, Paris, France. Opening act: Little Angels. Audio recording exists.

4/22/93: Le Zenith, Paris, France. Opening act: Little Angels.

4/25/93: Birmingham N.E.C. Arena, Birmingham, UK. Opening act: Little Angels. "Amnesty Is Granted" and "All Right Now" added to the set list for this show. Audio recording exists.

4/27/93: Sheffield Arena, Sheffield, UK. Opening act: Little Angels. Tony Jepson joins Van Halen for the encore.

4/29/93: Wembley Arena, London, UK. Opening act: Little Angels. Van Halen sets the record for the most seats sold on the day of a concert. The band performs "All Right Now" with Little Angels. Audio recording exists.

6/25/93: Pine Knob Music Theatre, Clarkston, MI. Opening act: Vince Neil.

6/26/93: Pine Knob Music Theatre, Clarkston, MI. Opening act: Vince Neil.

6/28/93: Riverbend Music Center, Cincinnati, OH. Opening act: Vince Neil.

6/29/93: Blossom Music Center, Cuyahoga Falls, OH. Opening act: Vince Neil.

7/01/93: Molson Park, Barrie, Ontario, Canada. This was the Canada Day .Festival. The bill included the Jayhawks, Alannah Myles, Kim Mitchell, and Vince Neil. During the encore, Ed played an Ernie Ball Music Man guitar painted with the Canadian flag. Audio and video recordings exist.

7/03/93: Darien Lake Performing Arts Center, Darien, NY. Opening act: Vince Neil. Audio recording exists.

7/04/93: Cayuga County Fairgrounds, Weedsport, NY. Opening act: Vince Neil. Audio recording exists.

7/06/93: Orange County Speedway, Middletown, NY. Opening act: Vince Neil. Audio recording exists.

7/07/93: Thames Music Center, Groton, CT. Opening act: Vince Neil. Audio recording exists.

7/09/93: Great Woods Center, Mansfield, MA. Opening act: Vince Neil. Edward meets Dr. Jim Schumacher, a neurosurgeon at Boston's Massachusetts General Hospital, who offered Edward brain surgery lessons in exchange for guitar lessons. Audio recording exists.

7/10/93: Great Woods Center, Mansfield, MA. Opening act: Vince Neil. Audio recording exists.

7/11/93: Jones Beach Amphitheater, Wantaugh, NY. Opening act: Vince Neil. Audio and video recordings exist.

7/13/93: Jones Beach Amphitheater, Wantaugh, NY. Opening act: Vince Neil. Audio recording exists.

7/14/93: Jones Beach Amphitheater, Wantaugh, NY. Opening act: Vince Neil. "Amnesty Is Granted" is added to the set list for this show. Audio recording exists.

7/16/93: Starlake Amphitheater, Burgettstown, PA. Opening act: Vince Neil. Video recording exists.

7/17/93: Merriweather Post Pavilion, Columbia, MD. Opening act: Vince Neil. Audio recording exists.

7/18/93: Merriweather Post Pavilion, Columbia, MD. Opening act: Vince Neil. Audio recording exists.

7/19/93: Starlake Amphitheater, Burgettstown, PA. Opening act: Vince Neil. Audio recording exists.

7/20/93: Blockbuster Pavilion, Charlotte, NC. Opening act: Vince Neil. Audio recording exists.

7/21/93: Hardee's Walnut Creek Amphitheater, Raleigh, NC. Opening act: Vince Neil. Audio recording exists.

7/23/93: Lakewood Amphitheatre, Atlanta, GA. Opening act: Vince Neil. Audio recording exists.

7/24/93: Starwood Amphitheatre, Antioch, TN. Opening act: Vince Neil. Audio recording exists.

7/25/93: Deer Creek Music Center, Noblesville, IN. Opening act: Vince Neil. Audio and video recordings exist.

7/27/93: Sandstone Amphitheatre, Bonner Springs, MO. Opening act: Vince Neil.

7/28/93: Riverport Amphitheatre, Maryland Heights, MO. Opening act: Vince Neil.

7/30/93: World Music Theater, Tinley Park, IL. Opening act: Vince Neil. Michael breaks a string during his solo and throws his bass to the ground before lighting it on fire. "The Love" is added to the set list. Audio recording exists.

7/31/93: Alpine Valley Music Theatre, East Troy, WI. Opening act: Vince Neil. Audio recording exists.

8/02/93: Buckeye Lake, Columbus, OH. Opening act: Vince Neil.

8/05/93: Starplex Amphitheater, Dallas, TX. Opening act: Vince Neil.

8/06/93: C.W. Mitchell Pavilion, Woodlands, TX. Opening act: Vince Neil. Edward causes a traffic jam after the show while trying to wave down passing motorists. Ed and Al's limo broke down on the way out of the venue, so the guitarist stood roadside with his thumb out trying to stop passing motorists so he could borrow a cellular phone. The brothers were eventually rescued from a throng of after-show autograph seekers when Al and Sammy's limo arrived on the scene.

8/07/93: C.W. Mitchell Pavilion, Woodlands, TX. Opening act: Vince Neil.

8/10/93: Fiddler's Green Amphitheater, Englewood, CO. Opening act: Vince Neil.

8/12/93: State Fairgrounds, Oklahoma City, OK. Opening act: Vince Neil.

8/14/93: Blockbuster Desert Sky Pavilion, Phoenix, AZ. Opening act: Vince Neil. Audio recording exists.

8/16/93: Park West Amphitheater, Park City, UT. Opening act: Vince Neil.

8/18/93: Portland Meadows, Portland, OR. Opening act: Vince Neil.

8/20/93: Shoreline Amphitheater, Mountain View, CA. Opening act: Vince Neil. Audio and video recordings exist.

8/21/93: Shoreline Amphitheater, Mountain View, CA. Opening act: Vince Neil. "Amnesty Is Granted" is added to the set list for this show. Audio recording exists.

8/22/93: Cal Expo Amphitheatre, Sacramento, CA. Opening act: Vince Neil. "Young Man's Blues" is added to the set list for this show. Audio recording exists.

8/24/93: Cal Expo Amphitheatre, Sacramento, CA. Opening act: Vince Neil. This show took place during the California State Fair. Audio recording exists.

8/27/93: Pacific Amphitheater, Costa Mesa, CA. Opening act: Vince Neil. Audio recording exists.

8/28/93: Pacific Amphitheater, Costa Mesa, CA. Opening act: Vince Neil. Towards the end of "Finish What Ya Started," all of the band members' wives took to the stage dressed in Playboy Bunny outfits. "Amnesty Is Granted" and "Young Man's Blues" added to the set list for this show. Audio recording exists.

8/29/93: Pacific Amphitheater, Costa Mesa, CA. This show was canceled.

Balance "Ambulance" Tour (1995)

Dubbed the Ambulance Tour by Eddie because of the hip and neck injuries sustained by himself and brother Alex, the *Balance* tour would prove to be the final tour with Sammy Hagar on lead vocals.

This tour also featured the band opening for Bon Jovi on the European leg of their tour. The reasoning behind this move was that the band needed to broaden their European fan base. What better way to do it than play alongside Bon Jovi, who are downright huge in Europe? A plethora of other bands also shared the bill on Van Halen's European dates, including Thunder, Ugly Kid Joe, Crown of Thorns, Slash's Snakepit, Die Doofen, The Pretenders, Skin, Otto, H-Blockx, and Little Steven.

The band added a new element to their stage show on this tour: the Jumbotron. Initially Alex's idea, this was the band's first time touring with a video production. The Jumbotron was a giant screen, similar to a television set, located above Alex. This was only the second time the setup had been used in arenas. Barbara Streisand was the first to use it in this manner. A six-man video team using four operating cameras and three point-of-view (POV) cameras, two of which were located on Al's drum kit, filmed the band, the crowd, and more, projecting the images onto the giant screen. The MTV-banned "Amsterdam" video was also shown on the Jumbotron and at the end of each show, the *Balance* cover twins would appear, saying their goodbyes to the audience.

Michael added a nod to J.S. Bach's "Toccata and Fugue" in D minor (recognized by many as the macabre organ piece from the Phantom of the Opera) to his bass solo on this tour. His bass setup included five Music Man 4-string basses; two in metallic gold, two transparent red, and one sunburst. Each was outfitted with a 2TEK bridge designed by Anthony and Linn Ellsworth and were otherwise stock with the exception of an added thumb rest and the removal of the three-position pickup selector switches (the pickups were hardwired for series-only operation). All the basses were strung with Ernie Ball Hybrid Slinky strings, gauged .045 to .105. Rig-wise, Michael used three racks of gear. The first housed Samson UR-4 and UR-5D wireless receivers. His main rack consisted of two Ampeg SVT-Pro preamps, a Bradshaw switching system, a Custom Audio Electronis 3+ Tube Preamp (for the bass solo), two Roland SDE-3000 digital delays (set to 579 and 279 milliseconds), two Boss SE-70 multi-effects units (for distorted flange), and an Ampeg SVT-3000 power amp (used as a spare). The third rack housed three Ampeg SVT-300 300-watt mono tube amps; two power a pair of Ampeg SVT810Es each, and the third was a spare. He also kept some standby units from previous tours including an ADA flanger, an Electro-Harmonix Bass Micro-Synth, a Colorsound fuzz, and a Roland DC-30 chorus/echo unit.

Prior to the start of the tour, Michael teamed up with Peavey and tried out a CyberBass, a bass-to-MIDI controller that connects to a rackmount sound module. The CyberBass was a precursor to a similar concoction known as a MidiBass. He considered using it during his bass solo, but didn't for unknown reasons.

Alex drank a homemade garlic and carrot drink each night before taking the stage, that had a tendency to leave a rather garlicky-smell all around him and his drum kit. This practice made Al the butt of many jokes. His solo featured a segment where he played against a recording of himself, showering the crowd with a rather Latinesque treat.

Edward brought "Franky" out on the tour during the first leg, but ended up not using it for unknown reasons. Edward also played one of his Ernie Ball Music Man guitars from time to time, which had black electrical tape covering the Music Man logo, probably due to the fact that he was now endorsing his new Peavey Wolfgang line. Early in the tour, Edward began to experience intense pain in his hip, which was later diagnosed as Avascular Necrosis. It was common to see him standing relatively still for most of these shows, even sitting on a red, white and blacked striped stool on more than one occasion. By tour's end however, he was much more active, either getting used to the pain or doing a hell of a job masking it. His solo featured several Roth-era song teasers including the verse section to "Mean Street" and the intro to "Runnin' with the Devil," as well as a nod to the 5-note communication sequence from *Close Encounters of the Third Kind.* The final leg of the tour featured the guitarist following in Al's footsteps: he also played against a recording of himself.

The band grossed a staggering $32.7 million in support of *Balance.* Other top grossing acts for the year included the Eagles with $56.6 million, the Grateful Dead, R.E.M., and Page & Plant.

Typical set list: • The Seventh Seal • Runaround • Top of the World • Amsterdam • When It's Love • You Really Got Me • Bass solo • Aftershock • Drum solo • Can't Stop Lovin' You • Ain't Talkin' 'Bout Love • Feelin' • Eagles Fly • Guitar solo • Why Can't This Be Love? • Finish What Ya Started • Right Now • Encore: • Panama • Dreams

3/11/95: Pensacola Civic Center, Pensacola, FL. Opening act: Collective Soul. MTV films "Spring Break Rocks" and Edward performs stone-cold sober as a recovering alcoholic for the first time in his career. Audio and video recordings exist.

3/12/95: Jacksonville Coliseum, Jacksonville, FL. Opening act: Collective Soul. Audio and video recordings exist.

3/14/95: The Thunderdome, St. Petersburg, FL. Opening act: Collective Soul. Several members of the World Wrestling Federation join the band backstage.

3/17/95: Miami Arena, Miami, FL. Opening act: Collective Soul. Audio recording exists.

3/18/95: Orlando Arena, Orlando, FL. This show was canceled.

3/20/95: Orlando Arena, Orlando, FL. Opening act: Collective Soul. Audio recording exists.

3/22/95: UNO Lakefront Arena, New Orleans, LA. Opening act: Collective Soul.

3/24/95: Reunion Arena, Dallas, TX. Opening act: Collective Soul. Outfitted with a large pair of earphones, Wolfgang Van Halen takes the stage to thunderous applause. He and Edward kick an inflatable beach ball back and forth. Audio and video recordings exist.

3/25/95: San Antonio Convention Center Arena, San Antonio, TX. Opening act: Collective Soul. Audio recording exists.

3/26/95: The Summit, Houston, TX. Opening act: Collective Soul. Audio recording exists.

3/28/95: El Paso Special Events Center, El Paso, TX. Opening act: Collective Soul.

3/29/95: Tingley Coliseum, Albuquerque, NM. Opening act: Collective Soul. Audio recording exists.

3/31/95: Thomas & Mack Arena, Las Vegas, NV. Opening act: Collective Soul. Audio recording exists.

4/01/95: America West Arena, Phoenix, AZ. Opening act: Collective Soul. Audio recording exists.

4/02/95: San Diego Sports Arena, San Diego, CA. Opening act: Collective Soul. Audio and video recordings exist.

4/04/95: Great Western Forum, Inglewood, CA. Opening act: Collective Soul. Audio recording exists.

4/05/95: Great Western Forum, Inglewood, CA. Opening act: Collective Soul. MTV films this concert and attaches the segment to news of Ed's gun incident. Ed also experiences major technical difficulties with his sound during the "Cathedral" portion of his unaccompanied solo and slams his guitar on the stage in disgust. Audio recording exists.

4/07/95: Oakland Coliseum, Oakland, CA. Canceled due to Sammy being sick.

4/08/95: San Jose Arena, San Jose, CA. Canceled due to Sammy being sick.

4/09/95: Arco Arena, Sacramento, CA. Canceled due to Sammy being sick.

4/14/95: Rosemont Horizon, Rosemont, IL. Opening act: Collective Soul. Audio recording exists.

4/15/95: Palace of Auburn Hills, Auburn Hills, MI. Opening act: Collective Soul. Audio recording exists.

4/16/95: Palace of Auburn Hills, Auburn Hills, MI. Opening act: Collective Soul. Audio recording exists.

4/18/95: Allen County Memorial Coliseum, Ft. Wayne, IN. Opening act: Collective Soul. MTV films an episode of Road Rules. (The cast spends the day as Van Halen roadies.) Video recording exists.

4/19/95: Rupp Arena, Lexington, KY. Opening act: Collective Soul. Audio recording exists.

4/21/95: Erwin J. Nutter Center, Dayton, OH. Opening act: Collective Soul.

4/22/95: Gund Arena, Cleveland, OH. Opening act: Collective Soul. Audio recording exists.

4/23/95: Charleston Civic Center, Charleston, WV. Opening act: Collective Soul.

4/25/95: Meadowlands Arena, East Rutherford, NJ. Opening act: Collective Soul. Audio recording exists.

4/26/95: Nassau Veterans Memorial Coliseum, Uniondale, NY. Opening act: Collective Soul. Audio recording exists.

4/28/95: The Spectrum, Philadelphia, PA. Opening act: Collective Soul. Audio and video recording exists.

4/29/95: Worcester Centrum, Worcester, MA. Opening act: Collective Soul. Audio recording exists.

4/30/95: Providence Civic Center, Providence, RI. Opening act: Collective Soul. Audio recording exists.

5/02/95: Buffalo Memorial Auditorium, Buffalo, NY. Opening act: Collective Soul.

5/03/95: Rochester War Memorial, Rochester, NY. Opening act: Collective Soul.

5/05/95: Colisee de Quebec, Quebec, QC. Opening act: Collective Soul. Audio and video recording exists.

5/06/95: Montreal Forum, Montreal, QC. Opening act: Collective Soul. Audio and video recording exists.

5/07/95: Knickerbocker Arena, Albany, NY. Opening act: Collective Soul. Audio recording exists.

5/13/95: Oakland Coliseum, Oakland, CA. Opening act: Shaw and Blades. Make-up for canceled 4/07/95 show. Audio and video recordings exist.

5/14/95: San Jose Arena, San Jose, CA. Opening act: Slash's Snakepit. Make-up for canceled 4/08/95 show. Audio and video recordings exist.

5/15/95: Arco Arena, Sacramento, CA. Opening act: Slash's Snakepit. Make-up for canceled 4/09/95 show. Audio recording exists.

5/24/95: Le Zenith, Paris, France. Opening act: Bad Moon Rising. Attendance: 20,000. Audio recording exists.

5/26/95: Weserstadion, Bremen, GER. This is the first show that Van Halen opened for Bon Jovi. The band would continue to open for Bon Jovi until 6/30/95. Ugly Kid Joe joined Van Halen as openers for this show.

5/27/95: Weserstadion, Bremen, GER. Die Doofen joins Ugly Kid Joe and Van Halen to open this show.

5/28/95: Goffertpark, Nijmegen, Netherlands. Little Steven joins Ugly Kid Joe and Van Halen to open this show. Audio recording exists.

5/30/95: Georg-Melcher Stadion, Essen, GER

6/01/95: Sportforum, Chemnitz, GER. Ugly Kid Joe opens with Van Halen.

6/03/95: Olympiahalle (Rock Im Park), Munich, GER. Other openers at this show included Hootie & the Blowfish, H-Blockx, Ugly Kid Joe, Slash's Snakepit, The Pretenders, and Otto. Audio recording exists.

6/04/95: Nurburgring (Rock Am Ring), Nurburg, GER. Other openers at this show included Hootie & the Blowfish, H-Blockx, Ugly Kid Joe, Slash's Snakepit, The Pretenders, Otto, and Little Steven. Audio recording exists.

6/06/95: Waldbuhne, Berlin, GER. Audio recording exists.

6/07/95: Waldbuhne, Berlin, GER

6/10/95: St. Jakob-Fussballstadion, Basle, Switzerland. Other openers at this show included Allison and Thunder. Audio recording exists.

6/11/95: Osterreich-Ring, Zeltweg, Austria

6/13/95: Estadio Olympico, Barcelona, Spain. The Pretenders join Ugly Kid Joe and Van Halen as openers. Audio recording exists.

6/14/95: Palacio De Los Deportes, Madrid, Spain. Van Halen headlined this show. The opening acts were Lizard and The Pretenders. Audio recording exists.

6/15/95: Stadion Avalade, Lisbon, Portugal. Crown of Thorns joined Ugly Kid Joe and Van Halen in opening this show.

6/17/95: Festivalsite Werchter, Werchter, Belgium. Little Steven joined Ugly Kid Joe and Van Halen in opening this show. Audio recording exists.

6/18/95: Flugplatz Lahr, Lahr, GER. Little Steven joined Ugly Kid Joe and Van Halen in opening this show. Audio recording exists.

6/20/95: Omnisports De Bercy, Paris, France

6/21/95: Cardiff Arms Park, Cardiff, Wales. Crown of Thorns and Thunder join Van Halen in opening this show. Video recording exists.

6/23/95: Wembley Stadium, London, England. Thunder joins Ugly Kid Joe and Van Halen in opening this show.

6/24/95: Wembley Stadium, London, England. Crown of Thorns and Thunder join Van Halen in opening this show. Audio recording exists.

6/25/95: Wembley Stadium, London, England. Crown of Thorns joins Van Halen in opening this show.

6/27/95: Gateshead Int. Stadium, Newcastle, England. Crown of Thorns and Thunder join Van Halen in opening this show.

6/28/95: Don Valley Stadium, Sheffield, England. Crown of Thorns and Thunder join Van Halen in opening this show. Richie Sambora performs "Rock and Roll" with Van Halen. This was the last show Van Halen opened for Bon Jovi. Audio recording exists.

6/30/95: Roskilde Festival, Roskilde, Denmark. The bill for this show included Cathedral (5:30pm), Van Halen (7:30pm), The Cure (10:00pm), and D.A.D. (1:00am). Audio recording exists.

7/15/95: Garden States Art Center, Holmdel, NJ. Opening act: Our Lady Peace. Audio recording exists.

7/16/95: Garden State Art Center, Holmdel, NJ. Opening act: Our Lady Peace. Audio recording exists.

7/18/95: Blossom Music Center, Cleveland, OH. Opening acts: Our Lady Peace and Skid Row.

7/19/95: Deer Creek Amphitheatre, Indianapolis, IN. Opening acts: Our Lady Peace and Skid Row. Audio and video recordings exist.

7/21/95: Sandstone Amphitheater, Bonner Springs, MO. Opening act: Our Lady Peace.

7/22/95: Riverport Amphitheater, Maryland Heights, MO. Opening act: Our Lady Peace.

7/23/95: Riverport Amphitheater, Maryland Heights, MO. Opening act: Our Lady Peace.

7/25/95: Tupelo Colesium, Tupelo, MS. Opening act: Our Lady Peace.

7/26/95: Starwood Amphitheatre, Nashville, TN. Opening act: Our Lady Peace. Audio recording exists.

7/28/95: World Music Theater, Tinley Park, IL. Opening acts: Our Lady Peace and Skid Row. Sammy Hagar forgets the words to "Eagles Fly." Audio recording exists.

7/29/95: Alpine Valley Music Theater, East Troy, WI. Opening acts: Our Lady Peace and Skid Row. Audio recording exists.

7/30/95: Target Centre, Minneapolis, MN. Opening act: Our Lady Peace. The Monks of Gyuto Tantric University, who provided the chanting at the beginning of "The Seventh Seal" on *Balance*, opened the show. (They had put on a performance of their own the night before.) The monks were taken by surprise once the band kicked into the song. Some of the unsuspecting holy men were so disoriented, they scrambled for cover, forgetting the plans made earlier at soundcheck. Led by Kevin

Dugan, the group was to exit the stage via stage right in single file, with tour manager Scotty Ross bringing up the rear. One monk jumped into the pits and another sat down on Alex's drum riser, apparently totally unsure of where he was supposed to go. Audio and video recordings exist.

8/01/95: Pine Knob Music Theatre, Clarkston, MI. Opening act: Our Lady Peace. "Foxey Lady" is added to the set list for this show. Audio recording exists.

8/02/95: Pine Knob Music Theatre, Clarkston, MI. Opening act: Our Lady Peace. "White Room" and "Foxey Lady" are added to the set list for this show. Audio recording exists.

8/04/95: Nissan Pavilion, Stone Ridge, VA. Opening act: Our Lady Peace.

8/05/95: Blockbuster-Sony Music Entertainment Center, Camden, NJ. Opening acts: Our Lady Peace and Skid Row.

8/06/95: Old Orchard Beach, Portland, ME. Opening act: Our Lady Peace. Audio recording exists.

8/08/95: Great Woods Center for the Performing Arts, Mansfield, MA. Opening acts: Our Lady Peace and Skid Row.

8/09/95: Great Woods Center for the Performing Arts, Mansfield, MA. Opening acts: Our Lady Peace and Skid Row. Audio recording exists.

8/11/95: Starlake Civic Center, Burgettstown, PA. Opening act: Our Lady Peace. Video recording exists.

8/12/95: The Polaris Amphitheater, Columbus, OH. Opening act: Our Lady Peace. "Outside Woman Blues" is added to the set list for this show. Audio recording exists.

8/13/95: Riverbend Music Center, Cincinnati, OH. Opening act: Our Lady Peace.

8/14/95: Nassau Veterans Memorial Coliseum, Uniondale, NY. Opening act: Our Lady Peace.

8/15/95: Nassau Veterans Memorial Coliseum, Uniondale, NY. Opening act: Our Lady Peace.

8/18/95: Molson Amphitheatre, Toronto, ON. Opening act: Our Lady Peace. Video recording exists.

8/19/95: Molson Amphitheatre, Toronto, ON. Opening act: Our Lady Peace. The Pay-per-view special is filmed. Audio and video recordings exist.

8/20/95: Frank Clair Stadium, Ottawa, ON. Opening act: Our Lady Peace.

8/22/95: Jones Beach Theater, Wantaugh, NY. Opening act: Our Lady Peace. Audio and video recordings exist.

8/23/95: Jones Beach Theater, Wantaugh, NY. Opening act: Our Lady Peace. Audio and video recordings exist.

8/25/95: Jones Beach Theater, Wantaugh, NY. Opening act: Our Lady Peace. Leslie West joins band to perform "Mississippi Queen." Audio and video recordings exist.

8/26/95: The Meadows, Hartford, CT. Opening act: Our Lady Peace.

8/27/95: Montage Mountain Performing Arts Center, Scranton, PA. Opening act: Our Lady Peace. Audio recording exists.

8/29/95: Merriweather Post Pavilion, Columbia, MD. Opening act: Our Lady Peace. Audio recording exists.

8/30/95: Classic Amphitheatre, Richmond, VA. Opening act: Our Lady Peace.

9/01/95: Hardee's Walnut Creek Amphitheatre, Raleigh, NC. Opening act: Brother Cane.

9/02/95: Blockbuster Pavillion, Charlotte, NC. Opening act: Brother Cane.

9/03/95: Lakewood Amphitheatre, Atlanta, GA. Opening act: Brother Cane.

9/11/95: Northlands Coliseum, Edmonton, AB. Opening act: Our Lady Peace.

9/13/95: Pacific Coliseum, Vancouver, BC. Opening act: Our Lady Peace. Audio recording exists.

9/15/95: Portland Civic Stadium, Portland, OR. Opening act: Brother Cane.

9/16/95: Gorge Amphitheatre, George, WA. Opening act: Brother Cane.

9/17/95: BSU Pavilion, Boise, ID. Opening act: Brother Cane.

9/19/95: The Delta Center, Salt Lake City, UT. Opening act: Brother Cane. Audio recording exists.

9/20/95: Fiddler's Green, Englewood, CO. Opening act: Brother Cane. Foul weather was afoot at this show. The band performed during a snowstorm, even getting involved in a playful snowball fight with the audience. The young boy featured on the *Balance* cover was brought on stage partway through the show and introduced to the crowd.

9/22/95: Kansas Coliseum, Witchita, KS. Opening act: Brother Cane.

9/23/95: Hilton Coliseum, Ames, IA. Opening act: Brother Cane. Audio recording exists.

9/24/95: Mark of the Quad Cities, Moline, IL. Opening act: Brother Cane.

9/26/95: Pyramid Arena, Memphis, TN. Opening act: Brother Cane.

9/27/95: Birmingham-Jefferson Civic Center, Birmingham, AL. Opening act: Brother Cane.

9/29/95: Woodlands Pavilion, Houston, TX. Opening acts: Brother Cane and Skid Row.

9/30/95: South Park Meadows, Austin, TX. Opening acts: Brother Cane and Skid Row.

10/01/95: Coca-Cola Starplex, Dallas, TX. Opening acts: Brother Cane and Skid Row.

10/03/95: The Myriad, Oklahoma City, OK. Opening act: Skid Row.

10/04/95: The Myriad, Oklahoma City, OK. Opening act: Skid Row.

10/06/95: Blockbuster Desert Sky Pavilion, Phoenix, AZ. Opening acts: Brother Cane and Skid Row. Peavey presents Michael Anthony with a gold-speckled bass in hopes of an endorsement deal. Audio recording exists.

10/07/95: Glen Helen Blockbuster Pavilion, Devore, CA. Opening acts: Brother Cane and Skid Row. Ed's guitar tech Matt Bruck and his band Zen Boy play outside as the crowd files into the Pavilion. Sammy dedicates "Eagles Fly" to his mother, who is watching the show from the stage. Mike performs with the Peavey bass received the night before for the very first time. Audio recording exists.

10/08/95: Selland Arena, Fresno, CA. Opening act: Brother Cane.

10/11/95: Lawlor Events Center, Reno, NV

10/13/95: Cal Expo Amphitheatre, Sacramento, CA. Opening act: Skid Row.

10/14/95: Shoreline Amphitheatre, Mountain View, CA. Opening acts: Brother Cane and Skid Row.

10/15/95: Irvine Meadows Amphitheatre, Irvine, CA. Opening acts: Brother Cane and Skid Row. Audio recording exists.

10/25/95: Yoyogi Olympic Pool, Tokyo, JAP. Audio recording exists.

10/26/95: Yoyogi Olympic Pool, Tokyo, JAP

10/27/95: Yoyogi Olympic Pool, Tokyo, JAP

10/29/95: Kokusai Center, Fukuoaka, JAP

10/30/95: Castle Hall, Osaka, JAP. Audio recording exists.

11/01/95: Budokan Hall, Budokan, JAP. Audio recording exists.

11/02/95: Budokan Hall, Budokan, JAP

11/04/95: Blaisdell Arena, Honolulu, HI

11/05/95: Blaisdell Arena, Honolulu, HI

Van Halen III Tour (1998)

This tour was planned from the beginning to be a departure from the usual Van Halen tour. The band was determined to visit more new places and to play a much more diverse set than ever.

The plan was to first visit New Zealand and Australia, places the band has never played, before returning to their usual stomping grounds in the U.S. and Europe.

The stage was a much more streamlined design than in previous tours. Essentially it consisted of a few risers, scaled down rigs (less aesthetics, more functionality), and a circus-like motif. This set up remained essentially the same throughout the tour, with the exception of the lighting system, which became more sophisticated after the initial overseas dates.

Alex's drum kit was probably the most noticeable thing on the stage. Bright yellow, the kit featured Sanskrit writing that spelled out "Van Halen" and "VHIII." The idea to use Sanskrit came from the band's art director Stine Schyberg. The kit consisted of a Ludwig 4-ply 16-by-24-inch bass drum, Ludwig 4-ply toms at 8-by-10-inches, 8-by-12-inches, 16-by-16-inches, and 16-by-18-inches, Ludwig Super Sensitive 6.5-by-14-inch chrome snare, Ludwig 3.5-by-13-inch piccolo, 13.5-inch and 12.5-inch congas, a cow bell, Paiste 2002 crashes at 16-inches, 18-inches, 18-inches (heavy), 20-inches, 20-inches (medium), Formula 602 heavy bell, 22-inch Signature Series dark ride with heavy bell, hi-hat consisting of a 15-inch Paiste 2002 top and a Paiste 2002 14-inch Sound Edge bottom, Yamaha 820 bassdrum pedals with a Roland electric kickdrum trigger, and 16-inch Calato Regal Tip Alex Van Halen Series double-butt sticks.

Ed used three main guitars, with a few extras thrown in on special occasions. All three guitars were Peavey Wolfgangs. The primary guitar, which was used throughout most of the show, was a stock Wolfgang with tobacco sunburst finish. The guitar he used for "Year to the Day" and his solo was a Wolfgang Special with a Fernandes Sustainer in the neck pickup position. The third guitar was a crème Wolfgang Special with a TransTrem used for "Fire in the Hole." Ed chose to use 35 to 45-foot George L chords on this tour instead of a wireless system. An attachment added to the bottom of the guitar bodies stretched the chord out away from the body to avoid becoming tangled. This tour also gave Ed the chance to test his new 5150 II prototype amp head. He used three 5150 cabinets on stage, two in his trademark red, black, and white striped pattern, and one yellow.

Effects were kept to a minimum. His rack consisted of a Lexicon PCM 70 for "Cathedral," two Roland SDE3000 Digital Delays, and an Eventide H3000 Harmonizer. His pedalboard included a 3-channel custom George Hardware bypass unit, an MXR M101 Phaser, an MXR M119 Flanger, and a wah pedal.

Taking a note from his brother, Ed used Sanskrit on his amps to spell out "Peavey."

Mike's setup included four main bass guitars. All were Peavey, two were 4-string (one tobacco sunburst and one gold) and two were 5-string (one metallic black and one sunburst). Unlike Ed, Mike chose to stick with a Shure wireless. His amp setup included two Ampeg SVT 300 power amps and an Ampeg SVT II Pro Pre/Power amp (for backup) with four bass cabinets (two per power amp). His effects rack, controlled by a custom-built Bob Bradshaw footswitch, consisted of two Roland DC30 analog chorus echoes, a Furman Powerswitch, a Klark Teknik Graphic EQ, an Ampeg SVP Preamp, two Boss SE70 Super Effects Processors, an SDE 3000 Digital Delay, an MXR Flanger, and an Electro Harmonix Micro Synthesizer.

The tour started out well down under and included an unusual feature the rest of the tour didn't. At some shows, during "Ain't Talkin' 'Bout Love," Gary would jump into the audience. When MTV filmed the 4/20/98 Sydney show, Gary continued this practice and even executed a half-faked fall down flight of stairs (it started out as real slip and Gary decided to go with the flow).

After the Australian tour the band did a short mini-tour of the U.S. before heading to Europe. The eight show mini-tour was a huge success. The shows were often packed with fans wanting to get the first look at the new lineup live and decide for themselves what kind of a show Mach III could provide.

The European tour was cut short when a piece of the ceiling at the Docks in Hamburg, Germany fell on Alex's arm during the soundcheck. Thankful to have only injured his arm, Alex wore a soft cast. The band was forced to cancel the remaining dates on the European tour. The venue where the incident occurred was condemned the next day.

The set list for this tour changed frequently and was probably the most varied the band has ever played. "Dirty Water Dog" was performed in Australia and Japan, but was left out of the U.S. set list.

When averaged the typical set list for the main North American tour looked like this: • Unchained • Without You • One I Want • Mean Street • When It's Love • Fire in the Hole • Why Can't This Be Love? • Romeo Delight • I'm the One • Drum Solo • Dance the Night Away • Jamie's Cryin' • Feel Your Love Tonight • Humans Being • Somebody Get Me a Doctor • Year to the Day • Guitar Solo • Right Now • Ain't Talkin' 'Bout Love • Josephina • Panama • Jump

4/10/98: Queens Wharf, Wellington, NZ. Opening act: Destiny. Audio and video recordings exist.

4/11/98: North Shore Events Center, Auckland, NZ. Opening act: Destiny.

4/14/98: Silverdome, Launceston, AUS. Opening act: Davo. Footage of this concert, including backstage footage, was shown on Australian television's Today Tonight. Video recording exists.

4/17/98: Melbourne Park, Melbourne, AUS. Opening act: Liquid. Sammy Hagar flyers and posters are posted all over Melbourne to advertise an upcoming Sammy Hagar concert. Posters, produced by the venue hosting Hagar, read "Sammy Hagar-Ex Van Halen." Audio and video recordings exist.

4/18/98: AIS Arena, Canberra, AUS. Opening act: Liquid.

4/20/98: Sydney Entertainment Centre, Sydney, AUS. Opening act: Gumption. MTV films this concert for an episode of Live from the 10 Spot. Muchmusic also broadcasts this concert and includes four more songs than the MTV broadcast. Audio and video recordings exist.

4/23/98: Newcastle Entertainment Centre, Newcastle, AUS. Opening act: The Poor.

4/24/98: Brisbane Entertainment Centre, Brisbane, AUS

4/27/98: Adelaide Entertainment Centre, Adelaide, AUS. Video recording exists.

4/29/98: Perth Entertainment Centre, Perth, AUS. Opening act: Hurricane Mary.

5/13/98: Woodlands Pavilion, Houston, TX. Opening act: Kenny Wayne Shepherd. Audio recording exists.

5/14/98: Starplex Amphitheater, Dallas, TX. Opening act: Kenny Wayne Shepherd. Audio recording exists.

5/16/98: Rosemont Horizon, Chicago, IL. Opening act: Kenny Wayne Shepherd. Ed uses a Wolfgang guitar with a Chicago Bulls logo on the body to close this show. Audio and video recordings exist.

5/17/98: Gund Arena, Cleveland, OH. Opening act: Kenny Wayne Shepherd. Audio recording exists.

5/19/98: Palace of Auburn Hills, Auburn Hills, MI. Opening act: Creed. Audio recording exists.

5/21/98: Fleet Center, Boston, MA. Opening act: Kenny Wayne Shepherd. Three songs from this show are broadcast on Real Rock TV. Audio and video recordings exist.

5/22/98: Madison Square Garden, New York, NY. Opening act: Creed. MTV's Mattrock producer Austin Reading proposes on stage to his girlfriend. The band obliges as a favor to Austin and Matt Pinfield who had just interviewed the band weeks earlier at the 5150 Studio for a special all-Van Halen episode of Mattrock. Audio and video recordings exist.

5/24/98: CoreStates Spectrum, Philadelphia, PA. Opening act: Fuel. Van Halen Day is declared in honor of the band's 22nd performance here. Audio and video recordings exist.

5/27/98: Helsinki Ice Hall, Helsinki, Finland. Opening act: Slumber.

5/29/98: Rock Im Park, Nurnberg, GER. The bill for this show also included Clawfinger, J.B.O., Therapy?, Bad Religion, Rammstein, and Ozzy Osbourne. Audio and video recordings exist.

5/31/98: Rock Am Ring, Nurburgring, GER. The bill for this show also included J.B.O., Deftones, Clawfinger, Therapy?, Bad Religion, Rammstein, and Ozzy Osbourne. Audio recording exists.

6/02/98: Huxley's Neue Welt, Berlin, GER. Opening act: Doro.

6/03/98: Docks, Hamburg, GER. This was the first show canceled due to Alex's injury. The remaining dates on the European tour were also canceled.

6/05/98: Karlshamn Rock Festival, Karlshamn, SE. Canceled.

6/06/98: Esbjerg Rock Festival, Esbjerg, DN. Canceled.

6/07/98: Tioren, Copenhagen, DN. Canceled

6/09/98: Wembley Arena, London, UK. Canceled.

6/10/98: NEC Arena, Birmingham, UK. Canceled.

6/12/98: Hallenstadion, Zurich, SW. Canceled.

6/13/98: Monsters of Rock Festival, Milan, Italy. Canceled.

6/14/98: Sportpark Boshoven, Bospop Festival, Weert, NL. Canceled.

6/16/98: Brabanthal, Leuven, BE. Canceled.

6/17/98: Le Zenith, Paris, FR. Canceled.

7/01/98: Desert Sky Pavilion, Phoenix, AZ. Opening act: Monster Magnet.

7/03/98: Del Mar Fair, San Diego, CA. Opening act: Monster Magnet. Audio recording exists.

7/04/98: Blockbuster Pavilion, Devore, CA. Opening act: Monster Magnet and Johnny Lang. Audio recording exists.

7/05/98: Shoreline Amphitheater, Mountainview, CA. Opening act: Monster Magnet. Audio recording exists.

7/07/98: Concord Pavilion, Concord, CA. Opening act: Monster Magnet. Video recording exists.

7/08/98: Arco Arena, Sacramento, CA. Opening act: Monster Magnet.

7/10/98: Rose Garden, Portland, OR. Opening act: Monster Magnet.

7/11/98: The Gorge, George, WA. Opening act: Monster Magnet. Audio recording

7/14/98: The Canyons, Park City, UT. Opening act: Kenny Wayne Shepherd.

7/16/98: Fiddler's Green, Denver, CO. Opening act: Kenny Wayne Shepherd.

7/18/98: Sandstone Amphitheater, Bonner Springs, KS. Opening act: Kenny Wayne Shepherd.

7/19/98: Riverport Amphitheater, St. Louis, MO. Opening act: Kenny Wayne Shepherd. Audio recording exists.

7/21/98: Riverbend, Cincinnati, OH. Opening act: Kenny Wayne Shepherd. Three people were stabbed outside this concert during the band's encore. By the time the encore was over the police and fire departments joined helicopters in evacuating the victims and seeking the suspects, who weren't caught (at least not on this night). Audio recording exists.

7/22/98: Deer Creek Music Center, Indianapolis, IN. Opening act: Kenny Wayne Shepherd.

7/24/98: Starlake Amphitheater, Pittsburgh, PA. Opening act: Kenny Wayne Shepherd. This show was broadcasted on the Album Network. Audio recording exists.

7/25/98: Polaris Amphitheater, Columbus, OH. Opening act: Kenny Wayne Shepherd. Video recording exists.

7/26/98: Hershey Park Stadium, Hershey, PA. Opening act: Kenny Wayne Shepherd.

7/28/98: Montage Mountain, Scranton, PA. Opening act: Kenny Wayne Shepherd.

7/30/98: Blockbuster Pavilion, Charlotte, NC. Opening act: Kenny Wayne Shepherd.

7/31/98: Coca-Cola Lakewood Amphitheater, Atlanta, GA. Opening act: Kenny Wayne Shepherd. Video recording exists.

8/02/98: Starwood, Nashville, TN. Opening act: Kenny Wayne Shepherd. Audio recording exists.

8/04/98: California Mid State Fair, Paso Robles, CA. Gary receives a bloody cut on the top of his head reportedly due to an encounter with a mic stand.

8/12/98: Molson Centre, Montreal, QC. Canceled.

8/13/98: Great Woods, Mansfield, MA. Opening act: Kenny Wayne Shepherd. This show was stopped after four songs. Gary experienced some problems with his voice and left the stage. After about fifteen minutes Ed and Al asked the crowd if they could come back the next night. Audio recording exists.

8/14/98: Great Woods, Mansfield, MA. Opening act: Kenny Wayne Shepherd. This show was added to make up for the 8/13/98 show. The full version of "Jamie's Cryin'" is played for the first time since the *1984* tour. Audio recording exists.

8/15/98: Jones Beach, Wantagh, NY. Opening act: Kenny Wayne Shepherd. Video recording exists.

8/16/98: PNC Bank Arts Center, Holmdel, NJ. Opening act: Kenny Wayne Shepherd. Video recording exists.

8/18/98: Walnut Creek Amphitheater, Raleigh, NC. Opening act: Kenny Wayne Shepherd.

8/19/98: Virginia Beach Amphitheater, Virginia Beach, VA. Opening act: Kenny Wayne Shepherd.

8/21/98: Nissan Pavilion, Bristow, VA. Opening act: Kenny Wayne Shepherd. Video recording exists.

8/22/98: Trump Marina & Casino, Atlantic City, NJ. Opening act: Kenny Wayne Shepherd. Audio recording exists.

8/23/98: SPAC, Saratoga Springs, NY. Opening act: Kenny Wayne Shepherd.

8/25/98: Darien Lake, Buffalo, NY. Opening act: Kenny Wayne Shepherd.

8/26/98: Molson Amphitheatre, Toronto, ON. Opening act: Kenny Wayne Shepherd. Audio and video recordings exist.

8/28/98: Classic Amphitheater, Richmond, VA. Opening act: Kenny Wayne Shepherd. Video recording exists.

8/29/98: Hartford Meadows, Hartford, CT. Opening act: Kenny Wayne Shepherd. Video recording exists.

8/31/98: New York State Fair, Syracuse, NY. Opening act: Kenny Wayne Shepherd.

9/02/98: Van Andel Arena, Grand Rapids, MI. Opening act: Kenny Wayne Shepherd.

9/03/98: Pine Knob, Clarkston, MI. Opening act: Kenny Wayne Shepherd.

9/05/98: Alpine Valley Music Theater, East Troy, WI. Opening act: Kenny Wayne Shepherd. Kenny Wayne Shepherd, his band, and roadies run out on stage during Alex's solo and begin dancing.

9/06/98: Float-Rite Park, Somerset, WI. Canceled.

9/15/98: House of Blues, Myrtle Beach, SC. Audio recording exists.

9/16/98: House of Blues, Orlando, FL

9/17/98: Sunrise Theater, Ft. Lauderdale, FL

9/20/98: Roberto Clemente Stadium, San Juan, Puerto Rico. Canceled due to Hurricane Georges.

9/25/98: Pedreira Paulo Liminsk, Curitiba, Brazil

9/26/98: Pacaembu Stadium, Sao Paulo, Brazil

9/27/98: Metropolitan, Rio de Janeiro, Brazil. These three South American dates were canceled just days after being scheduled due to a problem with a Brazilian promoter.

10/02/98: The Joint, Las Vegas, NV. Ed used his red, white, and black striped Wolfgang Special at this show. Gary dedicated "Josephina" to the memory or Matt Fourman, a long-time Van Halen fan. Audio recording exists.

10/03/98: The Joint, Las Vegas, NV. Audio recording exists.

10/13/98: Sullivan Arena, Anchorage, AK

10/16/98: Blaisdell Arena, Honolulu, HI

10/20/98: Sun Plaza, Hiroshima, JAP. Audio recording exists.

10/21/98: Kokusai Center, Fukuoka, JAP

10/23/98: Castle Hall, Osaka, JAP. Audio recording exists.

10/24/98: Rainbow Hall, Nagoya, JAP. Audio recording exists.

10/26/98: Sangyo Bunka Center, Iwate, JAP

10/28/98: Budokan, Tokyo, JAP. Audio recording exists.

10/29/98: Budokan, Tokyo, JAP

10/30/98: Budokan, Tokyo, JAP. "You Really Got Me" is added to the set list for this show. Audio recording exists.

11/01/98: NK Hall, Tokyo Bay, JAP

11/02/98: Yokohama Arena, Yokohama, JAP. Audio recording exists.

12/11/98: Roberto Clemente Stadium, San Juan, Puerto Rico. Make-up for canceled 9/20/98 show. This show was canceled due to Gary Cherone's strep throat.

Printed in the United States
65723LVS00003B/24